Strategic Management

 LOGIC & ACTION

ANNE SIGISMUND HUFF
Technische Universität Munchen
University of Colorado

STEVEN W. FLOYD
University of St. Gallen

HUGH D. SHERMAN
Ohio University

SIRI TERJESEN
Indiana University
Max Planck Institute of Economics

WILEY

JOHN WILEY & SONS, INC.

VICE PRESIDENT AND EXECUTIVE PUBLISHER	Donald Fowley
EDITORIAL PROGRAM ASSISTANT	Carissa Marker
PRODUCTION SERVICES MANAGER	Dorothy Sinclair
PRODUCTION EDITOR	Janet Foxman
EXECUTIVE MARKETING MANAGER	Amy Scholz
ASSISTANT MARKETING MANAGER	Carly DeCandia
CREATIVE DIRECTOR	Harry Nolan
DESIGNER	Hope Miller
SENIOR MEDIA EDITOR	Allison Morris
PRODUCTION SERVICES	Elm Street Publishing Services
ELECTRONIC COMPOSITION	Thomson Digital
COVER IMAGE	© René Mansi
CHAPTER OPENING IMAGE	© iStockphoto

This book was set in 10/12 Electra LH by Thomson Digital and printed and bound by RRD Crawfordsville. The cover was printed by RRD Crawfordsville.

This book is printed on acid-free paper. ∞

To order books or for customer service, please call 1-800-CALL WILEY (225-5945).

Library of Congress Cataloging-in-Publication Data

Strategic management : logic and action / Anne Sigismund Huff ... [et al.].
 p. cm.
ISBN 978-0-471-01793-6 (pbk.)
1. Strategic planning. 2. Management. I. Huff, Anne Sigismund.
 HD30.28.S73324 2009
 658.4'012—dc22

2008009618

10 9 8 7 6 5 4 3 2 1

··

This book is dedicated to our first teachers

Anne & David Sigismund
Boots & Ray Reed
Betty & Hugh Sherman
Nancy & Barry Terjesen

Contents

3 SERVING CUSTOMERS 57

5   COMPETING WITH RIVALS   125

8   THINKING GLOBALLY   235

Introduction

Strategy is no longer the exclusive concern of generals. It is not something you wait to think about until you are the president of an organization. You need to understand strategic thinking as a graduate entering the workforce and as a mid-level manager. Corporations, small businesses, non-governmental organizations, and public agencies—organizations of all kinds—are facing new challenges. Many of these organizations rely on their employees to help strengthen current ways of doing things and invent new ones. In other words, strategy is not an academic exercise, it is a way of thinking that can help you find and keep a good job.

This is a relatively short text written to acquaint you with important, research-based principles underlying strategic management. A wide range of organizational examples are part of the text, and worksheets at the end of each chapter facilitate further analysis. You are also encouraged to assess organizations around you and interview others to learn more. However, we urge you to move quickly to action as the best way to learn about this important subject.

The four of us are business professors, and we emphasize business strategy while recognizing that strategy is important for all organizations. We have used the material you will find here in at least a dozen countries to work with business undergraduates, MBAs, corporate executives, state employees, and not-for-profit managers.

Even with a focus on business strategy, it wasn't easy to condense the insights of a large field of research and practice into a few pages. An important complexity is that organizations increasingly work together to offer connected products/services/experiences that engage customers in the production process. Apple's iPod and iTunes offer a perfect example. Apple helped change the music industry with the iPod, creating opportunities for other companies to offer speaker systems and other complementary goods but also spurring competitors to offer alternatives. If music is important to you, if you chat about it online, offer opinions, share playlists with others, *you* are both enhancing and modifying these offerings.

Thirteen relatively brief chapters provide frameworks for understanding how to think and act strategically in this and other situations. Chapter 1 explains why explicitly defining (and redefining) strategy is important. Chapters 2, 3, and 4 suggest connections between the tasks of developing organizational capabilities, engaging customers and seeking entrepreneurial opportunities. Chapter 5 offers advice on analyzing competition and coopetition. Chapter 6 then emphasizes the importance of a business model specifying how resources to sustain the organization will be gathered.

The next three chapters look at the external context affecting strategy. Even if the business is small or oriented toward a local market, it is likely that some suppliers, buyers, and other entities in its environment will be part of larger international entities. Chapter 7 therefore considers corporate strategy. Chapter 8 talks about why and how strategists pursue their initiatives in more than one country. Chapter 9 moves to governance and social responsibility, issues that are not only in the public eye but also concern actors within an organization.

Chapters 10, 11, and 12 consider how to unite strategic ideas found in previous chapters. Chapter 10 discusses the flexible execution of strategy. Chapter 11 focuses on managing knowledge. Chapter 12 considers leadership at various organizational levels, returning to the idea that *you* will be increasing required to be a strategist.

Finally, Chapter 13 moves even closer to you, our reader. We describe some of the pressures on individual workers today and propose that individuals can use the strategic concepts found in this book for personal and career decisions. This is an important part of the book, not an aside. Every individual in a strategic situation is thinking at a personal level as well as a collective level, and it is important to remember that when making organizational decisions.

Acknowledgments

We are grateful to the many students who made helpful suggestions about ideas and exercises in this book over several years, and would like to especially recognize Michael Shimkus who sent comments on almost every chapter in this volume. Numerous colleagues also took time to compare views about strategic management. We are particularly grateful for thoughtful suggestions from formal reviewers, including:

BILL ANTHONY, Florida State University

JEFFREY BAILEY, University of Idaho

PAMELA BARR, Georgia State University

MOUSUMI BHATTACHARYA, Fairfield University

CHARLES J. CAPPS III, Sam Houston State University

RUSSELL COFF, Emory University

ANDREW CORBETT, Rensselaer Polytechnic Institute

DANIEL DEGRAVEL, California State University, Northridge

ROGER DUNBAR, New York University

FRANCES FABIAN, University of Memphis

MONIQUE FORTE, Stetson University

SUSAN FOX-WOLFGRAMM, Hawaii Pacific University

LES JANKOVICH, San José State University

JAMES MOORE, Louisiana State University

JOSEPH PEYREFITTE, University of Southern Mississippi

MICHAEL PITTS, Virginia Commonwealth University

DOUGLAS POLLEY, St. Cloud State University

MICHAEL RAPHAEL, Central Connecticut State University

CYNTHIA WAGNER WEICK, University of the Pacific

EDWARD WARD, St. Cloud State University

AL WARNER, Pennsylvania State University, Erie

Carola Wolf (a PhD student at the University of St. Gallen) deserves special mention for handling the many permission requests required to link our ideas to the scholarship of others. We are also indebted to David Stanley Chappell whose contacts with Wiley initiated this project, and who made many significant contributions to early drafts of the manuscript.

We think of the resulting volume as a 'travel guide' for those facing new situations. It is not the book with one compelling idea that you can pick up in an airport – these efforts can be inspiring, and often raise important issues, but a travel guide should cover more material and inform people with more varied agendas.

However, no book can tell you everything you need to know about strategizing in today's demanding circumstances. Much of that knowledge must be learned from experience. We try to give you a good start on an important and interesting journey, and we wish you well.

Anne Huff

Steve Floyd

Hugh Sherman

Siri Terjesen

Teaching Supplements

An Instructor's Manual has been designed to facilitate convenient lesson planning and includes sample syllabi, chapter outlines, and in-depth teaching notes. Approximately 300 PowerPoint slides give instructors the ability to integrate classroom lectures with a visual statement of chapter material. A test bank consisting of 60 multiple choice, true/false, short answer, and essay questions of varying difficulty also is available for each chapter. These comprehensive resources can be found on the Instructor Companion Site at www.wiley.com/college/huff.

Strategic Management

→ → → LOGIC & ACTION

1

Defining Strategy

Everyone is a strategist. We all act, every day, to achieve desired results—trying to avoid being the person left clearing the dishes after dinner, seeking a desired job interview, or demonstrating for a worthy cause. This book focuses on business strategists, whose purpose is to create something of value to customers or clients and make enough money doing so to stay in operation. Their activities are similar to those we all use to achieve our individual desires. They collect resources and organize activities to achieve their objectives. They learn from failure as well as success. They observe and sometimes try to duplicate what others achieve. As the world changes, their strategies change.

Strategic "success" is in the eye of the beholder. Because our primary focus is on profit-making firms in this book, we will describe "above-industry-average profitability" as an important measure of success. It is a widely used comparative measure of ability, and one that very few firms manage to maintain over time. When other goals are added (to be socially responsible as well as profitable, for example), the strategist's task becomes even more difficult.

· ·

The strategy field has developed a vocabulary that is essential for further discussion. This introduction focuses on the nature of strategy by answering three questions:

What are the characteristics of effective strategy?
Communicates a compelling purpose to others
Connects organizational strengths with environmental opportunities
Exploits current success while exploring new opportunities
Generates more resources than it uses
Coordinates and guides activities
Responds to new conditions over time

How are strategists influenced by other strategists? How do they lead others?
Five levels of strategizing are important within the organization
Stakeholders influence strategists across organizational boundaries

Why are the successes and failures of other organizations important?
Performance differences shape stakeholder expectations
Performance differences offer evidence from strategic experiments

We use examples to help clarify concepts and analytic frameworks throughout the book—our first is particularly interesting.

· ·

NAPSTER: AN IDEA THAT CHANGED THE WORLD

In the fall of 1998, Shawn Fanning, a computer science freshman at Northeastern University, began working on a program to help his roommate share MP3 music files. His first efforts were not very reliable, but they were enthusiastically received, and Shawn's friends began to send the program to other friends. The response was so positive that Shawn did not go back to his university in January. He continued to refine his revolutionary "peer-to-peer" file sharing system that allowed a user to find and download music from another user's computer. In May 1999, with an uncle, he founded Napster.com, a site that allowed registered users to share music files without charge.

The Internet was radically changed by Fanning's idea. A number of universities quickly blocked access to Napster and the similar sites that followed because student use started to dominate available bandwidth. Young users were not the only ones involved. One new website allowed individuals to share detailed needlepoint designs. Napster itself reported that many of its users were over 30.

However, the freely shared files frequently were the products of commercial enterprises, and Napster was quickly involved in heated discussions about copyright. On December 7, 1999, the company was sued by the Recording Industry Association of America (RIAA) and eighteen record companies. Various recording artists, including the well-known heavy metal band Metallica, supported the suit. Other musicians applauded Napster, arguing that the record industry was too controlling and that new music was more likely to find an audience on the web.

Fifteen months after its inception, more than 23 million Napster users were registered. At that point, in October 2000, BMG (the third-largest record company in the world) announced an alliance with the controversial company and proposed a monthly fee of $4.95 for unlimited downloading. However, many file sharers resisted even a nominal charge, arguing in various ways that music should be a free resource. The model did not get off the ground, and a court ruling in the same month made Napster vicariously liable for its users' copyright infringements. Eight months later, founder Shawn Fanning and CEO Konrad Hilbers abruptly resigned and Napster was gone.

Napster left a legacy. New file-sharing services, using different technologies, continued to facilitate downloading. In response, the RIAA launched 261 music piracy suits against individuals in the fall of 2003, including a mother whose 12-year-old daughter had downloaded music. Gradually, additional legal actions were taken in the United Kingdom, Australia, and other countries, though downloads are more difficult to trace with new technology. A further move was the development of digital rights management (DRM) software that blocked copying.

Meanwhile, Roxio bought the Napster brand name and technology for $5.3 million at a bankruptcy auction, and Napster2.0 emerged in 2004 under new ownership as a legal music-download service that now offers millions of songs for 99 cents each or a monthly subscription fee. By the beginning of 2008, Apple's slick iPod players and iTunes site were estimated to dominate 80 percent of the music scene following the same pricing scheme, but the game is not over. The major music labels have dropped DRM, which facilitates many new partnerships. Most observers expect Amazon to counter Apple's dominance with "more flexible pricing" and a more varied set of partners offering downloads. Whatever happens next, the billions of music and video files that have already been electronically downloaded around the world are ample evidence that an 18-year-old student's invention revolutionized not just the Internet but an important aspect of contemporary life.[1]

Napster's story shows the power of a business idea that meets an unmet need. It would be ideal if a book on strategic management could offer a list of such promising ideas. In fact your job as a strategist is to identify opportunities, just as Shawn Fanning did. An increasing number of organizations are looking for employees who have this skill.

The record companies' strong response to Napster makes the second important point that strategists do not play on an empty stage. Beneficiaries of the status quo are likely to join forces when the current way of doing things is upset, particularly when the potential consequences are as far-reaching as publicly available file-sharing technology. Conflict significantly increases the resources needed to further innovate and win. In addition, radical departures from the status quo often generate heated discussions about what is fair and ethical, the subject of Chapter 9.

A considerable body of strategic management research and experience helps explain who is likely to succeed in evolving competitive dramas like the one Napster helped initiate. We present some highlights in this text in the hope that readers will apply them to situations of interest. A globalizing, increasingly interconnected world offers opportunities with significant rewards for generating the kind of response that Napster did.

Of course, globalization is not the only dynamic shaping strategy. While some companies are growing larger from sales around the world, customers also are paying more attention to local efforts, from farmers' markets to indie films. They also are monitoring a wider range of outcomes, such as environmental impacts. Our excitement about strategic management is fueled by the possibilities of this complex setting. We want you to have a more sophisticated understanding of the nature of strategy before we look at details.

WHAT ARE THE CHARACTERISTICS OF EFFECTIVE STRATEGY?

When you think about your strategic choices, such as choosing a college, a major, or a job, you can probably identify a number of different objectives. It is likely that you are a logical and forceful actor about some aspects of these decisions, but also influenced by chance and the timing of events around you.

Determining organizational strategy is even more complex. We believe effective strategy has to do several things simultaneously:

1. Communicate a compelling purpose or vision to others
2. Connect organizational strengths with environmental opportunities
3. Exploit current success while exploring new opportunities
4. Generate more resources than it uses
5. Coordinate and guide activities
6. Respond to new conditions over time.

Strategy Communicates a Compelling Purpose or Vision to Others

> **Strategy** defines a desired objective and communicates what will be done, by whom, how, for whom, and why the output is valuable.

A basic definition of *strategy* is that it is a purposeful attempt to achieve an objective. Though it may take some time for a startup firm to come up with the details shown in Figure 1.1, a complete picture of strategy needs to include the following:

- What will be done—typically creating product(s), service(s), and/or experience(s)
- Who will do the work
- How (and often when and where) the work will be done
- Who will be offered the results
- Why customers or clients are expected to value and pay for what they receive.

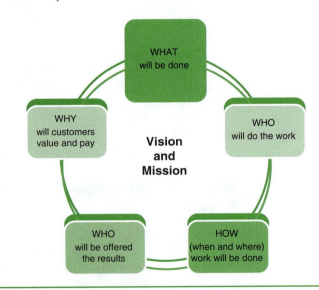

Figure 1.1 — A Visual Definition of Strategy

Vision statements provide a compelling image of what the company wants to become or do.

The dictionary definition of *vision* is "the ability to think about the future with imagination or wisdom."[2] *Strategic* vision more specifically provides a compelling image of what the organization is doing and why. Consider this statement from Google.

Never Settle for the Best

"The perfect search engine," says Google co-founder Larry Page, "would understand exactly what you mean and give back exactly what you want." Given the state of search technology today, that's a far-reaching vision requiring research, development, and innovation to realize. Google is committed to blazing that trail. Though acknowledged as the world's leading search technology company, Google's goal is to provide a much higher level of service to all those who seek information, whether they're at a desk in Boston, driving through Bonn, or strolling in Bangkok.[3]

The heart of this vision, in our minds, is providing "a much higher level of service to all those who seek information, whether they're at a desk in Boston, driving through Bonn, or strolling in Bangkok." It sets direction, but does not give employees and others very detailed information about what should be done, by whom, how, for whom, or why. A *mission* statement often provides this detail, and Google has one. Note that the following statement from Google's website addresses individual searchers, but also provides information of interest to advertisers, current and potential employees, stockholders, and the media.

Mission statements are more explicit than vision statements about what will be done, by whom, how, for whom, and why.

Google: Organizing the World's Information

Google's mission is to organize the world's information and make it universally accessible and useful.

As a first step to fulfilling that mission, Google's founders Larry Page and Sergey Brin developed a new approach to online search that took root in a Stanford University dorm room and quickly spread to information seekers around the globe. Google is now widely recognized as the world's largest search engine—an easy-to-use free service that usually returns relevant results in a fraction of a second.

When you visit www.google.com or one of the dozens of other Google domains, you'll be able to find information in many different languages; check stock quotes, maps, and news headlines; lookup phonebook listings for every city in the United States; search billions of images and peruse the world's largest archive of Usenet messages—more than 1 billion posts dating back to 1981.

We also provide ways to access all this information without making a special trip to the Google homepage. The Google Toolbar enables you to conduct a Google search from anywhere on the web. And for those times when you're away from your PC altogether, Google can be used from a number of wireless platforms including WAP and i-mode phones.

Google's utility and ease of use have made it one of the world's best known brands almost entirely through word of mouth from satisfied users. As a business, Google generates revenue by providing advertisers with the opportunity to deliver measurable, cost-effective online advertising that is relevant to the information displayed on any given page. This makes the advertising useful to you as well as to the advertiser placing it. We believe you should know when someone has paid to put a message in front of you, so we always distinguish ads from the search results or other content on a page. We don't sell placement in the search results themselves, or allow people to pay for a higher ranking there.[4]

Strategy is clearly a communication tool. Strategists must make sure that the right people know about the purpose of their organization and how it is being put into action. Aspects of this strategy must be clearly conveyed to salespeople, customers, managers, and other employees. In a typical business the board of directors, suppliers, partners, stockholders, and perhaps venture capitalists need to be informed as well. However, strategists in profit-making organizations such as Google are not the only ones who think about vision and mission. Individuals trying to realize personal objectives can think about strategy in this way. So can groups, non-profit organizations, networks, nation-states, and other entities.

Few actors need to know all components of strategy, and sometimes it is not a good idea to publicize details. When he was beginning to understand that his file sharing idea had promise, for example, Shawn Fanning benefited from the fact that the music establishment was not aware of his activities. As his purpose solidified, however, it was important that Napster attract an expanding group of users and employees. Eventually other groups had to understand what was being done, by whom, how, for whom, and why the outcome was valuable.

Napster is a wonderful example of how easy communicating a strategy can be. Fanning's vision was irresistible: share music without cost. Though illegal as initially formulated, the basic concept has had an amazing ripple effect. Strategists in other organizations often have to work harder to articulate purpose, but all successful strategists have to make their strategy compelling to others or they will not survive.

Strategy Connects Organizational Strengths with Environmental Opportunities

To recognize, develop, and evaluate strategic alternatives, it is important to look at the match between the capabilities of an organization and the environment where these capabilities might be used. Strategy connects a firm to individuals and other firms. They are all influenced by a broader environment of technological changes, economic realities, sociocultural values, and other forces. This macro context must be understood as the source of both strategic opportunities and threats to strategic success. A very general summary of this context is provided in Figure 1.2.

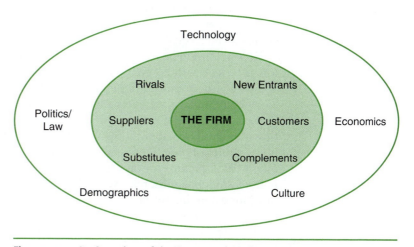

Figure 1.2 — An Overview of the Context of Business Strategy

This diagram appears again in Chapter 5, where it is discussed in more detail. At this point we merely emphasize that it is impossible to understand the sources of strategic ideas, or their outcome, without looking at the broader environment. Consider this example, from an interesting book called *Corporate Creativity*, by Professors Alan Robinson and Sam Stern.

A New Line of Business for Japan Railways East

When building a new high-speed line north of Tokyo, Japan Railways East was unexpectedly slowed by persistent flooding in a new tunnel. Specialists drew up plans to permanently divert the water, but the operation was stopped just in time, when a safety inspector suggested an alternative and much more strategic solution. Noting that workers had been drinking and enjoying the water, he proposed that the company bottle the water instead of draining it away.

In a relatively short period of time, Japan Railways East had vending machines on 1,000 rail platforms and was delivering bottled water to homes. Their advertising emphasized the long filtration that had taken place in the mountains and also noted the healthy minerals that the water had absorbed. It was an unplanned and unanticipated development that became a highly profitable new business, and solved what had been seen as a costly engineering problem.[5]

Several contextual issues are important in this short story. Demographic growth north of Tokyo was the opportunity that triggered Japan Railways East's decision to build a new rail line. The success of the new bottled water venture was a response to sociocultural changes leading individuals around the world to drink more water and be more concerned about its quality.

It is helpful to be more systematic about how these and other factors intersect with company characteristics. A worksheet for *SWOT analysis* can be found at the end of this chapter, the first of a series of tools included with every chapter. SWOT summarizes the *firm's* **s**trengths and **w**eaknesses, along with *environmental* **o**pportunities and **t**hreats. Thinking about organizational strengths and weaknesses helps strategists see themselves relative to their competitors. You might think Japan Railways East had no strengths for developing a bottled water business, relative to others already in the beverage business, for example, but don't forget that a captive market was waiting on railway platforms.

We hope you will take the time to apply SWOT to a situation you know. Research has shown that people learn more from activities that involve them directly. The worksheets found at the end of each chapter not only provide you with tools used in strategic analysis, but also give you a better understanding of the concepts we present and their value in action.

SWOT can be used in a static way that hides aspects of environmental change and new conditions within the firm. When used thoughtfully, it can summarize the evolution of strategy over time. It is particularly interesting to see how an apparent weakness in one setting might be changed into a strength by the introduction of a new strategy. This is a key issue facing many companies—such as Radio Shack.

**Worksheet 1.1:
SWOT
Analysis—A
Tool for
Identifying
Strategic Fit**

Staying in Tune with the Times at Radio Shack

Radio Shack moved from a retailing has-been in the United States to a force to be reckoned with in the electronics retail market in the 1990s. A major player in the 1980s as a vertically integrated manufacturing and retail enterprise, the company was blindsided by the rise of electronics superstores like Circuit City. Staffed by minimally trained sales clerks, these competitors offered deeply discounted prices on products that were often stacked on warehouse-style selling floors.

Radio Shack originally attempted to follow this trend with its Incredible Universe and Computer City superstores, but abandoned that strategy in 1997, shuttering all 17 Incredible Universe locations and selling its 90 Computer City stores to CompUSA. Unable to compete with the superstore concept, Radio Shack's new president, Leonard Roberts, chose an alternative strategy that identified the company's 7,000 retail outlets as its competitive advantage. Rather than manufacture products, the chain shifted its strategy to offer exclusive distribution of name-brand electronic products, especially wireless telephones and related goods, and it re-emphasized service as a way to support this new approach.

The company did have help. In 1996, Sprint was looking for a retail base from which to sell its wireless service, and Radio Shack offered an exclusive distribution opportunity. Radio Shack persuaded Sprint to contribute tens of millions of dollars toward upgrading its stores, in addition to providing needed advertising. As a result of further focus under Roberts, Radio Shack began to sell more wireless phones than its competitors Best Buy, Circuit City, Sears, and Montgomery Ward combined.

Unfortunately, the road continued to be rocky. In 2005 the company began a controversial program to monitor sales associates called Fix 1500. Then, in 2006, CEO David Edmondson resigned when it was revealed that he had doctored his résumé. The next hire, Julian Day, brought turnaround experience from Safeway, Sears, and Kmart. Though stock prices rose by 60 percent as a result, he took some heat when a large number of workers were notified via e-mail that they would be laid off.

By 2008, the company had more than 6,000 outlets around the world, and an important source of revenue was nonbranded kiosks in Sam's Club stores. Though Radio Shack is sometimes criticized for an "old fashioned" name and store design, Hoover's predicts that U.S. personal consumption expenditures on electronic goods will "grow at an annual compounded rate of 6.5 percent between 2007 and 2012." That's not bad, but some observers continue to question whether the company's business model works in a world of one-stop low-cost providers like Wal-Mart.[6]

Radio Shack is one of many companies that have significantly changed strategic direction in recent years. Imagine the difference in a SWOT analysis before and after Roberts took over. He and his team saw new opportunities in the external environment, especially the need for emerging wireless manufacturers to have effective retail outlets. Once an alliance strategy with Sprint was identified, old threats (notably warehouse-style competitors) became less important, but new ones had to be addressed. Strengths were also redefined: 7,000 small retail outlets had seemed a weakness, but they became a strength in the strategy adopted in the late 1990s, especially after the company's capacity for service delivery was improved. Yet five years later, store locations were less important as competitors across the industry began selling in convenient kiosks within larger retail locations.

Strategy Exploits Current Success While Exploring New Opportunities

Professor Jim March from Stanford University suggests that companies can follow two very different strategic paths when searching for opportunities.[7] *Exploration* strategies (like Japan Railways East's bottled water venture) find new ways to create value based on unfamiliar resources. In the process, strategists stretch their organization's capabilities well beyond what they were in the past.

Exploration strategies try to create new value from unfamiliar resources and activities.

Radical innovation is not, however, the only strategic opportunity. Indeed, as many Internet businesses illustrate, exploration is highly risky. The alternative to exploration is *exploitation*—a strategy that creates value by rearranging and improving established offerings. For example, exploitation strategies might seek better contracts with existing buyers or suppliers, use better equipment that reduces operating costs, or develop training programs that motivate workers and help them become more efficient. Improvements do not happen without attention and new activity, but when these efforts are successful, the effect can be additional value around an existing set of resources and activities.

Exploitation strategies try to create additional value using current resources and activities.

Because exploitation builds on what the firm already knows, it is often seen as less risky than exploration. Often this is an accurate assessment. An exploitation path can become a trap, however, when the environment changes.[8] In a dynamic environment, firms that merely do what they have done before quickly go out of business.

Strategy Generates More Resources Than It Uses

Strategy is much more than words; we suggest you look especially at the way money and other resources are deployed. It is equally important that strategy *generate* substantial resources—not only income, but reputation, employee commitment, brand identity, and other intangibles.

The balance between using and creating resources is critical. There is almost inevitably an imbalance at startup. Ultimately, however, customers, clients, or perhaps some third party must sufficiently value the outputs of strategy to pay for their creation. Unfortunately, quite a few organizations fail because the cost of their activities continues to exceed returns.

A strategic statement of "what, by whom, how, for whom, and why is it valuable" is therefore almost always an impressive achievement. Clever strategists leverage what they have in various ways, especially by connecting with other organizations. "Necessity is the mother of invention" is as true of strategy as it is of research and development (R&D), and invention is often needed to make inputs and outputs balance.

Strategy Coordinates and Guides Activities

Organizations exist to accomplish what individuals cannot effectively do on their own. Strategy is a helpful statement that indicates how individuals should work together. But there are limits to how much can be made explicit, even in very bureaucratic organizations. Strategists guide, rather than explicitly direct, activities within the organization and outside it.[9]

The word *guide* is critical. No statement can be detailed enough to tell many different people exactly what to do, especially when that statement is also supposed to be inspiring! Instead, strategy provides a general "recipe" that helps people make detailed decisions in their particular domain and coordinate with others. That logic is especially important in the unanticipated situations that inevitably arise.[10]

In other words, strategy should set off waves of compatible decisions that are important to achieving a given purpose. For example, after Fanning decided that his file-sharing concept was promising, he left college so that he could focus on programming, sought investor capital, incorporated, and moved to Silicon Valley. Strategic decisions in large companies can be traced in much more extensive progressions across functional specialties and geographic boundaries. Less strategic decisions are more contained and pertain to shorter periods of time.

Strategy Responds to New Conditions over Time

Our description of strategy so far has been rather straightforward. Strategy helps people focus attention on some things and de-emphasize others. Clarity is critical for influencing different people, in different places, across time. When strategy coordinates understanding and action in this way, it is a remarkable achievement—because there are many reasons why promising ideas do not proceed as planned.[11]

For example, many actors inside the organization and outside are simultaneously pursuing their interests. Customer needs and desires change and new competitors spring up to meet them. Sooner or later, because of these and other circumstances, even a compelling strategy has to be revised. Furthermore individuals and organizations often identify successful activities after they happen. All this means that strategic decision making in an inevitably changing world is more an ongoing process of *strategizing* than a one-time process of defining "what, by whom, how, for whom, and why it is valuable."[12]

Professor Henry Mintzberg, who teaches at McGill University, makes a useful distinction between *intended strategy* and *realized strategy*[13] that fits this idea very well.[14] Intended strategy is the plan before action begins; realized strategy reflects what is learned as events unfold. In our opinion, both kinds of strategy are useful. It is difficult to act, especially in groups of many individuals, without some kind of explicit statement of intention. That's intended strategy. But some of these

Strategizing is the ongoing process of discovering purpose, creating and using resources, and guiding supporting activities.

Intended strategy is the set of ideas, usually made explicit, that the strategist uses to inspire and direct activities.

Realized strategy is illustrated by the pattern of actual behavior over time.

ideas will not achieve desired results and so they cease to be used, while new insights and experiments that were not thought of originally will be incorporated into strategy over time.

The cumulative pattern of strategy can be difficult to follow. It takes time to understand new situations and assess the implication of many actions. Thus, strategists spend a great deal of time communicating strategy to those who must be involved. Clever observers (including competitors) often identify realized strategy more by looking at behavior than by examining verbal statements.

Figure 1.3 provides a summary of all six functions of strategy.

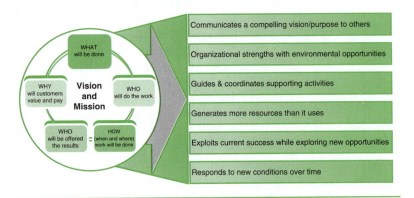

Figure 1.3 — Six Functions of Strategy

HOW ARE STRATEGISTS INFLUENCED BY OTHER STRATEGISTS? HOW DO THEY LEAD OTHERS?

The definitions and examples offered so far show that strategy is a relatively complicated response to a changing environment. It therefore should not be surprising that strategy is rarely developed by just one individual—such as the president or chief executive officer (CEO) of a firm. First, one person can rarely come up with all the ideas needed to define what, by whom, how, for whom, and why. Second, and more important, many different individuals, interest groups, and organizations care about and expect to have a role in specifying a firm's strategic objectives and activities.

Five Levels of Strategizing are Important within the Organization

Organizations vary in their formality and structure. Whatever form, structure provide channels of influence. Most organizations establish a hierarchy; a classic (simplistic and somewhat old-fashioned) example is shown in Figure 1.4. The arrows show that strategizing at any level within the organization will be affected by strategists both above and below.

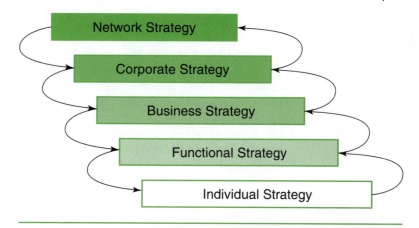

Figure 1.4 — Levels of Strategizing

Network strategy coordinates actions among allies that are not under the control of a single entity.

Network strategy develops within a group of organizations to achieve an objective that no single organization could achieve (or chooses to achieve) alone. Sometimes network strategy is formal and strict (contracts between buyers and suppliers, for example) but in many other cases it is informal. In all kinds of networking arrangements, however, the basic definitions of strategy just offered are still relevant. One example of a network strategy is the partnership of aerospace companies to design and build the Boeing Dreamliner.

Corporate strategy makes broad domain and funding decisions for a portfolio of business units.

In contrast to network strategy, *corporate strategy* develops within a single organization. Typically, the two most important foci of strategy at the corporate level are specifying the industries within which the business divisions of the corporation will compete, and allocating corporate resources to these divisions. The downward influence of corporate strategy thus determines the types of competitors encountered by a business and the resources available to compete with them. The corporate strategists' upward influence affects alliances with other organizations. An example of a corporate strategy is General Electric's goal to be either number one or number two in all of the markets in which it competes.

Business strategy defines what will be done, by whom, how, from whom and why to meet the goals of one organization, or one subunit of a diversified corporation.

Business (or organizational) strategy is generated within an independent business or within the division of a large corporation. Business strategy focuses on a single competitive arena or on a closely related set of arenas. Strategists at this level must influence the units that carry out strategy within their organization. Looking upward, business strategists are likely to influence external networks as well. For example, a business or organization strategist in Procter & Gamble's Duracell battery division focuses on how to compete in the battery industry, but that increasingly means connections with producers of goods that use batteries.

Functional strategy supports business strategy in areas such as information technology, human relations, research and development, and marketing.

Functional or operating strategy Functional strategists are coordinated by business-level strategy. In larger companies, functional units are likely to be established in information technology, human relations, finance, manufacturing, research and development, and marketing. These sub-units develop more detailed assessments of purpose and make more specific resource commitments than strategy at higher levels. Outsourcing can complicate the picture provided in Figure 1.4, as we will discuss in more detail in Chapter 5, but the basic interaction among strategic levels remains the same. An example of a functional strategy is a purchasing department's decision to implement an enterprise resource planning software package.

Finally, *individual strategy* potentially affects and is affected by all other strategic levels. The epilogue shows how the decisions of individuals can be analyzed using the frameworks we discuss in this book. A SWOT analysis, for example, can be highly relevant to personal career choices. You can also use SWOT analysis as a manager to predict how your employees might act in a new situation. Other important individual strategists (especially consumers) are outside the organization's formal boundaries, and their choices also affect the various levels of strategy.

Individual strategies direct efforts by individuals, inside or outside the organization, to protect and enhance their own welfare.

Stakeholders Influence Strategists across Organizational Boundaries

The overall conclusion to be drawn from the picture of interacting strategies shown in Figure 1.4 is that any given strategy will (and often should) be affected by strategy made in other parts of the organization. But this is not the only complication strategists face. Strategy is also the result of interactions with individuals and groups known as *stakeholders.* Some are likely to reinforce the organization's objectives, while others are likely to oppose its activities. They can be particularly influential when they form alliances that magnify their ability to influence the organization.

Stakeholders are potentially affected by an organization's activities and thus may attempt to influence its strategy.

Figure 1.5 provides the strategists' view of the environment we sketched more generically in Figure 1.2. If the expectations of the community, owners/stockholders, special interest groups, customers, partners, employees, governments, and suppliers are not met, some actors are likely to put a great deal of effort into trying to influence strategic decisions. Think of parents and teachers who work together to raise funds for school activities as an example from the public sector. Their cooperation may fit with the strategic plans of the school system very well. Parents working with lawmakers to legislate testing or impose other policy mandates on schools could be less welcome.

Figure 1.5 — Business-Level Stakeholders

Stakeholders vary in power and attentiveness, but even the possibility of positive or negative stakeholder activity affects the range of decisions strategists consider or execute. Whether they face an opportunity or a threat, stakeholders often affect how purpose is defined, how resources are gathered and used, and who benefits from this activity.

Each stakeholder is almost certain to see a given situation in a unique way because of their unique history and objectives. Further, not all actors have access to the same information or will attend to the same information. This complex, interactive, political environment makes it difficult to develop coherent strategy. A helpful starting point is to realize that every actor, inside and outside the organization, is trying to both make sense of the situation, and influence others to see the world in a way that fits the outcomes they prefer.

From the point of view of strategists at the business or organizational level, this tussle explains why coordinated action is important but also difficult. A classic problem for business level strategists, for example, involves reconciling inconsistent functional strategies that are likely to have incompatible objectives. The manufacturing unit typically wants to simplify product designs in order to smooth production, while the marketing department is likely to promote complex products to meet customer requests for new features. Business strategists try to address this kind of tension, but the welfare and strategic perspective of any one organizational group will never align perfectly with the needs of units established to achieve other purposes.

Sometimes inconsistencies are strategically useful. At the network level, for example, BMG kept its options open by maintaining participation in the RIAA lawsuit, even as strategists at the corporate level were working on a new business with Napster. Many strategists similarly explore new strategies with activities that are deliberately out of step with current strategy.[15] Fundamentally, however, strategy must limit the proliferation of inconsistent activities, because they make communication and coordinated activity so difficult.

Instead, strategists often try to create *synergies.*[16] They may, for example, build expertise in one functional unit by drawing on skills from other units. And strategists often rotate people through different job positions to promote understanding of the different pressures and contributions present in the business.

Synergies enable one resource to increase the impact of others.

Worksheet 1.2 can be helpful for developing strategy in situations that involve many different types of strategists. It relies on the very simple principle of identifying similar and dissimilar interests and trying to create positive links that are strong enough to counter inevitable negatives.

Worksheet 1.2: Stakeholder Analysis—A Tool for Working with Other Influential Strategists

At first, stakeholder analysis may seem overwhelming, given the large number of potential influences that could be identified. One approach is to limit the analysis to two groups: those that are the most active and those that seem most threatening. A broader base of analysis could be achieved in an organizational setting by dividing into work groups that focus on influential actors in different sectors in the environment. Stakeholder analysis would then identify the most important players for strategic consideration in each sector. The ultimate objective of stakeholder analysis, obviously, is to develop a compelling statement of strategy that will be acceptable to a large number of influential actors, while also inspiring and coordinating internal actions that are beneficial to the firm.

WHY ARE THE SUCCESSES AND FAILURES OF OTHER ORGANIZATIONS IMPORTANT?

Conversation about strategy cannot go very far without considering the strategist's *rivals.* These are the firms that compete for the same customers with similar offerings, often following similar strategies.

Rivalry means that stakeholders can compare organizations. Obviously, if a competitor provides outcomes that are much more attractive to customers, the firm must adapt or go out of business. Even before these choices are clear, however, if sources of capital or other influential stakeholders find one organization's strategy less compelling than others, survival is jeopardized.

Rivals offer similar products, services, or experiences to similar clients or customers.

It may seem paradoxical at first, but this basic reality means that interacting with strong competitors can strengthen a firm's capabilities—a theme that is developed further in Chapter 5. In this first chapter we simply observe that the performance of competitors is a valuable measure of strategic success and a source of models for potential adaptation.

Performance Differences Shape Stakeholder Expectations

Economic profit is the level of return after all costs of the unit's activities have been subtracted from revenue.

Economic theory proposes that over time, *economic profits* in a competitive arena will come together around an average figure as firms imitate each other, assuming that monopoly is not allowed. But the field of strategy refutes this view. Wherever there is rivalry, competitors try to differentiate themselves from one another. Research shows that profits tend to increase for firms that improve on, rather than just imitate, successful strategy.

Earning a profit means more than recovering the costs required to create it. Economic profit means recovering all costs: the costs of capital (shareholders' expected returns and interest on loans) along with something to reinvest in the business or use for other purposes.

The average return in an industry approximates what shareholders, analysts, banks, and other important stakeholders demand. By definition, only a few firms will be able to exceed this standard. The few firms that excel enjoy what is called *competitive advantage.* We know that a firm has an advantage because it has successfully competed for an above-average share of the industry's profits. Companies that consistently earn such profits (and/or meet some other performance standard important to stakeholders) have found a way to sustain their advantage.

Competitive advantage is revealed when a firm is more profitable than its rivals or exceeds them on other valued performance measures.

Competitive advantage is difficult to sustain over time, because rival strategists are highly motivated to copy success.[17] Nonetheless, there are a few impressive winners. As an introduction, Table 1.1 looks at return on assets, one way to think about economic performance.[18]

TABLE 1.1 RETURN ON ASSETS (ROA) IN FOUR RELATED INDUSTRIES (5-YEAR AVERAGE AS OF MAY 11, 2007)

Industry	Industry Average	Company	Company Average
Retail (Department and Discount)	8.6	Kohl's	12.2
		JC Penney	9.0
		Wal-Mart	8.7
		Tuesday Morning	8.2
		Target	7.7
		Sears	5.1
		Dillard	4.3
		Saks	−0.2
Retail (Specialty)	8.6	Costco	6.1
Retail (Grocery)	8.2	Whole Foods	9.4
		Tesco	7.9
		Safeway	5.7
		Kroger	5.4
Retail (Drugs)	7.0	Walgreens	11.8
		Rite Aid	0.4

Source: http://www.reuters.com. Accessed December 14, 2007.

The differences shown have significant consequences. Luck and differences among competitive environments partially explain why some organizations consistently outperform others, but most observers think that strategy accounts for performance variances like the ones shown. Boards of directors support or question corporate strategists based on this kind of comparison. Advice from investment analysts is based on this measure and a few others. Potential employees consider them. Current employees may stay or look for other jobs based on persistent comparisons.

Performance Differences Offer Evidence from Strategic Experiments

Laboratory scientists have confidence in their evidence because they can control the environment in which they experiment. Unfortunately for the strategist, the natural experiments that generate results like those shown in Table 1.1 are not as tidy. Still, comparative results like the ones shown are the only evidence of effective strategy available.

Wal-Mart may make more than companies such as Safeway and Kroger because along with groceries it also sells more expensive goods with higher margins. Surely there is more to it than this? Especially because Walgreens leads the group shown in Table 1.1? Most strategists spend a great deal of time thinking about comparisons like these. They try to make sense of them because they know their stakeholders are looking at similar figures as evidence about effective strategy. Strategists also need inputs to their own decision making.

Strategists consider the performance of their rivals in the hope of learning from their experience without the cost and time required to make their own experiments. Following the same logic, we offer many examples in this book. Although we know they will inevitably be a bit out of date by the time the publishing process is complete and you read them, the learning opportunities they offer should be taken seriously. If the questions they raise were easy to answer, strategic management would not be necessary, and the economists' expectation of regression to the mean would be borne out in fact. We know there are fascinating differences among organizational outcomes. This book provides frameworks for analyzing these results.

CONCLUSIONS FOR THE STRATEGIST

Strategy isn't always necessary. Dishwashing and other household tasks often are completed without maneuvering. Jobs sometimes are offered and accepted with little analysis on either side. Contributions to worthy causes are sometimes made without seriously examining the provider's operations. Entire organizations drift without participants seriously considering their purpose.

The authors of this book want something more. We want to live in reliably clean houses, find rewarding jobs, improve the world if we can, and influence what is done in the organizations where we work. That means we pay attention to strategy, and we hope that you, our reader, will too.

We have said that strategy establishes a desired objective and communicates what will be done, by whom, how, for whom, and why the output is valuable.

That seems straight forward, yet many strategies fail. The next five chapters help define a strategy that attracts enough resources for an organization to survive and prosper.

- Chapter 2 shows how **resources** can be developed and used to create competitive advantage.
- Chapter 3 describes how organizations create value for **customers** and provides ideas for drawing customers into the strategy process.
- Chapter 4 suggests that responding to **opportunity** brings needed energy and insight into the organization.
- Chapter 5 looks at **rivals** and the competitive environments they create.
- Chapter 6 discusses **business models**.

These are the basic building blocks of strategy. The chapters that follow add information about external and internal contexts that further affect the success of your efforts. Ideally you work, or will work, in an organization that actively seeks your inputs to strategy. Even if you do not, this book should be helpful for assessing the issues to which strategists around you are responding. We are confident that it won't be long before you identify your own contributions, and wish you well with this guide to strategizing.

Key Concepts

Strategy defines and communicates what an entity creates, by whom, how, for whom, and why it is valuable. It must also be a compelling statement of purpose that ultimately generates more resources than it uses and coordinates supporting activities while being responsive to changing conditions. Strategy is often communicated in a relatively general **vision** statement that provides a compelling image of what the organization should be. A more explicit **mission** statement often supplies more detail about what will be done, by whom, how, for whom, and why.

Strategies are more likely to succeed if they respond to or create opportunities in the environment, while minimizing threats. Successful

exploration strategies create new value with unfamiliar resources and activities. Successful **exploitation** strategies develop additional value from current resources and activities. Both kinds of strategy require recognizing an opportunity to turn a new idea into a successful venture.

Strategizing describes the ongoing process of discovering purpose, creating and using resources, and guiding supporting activities as new information accumulates. Consistent with this idea, it is useful to distinguish **intended strategy**, the set of ideas that the strategist uses to inspire and direct activities, from **realized strategy**, which is illustrated best by the pattern of actual behavior over time.

Strategists work at many levels in organizations. Each level can be expected to influence strategies developed at other levels. **Network strategy** coordinates actions among allies that are not under the control of a single entity. **Corporate strategy** deals with the broad domain and funding decisions for a portfolio of business units. **Business strategy**, the focus of discussion in this book, identifies specific competitive advantage(s) that can generate profit and other desired outcomes at the business unit or product level. **Functional strategy** supports business strategy in areas such as information technology, human relations, research and development, and marketing. **Individual strategies** are efforts by individuals, inside or outside the organization, to protect and enhance their own welfare.

More broadly, **stakeholders** (which are likely to include suppliers, employees, partners, customers, special interest groups, owners/ stockholders, local and perhaps international communities, and governments) are potentially influenced by organizational outcomes and thus may attempt to influence strategic activities. Strategy helps resolve differences of opinion among stakeholders. Ideally, the business strategist also finds **synergies** that enable one resource to increase the impact of others.

Strategists must pay attention to **rivals**, especially the firms that try to capture similar customers. Relative success is an important indicator of the viability of comparable strategies. **Economic profit,** the level of return after all costs of an organization's activities have been subtracted from revenue, is a particularly good performance indicator for profit making firms. **Competitive advantage** indicates that an organization is more profitable than its rivals or exceeds them on other measures valued by stakeholders.

Questions for Further Reflection

1. Choose a time frame (from one year to a lifetime) and describe your personal career strategy. What do you want to do, who needs to be involved in helping you, how will you proceed, who will benefit, and why will your efforts be valuable?

2. Identify five organizations that you admire, perhaps because they make a product you use or pursue a cause that is important to you. Using statements by organizational leaders found on the web, assess how compelling the public statement of each company's strategy is to you. Choose the one that you find least compelling and restate it.

3. Outline the network of organizations involved in delivering a widely used product or service. (You could choose part of the automobile industry, but consider being more venturesome. What about fresh flowers? Or football?) Using Figure 1.2, suggest environmental changes that might impact this network over time. Choose one actor in the network and think about how that actor might make sense of the changes you anticipate. Then, outline the efforts that actor might make to change current network strategy if the change in the macro environment you anticipate actually occurs.

WORKSHEET 1.1
SWOT Analysis—A Tool for Identifying Strategic Fit

In this activity, you use a worksheet to summarize the internal **s**trengths and **w**eaknesses of an organization you know (your employer, your school, your sports team, your church, etc.) in the context of environmental **o**pportunities and **t**hreats.

SWOT analysis has long been used as a tool for strategic analysis. If the analysis is done only once, it can be deceptively static. Comparative analysis is often a better thinking tool.

Step 1: Specify the organization and a time frame, then fill in your strategy summary and the four SWOT quadrants for the organization you wish to analyze.

Step 2: Identify which of the four boxes you were most uncertain completing, and brainstorm alternative answers.

Step 3: Put the most likely of these alternatives on one or more additional worksheets, and reconsider the other four categories in light of this anchor.

Step 4: Assess current strategy, given the fit revealed by these scenarios.

ALTERNATIVES

- Explore the SWOT implications of the most threatening or the most attractive ideas entered into the first worksheet.
- Fill out additional worksheets for competitors and compare them with your organization's current (or future) SWOT position.

SWOT Analysis Worksheet 1.1	Organization: Time Frame:
Analyst(s): Black = current (date _____) Blue = anticipated (date _____)	Strategy Summary:

Strengths	Weaknesses
Opportunities	Threats

WORKSHEET 1.2
Stakeholder Analysis—A Tool for Working with Other Influential Strategists

Step 1: Identify the most important groups and individuals that can affect the outcomes of an organization you know.

Step 2: Specify areas in which their interests are most likely to be supported and frustrated by current (or proposed) strategy.

Step 3: Brainstorm potential responses to these interests.

Working with Strategists Worksheet 1.2	Organization:
Analyst(s):	Strategy Summary:
Areas in which interests are likely to be supported by current/proposed strategy	Potential Interactions with specific stakeholders:
Areas in which interests are likely to be frustrated by current/proposed strategy	Potential Interactions with specific stakeholders:

NOTES

[1] Holahan, C. 2008. Sony BMG Plans to Drop DRM. *Business Week Technology* (January 4). Accessed January 21, 2008 at http://www.businessweek.com/technology/content/jan2008/tc2008013_398775.htm. To read Shawn Fanning's account of inventing Napster see Fredman, N. 2000. Shawn Fanning: Napster Founder and Former NU Student. *The Northeastern News* (October 18). Current news about Napster can be found at http://www.napster.com, accessed April 15, 2007. For background, see http://en.wikipedia.org/wiki/World_music_market and http://en.wikipedia.org/wiki/Napster, accessed April 15, 2007.

[2] http://www.askoxford.com/concise_oed/vision?view=uk, accessed May 5, 2007.

[3] http://www.google.com/corporate/tenthings.html, accessed May 5, 2007.

[4] http://www.google.com/corporate/, accessed May 5, 2007.

[5] Robinson, A., & Stern, S. 1998. *Corporate Creativity: How Innovation and Improvement Actually Happen*. San Francisco: Berrett-Koehler.

[6] An overview of Radio Shack and its competitive landscape can be found at http://www.hoovers.com/radioshack/–ID__11441–/free-co-competition.xhtml, accessed January 21, 2008. For an update on Radio Shack, see press releases at, http://www.radioshack.com. See also http://topics.nytimes.com/top/news/business/companies/radioshack_corporation/index.html?query=SAM'S%20CLUB&field=org&match=exact and http://en.wikipedia.org/wiki/RadioShack, accessed April 15, 2007. A satirical perspective can be found in Even CEO Can't Figure Out How RadioShack Still in Business. *The Onion* (April 23, 2007), accessed January 21, 2008, at http://www.theonion.com/content/news/even_ceo_cant_figure_out_how.

[7] March, J. G. 1991. Exploration and Exploitation in Organizational Learning. *Organization Science* 2: 71–87. For more on this topic, see McGrath, R. G. 2001. Exploratory Learning, Innovative Capacity, and Managerial Oversight. *Academy of Management Journal* 44: 118–131; Gupta, A. K., Smith, K. G., & Shalley, C. E. 2006. The Interplay between Exploration and Exploitation. *Academy of Management Review*, 49: 693–706.

[8] Leonard-Barton, D. 1992. Core Capabilities and Core Rigidities: A Paradox in Managing New Product Development. *Strategic Management Journal* 13: 111–125.

[9] Spender, J. C. 1989. Industry Recipes: The Nature and Sources of Managerial Judgement. Cambridge: Blackwell. Bower, J. L., & Doz, Y. 1979. Strategy Formulation: A Social and Political Process. In D. Schendel & C. Hofer (eds.), Strategic Management: A New View of Business Policy and Planning. Boston: Little, Brown.

[10] Huff, A. 1982. Industry Influences on Strategy Reformulation. *Strategic Management Journal* 3: 119–131.

[11] Dobni, B. 2003. Creating a Strategy Implementation Environment. *Business Horizons* (March-April), 43–46.

[12] Mintzberg, H. 2001. Decision Making: It's Not What You Think. *MIT Sloan Management Review* 42(3): 89–94.

[13] Mintzberg, H., & Waters, J. A. 1985. Of Strategies: Deliberate and Emergent. *Strategic Management Journal* 6: 257–272.

[14] Weick, K. E. 1995. *Sensemaking in Organizations*. London: Sage.

[15] McGrath, R. G., & MacMillan, I. C. 2003. *Discovery-Driven Planning*. Boston: Harvard University Press.

[16] Collis, D., & Montgomery, C. 1998. Creating Corporate Advantage. *Harvard Business Review*, 76: 3.

[17] Wiggins, R. R., & Ruefli, T. W. 2005. Schumpeter's Ghost: Is Hypercompetition Making the Best of Times Shorter? *Strategic Management Journal* 26: 887–911.

[18] Use the web for information on calculating ROA. For example, see http://www.answers.com/Return%20on%20Assets, accessed May 10, 2007.

2 Developing Resources

As individuals, we already know a lot about using resources. When we want something, we ask ourselves what is needed to achieve our goal. For example: "Do I have what it takes to become a competitive swimmer? Not just the skill, but the dedication, the coaches, and the travel money?" If resources are not at hand, we try to acquire them. Money is often important to achieving what we want, but everyday experience shows that money is not a substitute for the self-discipline, training, and commitment required to become a champion athlete. The objectives of organizational strategists similarly require financial resources, but also time, skill, and other inputs.

It is possible to use different resources to produce similar outcomes, just as swimmers with different genetic endowments will choose different coaches and use different practice routines. Like the athlete, the strategist must find a particularly effective bundle of resources and manage it over time to create sustainable competitive advantage.

This chapter answers the following questions:

Which firm resources are associated with competitive advantage?

How are competitive resources created and sustained?
   Branding
   Supporting activities
   Investment
   Position
   Accumulation
   Socialization

What risks are associated with resource accumulation?
   Uncertain capacity to accumulate resources
   Causal ambiguity
   Overcommitment
   External attribution

How is resource accumulation and deployment strategically managed?

The basic ideas behind effectively collecting and managing resources are straight forward. (Anyone could outline a workout schedule for a competitive swimmer on paper.) But living up to this vision and developing the skills to win are an entirely different matter. The problems and rewards of accumulating and using competitive resources are magnified several times at the business level. Consider Disney, a company that enjoys a remarkable set of resources.

THE IDEAL STAR

If you were choosing a performer to play the leading role in your blockbuster movie—purely from a business standpoint—what criteria would you use? How about a performer who is one of the world's best-known personalities, who is always ready and willing on a moment's notice, who doesn't require a formal contract, who never complains about anything, who doesn't even have an agent, and . . . whose rates are far below what all other actors demand?

Walt Disney Studios has dozens of such performers—classic names such as Mickey Mouse and Snow White, along with more recent stars such as the Little Mermaid, Simba, and Buzz Lightyear. The company has successfully used these characters in film, television, videotape, the Internet, consumer products, and theme park attractions. Over time, the characters' appeal has led to the development of a "Disney brand" that creates strong loyalty among customers. In the media business, nine out of ten projects fail. Disney's ability to create unique animated characters allowed it to produce top-notch entertainment at a low cost, with remarkably few failures for many years.

However, in 1997 Disney's financial performance took a significant turn for the worse. Michael Eisner, the company's CEO and an important force behind the effective use of its decades-old assets, explained the problem as the result of a few big clunkers at the box office, including *Hercules* and *Mission to Mars*. Some analysts thought the problem was deeper than that, stating that Disney's cherished animated film characters and the strategy of creating wholesome, family entertainment no longer resonated with contemporary American (or international) values.

Perhaps confirming Mickey Mouse's fading appeal in a changing world, Regis Philbin and the show *Who Wants to Be a Millionaire*? appeared to be Eisner's lifeboat in late 1999. In eighteen months it earned almost $1 billion for ABC and its parent, the Walt Disney Company. The stock market reacted favorably, but Regis and his show were not as unique or as durable as Donald Duck and Goofy. *Millionaire* was challenged by the CBS show *Survivor*, which was scheduled in the same time slot. On *Survivor's* first airing, 2.5 million more people watched the desert island performance than Regis's big-money game, and a number of similar shows followed close behind.[1]

Disney celebrated its fiftieth anniversary in 2005. Under new CEO Bob Iger, the company has been doing very well in the last few years, and the star performer is studio entertainment.[2] Pixar Animation Studios, purchased at the beginning of 2006, set box office records with *Finding Nemo* and *Shrek 2*. Its *Pirates of the Caribbean* trilogy, enhanced by computer-generated imagery, broke numerous box office records.

Disney also made headlines as the first media partner joining Apple to sell TV shows and movies on iTunes. An additional sign of success is that the company continues to be chosen as one of the best places to work by U.S. graduates. All in all, it is easy to conclude that Disney has found a place in the hearts of many people—and that an impressive group of cartoon characters still has a role to play.[3]

WHICH FIRM RESOURCES ARE ASSOCIATED WITH COMPETITIVE ADVANTAGE?

Disney illustrates one of the most enduring insights from strategy research: even the most ably supported advantage cannot be sustained forever. Some advantages can last over a significant period of time, however, and bring profit in many different ways. The strategist's job is to accumulate and utilize the *resources* that create these advantages. Differences in carrying out that job are a primary reason why some firms are more profitable than other firms in the same market.

> **Resources** are assets used to create and support offerings to customers or clients.

The Resource Based Theory of the Firm[4] provides useful vocabulary for thinking about why success tends to be associated with distinctive patterns of resources. From this perspective, an organization is a bundle of resources capable of creating value for shareholders and other stakeholders. Strategists are constantly trying to enhance their organization's resource bundle as environmental and internal circumstances change. Both theory and empirical evidence suggest that those who are better at identifying (and creating) changes in the world around them, then adjusting their resource mix accordingly, are more likely to perform above the average for their industry.

Figure 2.1 provides a brief summary of this logic. At the bottom of the figure are two kinds of resources—the basic building blocks of competitive advantage: *tangible* (physical) *resources* and *intangible* (not directly visible) *resources*.

> **Tangible resources** have a physical reality—examples are buildings, machinery, and supplies.

Most tangible resources are widely available and unlikely to create competitive advantage or meet performance demands of stakeholders by themselves. They are more likely to satisfy performance demands

> **Intangible resources** are not directly visible—examples are knowledge and reputation.

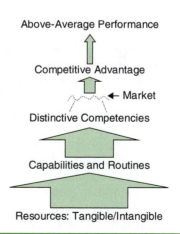

Figure 2.1 — Resource-Based Model of Performance

Capabilities are combinations of resources that create value.

when they are combined with intangible skills and knowledge to create *capabilities*. A simple example involves uniting an individual's hand-eye coordination with an automobile to end up with driving as a capability. The automobile without a driver provides little value; conversely, the ability to drive without an automobile is also of little use. The combination of the car (a tangible resource) and driving skill (an intangible resource) creates value.

Organizations collect, extend, and elaborate individual capabilities. The bundle of resources developed far exceeds the possibilities of individuals working on their own. Imagine being able to work with the talents that Walt Disney put together over the years—many of the best people wanted to work at his studio, and this must be seen as the foundation for his success.

Routines systematize the knowledge required to create and replicate capabilities needed by the organization.

Routines provide a way of systematizing the possibilities of the organization's bundle of resources. After all, Walt Disney couldn't live forever. Routines create "regular and predictable patterns of behavior in firms"[5] that persist over time, even as employees leave or enter the organization. Examples include procedures for ordering new inventory, advertising, accounting, and many other support activities as well as the procedures that directly create goods, services, and experiences. They are an important means of reproducing success, even though they can become disadvantageous if they persist when they no longer create value.[6]

Distinctive competencies are the organization's unique resources, capabilities, and routines.

Distinctive competencies are even more important for understanding profitability. Every organization has many resources, capabilities, and routines that are similar to those found in other organizations. Indeed, a large set of resources, capabilities, and routines are necessary to stay in business. Only a relatively small number of things that the organization does will be distinctive competencies. For example, Disney's signature style is a distinctive competency.

An important contribution of the resource base view was to put the spotlight on distinctive capabilities as a source of competitive advantage, as shown in Figure 2.1. As we said in Chapter 1, competitive advantage represents the ability of an organization to consistently outperform rivals in a given market. Enduring advantage is created by skillfully identifying distinctive competencies and combining them with other more widely available resources to attract and keep customers. The most widely used test of this relatively rare ability is economic profit that surpasses that of rivals—although other performance measures can also be important. Companies that consistently appear on lists of desirable workplaces, for example, have a competitive advantage.

The list of distinctive competences in a given organization is almost inevitably short because of the human will and ability to imitate. Humans (along with many other animals) have a remarkable tendency to modify their behavior after observing successful behavior by others, and sometimes this happens without conscious effort. In business settings, rivals deliberately match successful routines developed by other companies, and stakeholders often expect strategists to follow proven practices.[7]

Mimetic behavior is activity that follows patterns observed in the behavior of others.

This *mimetic behavior* is often strategic. Strategists can and should observe and learn from the skillful performance of others, and it makes sense to hire employees who have worked in companies with high performance. Strategists should also learn from customers, suppliers, distributors, and other intermediaries.

The firm with a distinctive advantage has to anticipate this mimetic process, which is one reason that no advantage can be expected to last forever. At the same time, the firm that copies should be cautious. Our globalizing, increasingly connected world tends to speed deterioration of advantage as firms follow each other's success. Only firms with less obvious and more difficult-to-understand resources, capabilities, and routines have a chance to elude the will to copy profitable strategies, at least for a time.

Socially complex activities arise from the interaction of individuals and other resources; they are difficult to understand, but result in more than the apparent sum of their parts.

Research suggests that distinctive competencies based on *socially complex activities* are particularly important, and thus we will focus most of this chapter on this aspect of resource development. Socially complex activities exceed the understanding of any one individual, even those who participate in them. They consequently are difficult for outsiders to understand or replicate; even former employees will find replication difficult.

Although we have been speaking in terms of corporate or organizational strategy, the same resource-based logic is applicable at other levels of strategic decision making. For example, it makes sense for a functional department focused on information technology to think about whether it has, or can obtain, competitive advantages when compared with other IT providers because outsourcing functions that do not meet the competitive advantage test has become easier and easier. Organizations certainly make mistakes in outsourcing decisions, but the basic logic of using the best suppliers (internal or external) is hard to refute.

Resource-based logic can also be applied at an individual level. It makes sense for people to think about and strategically develop their own bundle of resources, capabilities, and distinctive competencies. Almost everyone will be in the labor market multiple times within his or her lifetime. Many people choose, or are forced by circumstances, to alter their objectives. Each time this happens, an opportunity arises to revisit one's distinctive competencies and ask: Do I have a competitive advantage?

Worksheet 2.1:
A Tool for
Analyzing
Resources
. . . .

Worksheet 2.1 can be used to analyze resources at all levels, from the individual to the network, along with further instructions for its use. We encourage you to learn the resource-based vocabulary by using this worksheet, because it has proven to be a particularly useful way of thinking about strategy.

HOW ARE COMPETITIVE RESOURCES CREATED AND SUSTAINED?

One thing that makes strategy interesting is that different decision makers often come to entirely different conclusions about what combination of resources is most likely to bring them an advantage. Retail banking offers one example.

Royal Bank of Scotland: The Counterintuitive Strategy

Consolidation within the banking industry around the world has been rather dramatic in the last few decades. This has been accomplished primarily by large banks buying up smaller, regional banks and incorporating them into their systems. The usual strategy has been to rename the purchased banks under a single corporate name. Banc One, Bank of America, Citigroup, and Barclays are among the acquirers that have used this strategy to create a "supermarket" of services under one highly recognizable brand. Banks following this approach view the "umbrella brand" as a highly valued resource and invest considerable effort in developing it.

Royal Bank of Scotland Group (RBS) PLC has developed a different strategy. More like a "shopping mall" than a supermarket, RBS offers a variety of products under multiple brands.[8] For purposes of efficiency, the bank consolidates back office operations, but it views the acquisition process as collecting brands rather than killing them. In doing so, it creates competition among its own branches. Yet the company is described as being "one of the UK bank sector's star performers since taking over NatWest in 2000."[9]

In theory, maintaining multiple brands is a costly and inefficient strategy. However, behind the scenes, RBS supports a massive centralized technology and purchasing infrastructure that creates economies of scale. The bank believes that the cost of maintaining separate brands is worth the advantage gained by leveraging the identities of former competitors. The results support this belief. In 2007 the company was ranked fifty-forth in the Fortune Global 500.[10]

At the time we write this book, Royal Bank of Scotland's strategy has proven to be profitable and sustainable. An interesting comparative study of bank performance by Accenture, the consulting firm, compared RBS to other prominent banks in a way that underscores our emphasis on distinctive competence:

> Wells Fargo . . . sets the pace in distribution, Danske Bank [is a leader in] workforce superiority. Citibank's back-office scope and flexibility is a major competitive advantage, while Royal Bank of Scotland excels

at risk management and multi-brand management. It is important to note that in each case, the decision to concentrate resources and investment on one area is not at the expense of the other performance drivers. In fact, just the opposite is true. These institutions became high performers as a result of a strategic focus on, and a commitment to, elevating to excellence in at least one key skill set, while clearly demonstrating a general level of competence across the board.[11]

Many combinations of resources are possible. We define Disney's distinctive competitive advantage as the ability to consistently market and produce family entertainment at a relatively low cost. Underlying this competitive advantage is a unique pool of resources, capabilities, and routines, including a large cast of animated characters, and the routinized capability to make them remarkably lifelike performers in appealing scripts. In other words, Disney has more than the necessary resources to be in its business, and consumers reward its distinctive capabilities with above-average box office returns.

Resource-based theory has developed some indicators of the resources most likely to generate this kind of market advantage, using terms that are not often found in common conversation. That is not a bad idea from a strategic point of view, because strategists who master them may make it a bit harder for competitors to understand and copy their success. Resources are competitive resources because they have the following characteristics:

1. **Rare:** A resource that is widely available will not be distinctive.

2. **Nontradable:** A resource cannot be available for purchase in an open market; otherwise it will not remain rare over time.

3. **Nonsubstitutable:** If another resource can be substituted, the original resource loses its uniqueness.

4. **Inimitable:** The more difficult or costly it is to imitate a resource, the more likely it is to remain unique.

5. **Flexible:** A resource that can be adapted to new situations is much more likely to contribute to sustained advantage in a changing world.[12]

6. **Nonappropriable:** The profits generated by the resource must not be captured (appropriated) by others.[13]

A resource that meets one or more of these criteria may lead to a competitive advantage. The first four criteria are factors that preserve the unique, distinctive character of the resource. The fifth criterion listed, flexibility, is important in today's economy because rapid change is possible and often desired. There is considerable variance in the capacity of firms to ride the waves of change. Those that succeed often do so because they use resources, capabilities, and routines that can be adapted to different contexts and different times.

The sixth criterion, appropriability, assesses whether the firm or some other competitor realizes the value or profit from the resource. Appropriability should not be a serious issue for a firm that combines relatively rare, nontradable, nonsubstitutable resources in unique ways. But that is not always the case.

Who really earns the economic profit from Disney's consumer products? Disney does not manufacture a thing. Instead, it licenses other companies to do the manufacturing. Although Disney does not realize all the revenue from the toys, clothing, and so on that bear its name, the above-average royalty charged to manufacturers means that Disney—not the manufacturer— appropriates most of the profit from its unique brand name.

It is not easy to unravel how competitive advantage is generated with competitive resources that meet at least some of these criteria. The attempt often draws strategists into very specific functional-level activities. Attention to detail is worth it, however, in order to understand more about how firms differ, and why some are more profitable than others. In this chapter we highlight six aspects of creating sustainable advantage:

- Branding
- Supporting activities
- Investment
- Position
- Accumulation
- Socialization

Branding

A registered brand such as Disney's is obviously rare and nontradable, and in some markets, brand appears to be the single most important resource in determining market share. However, the value of this resource, and all others, depends on context. Table 2.1 estimates the percentage of customers loyal to a single brand across various products.

In the top categories, developing and managing brands is an obvious strategic priority. But why are brands in some markets so much more successful than others? And why are branding activities so different across companies, or even within the same company at different points in time? It is necessary to think about what lies *behind* brand name and other resources.

Strategists initiate different activities to create and maintain brand identity. They ask: What resources are at my disposal? What skills can I use or develop to create brand awareness? How can these be combined into more complex capabilities? What routines can I put into place to sustain my brand over time? Most important: How can I establish a brand image in the minds of my customers?

TABLE 2.1 THE VALUE OF BRAND AS A RESOURCE

Product	Percentage of Users Loyal to One Brand
Cigarettes	71
Mayonnaise	65
Toothpaste	61
Coffee	58
Headache remedies	56
Film	56
Laundry detergent	48
Beer	48
Automobiles	47
Shampoo	44
Soft drinks	44
Underwear	36
Television	35
Batteries	29
Athletic shoes	27
Garbage bags	23

Source: C. Schewe & A. Hiam, *The Portable MBA in Marketing* (New York: Wiley, 1998).

It is impossible to provide a recipe book for answering these questions, and they merge into the domain of marketing. From a strategic perspective, competitive resources, skills, and capabilities are unique to each company and meaningful only if customers feel other companies cannot match them. But these are not the only sources of advantage. Research also highlights the potential advantage of activities, investment, position, accumulation, and culture.

Supporting Activities

Specific people must do specific things to create a competitive resource. Think about your personal resources and capabilities. If you are a competitive swimmer, part of your performance has to do with certain genetic assets, such as strong lungs and broad shoulders. In addition, however, your ability has almost certainly developed from hundreds of hours of practice, coupled with specialized weight training and discipline in diet. Those who coach athletes (who are certainly strategists) try to make sure these activities take place regularly.

The idea that strategy is about creating and integrating activities around a common purpose is as old as the field itself.[14] We outline an

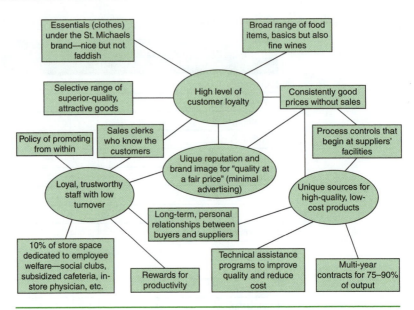

Figure 2.2 — Marks & Spencer's Activity System

Source: Analysis based on A. Montgomery, Marks & Spencer Ltd. (A). Harvard Business School Case No. 391089.

example in Figure 2.2. This set of interactions describes Marks & Spencer, a department store chain headquartered in the United Kingdom that long enjoyed a remarkable brand name and loyal customers, based on offering high-quality, relatively low-cost products.

Marks & Spencer: Unadvertised Advantage

BBC News describes Marks & Spencer as "the granddad of British consumer brands, spending most of the 20th century building up a reputation as the UK's most admired business."[15] The firm had not only a brand name for "quality at a fair price" and strong customer loyalty, but also very loyal employees. Typically, retailers face high turnover among employees, intense competition from rivals, and cost pressures from large brand-name manufacturers. Lord Marks of Broughton, chairman of Marks & Spencer from 1916 to 1964, articulated five principles that helped his company avoid these problems. One of his principles was to foster good relations with suppliers, staff, and customers.

Marks & Spencer concentrated on store-branded merchandise and built strong relationships with a network of suppliers to provide good-quality products at fair prices. The company sold only British-made goods and was the sole customer for many of these firms. They invested in technical assistance programs to help suppliers overcome cost or quality problems long before forging strong relationships with suppliers was fashionable.

> Other strategic decisions led to a series of unique investments in employee relationships, including 10 percent of store space dedicated to amenities such as employee social clubs and in-house medical care. These commitments helped reduce turnover among employees to exceptionally low levels. The firm created an environment where people knew each other well and it reinforced warm social relationships, not only among staff, but also with customers and suppliers. This, in turn, led to trust, reduced the costs of monitoring employees and suppliers, and solidified customer loyalty.[16]
>
> The customers, of course, were key. Marks & Spencer's St. Michael brand had a very strong reputation for fair value for money. The goods were available in stores across the United Kingdom, and returns were accepted even without a receipt. The company's reputation was so strong that it did not feel the need to advertise on television. At the end of the 1997/1998 fiscal year, it had a turnover of more than £8 billion, with pretax profits of £1.17 billion.[17]

If you have traveled in the United Kingdom, you may know that 1998 was a high point for the company, and the performance picture rapidly deteriorated thereafter. However, before updating the story we want to make two important points about the system that Marks & Spencer was able to assemble. First, it is the interconnections among activities that produce advantage. The ovals in Figure 2.2 show competitive advantages that result from combinations of very specific activities. One activity in and of itself may not have much significance, but in combination they produce a valuable resource.

Second, the choices that produced these activities must be different from the choices made by rivals if they are to yield competitive advantage. Other retailers in the United Kingdom, for example, emphasized manufacturer brands, and few provided employees with the kinds of perks found at Marks & Spencer. Many rivals offered broader, more fashionable lines of merchandise. It would have been natural for Marks & Spencer managers to broaden their product line to include trendier clothing and otherwise emulate strategies that seem to be succeeding in the marketplace. However, strategy is about doing things differently. That worked for a long time at Marks & Spencer,[18] though the formula shown in Figure 2.2 ultimately did stop providing an advantage.

Investment

Activity requires investment, and competitive advantage typically requires considerable investment. An important thing to learn from the success of companies such as Disney, Royal Bank of Scotland, and Marks & Spencer is that strategy is about saying no to many possible investments so that resources can be concentrated on creating and sustaining competitive advantage in well-specified ways.

Resource flows support current activity.

Resource stocks accumulate from investments over time to support competitive advantage.

Worksheet 2.2: Activity Map—A Tool for Connecting Strategic Investments

· · · · · · · · · · · · · · · ·

One of the metaphors often used to describe the process of managing investment in resources is filling a bathtub. The gush of water as it fills the tub can be seen as the flow of investments needed to create resources. At Marks & Spencer, *resource flows* include the company's investments in employee rewards.

The level of water in the bathtub represents the *resource stocks* that have accumulated from past investments, such as Marks & Spencer's high level of employee loyalty.[19] The resource stock underlies current competitive advantage. The resource flows determine whether an advantage will be sustained or whether, perhaps, a new competitive advantage can be developed.

Notice that the flow decisions—investments in resources—are very fine-grained. Unlike grand corporate strategies (the decision to spend millions on an acquisition, for example), flow decisions involve multiple investments in technical and administrative systems and other specific activities. The detailed decisions required to amass these resources are made by middle- and operating-level personnel, and in recent years analysts have come to see that they are critical to strategy.[20] At the same time, broad themes guide flow decisions; top-level managers, such as Lord Marks, typically develop these themes.

Breaking resources down into their component activities and the investments that support them helps maintain strategic consistency and focus across a wide range of more tactical investment activities. A tool for doing so can be found in Worksheet 2.2.

Position

Activity and investment take place in a specific time and place, and both time and place make a difference. Let's go back to your hypothetical swimming talents. If swimming is important to you, living in California might be considered a plus, because you could swim year round and there are many able coaches and many competitive swim teams to join. Serious athletes sometimes move to take advantage of this relatively unique environment and see their skills improve as a result.

On the other hand, you have to be very good indeed to win a regional meet in California. The same skill might take you further in a less competitive environment. Indeed, you might have a greater chance of becoming an Olympic athlete if you swim in a country where very few young people have the privilege of competitive training.

The choice (if you are driven to be a winner, and have the capacity to move) would seem to be obvious. But, as often happens in strategy, it is not that simple. You had better hurry no matter where you move. Better-trained, younger athletes are breaking today's records, and more and more countries are sending winners. The general point, of course, is that today's business strategists face increasingly competitive conditions and thus have more complicated choices to make.

We defer a more complete discussion until later chapters that focus first on entrepreneurship (in Chapter 4) and then on rivalry more generally (in Chapter 5). At this point we will only observe the following:

- Where activity and investment take place makes a difference.
- When activity and investment take place makes a difference.
- Some choices are much more likely to succeed than others.

A basic trade-off involves trying to improve skills and abilities by facing particularly demanding competitive environments, an expensive and risky position, versus increasing the returns from current capabilities by seeking more sheltered environments. Table 2.2 illustrates this trade-off between deploying and accumulating resources.

TABLE 2.2 DIFFERENCES BETWEEN RESOURCE DEPLOYMENT AND ACCUMULATION

	Deploying Resources	Accumulating Resources
Focus	Apply what we already know	Learn what we need to know
Time frame	Short to immediate term	Varies, but may be very long term
Expected results	Efficient execution of plan	Trying new things leads to both success and failure
Norms of behavior	Consistency and conformity	Divergence and creativity
Core assumption	Success is determined by the efficiency and effectiveness of resource allocation processes	Success is determined by the discovery and integration of new skills and ability

These differences became an important trade-off for Marks & Spencer as strategists used its accumulated resources to diversify. As it happened, an exploratory strategy moved the firm into international environments that were unexpectedly competitive. After the fact, Marks & Spencer strategists were judged to have made poor decisions at home as well, because they took their eyes off increasingly aggressive new entrants. In a remarkably short time they lost the esteemed position the company had long enjoyed.

The Fall of Marks & Spencer, 1998–2003

By 2003, Marks & Spencer had suffered a five-year decline in sales. The perception of the company slipped with remarkable speed from "assured quality" to "dowdy." The firm's collapse was a great shock to many, and a number of changes in positioning seemed responsible.

Diversification. In the 1990s, Marks & Spencer expanded throughout Europe, Canada, and the United States. Although the company enjoyed a strong reputation abroad, the firm encountered different retailing concepts that it failed to dominate with its operating strategy. After six years, strategists at Marks & Spencer reversed the diversification strategy. The company closed thirty-eight continental European stores, cut 4,000 jobs, eliminated its U.K. catalog business, and sold off its U.S. interests in Brooks Brothers. These measures resulted in a charge as high as $450 million.

Merchandising. The core business suffered during the period of diversification. Long recognized as one of the leaders in combining stylish fashion and food, Marks & Spencer slowly lost its trendsetting position in apparel. Department layouts and displays looked tired and outdated. New strategies, such as a lingerie joint venture with Agent Provocateur, flopped. The firm failed to achieve critical mass in new product areas such as mobile phones and digital media.

Competition. Other apparel retailers, such as The Gap, Next, H&M, and Topshop, hit the High Streets with more contemporary and trendy assortments targeted to younger audiences. Instead of being a leader, by 2000 Marks & Spencer was forced to be a follower.

Advertising. Various advertising campaigns flopped and reaffirmed the public's view that the retailer was out of touch.

Management. Problems with uncoordinated management practices and problems started to appear in the interfaces between top management, middle management, and front-line employees. Instead of acting together, the three groups were moving apart. Trust levels were falling, morale was fading, and people were becoming cynical and negative in their thinking and responses.[21] The closure of the Paris branch ended up in a legal wrangle. Longtime suppliers in the United Kingdom were dropped in favor of cheaper overseas suppliers; however, Marks & Spencer had not secured its supply lines before becoming reliant on overseas manufacturers. Empty clothing racks, especially in the key winter season, simply advertised to the market that the company had lost its way.

Clearly the retailing environment had become more challenging. The media and many other onlookers spent a great deal of time analyzing the firm's situation. As is often the case, many strategies could be recommended, but it is hard to find consensus about *how* strategists should regain the success they once enjoyed. Stuart Rose, appointed CEO in 2004, led a turnaround that included high-profile advertising and was knighted at the end of 2007 for his success in helping revitalize a major British institution.[24] A press release in 2005 indicated that "the outlook remains challenging, with tough economic and competitive conditions expected to continue. We are focused on delivering better quality, value and styling across all our product ranges, as well as improving service levels and store environment. We have made good progress, however, there remains much to do."[22] Strategies emphasized in other publications include the following:

- Refocusing on customers in three areas: product, service, and store environment
- Renegotiating supplier agreements and reorganizing buying teams
- Speeding delivery of high-quality product to stores
- Reducing stock commitments by more than 35 percent to increase flexibility
- Reducing clutter to make stores easier to shop
- Strengthening the Marks & Spencer brand with the launch of Your M&S
- Completing the sale of M&S Money to HSBC; acquiring per una (a brand of children's clothing); closing the Lifestore project; and returning £2.3 billion to shareholders
- Opening 31 Simply Food stores
- Emphasizing corporate social responsibility, including the use of fair trade products
- Implementing "green store" modernization plans[23]

Accumulation

We have already noted how long it takes to collect sufficient stock of some resources, particularly some kinds of intangible assets and technical capabilities. Table 2.3 provides some interesting evidence about how long a company should expect to work before developing some of the most valuable assets.

TABLE 2.3 AVERAGE REPLACEMENT PERIOD OF SELECTED INTANGIBLE RESOURCES

Intangible Resource	Replacement Period (Years)
Company reputation	10.8
Product reputation	6.0
Employee know-how	4.6
Networks	3.4
Supplier know-how	3.1
Databases	2.1
Distributor know-how	1.6

Source: R. Hall, 1993. The Strategic Analysis of Intangible Resources, *Strategic Management Journal* 13: 135–144.

The necessity of commitment may seem obvious from this evidence, but considerable subtlety is involved. Amazon faced a particularly difficult situation in its first years of operation as it tried to manage inventory.

Amazon's Stockpile

After hitting a high of $107 per share in December 1999, Amazon's stock lost more than half its market value by mid-2000. At that point, an analyst at a leading Wall Street investment bank issued a stinging financial analysis—essentially saying that the company was draining cash at a rate that threatened its survival. One of the biggest problems, according to the analyst, involved resources.

In its first few years, Amazon's managers accumulated talented programmers and marketing skill. As the product line expanded from books to other goods, warehouses and distribution centers were built all over the United States and ultimately around the world. But strategists failed to accumulate necessary inventory management skills and systems. As a result, they lacked the capability to estimate the amount and kind of inventory to order, and unsold inventory does not generate cash. Sales grew 170 percent in 1999, but inventory swelled by 650 percent! Basically, this new economy company was struggling because it lacked an old-economy competence.[25]

It took some time, but Amazon acquired key old-economy competence and significantly expanded its initial strategy—based on its previous weakness. *Business Week* reported that the company was "morphing into a tech company . . . as much Microsoft . . . as Wal-Mart." After intense concentration on information technology, Amazon's distribution centers were reported to be able to handle triple the volume that they could in 1999, at half the cost. In fact, Amazon began managing the e-commerce business of other retailers.[26] At the heart of this success is a supply-chain management system that *Information Week* described as the most sophisticated in the world.[27]

Socialization

One more point about the accumulation of resources is important: new employees are hired because they possess needed personal skills, but their contribution to the organization's competitive position cannot be assumed. They may arrive knowing how to carry out an assigned job in a general way, but they do not know how to work in a way that fits their employer's particular competencies. Nor is it possible to just give them detailed instruction, because even the simplest job cannot be totally described. Conditions vary; things happen that have never happened before; socially complex routines are not fully understood and so cannot be formally taught.

The *socialization* of employees and other actors helps them understand why resources are valuable and how they are accumulated. Employees have to learn how things are done in a new job, how to solve the problems that inevitably arise, what kinds of new solutions are likely to be appreciated, and how they can best coordinate their activities with others. They do that by receiving formal instruction, but also by paying attention to people around them and having people pay attention to them. Employees make inferences from what they hear and see and compare their ideas with others. Stories are told and interpreted; activities are physically demonstrated.

Ideally, employees come to identify with the work of the organization and invest effort and creativity that goes beyond their job description. But whether or not this occurs, whether or not their experience in the organization is positive, their work continues to be shaped by the social setting. Understanding how this inevitable socialization occurs and influencing it in a positive direction is critical to the accumulation of competitive resources.

WHAT RISKS ARE ASSOCIATED WITH RESOURCE ACCUMULATION?

Both Marks & Spencer's diversification difficulties and Amazon's problems with distribution illustrate why it is important to understand the sources of strategic risk. *Strategic risk* comes from uncertainty about the availability of resources as well as the cause-and-effect relationships of a desired strategy.

Think of the career path you have chosen. If you have spent the last several years honing your business skills, it's not likely that you're going to become a competitive swimmer. Prior decisions about what you wanted to do with your life now constrain the options realistically available to you. After founder Jeff Bezos spent several years building Amazon around a business model that assumed physical presence wasn't necessary, it wasn't easy—some thought it was impossible—to accumulate a different set of capabilities in time to meet the competitive challenge of more traditional retailers. Each strategic choice involved risk. Theorists highlight four contributing factors: uncertain capacity to accumulate assets, causal ambiguity, over commitment, and external attribution.

Uncertain Capacity to Accumulate Resources

Our examples illustrate how complex the resource picture can become. Limited availability of key resources and difficulties evaluating resource quality are problematic. In addition, a single distinctive competence is likely to involve coordination across many activities located in several functional departments (procurement, marketing, customer service, warehousing, shipping), dozens of specific activities, and hundreds (if not thousands) of individual people. Limited capital, lack of experience, problems with communication, and lack of motivation make organizing these activities difficult.

Causal Ambiguity

Accumulation can be problematic, but strategists often face the greater difficulty of not knowing in advance precisely which skills, systems, people, and activities are going to be critical as markets evolve (the topic of Chapter 6). It may be easy to see after the fact which pieces are missing, but in real time that insight is much more difficult to achieve. Resource-based theorists assert that most competitive resources are socially complex and have *causal ambiguity*. Even within the firm, strategists are unlikely to fully understand whatever magic they currently enjoy. To the extent that they do not, strategists are unable to deliberately support or replicate success.

> **Causal ambiguity** refers to the lack of readily apparent connection between a firm's activities and its competitive success.

The basic point is that risk cannot be avoided; complexities and ambiguities surround all resource investment decisions. That is good news, in a way. Uncertainty and risk protect competitive advantage from imitation. After all, if managers inside the firm could precisely articulate all the ingredients of distinctive competence, then why couldn't their rivals do the same thing? The very complexities of resource accumulation are what help isolate successful firms from their competition.[28]

Overcommitment

Another significant risk is associated with exploiting the current stock of resources. Many organizations become almost blindly committed to their present course of action, even when changing circumstances encourage them to learn new things.[29] Managerial psychology plays a significant role. Those responsible for deploying a set of resources in support of a known, successful strategy are not likely to value someone else's idea to try something radically new. Why tinker with success? Current customers seem happy. Unfortunately, a focus on producing efficiency distracts managers from seeing the potential of learning or understanding how a new idea might contribute to a new capability. This myopia is efficient in the short run, but in the long run increases strategic risk.

External Attribution

The final problem of resource accumulation that we will mention is also associated with how managers think. Research suggests that when things go well, people attribute success to their own efforts. When things do not go well, almost all of us tend to focus on external sources of the problem.[30] The competitor that can rise above this human tendency has a promising future. Consider the following comparison.

Strategy and the Weather

After World War II, the trucking industry became a major carrier of goods in the United States, considerably diminishing the railroads' share of the business. Two well-known firms, the Rock Island Railroad and the Chicago and Northwestern Railway (C&NW), were affected by this downturn, but they differed in the way they interpreted it. In letters to shareholders and speeches to analysts, Rock Island emphasized the impact of more favorable federal regulation of the trucking industry and noted a variety of unfortunate circumstances, including several years of unusually bad weather, that slowed business in various sectors of the economy. It spoke of declining traffic as a "temporary economic adjustment, which will be of comparatively short duration."

Strategists at the C&NW had a different interpretation of the same environment. They thought the railroad's declining share of traffic was likely to be permanent and signaled the need for internal change. Several different issues were seen as problematic, especially high wage/ revenue ratios. But steps were taken in almost every phase of the business, from maintenance to finance, that strengthened the company's competitive position. It took at least six years to "unlearn" past ways of doing things and put new practices into place, but the company survived, while parts of Rock Island were ultimately acquired by a stronger railroad and the rest of the company was liquidated.[31]

In this and many other cases, a big part of the risk in strategic decisions results from how strategists perceive the circumstances around them. What is even more interesting about the railroad story, however, is that different managerial perceptions can create different business environments. C&NW saw the environment as somewhat controllable, and on this basis, it developed a strategy that created a more controllable environment. Rock Island saw the world as virtually uncontrollable, and on this basis, it did not act.

HOW IS RESOURCE ACCUMULATION AND DEPLOYMENT STRATEGICALLY MANAGED?

Although luck may play a role in the resource endowments available to a given company at a point in time, it is the strategists' job to capitalize on luck, and when possible strategists must transcend it by managing the current resource base and developing new competencies over time. The following steps are suggested as an extended exercise to conclude our discussion of competitive advantage. They oversimplify the strategic thinking that occurs in most organizations, but highlight key aspects of formulating a resource-based strategy.

Step 1: Attend to Necessary Resources

There are many choices in how a given product or service might be produced, and successful competitors often find unexpected means of doing so. Although there are very few absolutely necessary resources, as a practical matter most companies use many similar ones, and a firm that lacks a particular resource, or an acceptable substitute, can be in trouble. That is the lesson of Amazon and its early difficulties with distribution.

Step 2: Determine Competitive Advantage (If Any)

Start with the question: Does the firm have a competitive advantage? The first clue lies in economic profit or some other widely valued performance measure. Remember that economic profit means above-average returns. If there is no current advantage, then focus the analysis on the intended or potential advantage of the organization. Remember also, as Marks & Spencer's story reminds us, that a historical advantage may no longer be creating value for your organization.

Step 3: Define Distinctive Competencies

The next step in the analysis of competitive advantage involves linking high performance with more specific firm attributes. It is not enough to talk in generalities about "what we do especially well." Value is relative. For example, a company that feels it provides exceptional service may find, when customers are closely questioned, that its service levels are really not that different from their competitors'. Strategists must beware of the tendency to overestimate their own prowess; too often improvements across the industry are interpreted as a company gain. Identifying distinctive competence involves external comparisons.

Step 4: Decompose Distinctive Competencies to Focus Investment

Once a list of distinctive competencies has been developed, each one should be broken down into its constituent parts. Activity system analysis (Worksheet 2.2) or some equivalent is helpful in this regard. For example, the activity system in Figure 2.2 highlights customer loyalty, trustworthy staff, and strong supplier relationships as the result of distinctive competences Marks & Spencer enjoyed until the late 1990s. Once competencies like these are identified it is important for managers to understand the relationship between stocks (resources) and flows (investments to create resource). Without such an analysis, it would be easy to lose track of the investments that support an important capability or routine.

Step 5: Look for Opportunities to Leverage Resources

Once one understands the relationships between a set of resources and distinctive competence, two logical questions arise: Can deployment of the resource be profitably expanded within this arena (an exploitation strategy)? Are there new arenas in which current and new resources could profitably be deployed (an exploration strategy)?

Step 6: Plan for the Ongoing Renewal of Resources

Many things can diminish the value of a particular resource. For example, sustaining a successful retail operation requires an ongoing series of investments in human resources, typically including above-average compensation and employee benefit programs. If other companies begin to match or exceed a retailer's employment package, talented salespeople are more easily attracted away.

Step 7: Watch Out for Competence-Destroying Change and Capitalize on Competence-Enhancing Change

Anyone who watches a company's fortunes over time recognizes that a major jolt sometimes comes along—a jolt that undercuts the value of a resource to the point at which no amount of incremental improvement restores advantage. These *competence-destroying changes* often involve new technology, significant regulation or deregulation, or the emergence of new competitors. For example, since the web made the process of arranging airline, hotel, and car rental reservations so easy, many large corporations have terminated their contracts with outside travel agents and trained people in-house to make travel arrangements. The fact that these activities no longer need to be outsourced has been a major blow to travel agencies.

Competence-destroying change in the environment reduces or extinguishes the value of past asset stocks.

Web-based technology is destroying the value of many competitive resources of the past. These changes are spreading across industries, including financial services (where intermediaries are the target), entertainment (where broadcast networks are suffering), and industrial production (where buying on the web destroys distributors' bargaining power). The Internet may be one of the biggest competence-destroying changes ever observed; it certainly affects strategy at all levels of analysis. We will continue to consider these changes because they are particularly relevant to today's strategist.

However, it is important to remember that some changes in the competitive environment can enhance a firm's resources. Such *competence-enhancing changes* are exactly what a Darwinian evolutionist would expect. Just as a change in climate, say colder weather, disadvantages some species but favors others, so too every environmental change creates winners as well as losers. The important difference is that the strategist can perhaps do more to take advantage of large-scale changes in environmental opportunity than species with or without fat, fur, and other decisive characteristics.

Competence-enhancing changes in the environment increase the value of resource stocks.

CONCLUSIONS FOR THE STRATEGIST

Every strategist inherits a stock of resources that have accumulated over time, including his or her own personal assets. The strategist must consider how to do the following:

- Fully exploit the potential of these resources
- Invest in their maintenance and improvement
- Summon the will to leave them behind when assets more appropriate to changing conditions must be developed.

Valuable competitive resources are flexible. They are like shocks in a car that buffer travelers from many bumps in the road. You know that Marks & Spencer continues to be pressured by cut-rate retailers and high-value brands. It has to refurbish past resources but also develop new ones to meet these challenges. Disney is similarly changing its strategy in the face of a changing competitive environment. Its characters are still among its formidable assets, but they are increasingly augmented by other resources.

The fact that current competence and the resources that support it tend to erode is one of the most enduring and generalizable observations of strategy. It is not just that competitive resources cannot last forever; it is also that the resource-based strengths of the past tend to become weaknesses in the future. Distinctive resources in particular become anchors that are very difficult to leave behind.

Thinking about current and potential resources is the first subject in what we call the "heart" of strategy. In the next chapters we focus on four additional topics that also must be considered before strategy can be defined. In Chapter 3 we attend to the needs and desires of current and potential customers. In Chapter 4 we add the challenge of identifying opportunity. In Chapter 5 we look at rivals and draw on economic theories that expand the resource perspective. In Chapter 6 we consider how this analysis will change over time.

Key Concepts

Resources are assets that can be used to meet performance demands. They are often subdivided into **tangible resources** that have a physical reality, such as buildings, machinery, and supplies, and **intangible resources** that are not directly visible, such as knowledge and reputation.

Capabilities are combinations of resources that create value. They tend to be valuable if they become **routines**—regular and predictable patterns in organizational behavior that persist over time even though the individuals involved change.

Many similar resources, capabilities, and routines are used by all (or virtually all) industry participants. Although it seems unlikely that success can be achieved without them, strategists are advised to pay particular attention to **distinctive competencies**—the resources, capabilities, and routines that are unique to their organization. The process of generating competitive resources must, by definition, be difficult, or all competitors would quickly be able to copy any activity which is rewarded in the market. Although it is not easy to understand how competitive advantage is achieved, the distinctive competencies that yield advantage must be expected to erode over time because of **mimetic behavior** by competitors, who follow patterns observed in the behavior of others. **Socially complex activities** are particularly difficult to understand and hard to imitate. These tend to be important components of distinctive competencies.

Theory and empirical research suggest that a resource is more likely to be competitively useful if it is **rare** or not widely available, **nontradable** on the open market, **nonsubstitutable** by alternative resources, **inimitable** or unique, and **flexible** or adaptable. The benefits these resources bring must also be **nonappropriatable**; that is, they cannot be captured by other actors, such as competitors.

Investment creates a **resource flow** that feeds current organizational activity. That flow can be usefully distinguished from **resource stocks**, which are the result of investments and activities over time. The latter typically supports sustained competitive advantage. The deployment of resources and the possibility of accumulating additional resources depends on the position of the firm. Resource accumulation requires time and does not happen automatically. The **socialization** of employees and other actors, through direct communication and informal interaction, is an important contribution to building understanding of why resources are valuable and how they are accumulated.

Strategic risk is an estimate of strategists' uncertainty about outcomes associated with the strategic activities they undertake. **Causal ambiguity** refers to the lack of readily apparent connections between a firm's activities and its competitive success. In addition to the problems of limited human understanding, risk comes from the possibility of **competence-destroying change** in the environment that reduces or extinguishes the value of past asset stocks. Some firms, however, will benefit from **competence-enhancing changes** that increase the value of their resources, just as Darwinian evolutionists predict.

Questions for Further Reflection

1.   Choose a personal goal. What resources do you have to achieve it? Do you need others? What activities support them? What investments are needed (and when should they be made?) How should you position yourself? Would branding activities be helpful?

2. Identify a startup organization that you know firsthand or from information on the Internet. Specify its strategy as you understand it. Identify key activities necessary to support the strategy and the resources needed to carry it out. Do you think current strategy is realistic?

3. Identify a battle between competitors. (For example, in the next chapter we will look at Nike versus Adidas.) Does either company have a competitive advantage? How long do you expect the advantages you identify to last? What would you suggest as a strategic advisor hired by one of these competitors?

WORKSHEET 2.1
A Tool for Analyzing Resources

The Resource-Based Theory of the Firm offers a useful vocabulary for understanding current advantage and future potential. These are inevitably comparative assessments. The columns in Worksheet 2.1 (which should be labeled) can be used in various ways to compare key resources and capabilities.

Option 1: Specify a level of analysis and compare your resource pool (column 1) with the resources of two competitors (columns 2 and 3). You might consider comparisons with nearest competitors or industry leaders.

Option 2: To summarize strategic effort, compare your organization's resources at a point in the past (column 1) with present resources (column 2) and the resources you and others are trying to develop by some specific date in the future (column 3).

Option 3: To assess your personal fit with your job setting, put the resources you use in your job in column 1, the resources of your unit in column 2, and the resources used by your organization in column 3. Use a second color to add personal resources that are not currently in use and consider one or more of the following questions:

1. Are there additional ways in which I could add value with my current resources?

2. Are there opportunities to combine my skills with the skills of others?

3. How can I extend my personal resources in this environment?

4. What other jobs (in this organization or others) might utilize different combinations of resources or teach me more?

Resource Analysis Worksheet 2.1	Organization: Time Frame:
Analyst(s): Black = current resources (date _____) Blue = anticipated resources (date _____)	**Strategy Summary:**

Tangible Resources			
Intangible Resources			
Capabilities			
Routines			
Distinctive Competencies			
Competitive Advantages			

WORKSHEET 2.2
Activity Map—A Tool for Connecting Strategic Investments

Identify an organization's primary competitive advantage and the activities and investments that create it.

Step 1: Put the name of the primary competitive advantage in a circle in the center of this worksheet. (If you are not sure that there is a competitive advantage, identify the distinctive competence that is the most promising contributor to future advantage.)

Step 2: In black pen, list and connect activities that generate this competence.

Step 3: In blue pen, list and connect the investments that support this competence.

Step 4: Circle, in red, the distinctive competencies on your map. We reiterate a caution in the text: research shows that actors tend to overestimate the extent of their distinctive competencies. Ask yourself:

- Are you confusing hope or intention with actual results?
- Do you have supporting evidence that supports your claims?

Step 5: On one or more copies of your map, use a fourth color to brainstorm additional resources and investments that might further reinforce your advantage, focusing especially on the development of distinctive competencies.

ALTERNATIVES
- Put two competencies on the same page and consider their connections.
- Focus on the results of your distinctive competency by drawing arrows that point to its consequences for customers and other stakeholders.

Competitive Advantage Analysis Worksheet 2.2	**Organization:** Time Frame:
Analyst(s): Black = activities Blue = investments Red (circled) = distinctive competence Fourth color = strategic additions	**Strategy Summary:**

NOTES

[1] Grover, R. 2000. Wow, Is That the MTV Crowd Peeking at CBS? *Business Week* (June 26). http://www.businessweek.com/bwdaily/dnflash/june2000/nf00609d.htm, accessed February 29, 2008.

[2] How Bob Iger Unchained Disney. *Business Week*. (February 5, 2007). http://www.businessweek.com/magazine/content/07_06/b4020085.htm?chan=search, accessed November 28, 2007.

[3] Gerdes, L. (2006), Hello Mickey. *Business Week*. (May 4).

[4] Penrose, E. T. 1959. *The Theory of the Growth of the Firm.* Oxford, England: Blackwell; Penrose, E. T. 1985. *The Theory of the Growth of the Firm Twenty-Five Years After.* Acta Universitatis Upsaliensis, Studia Oeconomiae Negotiorum, 20, Uppsala; Barney, J. B. 1991. Firm resources and sustained competitive advantage. *Journal of Management* 17(1): 99–120; Wernerfelt, B. 1984. A Resource-Based View of the Firm. *Strategic Management Journal* 5: 171–180; Lado, A. A., Boyd, N. G., Wright, P., & Kroll, M. 2006. Paradox and Theorizing within the Resource-Based View. *Academy of Management Review* 31: 115–131.

[5] Nelson, R., & Winter, S. 1982. *An Evolutionary Theory of Economic Change.* Cambridge, MA: Harvard University Press.

[6] Dougherty, D. 1996. Sustained Product Innovation in Large, Mature Organizations: Overcoming Innovation-to-Organization Problems. *Academy of Management Journal* 39(5): 1120–1153.

[7] DiMaggio, P., & Powell, W. W. 1983. The Iron Cage Revisited: Institutional Isomorphism and Collective Rationality in Organizational Fields. *American Sociological Review* 48: 147–160.

[8] For a history of RBS, see Hoover's, Inc. 2007. The Royal Bank of Scotland Group plc, Hoover's Profile. http://www.answers.com/topic/the-royal-bank-of-scotland-group-plc?cat=biz-fin&print=true&lsc=false, accessed November 28, 2007.

[9] http://investing.thisismoney.co.uk/cgi-bin/digitalcorporate/thisismoney/security.cgi?ticker=RBS, accessed May 5, 2007.

[10] http://money.cnn.com/magazines/fortune/global500/2007/snapshots/7637.html, accessed January 21, 2008. See also Portanger, E. 2003. Royal Bank's Road to Riches: Stay Divided, Conquer. *Wall Street Journal* (September 23): A1, A10.

[11] The Point—New Tool of the Bank Trade. 2005. www.accenture.com/xd/xd.asp?it=enweb&xd=industries%5Cfinancial%5Cpoint27%5Cfsi_thepoint27.xml.

[12] Barney, J. 1995. Looking Inside for Competitive Advantage. *Academy of Management Executive* 9(4): 49–61.

[13] Penrose, E. 1959. *Theory of the Growth of the Firm.* Oxford, England: Blackwell; Wernerfelt, B. 1984. A Resource-Based View of the Firm. *Strategic Management Journal* 5: 171–180.

[14] Andrews, K. 1971. *The Concept of Corporate Strategy.* Homewood, IL: Irwin.

[15] M&S: A Brand New Challenge. BBC News. (July 23, 2001). http://news.bbc.co.uk/1/hi/business/597830.stm, accessed February 29, 2008.

[16] Montgomery, A. 1991. Marks & Spencer, Ltd. (A). Harvard Business School Case No. 391.

[17] Marks & Spencer Profits Top Expectations, BBC News. (May 19, 1998). http://news.bbc.co.uk/2/hi/business/96531.stm, accessed November 28, 2007.

[18] Porter, M. 1996. What Is Strategy? *Harvard Business Review* 74(6): 61–79.

[19] Dierickx, I., & Cool, K. 1989. Asset Stock Accumulation and Sustainability of Competitive Advantage. *Management Science* 35: 1504–1511.

[20]Jarzabkowski, P. 2005. *Strategy as Practice: An Activities-Based Approach*. London: Sage.

[21]Goodman, M. 2000. When Mediocre Management Frustrates Talent. *Strategic Direction:* (November–December): 18.

[22]http://www2.marksandspencer.com/thecompany/mediacentre/pressreleases/2005/fin2005-05-24-00.shtml, accessed November 28, 2007.

[23]Marks & Spencer, 2005. Annual Review and Summary Financial Statement, p. 3. http://en.wikipedia.org/wiki/Marks_%26_Spencer, accessed November 28, 2007.

[24]Marks and Spencer's Rose Honoured. BBC News (December 29, 2007). http://news.bbc.co.uk/2/hi/business/7163235.stm, accessed January 21, 2008.

[25]Can Amazon Make It? *Business Week* (July 10, 2000): 38–45.

[26]Reprogramming Amazon. *Business Week* (December 22, 2003).

[27]Bacheldor, B. 2004. From Scratch: Amazon Keeps Supply Chain Close to Home. *InformationWeek* (March 5).

[28]Lippman, S. A., & Rumelt, R. P. 1992. Demand Uncertainty, Capital Specificity, and Industry Evolution. *Industrial and Corporate Change* 1(1): 235–262.

[29]Floyd, S., & Wooldridge, B. 2000. *Building Strategy from the Middle: Reconceptualizing the Strategy Process*. Thousand Oaks, CA: Sage.

[30]Dutton, J. 1993. Interpretation: A Different View of Strategic Issue Diagnosis. *Journal of Management Studies* 30(3): 339–358.

[31]Barr, P. S., Stimpert, J. L. & Huff, A. S. (1992). Cognitive Change, Strategic Action, and Organizational Renewal. *Strategic Management Journal* 13: 15–36.

3

Serving Customers

You have excellent training to be a strategist: you have been a customer all your life. But many strategists confuse their experience and their customers' experience, and too few focus on customers as the basis of their strategy. We argue in this chapter that it is critical to collect (and continue collecting) information from the people your organization serves, and then use it!

Organizations exist to provide value to some client or customer group. That might seem obvious, but it is easy for those inside the organization to focus on day-to-day activities that keep them far away from the recipients of their efforts. Without a strong customer connection, strategists are at risk of developing organizational competencies that have little or no market value.

Strategists with a strong customer orientation also focus on employees. They consider the resources and activities that help employees understand changing desires of current customers and assess whether they might profitably serve new customers. However, as with other things in life, a positive idea can be taken too far; companies still must make money while attending to customer needs.

* *

This chapter puts what customers value at the center of strategic thinking by answering five questions:

Why is the customer relationship increasingly critical?
Customers are becoming more sophisticated and demanding
New technology allows new forms of customer contact
Competitors are raising expectations
Coproduction is increasing

What is a service mentality?
Organizational activities matched to customer needs and desires
Customers seen from a positive perspective
Employees who understand that their success comes from service
A climate that supports and reinforces service

What are the guidelines for a customer-based business model?
Definition of the business in customer, not production, terms
Clarity about the needs to be satisfied
Choices about how needs will be satisfied

How do companies gather data to identify and understand their customers?
Analyze customer experience
Map customer perceptions of the market
Track marketing information
Anticipate the consequences of demographic trends

Involve customers in design and selection
Use ethnography techniques
Can the customer connection be overemphasized?
Service levels have to fit strategy
Some customers are too expensive to serve
Today's happy customers are not necessarily tomorrow's customers

Smart companies have always paid attention to their customers' buying decisions as one important indication of needs and trends. New technology is allowing not just more detailed tracking, but new ways of directly interacting with customers at the point of purchase. Shoes provide an interesting example.

MASS CUSTOMIZATION OF ATHLETIC FOOTWEAR: A "WIN-WIN" TREND?

For decades, the general public's athletic footwear selection was limited to seasonal mass-produced styles, sizes, and colors. Only world-class athletes were able to purchase footwear designed for their specific needs. In late November 1999, Nike began to reverse the situation with the NIKEiD range. Customers everywhere had the chance to select shoe color and an eight-character embroidered name for a 5 percent price premium.

Six months later, Adidas pilot-tested a much larger range of mass customization options with the mi adidas line of soccer boots offered in select retail outlets in six major European cities. Adidas "fitting experts" scanned customers' feet to measure their exact length, width, and pressure distribution. Customers could try on basic prototypes fit to each foot. After selecting personal fit preferences, customers used the PC to view and select shoe material, an embroidered monogram, and stud profiles. They also chose the color of the main boot, outer sole, stripes, and collar. A 50 percent premium was charged. The shoes were built in one of three factories in Indonesia or China and delivered in approximately three weeks.

A significant number of customers loved the idea of having a say in the design and fit of their footwear. Adidas benefited by observing customer preference and aggregating this into market research information. The findings were used to improve the customized product line and to forecast customer demands for standard lines. Some information, such as preferred color combinations, was particularly helpful on a regional level. The experience increased customer loyalty through satisfying final products and a trouble-free reordering system.

Following the successful pilot, Adidas provided its technology to many more retail stores and extended the product line to include running shoes, tennis shoes, and golf clubs. Products are now sold through special events, in traditional retail outlets, at major sporting contests, and online.

> Not surprisingly, competition increased. NIKEiD expanded to allow consumers to select a number of different features for running, basketball, and cross-training shoes that it sells online. In 2006 the company announced the iPod Sports Kit.[1] The Apple website suggests:
>
> > You don't just take iPod nano on your run. You let it take you. Music is your motivation. But what if you want to go further? Thanks to a unique partnership between NIKE and Apple, your iPod nano becomes your coach. Your personal trainer. Your favorite workout companion. Introducing Nike + iPod.[2]

✱ **Mass customization** allows a large number of customers to personalize product characteristics.

Mass customization improves product delivery not just to those with special needs or sensitivity to fashion, but also to those who would like to repurchase the very same product over time. However, the strategy has blurred traditional retail boundaries, with some controversy around who "owns" particular customers and information about them—the manufacturer, the retailer who initially customizes the product, or the retailer who subsequently takes follow-up orders? Further, the profit consequences of mass customization are not always clear. The setup costs can be high, and not all customizers have been able to develop the new skills and contacts required.

Although some companies that tried mass customization, such as Levi Strauss, have now exited the market, we believe that customization is part of an irreversible trend. Customers are increasingly savvy. They want and expect more. Strategists have to keep track of and anticipate these demands. They use a *customer-based strategy* with the assumption that satisfying customers will also maximize success in reaching more traditional performance goals, including returns to stockholders.

Customer-based strategy focuses on identifying and serving customer needs and desires.

WHY IS THE CUSTOMER RELATIONSHIP INCREASINGLY CRITICAL?

Customer contact is a measure of the amount of user involvement in planning, executing, and delivering a good or service.

Different businesses have different levels of *customer contact*, as suggested in Table 3.1.[3]

TABLE 3.1 THE RANGE OF TRADITIONAL CONTACTS WITH CUSTOMERS

Low Contact	Medium Contact	High Contact
Mining	Retail outlets	Gourmet restaurants
Farming	Public transportation	Health centers
Manufactured commodities (e.g., chemicals)	Fast-food chains	Real estate agents
	Libraries	Caregivers (e.g., day care)

Attention to producing tangible goods has always dominated the management of businesses on the left side of this table, while customer relations were more important for businesses on the right side. Traditionally, customer contact tended to be seen as a cost to be minimized by firms operating in industries on the left of the table, while it became a possible source of advantage toward the right.

Today, these distinctions are increasingly tenuous, and contact with the customer is becoming more important for almost all organizations. As a result, the ownership and manipulation of physical capital, once considered the engine of economic growth, has been economically dominated by the *intellectual capital* used to supply more integrated products and services. Several different things are happening: customers are becoming more sophisticated; new technology is allowing for new ways of customer contact; competitors are raising expectations; and coproduction is increasing.

> **Intellectual capital** summarizes the knowledge, skills, and capabilities used by an organization to produce goods and services.

Customers Are Becoming More Sophisticated and Demanding

Twenty-first-century customers often know what they want. Comments from other customers (often on the web) provide widely available information before a buying decision is made. Contemporary life also provides more opportunities for consumption. In many countries people assume they will have twenty-four-hour, seven-days-a-week access to their bank accounts, for example. In the United States, customers with relatively modest holdings expect personal bankers to offer financial planning services and other support from a single point of contact. Twenty years ago, only the very wealthy invested money directly in the stock market. Now, more than 50 percent of American consumers have bought and sold stocks, bonds, or mutual funds. For retail banks, this means that customers demand access to a much wider array of services, well beyond the personal checking and savings accounts of their parents' generation.

Customer demands are increasing in every sector we can think of. For example, doctors are more and more likely to see patients who know (or believe they know) more about their particular ailment than the professional they visit. But this is not the only challenge facing the health care industry. As Figure 3.1 shows, physicians and nurses typically see the value they add to health care in terms of medical expertise and technology. Customer surveys, however, show that customers' perceptions of value in health care are much broader. In fact, patients may be relatively unconcerned about the technical quality of physicians' services. They take for granted that the doctor is properly trained. (When was the last time you queried your physician about his or her credentials?) Instead, patients' perceptions of value include whether the physician seems caring and friendly, whether the exam room is comfortable, whether the physician is on time for appointments, and even whether convenient parking is available.

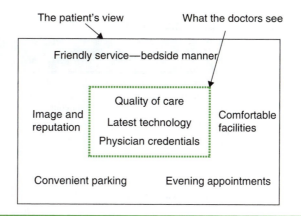

Figure 3.1 — Perceptions of Desirable Attributes of Health Care Services

These first examples come from business relations with individual customers. If we add the vast increase in business-to-business services, the changing nature of customer relations is even more important. Many companies are outsourcing activities in which they do not have a competitive advantage, for example, but outsourcers can be very sophisticated customers because they have experience in carrying out the activities that they now seek to buy in the marketplace. They not only know what they want, they have direct knowledge about the processes and costs involved.

So much research on perceptions of product and service quality has been done that it is difficult to succinctly summarize.[4] Table 3.2 provides an overview of key factors that customers tend to care about.

TABLE 3.2 FEATURES THAT CAN AFFECT CUSTOMER PERCEPTIONS OF THE QUALITY OF AN ORGANIZATION'S GOODS OR SERVICES

Goods	Services	Environment (Actual or Virtual)
Cost/performance (value received from core attributes of the good)	Professionalism (knowledgeability of service provider)	Accessibility (ease of locating and navigating provider site)
Features (available extras)	Concern/responsiveness (interest in meeting customer's needs)	Ambience (tangible features of the site that may or may not receive conscious attention)
Functionality (ease of use in comparison to value received)	Fit (match between customer needs and services provided)	
Constraints (limits on what can be done with the product)		Security (ability to protect welfare of site visitors)
	Interaction (willingness to accept input and share control decisions)	Novelty (newness in comparison to past experience)

(continued)

TABLE 3.2 (CONTINUED)

Goods	Services	Environment (Actual or Virtual)
Reliability (probability of malfunctioning)	Trustworthiness (ability to keep promises and maintain confidentiality)	Personnel (appearance and behavior of employees)
Serviceability (ease of maintenance and repair)	Flexibility (capacity to respond to additional or altered information)	Customer commonalities (buyers' perceptions of their similarities and differences compared to other buyers)
Aesthetics (attractiveness of design, touch, smell, etc.)	Recovery (individual and organizational skill in solving problems)	
Speed (time elapsed between order and delivery)	Reputation (recognition of service quality by others)	
Reputation (product recognition by others)	Cost/value received (perception of benefits gained)	

Source: Based on S. Schneider & S. S. White, *Service Quality* (Thousand Oaks, CA: Sage, 2004), Chapter 2.

Note that customers make judgments about tangible, physical characteristics that might be objectively confirmed by others. They also make judgments that are more subjective, comparative, and potentially idiosyncratic. As the line between goods and services blur, and both are included in a bundle that includes experiences like "novelty", the categories listed increasingly overlap. Furthermore, what one observer would find a positive (for example, "many people buying this product or using this service look like me"), others might find a negative. The details can be worked out only in the context of a particular company's activities, at a particular point in time, with a specific set of consumers.

New Technology Allows New Forms of Customer Contact

New technologies enable more contact with customers, but also lead customers to expect more contact. New information technologies, in particular, cause firms to re-examine how they can create value for customers. For example, the Internet is a competitive threat to large brick and mortar retailers such as Barnes & Noble and Borders bookstores. As we know, a search engine can provide a consumer with many more product choices than a brick and mortar store, no matter how big that store is physically. In order to compete, bookstores are developing *experience-oriented strategies*. They often provide coffee, easy chairs, and products that might appeal to literary clientele. They also offer sales online, with returns in the store, something an e-tailer such as Amazon cannot match. This is an important trend, one we discuss in more detail later in the chapter.

The connectivity and scope provided by the Internet has changed the nature of almost all business. Consider newspapers, a business with

Experience-oriented strategies support the process of consuming an organization's offerings.

mid-range customer contact in Table 3.1. In the established business model, journalists create copy; editors make decisions about content; supervise layout, and control the appearance of the paper; and the results are transmitted to presses that create the physical product. Then, using an extensive distribution system, the paper is delivered to individual homes, newsstands, libraries, and many other venues on a daily basis. Today's newspapers exist for three reasons: (1) they have sufficient product circulation, (2) they can use circulation numbers to attract advertising revenue, and (3) they have found ways to create economies of scale in printing and distribution.

As we all know, the growth of television undercut this model with visually dramatic and timelier reportage. But most television news offers relatively little detail in comparison to print, and a significant though shrinking newspaper market still exists.

Now television viewing is declining. With the availability of the Internet, customers for news can act as their own editors, choosing what personally interests them from a variety of media. Only the stories and features that are likely to interest them need to be sent to their personal computer at work or at home. Classified advertisements also are a natural online product; the ads can be placed with respect to users' activities and are more easily updated online. Meanwhile, distribution and printing costs are relatively small.

Although the Internet is the driving force in this example of changing relations with customers, many other technological changes are also changing the world economy. Travel and transportation are increasingly economical. Manufacturing can be carried out on a smaller and smaller scale. The materials available for manufacture are increasingly sophisticated. Trained workers are more available around the globe. These and other drivers of a changing economy are bringing the customer into closer contact with organizations. Companies can do more for their customers, closer to the time and place of desired delivery, in more varied forms.

Competitors Are Raising Expectations

Increasing contact with customers is also driven by competition. In the next three chapters we discuss the changing face of rivalry; in this chapter we simply note that the search for competitive advantage has led firms to increase their efforts to connect with particular customer groups they can serve well.

As goods become more information intensive and interactive, one especially important move is to increase service offerings. That trend includes manufacturing firms. For example, when airlines order a new Boeing jet, they do not get GE engines, they get a fixed-price maintenance agreement from GE charged at so many dollars for each hour of flight. Airlines really do not care about owning engines; what they want is a guarantee that they will be able to be in the air earning revenue. They now get that from a traditional manufacturer, GE, with a new sense of service. Rather than a remote relationship through a second party (Boeing), GE has a direct connection with the airline customers that use their products. Ideally, more knowledge leads to better service and greater profits.

The same story can be found in almost every industry, even the manufacture of commodities. Consider the following service strategy from the chemical industry.

Sharing Environmental Costs

Specialty chemicals were traditionally sold in bulk to automobile manufacturers, which used them in different production processes. The chemical companies charged the automobile firms by the quantity of the material used; they maximized their profitability by maximizing the amount of chemicals they sold and by minimizing production and transportation costs. Customers were motivated to purchase only the chemicals needed to complete the production process, while meeting their quality standards. An apparently unrelated issue was that the automobile manufacturer was responsible for the environmental costs associated with using chemicals.

The result of the traditional buyer-seller relationship was that there was no incentive for chemical companies to invest in research to develop less environmentally harmful products. Today, however, the chemical buyer and seller are much more likely to have cost-sharing arrangements in which the automobile manufacturer never actually purchases or handles chemicals. Instead, the chemical supplier performs the production process that uses the application of its chemicals at the auto manufacturer's site. The chemical company takes responsibility for maintaining a prescribed level of quality for production at a fixed price. If they can reduce the costs associated with this production process by making the process more efficient (including reducing the costs associated with hazardous waste), then both parties share in the savings.[5]

In short, instead of selling and buying products alone, many manufacturers are selling services and purchasing services alongside tangible goods. At the same time, service firms often offer more products than they did in the past. Hotels, for example, have started to sell the robes, cosmetics, shower curtains, and even beds found in their rooms. This is possible because of partnerships with manufacturers, which results in customers receiving more extensive service.

Coproduction directly involves customers in the creation of the goods, services, or experiences they consume.

Coproduction Is Increasing

At the extreme, the line between customer and seller blurs, and *coproduction* with customers begins to take place.[6] We began this chapter by referring to mass customization, an idea that has grown tremendously in popularity. Dell is an outstanding example. Its basic business model is to have customers select desired features of laptops, PCs, printers, and other technology goods it offers online. Toys (Mattel, Lego), jeans (Lands' End), and cosmetics (Procter & Gamble) are among the broad range of other products that offer customer design involvement.

Coproduction is often a subtle form of *cost sharing*. For example, airlines often ask customers to check themselves into flights they have prebooked: once an identifying credit card is entered into a special service kiosk, the customer checks and prints boarding cards. In fact, self-service can be found everywhere in America—as customers clear their tables in fast-food restaurants, pump gas and clean their windows at gas stations, and check out the goods they chose from shelves in grocery stores. In some cases, consumption accompanies such participatory acts—in self-guided museum tours and interactive theater, for example. In other cases, the coproducing customer benefits from faster, cheaper, or more personalized exchange.

Closer customer involvement in the creation and consumption of goods and services can also be found outside the retail arena. Cisco Systems, the largest manufacturer of the electronic routers and switches that constitute the Internet backbone, is a good example. Cisco dominates many of the markets it is in,[7] but the company did not achieve success by itself—its customers are an important part of the picture.

Cost-sharing strategies allocate costs between members of an alliance, including alliances between customers and producers.

Coproducing Networks

Cisco manufactures products that allow computers to talk to each other on networks and the Internet. Its customers are mostly large businesses and public-sector organizations that are building networks to support their increasingly complicated activities. Cisco has built its strategy on the notion that it sells complex equipment to technicians and engineers in these technology-intensive settings. The key to selling in such a situation is to provide a product that fits the customer's design criteria. To create the necessary relationship between its own engineers and the customers, Cisco holds "networking parties" where technicians get to know each other. Cisco also frequently becomes a partner with its customers, forming joint ventures such as one with KPMG that offers network-consulting services.

Cisco doesn't just give lip service to customer service; it has invested millions of dollars in an online customer service website. This is not your ordinary help desk. The system allows customers to ask sophisticated questions about Cisco's technology, including how it fits with their own system's architecture. Engineering aids make navigating the system easy for customer engineers, and the net result is that customers essentially write their own order.[8]

Most important from the customer's perspective, the same system allows customers to diagnose and solve technical problems for themselves—getting answers much faster than if they wait for a voice on the phone or (much worse) the arrival of an on-site technician. In data transmission, seconds of downtime mean millions of dollars lost (not to mention unhappy users). In this case, the best way to serve the customer is through the customer's own technical service staff.[9]

WHAT IS A SERVICE MENTALITY?

Many people know that services are beginning to dominate economic activity.[10] In the United States and in Europe, approximately 80 percent of high-wage employment and 73% of low-wage is generated by providing services.[11] The numbers would be even higher if statisticians could calculate the growing service content of goods produced in other sectors. We want to be sure you know what service means.

Organizational Activities Matched to Customer Needs And Desires

As noted in the introduction to this chapter, perhaps the most important imperative of a service perspective is the move from what Peter Drucker calls an internal perspective to an external one. Table 3.3, expanded from a book called *Customer-Centered Strategy* by Professor Mark Jenkins, suggests the significant difference in questions asked by the strategist.

TABLE 3.3 THE CONTRAST BETWEEN INTERNAL STRATEGIC QUESTIONS AND EXTERNAL STRATEGIC QUESTIONS

Internal Perspective	External Perspective
What are our competencies and strengths?	What are the characteristics of our customers?
What are our weaknesses?	What are customers' values?
How do we stack up against the strengths and weaknesses of our competitors?	What is the customers' price sensitivity?
	How do our current customers identify and rank providers of what they want?
	What kind of future customer groups will we be able to serve?

Source: M. Jenkins, *Customer-Centered Strategy: Thinking Strategically about Your Customers* (Philadelphia: Trans-Atlantic, 1997).

Of course, strategists need to ask the questions in both columns, but as we noted at the beginning of this chapter, companies often have great difficulty moving from an internal to an external focus. Giving more thought to issues in the column on the right often leads to a significant change in strategy. An illustration can be found in this story from a traditional customer-contact business.

The Town Librarian and the Latchkey Children

The town librarian was becoming increasingly concerned. Each day at about 3 p.m., a flood of schoolchildren came into the library's reading rooms. At about 5 p.m. the tide of children began to turn. By 6 p.m. the library was quiet once again. A survey revealed that the library was being used as an informal day-care center for "latchkey" children (so called because they would have to use their own key if they went home after school while their parents were at work.)

The reading rooms, quiet and sparsely populated most of the day, were becoming increasingly noisy and crowded. Books, particularly fragile paperbacks, were left in untidy heaps on library tables or on the floor with spines cracking. Tired assistants faced mountains of reshelving before they could leave for the day. The constant traffic to the bathrooms kept the janitor busy with special efforts to keep them neat, clean, and well stocked.

One library that felt the pressure had a budget funded from general revenues by the town's budget committee. The budget committee had not increased the library's budget for two years, even to keep up with inflation. It might be expected that staff would feel it was not the library's job to care for latchkey children. This is a task that should be done by parents or perhaps other day-care providers. What should the town librarian do?[12]

The librarian's easiest response in this brief example would seem to be establishing new rules that require children to be accompanied by adults when visiting the library. An entrepreneurially oriented strategist, on the other hand, saw the situation just described as an opportunity to create greater value for customers. A library is traditionally defined as a place to keep books and make them available to the public. To that end, libraries have elaborate inventory and recording systems that track where books are and which patrons have borrowed them. But is this the only way to interpret the library's mission? Is there an opportunity to redefine the mission to provide greater value to customers?

The strategic librarian decided to enhance the value provided by her organization. She emphasized that the library was part of the educational and cultural assets of the town—a potential provider of chamber music performances as well as book review clubs and places for students to study. More specifically, the influx of latchkey children was reassessed as a chance to encourage reading and a love for books among the library's future customers. The library began to offer story hours and art classes. Volunteers, especially retired people, were brought in to work during after-school hours to help cover expenses. As a result, the citizens voted for an increase in their local taxes so that the library could improve the services it was offering to the community.

Customers Seen from a Positive Perspective

The librarian's dilemma was successfully resolved only because the library stopped seeing after-school visitors as a problem. It is easy to view people outside the organization in a negative light. Customers in particular often want things the organization does not and perhaps cannot provide. Different individuals and groups can make contradictory demands. They often present urgent requests that the company did not anticipate.

Various responses to these potential difficulties are possible; some of them are defensive, even hostile. Indeed, strategy is often seen as intrinsically competitive, and many of its well-known principles come from the military, where strategy helps determine life-and-death contests. Military success is often fueled by the energy that comes from defending home and property, a perspective that puts the organization and its allies on center stage.

Business strategists often take the same perspective, and Chapter 5 summarizes some important thinking about the need to "defend" profits from the demands of buyers and suppliers. In this chapter, however, we want to emphasize that the traditional military mindset does not work well with a customer-centered strategy. It is hard to think about truly pleasing someone who is viewed (even subconsciously) as the enemy.

This raises one of the inherent complexities of strategy: the strategist must balance requirements for survival of the organization with requirements for serving the customer. Paying attention to only one set of requirements is very likely to subvert the other. Yet the successful middle ground, in our view, increasingly puts the customer at the center of strategy, and that requires a *positive model of human behavior*. Not only customers, but also suppliers, distributors, and especially the company's own employees must be assumed to be well-meaning. Encountering a few people with ill will is almost inevitable, but they must be treated as special cases. It is important that dealing with outliers does not jeopardize a basically positive mindset.[13]

> **Positive models of human behavior** assume that most people are intrinsically well-meaning in their interactions with others.

More specifically, successful customer-centered strategists do the following:

- Respect customers as capable of identifying and making decisions about their needs[14]
- Assume that the needs and interests of the customer will change and require adaptation by the organization
- Adopt a partnership perspective in responding to customer needs.

These are viable principles for a wide range of organizations—including those with business-to-business strategies and those that serve children, the mentally ill, and other customers who traditionally have not been given a voice in service delivery.

Customer-centered strategists assume that positive principles will need organizational support to become practical.[15] They do not assume, as we will describe at the end of the chapter, that all customer requests can or should be fulfilled. Nonetheless, the central idea is that by meeting customer requests, even those that initially seem difficult or impossible, the organization is likely to be in a better, more financially sound position in the future.

Employees Who Understand That Their Success Comes from Service

A third key component of a service mentality involves employees. It is difficult for people who are not happy to happily serve customers. That would seem obvious, but it is an observation that makes significant demands on the strategist. The basic guidelines for trying to make employees happy mirror those just suggested for successful interaction with customers: respect, adaptation, and partnership. The field of human resource management is devoted to choosing and supporting effective employees, and thus in this strategy text we will not cover the subject in depth. However, the link between employees and customers must be made clear by management if people within the organization are to gain satisfaction from serving customers.

As an example, we return to Cisco. Its service success depends not only on connecting strongly with customers, as described earlier in this chapter, but also on a strong connection with employees.

How Cisco Keeps Its Employees Happy

Faced with the need to attract and retain the best technical minds in the very competitive Silicon Valley job market and other sites, Cisco developed a distinctive competence in satisfying employees as a way to achieve distinctive customer satisfaction. The company regularly shows up on lists of the best companies to work for,[16] and it has made good use of its Internet expertise in keeping employees happy. The employee services website provides speedy access to the company database of résumés and job positions. Employees can directly access their personnel files. They can find information about stock options and other benefits (almost all employees are shareholders). The site also catalogs company learning programs and allows employees to book training on their own.[17] It fully reimburses tuition up to an annual maximum of $7,500.[18]

The match between employee success and customer service is also made clear. A customer-oriented mentality is central to Cisco's culture, and customer satisfaction is a major part of performance appraisal and compensation for managers and employees alike. Early in its history, Cisco established a customer advocacy function. That means that "anyone in the company can ring the bell" if he or she finds a dissatisfied customer. All employees thus have a responsibility for carrying out a central feature of the firm's strategy. Making this critical activity part of data kept and shared emphasizes its centrality to the way the company operates.[19]

A Climate That Supports and Reinforces Service

Happy employees do not automatically make customers happy. The culture of the organization, as well as its processes and systems, must highlight the importance of customer service and support its delivery. *Organization "climate"* is a concept that tries to capture the overall experience of employees at work; a *service climate* more specifically creates the expectation that customers will be respected and served. Strategists provide the tools and relationships that help that happen. They establish practices, policies, and procedures that are actually used by their employees. Potential contributions to that climate, identified from the research literature, are outlined in Table 3.4.

Service climates support and reinforce satisfying customers.

TABLE 3.4 CONTRIBUTIONS TO SERVICE CLIMATE

Dimension	Requirements for Effective Service
Equipment	Reliable tools for customer support are available.
Training	Purpose and methods of customer contact are made clear.
Personnel	A sufficient number of staff are trained in customer support and made available to customers.
Systems for work processing	Processes for interacting with customers are in place.
Record keeping	Records of past contacts are available.
Evaluation and learning	Outcomes of transactions are recorded and evaluated.
Reward	Service success is recognized.
Management	Successful practices are routinized through subsequent training and system modifications. Problems and anomalies are addressed.
Communication and marketing	Customers are aware of the purpose and benefits of the organization's efforts.

Source: Based on S. Schneider & S. S. White, *Service Quality* (Thousand Oaks, CA: Sage, 2004).

Clearly a lot of tools and activities are needed, but the strategist does not have to do it all. Just as customers can be effective participants in production, so can employees. The people on the "front line" of service are the ones who have the detailed knowledge to make a customer-centered strategy a success.[20]

WHAT ARE THE GUIDELINES FOR A CUSTOMER-BASED BUSINESS MODEL?

More and more organizations are developing a customer-oriented definition of their business. Doing so, as Figure 3.2 from Derek Abell shows, means addressing three fundamental questions.

Figure 3.2 — Abell's Model of Business Definition

Source: D. F. Abell, *Defining the Business: The Starting Point of Strategic Planning* (Upper Saddle River, NJ: Prentice-Hall, 1980).

Definition of the Business in Customer, Not Production, Terms

The purpose of Abell's first question, "Who is being satisfied?" is to elicit a clear description of what the customer values. Unless a product or service satisfies specific needs or wants, it cannot be expected to generate revenue. That means the customer should drive vision and mission; although other stakeholders are important to business success, especially shareholders and employees. The account that follows is a reminder of how even companies that satisfy their customers at one point in time can lose contact.

Encyclopedia Britannica Loses a Long-Standing Business

Encyclopedia Britannica established one of the best-known brands in the world by selling multivolume sets of encyclopedias. In the 1990s, however, its sales declined by more than 50 percent. Its nicely bound volumes sold for $1,500–$2,000. That was hard to justify compared to Microsoft's Encarta CD-ROM, which sold for $50 or came free with the purchase of many computers with a CD drive.

Encarta, a licensed product from the publishing company Funk & Wagnall's, had traditionally been sold in grocery stores. When Encarta was first introduced, Britannica did not respond. Decision makers thought that an electronic encyclopedia was an inferior product, a toy, and believed customers would be able to easily see the greater benefits of their offering.

They were wrong. Britannica misunderstood both its competitors and its customers. It was not competing against Encarta, with its vastly different cost structure; it was competing against the computer. The parents who once invested in the leading encyclopedia (long considered the best home learning tool for children) now used their money to buy what they considered an even more vital learning tool, a computer. Encarta just came along as a "free" additional feature.

When decision makers at Britannica finally recognized the competitive threat this new bundle of products posed, they decided to give away a CD version of their encyclopedia with the purchase of a printed version, and to sell the CD-ROM version for $1000. As you probably know, this strategy was not successful. Facing tough on-line competition from Wikipedia and a review by the well-regarded journal *Nature* that showed that Wikipedia citations were close to encyclopedias in accuracy,[21] Britannica continued to decline and was sold to new owners. They developed an online encyclopedia at www.britannica.com, which features contributions from leading scholars, including several Nobel Prize winners, daily updates, and links to the *New York Times* and the BBC. That is an advance in content compared to previous paper volumes, yet competitor Wikipedia is regularly cited as one of the top ten sites visited on the web—demonstrating the success of a very different model of how information can be gathered.[22]

Clarity about the Needs to Be Satisfied

Defining the customers who are most strategic to serve can be difficult.[23] The question of *what* needs or wants to satisfy can be even harder. Consider a mundane product such as an elevator. The customer is multifaceted. A manufacturer must think about the owner or developer of the building, the general contractor who builds the structure (and actually purchases the elevators), the architect who designs and selects the elevators, the companies who lease space in the building and, of course, the users of the elevator. Otis significantly increased its revenue when it decided which of these customers it would focus on serving.

Moving Up by Narrowing Down

At Otis Elevator, the worldwide leader in "vertical transportation" for high-rise buildings,[24] strategists look at their customers' experience and see opportunities to satisfy well after the purchase phase. Indeed, Otis has built the profitability of its business by emphasizing excellent service downstream. Otis strategists decided to focus on the elevator in use and its maintenance, rather than the obvious point of purchase, where price competition is rampant.

The company is proud to say that it knows an elevator needs service before the customer. It achieves this by placing a computer chip in the elevator's operating system that reports maintenance issues back to Otis. Ready to respond is a massive corps of factory trained service representatives stationed around the world.[25]

In addition to the complexities of purchase and use by multiple customers, most companies serve many different market segments and in each of these (by definition) customer demands differ. Targeting segments is an important strategic decision, and tracking and analyzing them is essential to the bottom line. Some segments grow faster than others, and some are more profitable than others.

This is the domain of marketing strategy. As an overview, we will simply note that market segments can be defined by attributes of the product, attributes of the customer, or both. Figure 3.3 lists typical segments in the automobile industry. Figure 3.4 shows how product and buyer attributes (in this case, geographic location) can be used to create a segmentation matrix. The purpose of creating a segmentation matrix is to identify the segments that the organization currently serves or would like to serve, to evaluate the attractiveness of each segment, and to design a strategy for competing in chosen segments.

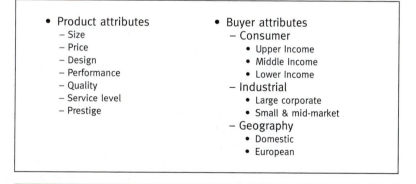

- Product attributes
  - Size
  - Price
  - Design
  - Performance
  - Quality
  - Service level
  - Prestige

- Buyer attributes
  - Consumer
    - Upper Income
    - Middle Income
    - Lower Income
  - Industrial
    - Large corporate
    - Small & mid-market
  - Geography
    - Domestic
    - European

Figure 3.3—Consumer Dimensions for Segmentation of the Auto Industry

Other characteristics can be used to segment markets, including age, gender, occupation, education, religion, and nationality.

	North America	Western Europe	Eastern Europe	Western Asia	China	Southeast Asia	Central Asia	Africa
Passenger sedans (luxury)								
Midsize passenger sedans								
Sport-utility vehicles								
Passenger minivans								
Delivery vans								
Heavy trucks								
Specialty vehicles								

Figure 3.4 — Buyer and Product Attributes

Buyer behavior, which includes factors such as extent of use, degree of brand loyalty, usage rate, benefits sought, and lifestyle, is also a common way to measure and identify segments. Again, the strategic decision is whom the organization can best serve, based on the best combination of what customers want and what the company can provide.

Choices about How Needs Will Be Satisfied

As the strategist considers who might be served and what needs might be met, Abell's third question about *how* needs will be met takes us back to the notion of distinctive competencies. Strategists ask: What do we as an organization do that the customer specifically values? But they also ask: How do we do it differently and better than the competition? What resources are required to meet the needs we have identified now and in the future? These questions direct attention back to internal resources—it does little good to seek a business definition that is customer oriented if the organization lacks the capability to deliver on customer needs with attractive products and services.

At the beginning of Chapter 2, we discussed Disney, a vast company that has established itself as a trusted guide to family entertainment.

Disney offers its customers vacations, films, videos, books, music, sporting events, and other family activities. But independent firms produce most of the products and services that Disney offers for sale. The most important role that people at Disney perform is selecting products that will enhance its reputation for high-quality entertainment. The organization concentrates on the job of maintaining the trust of families worldwide for quality products and services.

Synergy enables one resource to increase the impact of others.

They are looking for *synergy*. Ideally, some of the same resources can be leveraged in multiple segments. Brand names help this happen. For example, although the Mercedes emblem has different meanings for different segments (prestige in luxury cars, dependability in heavy trucks), the brand has value as a quality image that crosses all of Daimler AG's segments. That allows the firm to expand its business by leveraging a pool of resources into new market segments. Disney does the same thing in its multiple markets.

Once again we suggest that you gain some direct experience with considering how a company can grow by meeting multiple customer needs. Worksheet 3.1 will help drive home the key ideas of the chapter.

Worksheet 3.1: The Growth Matrix—A Tool for Expanding Product/Service/ Experience

HOW DO COMPANIES GATHER DATA TO IDENTIFY AND UNDERSTAND THEIR CUSTOMERS?

Satisfying the customer is a moving target. Too often, firms lose track of what the customer really values. It is much easier to focus on the physical product or technology and to assume it suits customers than to really engage with customers in all of their complexity. Neglecting to stay connected with customers is particularly easy for a company that has been successful for some time. Strategists can believe that they know what their customers value, while their customers' perceptions of value changes over time. We have already described Encyclopedia Britannica as an example of such a value shift.

To make life more difficult for the strategist, customer composition itself is often changing. In part this has to do with strategic choices deliberately made by the organization. We have just pointed out, for example, that resources have more value when they are leveraged across multiple markets. Seeking synergy, businesses may expand their customer base or emphasize new markets or new market segments. When they succeed, the definition of customer value is almost certain to change, and the resources required to serve the customer are likely to shift. If the overall customer-based strategy is not reassessed, financial benefits from expanding the market are unlikely to develop. Four activities may be particularly helpful: analyzing customer experiences with a product or service, mapping customer perceptions of the market, tracking marketing information, and anticipating the consequences of demographic trends.

Analyze Customer Experiences

Although the key exchange between buyer and seller is an economic transaction, in reality there are many more points of customer contact. Each offers an opportunity to learn about the customer, or for the customer to learn about the organization. *A customer experience map* may lead to insights about what customer satisfaction and behaviors really mean—or could mean—as a basis for competitive advantage.

Figure 3.5 offers an example of such a map, with some questions that might provide useful input to customer-centered strategy.

A customer experience map summarizes contact with a product or service from a customer's perspective.

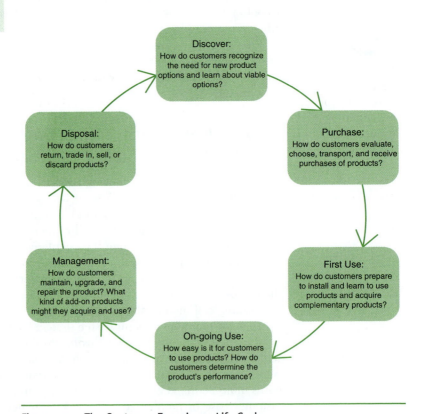

Figure 3.5 — The Customer Experience Life Cycle

It can be helpful to ask customers directly about how they use a product or service. Customers often offer valuable insights. It is also true, however, that busy customers may not think directly about their experience. Strategists therefore need to observe and infer experience from more general evidence.[26]

Map Customer Perceptions of the Market

One method strategists can borrow from marketers to help understand the connection between products and customers is to develop a visual *customer perception map* of the market. Doing so typically involves choosing important dimensions of customer behavior or characteristics, measuring customer responses along these dimensions, and then plotting responses on a grid that represents the perceptual space in which products or services exist.

In aggregate, customer perception maps may suggest overly crowded territories where too many rivals are competing for the same segment, or they may reveal opportunities where there are underserved or unrecognized needs. Figure 3.6 illustrates such a map for the automobile industry.

> **Customer perception maps indicate market distinctions made by a significant number of customers or potential customers.**

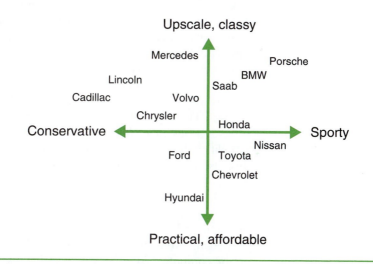

Figure 3.6 — Customer Perception Map of the Automobile Industry

Notice that the map uses subjective terms such as *classy* and *practical* to define a market. These words come directly from customer descriptions of the product. Perception maps are intended to trace how customers think about the competitive space and to give manufacturers information to position, or reposition, product offerings. The purpose of re-positioning strategies is to seek out more profitable segments or to increase the differentiation or "space" between one product and others.

Thus, in the automobile industry, it might make sense for Saab to reposition if it wants to differentiate itself from Volvo on the one side and BMW on the other. That might mean incorporating the high safety standards of Volvo with an updated BMW styling package. Note too, that the upscale, conservative segment is particularly well represented in the automobile industry; that makes sense because baby boomer consumers with big disposable incomes value such cars though it is jeopardized by rising prices of gasoline. The sporty, practical segment appears to be underserved. Perhaps this is because competing in the lower right corner of the grid is difficult (manufacturing a sporty but affordable car) or unprofitable (avid consumers tend to be young men who don't have a lot to spend). The overall point is that it doesn't make sense to assume that it will be strategic to fill every hole in a map like this, but such a map does offer important evidence for choices that should be less contested. (Unless, of course, your competitor is working with a similar map and aiming toward the same uncontested space!)

Track Marketing Information

Tracking elusive information about the customer has become a major activity. Most companies have specialists to gather and analyze detailed information about customers. Customer satisfaction surveys are obvious examples of this search for data.

But how can companies identify shifts in interests? Ideally strategists find clues before a trend is obvious to most consumers. Smart strategists create as well as respond to demand by reinforcing new interests and behaviors. The sources of information for this kind of strategy are often indirect. For instance, do you ever wonder why you keep getting offers for credit cards, even after you turned the last several offers down? That is because data from every transaction you make is collected. Credit card companies, like American Express, analyze customer statements and then sell mailing lists to customers of their own who seek buying patterns that match what they are trying to sell. If you have purchased a house, leased a car, taken out a mortgage, or done anything else that might change your status, you are especially likely to get a mailing. In fact, the computer system at American Express collects more than 450 pieces of information on every one of its cardholders. The data is updated weekly and used to target marketing for all kinds of products—magazines, cruise vacations, and exercise videotapes, among others. The company's website generates sales in travel and other kinds of purchases. But equally important, each site visit offers an opportunity to learn one more thing about the customer's preferences by monitoring his or her electronic visits.

In their efforts to gather similar consumer data, several companies have been accused of invading people's privacy. For example, Microsoft provides a Media Player in its software suite that has what some consumers say is a privacy-invading feature. Media Player keeps a log, stored in the user's own computer, of the DVDs that the computer plays. The software sends this log back to Microsoft, which sells it to other companies that match the interests of the consumer with movie and music advertisements that subsequently pop up on the user's screen.

These examples flag an ethical issue: technology has allowed companies to capture vast amounts of personal information about customers without their knowledge and use it to build detailed dossiers on individuals. We will return to this issue in our discussion of corporate social responsibility in Chapter 9.

Anticipate the Consequences of Demographic Trends

As a last source of information that can help companies develop customer-based strategies, consider demographics. Virtually every company is affected by demographic changes in the population. Changes in age, birth rate, work behavior, and ethnic mix in a population will be reflected in profound changes in the customers available to serve and what they will expect.

For example, the financial collapse of the 1930s depressed birth rates in the United States for almost fifteen years. Then, after World War II, the birth rate grew at an unusually high rate, producing what was later called the baby boom. Since the 1970s, the U.S. birth rate has been dropping. Perhaps more interesting, the age at which the first child is born has been increasing. When the baby boom generation reached its thirties and forties in the 1980s and 1990s, these dynamics affected size and timing of the next "baby boomlet."

The ripple effects of uneven birth rates are enormous. At present, and for the first time in U.S. history, the largest segment of the population is also the most affluent and has the most political power. Furthermore, in the United States and every other developed country, but also in China and Brazil, the birth rate is now well below the replacement rate of 2.2 live births per woman of reproductive age. The decline in the young population is changing markets in fundamental ways. Growth in family formation has been the driving force in all domestic markets in the developed world. The mass market that emerged in all rich countries after World War II has been youth-determined from the start. It has now become middle-age-determined, or perhaps more accurately, split into two—a middle-age-determined mass market and a much smaller youth-determined one.

Because the supply of young people is dramatically decreasing, new employment patterns designed to attract and hold on to the growing number of older educated people is expected to become increasingly important. At the same time, although politicians everywhere still promise to save the existing pension systems, it is highly likely that in another decade or two people will have to keep working until their midseventies.

All of this suggests that new business opportunities will rise in the areas of health, entertainment, travel, and financial services in particular. For example, as people continue to age and live longer, there will be demand for medical and health advice, medications, treatments, and diet and exercise plans. With regard to entertainment, experienced consumers will want to travel to unique parts of the world and seek educational experiences, excitement, and aesthetic pleasures they have not experienced before. Financial services will be expected to keep pace—providing opportunities for individuals to manage the assets that make these experiences possible.

Worksheet 3.2 offers an opportunity to explore alternatives in the context of a particular product or service.

Worksheet 3.2: Customer Survey—A Tool for Understanding Buyer Experience

Involve Customers in Design and Selection

The discussion of Adidas and Nike that initiated this chapter suggests how customers can become more actively involved in product decisions. The next step is to involve customers in more strategic decisions. Professor Frank Pille, who co-directs the MIT Smart Customization Group and works at the University of Aachen in Germany, has devoted his career to developing this idea.[27] He is particularly interested in how customers can begin to make the research and design decisions once seen as a major company capability. Here is an intriguing example:

> Crowdcasting broadcasts a company's problem to a specific—and carefully chosen—group. Think of . . . crowdcasting as a private backstage party you can't get into if you're not on the list. In Idea Crossing's Innovation Challenge, contestants sign confidentiality agreements, and their strategic solutions become the property of the corporate sponsors. At the 2004 Innovation Challenge, Sprint executives asked participants to devise new services featuring high-speed wireless technologies; last year IBM searched for ways to market itself to businesses in China and India—countries that send large contingents of MBA students to the event.[28]

Use Ethnography Techniques

An increasing number of companies are using anthropological tools to understand the customer's world. This approach assumes that customers may be unable to articulate their needs and desires, or may not be interested in doing so. Storylistening, pioneered by Olaf Rughase, is one promising technique.[29] The purpose is to gather data about the customer's world from very general customer accounts without using preconceived categories. A compatible approach focuses on observing customer activities. Ethnography, the description of people and activities in specific places, is especially valuable when moving into markets with which strategists have little previous experience.[30]

Whatever tool is used to gather data, the overall intention is summarized in Figure 3.7. It suggests that there is a natural interplay between the issues discussed in Chapter 2 and those discussed in this chapter. Constant interaction allows strategists to think about different ways customers can be served, alternative customer groups to be served, and possible market evolution.

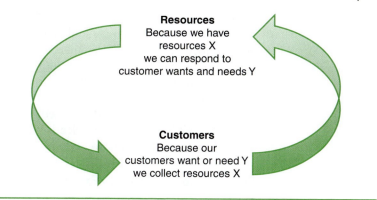

Figure 3.7 — The Interplay between Resources and Customer Information

CAN THE CUSTOMER CONNECTION BE OVEREMPHASIZED?

We are enthusiastic about engaging customers and believe that closer customer contact characterizes today's competitive environment. However, no organization has infinite resources to serve customers. The following issues seem particularly important in thinking about this aspect of strategic decision making.

Service Levels Have to Fit Strategy

The Nordstrom department store chain is famous for offering outstanding customer service that fits its upscale merchandise and facilities. During the Christmas shopping season, for example, a live pianist plays a grand piano, and wine is served in most store lobbies. There are also legendary stories of customers having been served well beyond their expectations. For example, one of the authors of this book found himself in urgent need of a haircut while visiting San Francisco. The nearby Nordstrom's salon was booked for the day, but the accommodating manager not only suggested an alternative, he also called the competitor and made the appointment! At the time, your author couldn't help thinking, "Why aren't all my retail experiences like this?"

But this level of customer service is clearly not appropriate for all retailers. Wal-Mart, for example, is not in a position to offer the same level of service and expertise on the shopping floor as Nordstrom does. Wal-Mart follows a low-cost strategy, and paying store clerks what Nordstrom pays would undermine its competitive advantage. Yet to increase the customer's perception of service, Wal-Mart stations greeters at the store's entrance. Usually part-time semiretired workers, these greeters offer a friendly, low-cost way to enhance the customer's experience.

The contrast between Nordstrom and Wal-Mart shows that the level and kind of customer service should be driven by strategy. The strategy must be focused on using customer service as a means of *adding value*, which means that the customer is willing to pay for the level of service provided. American Express reflects this distinction in how it charges for its card services—$36 for the basic card (most service is delivered through automated phone or Internet systems) versus $300 for platinum (the wait for telephone service is virtually nil and members have twenty-four-hour access to concierge services).

Some Customers Are Too Expensive to Serve

A somewhat cynical *80/20 rule* is often reported by service providers: "80% of my effort goes to serving 20% of my clients." To the extent that such a significant imbalance exists, and the resource-eating group can be encouraged (retrained, restricted) to decrease their demands, profits will rise.

Organizations have to be careful that their activities do not increase the percentage of overly expensive customer demands. An online survey, for example, may give the impression that the customer will receive a personal reply. If thousands of customers respond, the organization may not have that capacity.

One of the foremost advocates of quality customer service identifies an even more problematic group of undesirable "jaycustomers": the thief, the rule breaker, the belligerent, the feuder (who gets into arguments with others), the vandal, and the deadbeat.[31] The wise strategist obviously tries to avoid such customers, because they use resources that could be used in more productive ways.

Even committed and well-meaning customers can create unrecoverable costs. Mass customization, the interesting strategy mentioned at the beginning of this chapter, is one example. Working with customers as discrete individuals with different needs by definition means variability, and variability has a cost. Mass customizers often justify the cost of contact by treating the exchange not just as a sale but as a chance to learn about potential customer needs and interests in a larger market. However, learning about customers and then using that knowledge also has significant cost for the organization. Experience suggests that few organizations have the capacity to process the customer information that is available to them.

Strategists can reduce unnecessary variability by structuring encounters and providing orienting information in an accessible form before contact is made.[32] Examples can be found everywhere: improved setup instructions for goods that must be assembled, increased information provided before stressful events such as surgery, and so on. Although information from the organization helps, organizations also create venues where customers inform each other (such as student-to-student tutoring and support groups). If monitored, these encounters can reinforce the customer relationship and also reduce costs.

Today's Happy Customers Are Not Necessarily Tomorrow's Customers

We have already discussed the widely accepted truism that success at one point in time can become the anchor that keeps an organization from identifying new needs in the marketplace and succeeding at a later point in time. Clayton Christensen, a professor at Harvard University, is well known for arguing that technically sophisticated customers are currently attractive sources of information but they can tie the firm to a particular knowledge base and give them little experience with other emerging technologies.[33]

Within reason, strategists may therefore choose to spend resources interacting with customers who do not bring significant current returns to the business. The justification (which of course must be examined) is that they are exploring options that may be valuable in the future.[34]

Strategists must also think about noncustomers. Yellowtail is an Australian wine that leaped ahead of its competitors to become American's number one import within a few years after its introduction. Strategists did that by breaking industry tradition and thinking about people who do *not* buy wine. They found that people who drank beer and hard liquor did not like the taste of wine, and were put off by the snob factors associated with wine. A sweeter wine with a wallaby on the label significantly expanded the market.[35]

CONCLUSIONS FOR THE STRATEGIST

As a strategist, you must remember your own customer experiences, but not rely on them. Customer needs tend to vary widely across various segments or groupings. Understanding and mapping varied customer experience allows the strategist to provide organizational products and services at various points in this process.

As a general rule, the most important way to stay in touch with customers is to engage them as they experience your product or service. Smart strategists tend to ask their customers questions. They track their behavior in detail. They engage customers and set up situations in which customers are willing to coproduce products, services, and experiences that they then pay for. This is the information that fuels innovation and entrepreneurial response—the subject of our next chapter.

Key Concepts

Customer-based strategy focuses on identifying and serving customer needs, often with the assumption that satisfying customers will also maximize success in reaching more traditional performance goals, particularly stockholder value. Ideally this results in unique **intellectual capital**—knowledge, skills, and capabilities that an organization can use to produce goods, services and experiences for its competitive advantage.

All companies can use a customer-based strategy, including those that use **mass customization** to allow a large number of customers to personalize product characteristics and those who use **experience-oriented strategies** to emphasize the process of consuming their offerings.

A customer-based strategy requires **customer contact, which** is measured by user involvement in planning, executing, and delivering a good, service, or customer experience. It can lead to **coproduction,** which directly involves customers in the creation of the goods and services they consume. This is typically a **cost-sharing** strategy that allocates costs between customers and producers.

We suggest that **positive models of human behavior** (which assume most people are intrinsically well-meaning toward others) are required for almost all successful customer-centered strategies. One goal is the achievement of **synergies** that enable one resource to increase the impact of other resources.

Service is an increasingly important component of company activities, and companies with a positive **service climate** have established practices, policies, and procedures for successfully interacting with customers that are actually used by their employees. Finally, a service-oriented strategy almost always involves collecting data from and about customers. A **customer experience map** summarizes contact with a product or service from a customer's perspective. A **customer perception map** indicates distinctions they make about products in a specific market. Both can be used as a basis for identifying underserved customer needs for further strategic consideration.

Questions for Further Reflection

1. Analyze one of your experiences as a satisfied customer. What strategies did the company follow to please you? Would you appreciate other reinforcing offerings from this company? Can you identify several other kinds of customers who must be satisfied in different ways?

2. Find a company that has recently changed its strategy significantly (airline companies that no longer serve food, for example, or grocers that deliver online orders). Which customers are likely be more or less served by this change in direction? Can you suggest ways to improve the likelihood of success by intensifying customer orientation? Does the company risk providing too much service?

3. Identify an industry that is beginning to produce services or products that have not been offered before. (Think of a new type of Internet service, for example, or an innovative product introduction in a sport that interests you.) Do you see an opportunity for a new complementary business? (Industries

in transition tend to offer more new opportunities than more established ones.) Is there a potential for coproduction with customers? What valuable information would you expect the company to gain from close contact with customers?

WORKSHEET 3.1
The Growth Matrix—A Tool for Expanding Product/Service/Experience

A great deal of research suggests that strategists tend to follow the path established by previous decisions, but you have alternatives. This worksheet compares moves in three different directions.

Step 1: In the top left corner of this matrix, list the markets currently served by a specific organization that interests you.

Step 2: Move to the top middle section of the matrix and think about existing products from your company and its current competitors.

Step 3: Consider possible extensions of current products/services in this market and list them in the top right corner. You are trying to add options that go beyond current product/service/experience offerings that meet needs you know exist in current markets.

Now consider options with much greater strategic risk.

Step 4: Identify new markets that your company might serve in the bottom left corner of the matrix.

Step 5: In the bottom middle section, identify any existing products/services/experiences serving these markets.

Step 6: In the bottom right section, identify plausible new offerings in new markets.

EXTENSION
- Role-play the most important competitor of the company you chose, and follow the preceding steps for that organization.

Growth Matrix Worksheet 3.1	Organization: Time Frame:
Analyst(s): Black = current portfolio Blue = possibilities Red (circled) = greatest performance potential	**Strategy Summary:**

Existing Markets	Existing Products	New Products for Existing Markets
New Markets	Products Currently Serving New Markets	New Products for New Markets

WORKSHEET 3.2
Customer Survey—A Tool for Understanding Buyer Experience

Customers make judgments about both the intangible, physical characteristics of a product, service, or experience and the subjective aspects. Consider how customers evaluate a specific company's offering.

Step 1: Identify product/service/experience combination that is purchased.

Step 2: Interview several customers and fill in the table of customer perceptions.

Step 3: Think of how the product/service/experience might be improved to meet customer needs. Complete the right column with these ideas.

Step 4: Circle the ideas for improvement that are most feasible. Star the ideas that might lead to the greatest market.

ALTERNATIVE
- Select a product. Focus on improving the following characteristics: cost/performance, features, functionality, constraints, reliability, serviceability, aesthetics, speed, and reputation.

Customer Survey Worksheet 3.2	Organization: Service Time Frame:
Analyst(s):	Strategy Summary:

	Customer Perception	How to Improve Perception
Professionalism (know-how of service provider)		
Concern/responsive-ness (interest in meeting customer needs)		
Fit (match between customer needs and services provided)		
Interaction (willing-ness to accept input and share control decisions)		
Trustworthiness (ability to keep promises and main-tain confidentiality)		
Flexibility (capacity to respond to additional or changed information)		
Recovery (individual and organizational skill in solving problems)		
Reputation (recog-nition of service quality by others)		
Cost/value received (perception of benefits gained)		

NOTES

[1] See http://www.sfgate.com/cgi-bin/article.cgi?f=/c/a/2006/05/24/BUG5TJ0UVH1.DTL and http://www.engadget.com/2006/05/23/apple-and-nike-launch-29-ipod-sport-kit/, accessed May 5, 2007.

[2] Quote from http://www.apple.com/ipod/nike/, accessed May 5, 2007. See also Berger, C., Moeslein, K., Piller, F., & Reichwald, R. 2003. Co-Designing the Customer Interface: Learning from Exploratory Research. TUM Business School Working Paper no. AIB37; http://www.miadidas.com, accessed March 1, 2008.

[3]See a similar table in Chase, R. B., Northcraft, G. B., & Wolf, G. 1984. Designing High Contact Service Systems: Application to a Savings-and-Loan. *Decision Sciences* 5(4): 542–556.

[4]See especially work on SERVQUAL by Parasuraman, A., Zeithaml, V., & Barry, L. 1988. SERVQUAL: A Multi-item Scale for Measuring Consumer Perceptions of Service Quality. *Journal of Retailing* 64: 2–40; Parasuraman, A., Zeithaml, V., & Barry, L. 1994. Reassessment of Expectations as a Comparison Standard in Measuring Service Quality: Implications for Further Research. *Journal of Marketing* 58: 111–124.

[5]Rifkin, J. 2000. *The Age of Access*. New York: Penguin.

[6]Zeithaml, V. A., & Bitner, M. J. 2000. *Services Marketing: Integrating Customer Focus across the Firm* (2nd ed.). Boston: McGraw-Hill. For an approach that takes the idea of coproduction one step further, see Prahalad, C. K. 2004. *The Future of Competition: Co-Creating Unique Value with Customers*. Boston: Harvard Business School Press.

[7]Cimilluca, D. 2007. Cisco's Growing M&A Appetite. *Wall Street Journal Online* (April 9). *http://blogs.wsj.com/deals/2007/04/09/ciscos-growing-ma-appetite/*, accessed May 5, 2007.

[8]See Cisco Customers, http://www.cisco.com/public/regben_cust.html, accessed November 29, 2007.

[9]Morgridge, J. P., & Heskett, J. L. 2000. Cisco Systems: Are You Ready (A). Harvard Business School Case No. 901002.

[10]An excellent map on labor force by sector around the world can be found at http://en.wikipedia.org/wiki/Image:Gdp-and-labour-force-by-sector.png, accessed May 5, 2007.

[11]The Characteristics and Quality of Service Sector Jobs, p. 107. http://www.oecd.org/dataoecd/11/15/2079411.pdf, accessed May 5, 2007. See also economic census data from the U.S. Census Bureau, U.S. Department of Commerce.

[12]Adapted from Moore, M. H. 1995. The Town Librarian and the Latchkey Children. *In Creating Public Value: Strategic Management in Government*, Chapter 1. Boston: Harvard University Press.

[13]Two useful websites that collect ideas from practice and research from a positive point of view are http://www.bus.umich.edu/positive/ and http://appreciativeinquiry.case.edu/, accessed May 13, 2007.

[14]Lengnick-Hall, C. A. 1996. Customer Contributions to Quality: A Different View of the Customer-Oriented Firm. *Academy of Management Review* 21(3): 791–824.

[15]Pugh, S. D. Dietz, J., Wiley, J. W., & Brooks, S. M. 2002. Driving Services Effectiveness through Employee-Customer Linkages. *Academy of Management Executive* 16: 73–84.

[16]Moos, T. T. 2007. Cisco Praised for Innovative Employee Programs (November 20). http://newsroom.cisco.com/dlls/2007/ts_112007.html, accessed November 29, 2007.

[17]Morgridge, J. P., & Heskett, J. L. 2000. Cisco Systems: Are You Ready (A). Harvard Business School Case No. 901002.

[18]Cisco Systems: Leading Maker of Networking Products and Services. http://nyjobsource.com/cisco.html, accessed November 29, 2007.

[19]http://newsroom.cisco.com/dlls/tln/exec_team/elfrink/perspectives.html, http://www.businessweek.com/1999/99_40/b3649012.htm, and http://www.e-consultancy.com/knowledge/whitepapers/82535/building-customer-loyalty-through-cisco-s-customer-advocacy-group.html, accessed May 5, 2007.

[20]See Floyd, S., & Wooldridge, B. 2000. *Building Strategy from the Middle: Reconceptualizing Strategy Process*. Thousand Oaks, CA: Sage.

[21]http://www.nature.com/news/2005/051212/full/438900a.html, accessed May 13, 2007.

[22]Downes, L., & Mui, C. 1998. *Unleashing the Killer App: Digital Strategies for Market Dominance.* Boston: Harvard Business School Press. For an overview of Wikipedia use, see Rainie, L., & Tancer, B. 2007. Wikipedia: When in Doubt, Multitudes Seek It Out. *Pew Research Center Publications* (April 24). http://pewresearch.org/pubs/460/wikipedia, (accessed January 21, 2008). See also Wikipedia's extensive entry on Encyclopedia Britannica at http://en.wikipedia.org/wiki/Encyclop%C3%A6dia_Britannica, accessed January 21, 2008.

[23]Schneider, B., Ehrhart, M. G., Mayer, D. M., Saltz, J. L., & Niles-Jolly, K. 2005. Understanding Customer-Organization Links in Service Settings. *Academy of Management Journal* 48: 1017–1032.

[24]See Otis Fact Sheet 2007, http://www.otis.com/corp/pdf/Otis_Fact_Sheet_2007.pdf, accessed November 29, 2007.

[25]Litt, M. 1997. Otis' Elevator Network Reaches New Heights. *Network Computing* 8(15).

[26]The customer services life cycle concept was initially described in: Ives, B. & Learmonth, G. 1984. The Information System as a Competitive Weapon. *Communications of the ACM*, 27,12, 1193–1201.

[27]http://www.aib.wiso.tu-muenchen.de/piller/, accessed May 5, 2007.

[28]Haiken, M. 2006. Want Fresh Ideas? Try "Crowdcasting" : It May Sound Like Just Another Corporate Buzzword, but Crowdcasting Is How DaimlerChrysler, Hilton and American Express Are Aiming to Get a Competitive Edge (November 21). http://money.cnn.com/2006/11/20/magazines/business2/crowdcasting_whatworks. biz2/?postversion=2006112106, accessed May 5, 2007. Also see http://innovationzen. com/blog/2006/08/01/top-10-crowdsourcing-companies/, accessed May 20, 2007.

[29]Rughase, O. 2002. Linking Content to Process: How Mental Models of the Customer Enhance Creative Strategy Process. In A. Huff & M. Jenkins (eds.), *Mapping Strategic Knowledge*, p. 46–62 London: Sage. http://www.sr-partners.com/pdf/Linking%20_ content_to_process.pdf, accessed May 21, 2007.

[30]Nussebaum, B. 2005. Innovation in China and Asia Is Getting Hot. *Business Week* (November 27). http://www.businessweek.com/innovate/NussbaumOnDesign/ archives/2005/11/innovation_in_c.html, accessed May 21, 2007.

[31]Lovelock, C. H., & Wright, L. 2002. *Principles of Service Marketing and Management* (2nd ed.). Upper Saddle River, NJ: Prentice-Hall.

[32]Chase, R. B., & Stewart, D. M. 1994. Make Your Service Fail-Safe. *Sloan Management Review* 35(3): 35–44; Lengnick-Hall, C. A. 1996. Customer Contributions to Quality: A Different View of the Customer-Oriented Firm. *Academy of Management Review* 21(3): 791–824.

[33]Christensen, C. M. 2003. *The Innovator's Dilemma: The Revolutionary Book That Will Change the Way You Do Business.* Boston: Harvard Business School Press.

[34]Hamel, G. 2000. *Leading the Revolution.* Boston: Harvard Business School Press.

[35]Kim, W. C. & Mauborgne, R. 2005. *Blue Ocean Strategy.* Boston: Harvard Business School Press.

4 Seeking Opportunity

Would you like to start your own business? Are you hoping it will make you rich? Or are you the kind of person who values security and wants to avoid an uncertain environment? The epilogue of this book suggests that employment security is increasingly unlikely. We therefore urge everyone to anticipate changing jobs and acquire a range of skills to manage his or her career. In this chapter we make the same argument to organizational strategists.

As new technology develops and customer needs change, there is an increasing possibility that another individual or organization will find a better way of providing the products, services, and experiences you deliver now. A core part of what it means to be a strategist is therefore to think and act like an entrepreneur. Whether you are motivated by the need to defend an existing competitive position or the desire to establish a new one, the very heart of strategy is about inventing new ways to connect resources and customers.

· ·

We explore the importance of continually thinking about new opportunities by considering three important questions:

What signals the capacity to develop opportunity?
Characteristics of individuals who recognize and develop opportunities
Teams that develop opportunities
Capabilities of organizations that develop opportunities

What are the processes of opportunity development?
Recognizing opportunities
Finding resources
Managing innovation

What are the differences between small firm and corporate entrepreneurship?
Small firm entrepreneurship
Corporate entrepreneurship

Is ambidexterity the answer?

The basic idea is that all strategists must be opportunistic, though obviously some environments require more attention to new opportunities than others. Consider Jeff Bezos, the entrepreneur who started Amazon and who continues to aggressively seek opportunities for his established business.

· ·

JEFF BEZOS AND AMAZON.COM

Jeff Bezos made the decision to start Amazon.com after reflecting on "regret-minimization." He imagined himself at age 80 looking back on his life: "Would I regret having given up an almost certain multi-million dollar bonus [if I remain with my current employer] to go out and start my own company? . . . Of course I wouldn't. At age 80, I doubt if I will even remember the bonus. But if I . . . pass up the chance to participate in a historic opportunity like the development of the World Wide Web, I would . . . [regret] it for the rest of my life."[1]

Bezos spoke to his parents, who agreed to loan him $300,000 from their retirement savings to pursue the opportunities created by the Internet. He and his wife, MacKenzie, then left New York for a new life in a rented two-bedroom house in the Seattle suburb of Bellevue, Washington. Jeff converted the garage into a workspace and with a small team of collaborators spent more than a year creating the Amazon.com website and developing the database programs to support it. The website was tested by 300 friends and family members in June 1995 and became available to the public the following month.

In the first thirty days, Amazon sold books in fifty states and forty-five countries. Brick-and-mortar competitors, such as Borders and Barnes & Noble, were slow to respond. They had little sense of the opportunities the Internet provided or the competitive threat posed by the likes of Amazon.

The company went public in May 1997, the same year that Barnes & Noble opened its online store. By 1998, Amazon.com had 4 million customers and was valued at $6 billion—more than Borders, Barnes & Noble, and all of the other independent booksellers combined. At that point, Amazon began selling videos, toys, and electronics. It also launched ventures in the United Kingdom and Germany.

By the end of 2007, Amazon had net sales of $ 10.7 billion, 44 percent of which originated from outside the United States. It boasts that it has "Earth's biggest selection," selling items as varied as cameras and outdoor plants. Some analysts have argued that Amazon should focus on its core competence—books. But the "everything" concept has proved successful. That includes retailers such as Target (a partner since 2001) along with smaller third-party sellers make up approximately 28 percent of all sales on Amazon.

Although it took Amazon seven years to turn its first profit, $256 million in 2003, the profit picture is still rockier than some investors had hoped as the company continues to pursue new opportunities. For example, Amazon recently unveiled a new service called Unbox, through which customers can download content from six major studios and several TV channels.[2] Almost simultaneously, Steve Jobs announced a very similar service at Apple, showcasing the exclusive deal with Disney we mentioned in Chapter 2.[3] A key controversy in the new market is pricing—Amazon is narrowing margins, even of mass retailers like Wal-Mart. Another uproar has to do with consumer rights—to date the content Amazon offers remains the property of the seller, at a price that the seller determines.[4] Clearly the contours of opportunity, and the route to profits, are still being explored.[5]

WHAT SIGNALS THE CAPACITY TO DEVELOP OPPORTUNITY?

The founding of Amazon illustrates how an insightful individual, evolving opportunities, and a pool of potential resources shape strategic action. Uncertainty abounds—about customer needs, resource availability, and the specific offerings that will make a profit. Jeff Bezos, the entrepreneur, initially recognized an opportunity to provide books from online orders. He initially coordinated resource development in his garage. Over time, Amazon acquired additional resources to support growing numbers of customers, products, and sales. As the firm met success, it "co-evolved" with the Internet, changing the nature of available opportunities as it changed itself.[6]

The ongoing story of Amazon also illustrates that recognizing and developing opportunities continues to be important for established companies. One example from the early days of the company involves the resource gap that emerged as Bezos and his staff began to recognize the weaknesses of their virtual bookstore. Initially, they thought book publishers could ship directly to customers based on orders from Amazon. This "drop shipment" approach meant that Amazon would rarely take physical possession of what it sold. Bezos and his team reasoned that it was a good idea to minimize inventory costs and maximize inventory turnover by being a virtual seller. Unfortunately, the book suppliers (publishers or distributors) did not always respond as quickly as expected, coordination problems developed, and in the end the virtual model increased stockouts and lengthened delivery times to customers.

To reduce these problems, Amazon began to take on some inventory. This created more problems. The lack of well-located physical warehouses and inadequate logistical systems slowed Amazon's inventory turnover and further frustrated its efforts to turn a profit. By 2000, Amazon's inventory turnover was less than half that of its brick-and-mortar rivals. Fortunately, the Amazon team acted to close this gap by securing the necessary resources, including a network of warehouses dispersed around the world and innovative software that manages orders and deliveries.

Bezos was responding to the opportunity provided by growing Internet usage. But recognizing and responding to a trend does not always produce profits. The failure of so many Internet-based businesses (the "dot-bomb" phenomenon) is proof that many did not understand the opportunity (and risk) of the Internet. *Strategic* entrepreneurship means recognizing *profitable* opportunities—building a business and achieving competitive advantage, as shown in Figure 4.1.

Figure 4.1 — Developing a Strategic Opportunity
Source: Adapted from J. Timmons, as cited in B. Bygrave & A. Zacharakis, *The Portable MBA in Entrepreneurship* (3rd ed.; New York: Wiley, 2003).

An opportunity is a chance to offer a new or better product, service, or experience to customers. Skill in opportunity recognition can be found in entrepreneurial individuals, teams, and organizations that threaten established businesses. Thus even strategists enjoying tremendous competitive advantages must understand the sources of new ideas and how they are developed.

Characteristics of Individuals Who Recognize and Develop Opportunities

Research shows that entrepreneurial individuals are not quite the same as the rest of us. *Entrepreneurs* tend to have a stronger need for achievement, higher risk-taking propensity, greater perseverance, more commitment to a task, bigger vision, higher creativity, and more tolerance for ambiguity. Individuals who want to become entrepreneurs also tend to have more positive attitudes toward risk and independence.[7] The entrepreneur can be an individual working alone, but often *entrepreneurial teams* bring a pool of competencies to a new venture.

Individuals who are able to develop *an innovation* into a market offering are also leaders. Facing risk and tackling the challenges of a new venture requires immense courage and energy. Their most important entrepreneurial characteristic is the ability to imagine a future reality in

Entrepreneurs recognize opportunities, assess fit between market and their company, find and combine resources, develop innovative solutions, take risks, and strive to make a profit.

Entrepreneurial teams are groups of individuals who bring their collective and often complementary skills and resources to a new venture.

An innovation is a new idea that is brought to market.

the form of an innovative product, a new business process, or an entirely new industry. Yet realizing that vision requires other leadership skills, including the ability to learn and the ability to teach.

Figure 4.2 summarizes entrepreneurial leadership roles. Some individuals developing a new opportunity are creative and innovative; others are more adept with management skills and business know-how. Combining these two dimensions produces four roles: promoters, inventors, managers, and transformational leaders. Although *transformational leader* is an attractive description, and critical for the development of a new opportunity, in reality all four roles are likely to be required to bring a new idea to market.

Entrepreneurial leadership.

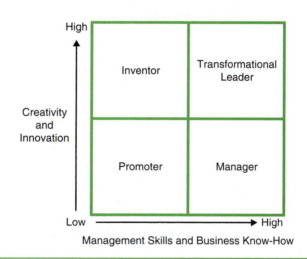

Figure 4.2 — Entrepreneurial Leadership Roles

Source: Adapted from J. Lange, presentation to Governor Craig Benson's Entrepreneur's Workshop (2003).

The individuals who recognize and develop opportunities come from all sectors of society. A recent college graduate who sets up her own software company may be an entrepreneur. But likewise, vendors on the streets of New York City, retailers at the local farmer's market, and yoga enthusiasts opening new studios are all potentially developing new opportunities.

Historically, women and minorities have been underrepresented among entrepreneurs. Women own approximately 28 percent of small businesses in the United States. Racial minorities own 15 percent—including Hispanics (6 percent), Asians and Pacific Islanders (4 percent), Blacks (4 percent), and American Indians and Alaska Natives (1 percent). These percentages are below the representation of these groups in the overall population. Current research suggests that minorities and women tend to be less ambitious about the amount of initial capital they need and have smaller, slower growing businesses.[8] There is no reason to believe that minority entrepreneurs' underrepresentation and underfunding have anything to do with innate ability, however, and women and minority-owned businesses are increasingly important in the U.S. and world economies. Although there is no country in the world where women are *more* active in entrepreneurship than men, there are a few where they come very close, including Thailand, China, and South Africa.[9]

Before concluding the discussion of individual entrepreneurs, it also is important to recognize that despite hits such as Amazon, success rarely comes from a first "blockbuster" project. The typical scenario is a series of entrepreneurial efforts over time, some of which fail. Among the other attributes of entrepreneurs, it is therefore important to add *persistence.* Can you visualize yourself as a *serial entrepreneur* who continues to recognize and develop opportunities? Consider Sally Edwards's experience.

Serial entrepreneurs start a number of entrepreneurial efforts over time.

Serial Entrepreneur: Sally Edwards

Sally Edwards graduated from the University of California at Berkeley with a degree in exercise physiology and a secondary teaching credential in 1970. After volunteering for two years with the American Red Cross in Vietnam, Sally returned home to a teaching position. After three years, she yearned to try something different that would match her interests in people and sports. In 1976, with $3,000, the 28-year-old cofounded Fleet Feet, a specialty running store, in a Victorian-style house in Sacramento, California.

Over the next seventeen years, Sally expanded the franchise to forty locations in fifteen states with more than $20 million in annual sales. In the process, she completed an MBA at National University in Sacramento. Finally, in 1998, she sold Fleet Feet and took time off to travel around the world.

Sally returned to California with renewed energies and ideas and cofounded Yuba Shoe Sports Snowshoes, which she then sold three years later. This serial entrepreneur's latest venture is Heart Zones, a fitness education company that teaches people how to use heart rate monitors to stay healthy. Heart Zones services have recently expanded to firms that are interested in lowering employee stress levels.

Sally is an entrepreneur who likes to start new businesses, but turns to other managers for the daily operations: "I am now interested in empowering others and not [being] involved in the business on a day to day basis." When asked what advice she has for business school students, Sally said, "It's important to follow your heart and do something that you love and that you are good at."[10]

Teams That Develop Opportunities

Although individual entrepreneurs are important, Sally Edwards's experience and that of many others suggests that most of the time opportunity development involves more than one person. Few individuals, after all, have all of the skills and knowledge necessary to maximize the chances of success for a new venture. For example, an individual who identifies a new technology may have a scientific or engineering background but lack business skills. If savvy, he or she will seek partners who know about accounting, finance, and management systems. A number of now-famous companies were founded by technical-business pairs, including Honda Motor Company, Genentech, and Hewlett-Packard.

The competencies needed within the team can be defined only in terms of the new venture itself. According to Ed Catmull, president of Pixar Animation Studios, "If you give a great idea to a mediocre team, they will screw it up. But if you give a mediocre idea to a great team, they will fix it or throw it away and come up with something different."[11] Elaborating on the ideas expressed in Figure 4.2, teams not only need to cultivate skills in opportunity recognition and creativity but also must develop in areas such as operations and administration.

The competencies of the initial team represent the "gene pool" from which the venture's future distinctive competencies will evolve. More specifically, without the right mix of people in the core team, a new venture is unlikely to develop a competitive advantage. For this reason, potential investors look very carefully at who is on the management team, and many venture capitalists identify the people involved as one of most important considerations in their decision to invest.[12] Corporate strategists evaluating new ideas proposed to their business units are similarly evaluative.

Capabilities of Organizations That Develop Opportunities

Although individuals and teams are key actors in the development of a new product, service, or experience, the organizational context also has a critical role to play. The concept of *entrepreneurial orientation* has been developed to describe an organization's ability to recognize and respond to new opportunities.[13]

Entrepreneurial orientation describes an organization's ability to promote autonomy, innovativeness, proactiveness, competitive aggressiveness, and risk taking.

Autonomy   Some organizations find it quite difficult to recognize new opportunities. The financial controls and management systems necessary for keeping an established business efficient will almost certainly interfere with the freewheeling, creative efforts of entrepreneurial-oriented individuals and teams. Later in this chapter we will describe how new venture divisions or other independent units can be established in larger organizations to shelter entrepreneurial activity from bureaucratic controls. These relatively autonomous work units enable creative thinking and risk taking even while established businesses are more controlled.

Innovativeness   Firms that bring new ideas to market are able to break away from existing technology and conventional practice to grasp state of the art concepts. Innovation may be on several levels: technology, product-market, or administrative process. A breakthrough or *radical innovation* may completely transform a company or an industry. An example of a radical innovation is the introduction of digital photography, which displaced the need for instant photography and also most chemical photography. Another example of a radical innovation would be the introduction of a personal flying craft that would replace cars, just as cars were a radical innovation replacing horses. *Incremental innovations* enhance current products or processes and make up about 85 to 90 percent of a firm's product development portfolio.[14] An example of an incremental innovation is the shift from black-and-white to color televisions. Another example is how several major dental product manufacturers have added whitening ingredients to their toothpastes. Although radical and incremental innovations differ in many respects, including the amount of autonomy they tend to require, both offer opportunities.

Proactiveness   An organization is likely to develop new opportunities to the extent that it responds proactively to future environment changes affecting customer needs and desires. In addition, entrepreneurial organizations do not wait to see what rivals do. Instead, they are more likely to pursue *first-mover* status by introducing a new product or service ahead of other firms. As a result, their offerings are more likely to be associated in the customer's mind with the product category, and they have a head start on becoming the market leader. An example of a first mover is Napster, mentioned in Chapter 1.

It should be noted, however, that choosing to be a *second mover* can also be proactive, because this strategic position offers the opportunity to learn from first movers. As one example among many, consider the development of mobile phones, with market share increasing among companies that brought later, but more sophisticated, models to market.

Competitive Aggressiveness   *Competitive aggressiveness* refers to a firm's willingness to take on its competitors. Organizations that develop new ideas do not shy away from rivals or seek to defend established positions. Some hope to take market share from others. Typically, they are more willing than other organizations to engage in aggressive techniques

Radical innovations are a significant departure from currently available product or service offerings.

Incremental innovations contribute to the improvement of existing product or service offerings.

First movers in a new product or service category can potentially define an innovation's characteristics in the minds of buyers, gaining valuable name recognition and brand loyalty.

Second movers have the potential advantage of learning from and improving on the efforts of first movers.

such as price cutting. Even the firms that try to establish a new market often cannibalize existing offerings. Think of mobile phones' impact on the profitability of landlines, roadside kiosks, and hotel phone services.

Risk Taking   The kinds of organizations we are profiling embrace risk taking of all kinds—financial risk, business risk, and personal risk. This willingness to gamble often gives them an advantage over more conservative organizations. Entrepreneurial firms are more likely to launch a product based on new technology, for example, while others wait to see if the technology can be "proven." It would be a mistake, however, to assume that entrepreneurs are inevitably gamblers. Often they spend considerable effort assessing risk and acquiring the information needed to reduce it.

In summary, the capacity to recognize and develop a market opportunity can be found in individuals, teams, and entire organizations. In many ways, it is the essence of what it means to be a successful strategist. But what do these innovators actually do?

WHAT ARE THE PROCESSES OF OPPORTUNITY DEVELOPMENT?

Many people interested in business strategy hope for a "big win." We all know that the odds of identifying that kind of opportunity are not that promising, but real-life examples feed our dreams. Consider the phenomenal growth of Crocs Footwear.

Crocs Feed a Fad

"Crocodiles are tough and strong animals with no natural predators. Crocodiles are equally good in land and water and live for a very long time, a great description of our Crocs shoes!" according to the crocs.com website.[15] You have probably seen their "incredibly ugly" but "incredibly comfortable" shoes on an incredibly broad range of people—kids, grandmothers, nurses, and beach volleyball players, not to mention celebrities Matt Damon, Jennifer Garner, Teri Hatcher, James Gandolfini, Jack Nicholson, and Al Pacino.[16] Founded in July 2002, the company sold $1 million worth of shoes in 2004, $100 million in 2005, and more than $300 million in shoes and related accessories in 2006.[17]

That's pretty good for three buddies who thought they could sell a new boating shoe. Their initial insight was that the new spa shoes one of them brought on a sailing trip had good traction and didn't mark the deck. The first prototypes from the company they founded were almost instantly successful in the boating market, but as many consumers know, the shoe quickly attracted a much broader following. Some feel that the timing was right—many people had been wearing sport shoes for nonsporting activities, but the most stylish offerings are expensive. The first Crocs, in contrast, were sold for $19, and low prices have been retained even at Nordstrom's and other classy outlets.

This kind of growth leads to major supply problems, as well as inevitable imitation. The founders purchased the Canadian company that produced the original spa shoe and its patents and acquired the factories that were initially making the shoe and the suppliers of the proprietary resin from which the shoe is made. That allowed them to win lawsuits against several imitators and provided a basis for setting up additional production facilities in Mexico, China, and other locations as demand skyrocketed.[18]

Although the demand is in part the result of a fad that cannot be expected to last, a more sustainable market may be medical. All shoes have arch support, which differentiates Crocs them from simple thongs. Three models have been expressly developed for users with special needs, including a shoe for diabetics. A recent article in the *Washington Post* reports that Crocs "are featured prominently on the Web site of the . . . American Podiatric Medical Association [APMA] (http://www.apma.org/) . . . [and] have been awarded the APMA Seal of Acceptance. The APMA takes special note of the fact that Croslite [the material used in making Crocs] 'warms and softens with body heat and molds to the users' feet, while remaining extremely lightweight.'"[19] The resin also resists bacteria and fungus.

Two other growth areas are international sales and new products. In addition to clothing and objects such as garden kneelers and spa pillows made from Croslite, the company continues to develop new models of footwear, including a high-fashion line called YOU introduced in late 2007. The company website does a good job of expressing the core idea that guides these developments:

> Despite our rapid success, we still stand behind to the core values of Crocs Footwear. We are committed to making a lightweight, comfortable, slip-resistant, fashionable and functional shoe that can be produced quickly and at an affordable price to our customers.[20]

The founders of Crocs had an initial business plan, but clearly that intended strategy was quickly overtaken by success that no one could predict. Their realized strategy had to account for issues that many less fortunate start-ups do not have to face. Nevertheless, it is possible to identify three common processes in opportunity development: recognizing opportunity, finding resources, and managing innovation.

Opportunity recognition involves discovering an idea and forming it into a business concept.

Recognizing Opportunities

The first part of *opportunity recognition* is often called *discovery*. It represents the basic insight underlying a new business idea. This insight might come from an unanticipated "Eureka moment," such as the recognition of how well a spa shoe performed on a sailboat, or from a more disciplined deliberation. For example, strategists can consider the characteristics of the macro environment reviewed in Chapter 1. They can actively scan the environment for technological, political/legal, economic, demographic, and cultural trends. An example of the latter process can be found in the work of Sergey Brin and Larry Page, two computer science students at Stanford University who exhaustively researched the process of data mining on the Web and then developed proprietary technology to perform Web searches better and more efficiently. They later commercialized the system in the form of a new business venture: Google.com.

Another example is Canada's Cirque du Soleil, whose performances have been seen by 40 million people around the world and whose revenues, after just two decades, exceed those achieved by Ringling Brothers and Barnum & Bailey after a century of operations. Rather than emulate existing firms, Cirque du Soleil "reinvented" the circus by focusing on human performance and appealing to a new customer audience of adults and corporate clients. INSEAD business school professors Chan Kim and Renée Mauborgne use the term *blue ocean* to describe the uncontested market space that Cirque du Soleil and other entrepreneurial organizations have created. Blue oceans are "industries not in existence today—the unknown market space, unconstrained by competition." In contrast, *red oceans* "represent all the industries in existence today—the known market space. In red oceans, industry boundaries are defined and accepted and the competitive rules of the game are well understood."[21]

After discovery, the business potential of an idea must be evaluated. Idea formation—the process of evaluating, formulating, and refining a business idea into a business concept or business model—is a process we describe in much greater detail in Chapter 6. Typically, external circumstances play a big role in the extent to which a business model becomes a viable venture. Timing, the *synchronicity* of the entrepreneur's discovery with market need or market interest, plays a *huge* role.

Whether an idea is viable as a business concept depends on whether it is:

- Attractive—meets a market need
- Attainable—doable
- Value creating—likely to produce a profit

If an idea meets these basic criteria, it may be said to be a viable business concept. Typically, more formal *feasibility analysis* then solidifies the definition of the opportunity. That involves evaluating the skills and readiness of the individual strategist and team, as well as determining

Synchronicity is the time-sensitive match between the entrepreneur's recognition of opportunity and occurrence of market need.

Feasibility analysis evaluates the human and financial resources available for launching a new venture.

the availability of and access to the resources required for launching the new venture.

Finding Resources

Entrepreneurial firms are often challenged by a lack of resources. Depending on the nature of the business, 20 to 40 percent of new ventures fail within their first year. By year 2, the failure rate jumps to 30 to 60 percent, and by year 10 it's a whopping 90 percent.[22] Most of these businesses fail for lack of resources. The firms that succeed fit their strategies to their resource profiles.[23]

As discussed in Chapter 2, firms are bundles of resources, including employees, financial capital, brands, and physical facilities. New firms must determine the need for, and then acquire, these varied resources. How much financial capital is typically needed? One of the things that make Crocs Footwear such a compelling story is that its growth was supported by $239 million earned in the largest initial public offering ever attempted in the footwear industry. Surprisingly, very little cash is involved in the more typical initial start-up. Of current Fortune 500 firms, 25 percent began with less than $5,000, 50 percent with less than $25,000 and 75 percent with less than $100,000. In fact, fewer than 5 percent of Fortune 500 firms began with more than $1 million.[24] Clearly, financial capital is not the only resource required to turn an idea into a business.

Figure 4.3 shows that in addition to physical and financial capital, those who develop a new opportunity also need human resources

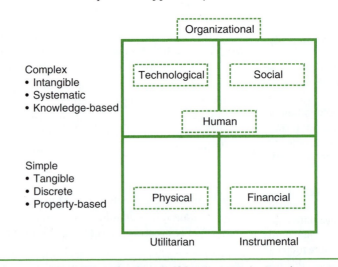

Figure 4.3 — Varied Resources Required for Opportunity Development

Source: Adapted from C. G. Brush, P. G. Greene, & Hart, M. M., From Initial Idea to Unique Advantage: The Entrepreneurial Challenge of Constructing a Resource Base, *Academy of Management Executive* 15: 64–80.

(managers and employees), social capital (relationships with other individuals and firms), technological resources (know-how), and organizational capital (routines, capabilities, and competencies) to be successful. As the figure suggests, these resources can be classified in terms of whether they are simple or complex and whether they are used in the operations of the venture (*utilitarian resources*) or acquiring needed inputs (*instrumental resources*). The second category includes financial capital used to acquire opportunity-specific inputs, including technological resources.

The point of Figure 4.3 is to remind those who try to develop a new opportunity that success requires the accumulation of all five types of resources. Moreover, although simple resources may be essential, we know from Chapter 2 that such resources are easily duplicated. Acquiring complex resources is central to developing advantage.[25]

The paths that entrepreneurial strategists follow to accumulate necessary resources vary. Some start with financial capital in their bank account. Others rely on relationships with bankers, venture capitalists, or family members to gain needed financing. In fact, studies of new ventures have demonstrated that the *social capital* available from relationships plays a big role in predicting a new venture's success.[26] Although many different paths are possible, entrepreneurs who ignore the need for one or more of these resources are likely to be disappointed.

Managing Innovation

Some strategists identify new opportunities by considering characteristics and changes in customer groups, as described in Chapter 3. Others discover opportunities by observing changes in the larger macro environment, including technology and social systems. One distinction useful for brainstorming is the difference between *product innovation* and *process innovation*. Particularly interesting innovations have begun to combine these conceptually distinct alternatives, as you will remember from the discussion in Chapter 3 of Otis Elevator's reorientation from selling machinery to servicing elevators.

As products and services blur and organizational processes change to support new offerings, an interesting conceptual distinction involves the extent to which entrepreneurial ideas depart from what is currently available in the marketplace. As we mentioned earlier, incremental innovations that utilize current capabilities are at one end of a simplifying continuum; they are a relatively small step away from existing offerings. Radical innovations, on the other hand, are very different from current products and services. These are riskier explorative ideas that require a good deal of strategic attention (and luck) to succeed. Radical innovations are likely to involve the development of new resources, including new networks of suppliers, distributors, buyers, and complementary

Utilitarian resources are required to produce a good or service.

Instrumental resources are not directly required to produce a good or service, but are helpful for acquiring needed resources.

Social capital is the resource pool available from relationships with others.

Product innovations are changes in the product or service offered to an existing or new market.

Process innovations do not change the offering itself, but change the way in which the organization operates.

Competence-destroying innovations make existing product or service offerings obsolete.

products. If successful, they will be *competence-destroying innovations* for firms currently active in the market, and thus likely to be actively resisted, once their potential is recognized. One part of the strategist's job in established companies is to anticipate and counter newcomers; strategists in the challenging firm must counter these moves.

Though we have just offered a set of academic terms, the world is full of excellent practical illustrations. In transportation, for example, the invention of the airplane was one of a long line of competence-destroying innovations from the perspective of those providing transportation by rail, bus, ship, and automobile. At a more refined level of analysis, the significant increase in size of the Airbus 380, which can hold more than 850 passengers in economy configuration,[27] is a more incremental innovation. It is still potentially competence-destroying for Boeing, however, because it can carry so many more passengers than the fleet they offer to buyers.

All of this is part of a process that can be predicted in general terms. Figure 4.4 summarizes the observation that the performance of any given solution (such as Boeing's 747) tends to peak over time as the limit of a given technology is reached. Strategists then tend to put their effort into a new technology. Initially this new effort is unlikely to yield the performance benefits of current technology, but a successful contender provides greater benefits over time.

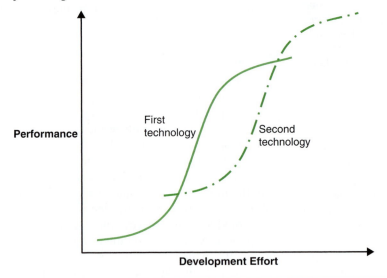

Figure 4.4 — Technology S-Curves

The profit made from performance improvement from the second technology is driven by the number of users who adopt it. In the case of a successful innovation, the first few innovative users are followed by a greater number of adopters. Marketing strategy is centrally important to reaching these early buyers, whose needs and interests vary.

Everett Rogers suggested some time ago that the adoption of a successful innovation tends to follow an S-curve of its own, as shown in Figure 4.5.[28] A relatively small number of adventurous *innovators* are drawn to new products by companies that successfully communicate the unique features of their innovation. A more difficult marketing task is to entice a larger set of *early adopters* to the new product, service, or experience. They tend to be more evaluative; though they are also drawn to the innovation's new features, they do not adopt unless the benefits of a new offering are clear. This group tends to include many opinion leaders. They are important for attracting the *early majority users*, who, according to Rogers and others,[29] adopt a new innovation only if they can be shown that it is relatively easy to use, reliable, and consistent with existing ways of doing things. Attracting the *late majority users* and *laggards* requires persuasive communication about these features. These potential users are primarily drawn by the simplicity and cost-effectiveness of an increasingly familiar and no longer "new" product, service, or experience.[30]

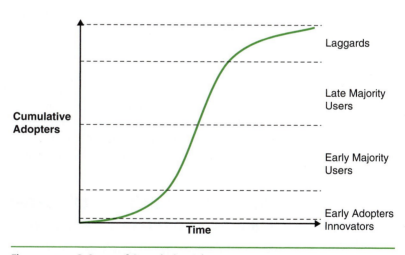

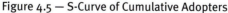

Figure 4.5 — S-Curve of Cumulative Adopters

A critical area of innovation management is to learn from users. *Lead users* are particularly important to identify. Their profile is similar to the bulk of adopters, but they are motivated to help the entrepreneurial organization meet their needs. The term was coined by MIT professor Eric von Hippel. His idea is that lead users, a term that includes customers and noncustomers, are passionate about meeting certain needs or desires. Often they have invented solutions themselves and are typically willing to discuss their ideas and inventions with producers.[31]

Lead users are similar to the majority of an innovation's users and are willing to help the producers improve their product, service, or experience.

Worksheet 4.1: S-Curve Analysis—A Tool for Explaining User Characteristics

How do the first adopters differ from the next set of users? Can you anticipate the demands of late adopters? Given our emphasis on connecting with customers, it won't surprise you that we suggest you take the time to fill out Worksheet 4.1. It encourages you to think about how a wide range of customers might contribute to a specific product or service that interests you.

Before concluding this discussion of managing innovation, we will remind you that in today's world, wise strategists also seek inputs from trusted suppliers in developing a new opportunity. For highly technical products, the supplier may even locate an office at the producer's site to maximize their involvement. Automobile and aircraft manufactures have become particularly reliant on these partnerships. One advantage they gain is more diverse ideas for innovation. Boeing makes the following claim:

> Supplier diversity is key to doing business in the global century. As Boeing increasingly focuses on its core competencies in high-end design, engineering, and systems integration, we need suppliers that are highly focused on their own core competencies, continually striving to create additional value in everything they do. Small and diverse companies have proved in competition that they bring innovation, flexibility, and strength to our supply base, as well as a passion for helping Boeing deliver the strongest possible solutions to our own customers.[32]

This statement reflects a core idea in opportunity development. Many new ideas come from smaller, more flexible firms. If you are attracted to this role, however, you should remember that although the economic system as a whole benefits from a diversity of ideas, the entrepreneurial pool includes many failures as well as a few successes.

WHAT ARE THE DIFFERENCES BETWEEN SMALL FIRM AND CORPORATE ENTREPRENEURSHIP?

Many of the ideas we have just presented come from studies of entrepreneurship, which people often believe is restricted to relatively young and small companies. However, opportunity development is also important to large established organizations. Not all of these companies are like Boeing, whose strategy depends on new product development. *Intrapreneurship* or *corporate entrepreneurship* is increasingly important to all organizations. The process and behaviors involved are remarkably similar to those we associate with entrepreneurship in smaller firms, though there are some important differences that we describe after a review of the classic small firm situation.

Small Firm Entrepreneurship

Small and medium-sized enterprises (SMEs) are an engine for economic growth. In the U.S. economy, SMEs produce 75 percent of new jobs and 55 percent of America's technical innovation. Approximately 52 percent of U.S. workers are employed by firms with no more than 500 people. In addition to 5.7 million firms in America with less than 100 employees, nearly 18 million Americans consider themselves self-employed.[33] In other countries, self-employment and SMEs play an even larger role in the local economy.[34]

Many small businesses are not entrepreneurial, but as we have already observed, entrepreneurs in small business can often respond more quickly to industrial and economic changes than entrepreneurs in larger businesses. Without the bureaucracy and public oversight typically found in larger firms, small firms tend to be more nimble and more flexible. Therefore, small firms tend to lead the way in generating new ideas for an industry or group. But with all their flexibility, small firms lack the experience, industry recognition, and customer familiarity that larger firms command. They are therefore highly vulnerable to competition from large, established competitors.

The vulnerability of size is increased by the uncertainties associated with all new ventures (whether a significant need exists, what resources are needed to satisfy that need, and how to match the two—as depicted in Figure 4.1). These problems explain the low survival rates of new ventures. The effect is so prevalent that economists describe it with a special term: *liability of newness*.

One of the most obvious differences between new or small firms and larger, more established firms is differential access to financial capital. Established firms can draw on their own treasury to support a new business concept. In contrast, the capital base of small firms is typically quite meager. The financing needed to start up the new venture (*start-up capital*) may come from a variety of sources, such as banks, friends, family, other personal contacts, venture capitalists, corporate partners, and angel investors. *Bootstrapping* entrepreneurs rely instead on their personal financial resources in the start-up phase.

Once the firm has begun to conduct business and generate sales, the chances of obtaining outside financing from venture capitalists, banks, and other public sources increase. Venture capital, a form of private equity financing, has advantages and disadvantages. One advantage is that venture capital enables more rapid growth than might otherwise be possible. *Venture capitalists* are likely to invest in early stages of development, taking risks that bankers or the general public would not consider. Venture capital financing also provides access to the advice and expertise of the financiers. Many venture capitalists have deep knowledge about specific industries or technologies that can be crucial

Liability of newness recognizes the vulnerability that comes from lack of experience, industry recognition, and customer familiarity.

Start-up capital is the financial requirement for initiating a new venture.

Bootstrapping is the use of an entrepreneurial individual's personal resources to finance a new business.

Venture capitalists are investors who search for and provide capital to entrepreneurs.

to new venture success.[35] They also bring the kind of experience and business acumen that many individuals recognizing a new opportunity lack. Venture capital investments typically range between $500,000 and $5 million.

Venture capital usually comes with conditions, however. Backers may require membership on the board or a significant ownership stake in a company formed to realize a new opportunity. Once a venture capitalist is involved, initial partners are no longer free to do whatever they please. Conflicts may arise between what the founders want to do and what the venture capitalist thinks is best. This kind of conflict may seem to be a disadvantage, but research suggests that disagreements about the business between entrepreneurs and venture capitalists may actually be beneficial to the venture's performance, because it airs and potentially resolves problems.[36]

Entrepreneurs may also pursue less traditional sources of financing, such as leasing equipment or real estate, bartering noncash items to exchange for goods and services, seeking credit from suppliers, and even using credit cards. Still another financial option comes from *angel investors*, private individual investors who provide seed capital to early-stage ventures, especially firms that have demonstrated capability. The average angel investor provides $37,000 of funding to a new venture. In addition to money, angels typically offer expertise, experience, and contacts. Once established, a new venture may also seek funding through an *initial public offering* (IPO), in which company stock is sold to the public.

Some forms of opportunity development do not require a brand new start-up. The most common of these is *franchising*. A franchise is a "business opportunity by which the owner, producer, or distributor for a service or trademarked product (the franchisor) grants exclusive rights to an entrepreneur (the franchisee) for the local distribution of the product or service, and in return receives a payment or royalty and conformance to quality standards."[37] Franchising plays a significant role in the U.S. economy, employing 8.5 million people, constituting 42 percent of all retail sales, and accounting for 20 percent of the gross domestic product. Familiar examples of franchised businesses include McDonald's and many other chain restaurants, small retailers such as The Body Shop, and service firms such as Meineke Mufflers.

Franchising has several advantages. In a successful operation, the most important thing gained by the *franchisee* is the knowledge of how to run the business and make a profit. Often a franchisee also gains national advertising, a good brand, and the consumer recognition that these activities produce. These benefits come at a price, of course, in the form of the fees and royalties assessed by the franchisor. Using resource-based theory, the problem with this opportunity from the franchisee's point of view is that the franchisor often appropriates most of the profit.

From the perspective of the *franchisor*, franchising can be seen as a way to grow. A small firm can become a large firm if a new venture

Angel investors are private individuals who provide seed capital to early-stage ventures.

Initial public offerings (IPOs) sell stock in a new venture to individual and institutional investors.

Franchising is an opportunity to obtain exclusive rights to a brand and business model in a specific locality in return for a royalty.

is imitatable and sufficiently attractive to small-business entrepreneurs. This requires a logic whereby the venture is reproduced over and over again across different geographic regions. Consider the late Dame Anita Roddick's experience with The Body Shop.

The Body Shop

Born in the small English seaside town of Littlehampton in 1942, Anita Roddick grew up working at her family's Italian restaurant. This early entrepreneurial experience and a period of travelling that she describes as a "university without walls" served her well in 1976, when her husband, Gordon, left for a ten-month horseback-riding trip through South America. Anita had to provide for her two young daughters and decided to sell handmade cosmetics from ingredients she put together in her garage. She started with only fifteen products, but packaged these into five different sizes to the give the appearance of having many more.

The products were popular, and Roddick raised the capital for a second store by selling half of the business for $8,000. Looking back, she says that "running that first shop taught me business is not financial science, it's about trading: buying and selling. It's about creating a product or service so good that people will pay for it."[38]

By the time Gordon returned home, he found his wife running a thriving business and suggested that The Body Shop begin offering franchises. By 1978, Body Shop franchises were open across the United Kingdom and Europe, with the first foreign store established in Brussels.

From the beginning, Anita promoted The Body Shop as an experiment in "profits with principles." The company campaigned for Greenpeace, shunned advertising, and promised only natural products that were not tested on animals. These values attracted many potential entrepreneurs as franchisees. The Body Shop grew rapidly and went public in 1984. International expansion continued with a store in New York opening in 1988. In 1994, The Body Shop Direct was launched to sell directly into homes.

In 1997, Roddick tried but failed to turn The Body Shop into a charity.[39] By 2002, Anita and Gordon had resigned as cochairs to be non-executive directors and "creative consultants." The Body Shop expanded in Asia and South Africa and launched an Internet business. Approximately 70 percent of all stores were owned by franchisees.

Then the company agreed to an offer from L'Oréal, the French cosmetics giant. The acquisition was widely condemned, because both L'Oréal and Nestlé, owner of 25 percent of L'Oréal stock, had been criticized for animal rights abuses. An industry website reported, however, that "Body Shop sales continued to climb. The announcement was made alongside the figures for the full financial year, which revealed that sales reached $1.5 billion. A spokesperson said the figure was mainly driven by the addition of 88 new stores worldwide, as well as a strong growth in its Internet sales in the U.S., along with a good response to its Body Shop at Home channel."[40]

Unfortunately, Anita Roddick died on September 10, 2007, of a massive heart attack. Tony Juniper, director of Friends of the Earth, wrote in the *Evening Standard* that "Anita did more than run a successful ethical business: she was a pioneer of the whole concept of ethical and green consumerism. There are quite a few business people today who claim green credentials, but none came anywhere near Anita in terms of commitment and credibility."[41]

Corporate Entrepreneurship

> **Corporate entrepreneurship** is an effort by enterprises with large, established businesses to discover new opportunities.

Also termed *intrapreneurship*[42] or *internal corporate venturing, corporate entrepreneurship* means bringing entrepreneurial processes into a large, existing enterprise. Corporate entrepreneurs have certain advantages and disadvantages compared to small firm entrepreneurs. Most important, they benefit from the firm's existing resources, including financial capital but also their current capabilities and competencies.

The Body Shop provides a clear example of the continuing need to pursue new opportunities. Cosmetics.com reports that "sales [have] been boosted by product innovation, [including] a number of new launches" along with "a comprehensive restructuring programme to up production efficiencies."[43] Increasing size requires and facilitates many such changes, but those seeking new corporate opportunities face disadvantages too. Estimates vary, but more than half of corporate ventures fail. Some put the failure rate (in terms of managers' expectations for profitability) between 60 and 85 percent.[44] The Irish drinks producer Diageo offers several examples of apparently plausible ideas that did not add value to the parent company.

Failed Corporate Venturing at Diageo

Diageo is a Dublin, Ireland–based premium drinks conglomerate whose major brands include Guinness, Baileys, Smirnoff, and Johnnie Walker. In July 2000, Diageo established a New Business Ventures (NBV) unit run by Graham Sumeray. The unit's mandate was to create businesses in other sectors while increasing demand for core products.

One failed venture was an attempt to leverage the Guinness brand by offering Ireland travel packages and theme tours to customers in the United States. An in-bar TV venture, Translucis, was sold in 2003. Another failed venture was a wireless media channel called Nightfly. The entrepreneurial idea was to use mobile phones as a marketing channel; customers were to be signed up for the service in local bars and restaurants. Launched in 2000, Nightfly closed three years later. According to Sumeray, "The conclusion of our review was that the business needed a partner to take it to the next stage. We had several offers on the table, but none were compelling enough, so we decided to close the business."[45]

Diageo's experience demonstrates that even with resources, including very strong brands, developing new opportunities is risky. In November 2003, the company closed the NBV unit to refocus on its core business.[46]

What is it about large organizations that seems to defeat corporate new ventures? A key issue seems to be difficulties of moving beyond past success. Sources of current success (core competencies or core capabilities) become sources of *inertia* that make corporate venturing less likely;[47] theorists have called this the *core rigidities* problem.

Inertia
is the tendency
to continue in a
current state.

Core rigidities
are sources of
current success
that make
new-venture
development
difficult.

As we saw in Chapter 2, organization structures and processes represent important elements of an organization's core capabilities. These organizational assets are highly specialized and are critical supports for a profitable business. But the same structures and processes, by definition, will be misaligned with the strategy needed by a corporate venture in a new competitive context. They are almost inevitably rigidities standing in the way of a new venture that will require other structures and processes. Consider the difference between the requirements of running a national financial newspaper, such as the *Wall Street Journal*, and running a financial information website, such as www.wallstreet-journal.com.

The Complex Face of News Delivery

In the print edition of the *Wall Street Journal*, printing technology dominates operations; in the interactive edition, Web-based computing is key. In print, news is delivered on a daily basis—reporting often reflects back over months or even years. On the Internet, news is delivered *now*, "in real time." This changes not only delivery and distribution processes but also the production processes (writing for real time versus journalistic analysis). In terms of processes and core activities, these are quite different businesses.

In addition, the key to making money with news on the Web is not just selling information. In fact, people are often unwilling to pay for information, because it is so freely available on the Web. The key in such a business is customization, value-added services, product sales, and advertising. All of these are driven by technology.

The challenge for management at the *Wall Street Journal* has been not only to learn how to compete on the Internet but also to prevent the core rigidities of the print edition from undermining the development of the interactive edition. Structurally, for example, the interactive edition needs technologists as decision makers, because technology drives new products and services on the Web. Journalists, not technologists, are dominant in the leadership of the *Wall Street Journal*. By background and experience, they are in a poor position to make the judgments it takes to succeed in the highly competitive Internet format.

The solution to the core rigidities problem for the *Wall Street Journal* and many other large corporations is structural isolation: the corporate new venture is developed separately from the structure, systems, controls, or culture of the parent organization in order to promote corporate entrepreneurship. Thus, the interactive edition is a separate subsidiary of the *Wall Street Journal*, complete with all of the functions and support of an independent business. Reports suggest that it is successful. Indeed, it is one of few news and information website to be making money.

Many large corporations have launched successful new ventures. General Electric, for example, has capitalized on its position as a manufacturer of jet engines in the development of its business in equipment financing. Similarly, Walt Disney has exploited its brand and even specific characters across a wide range of different markets, including animated shorts, motion pictures, theme parks, television shows, and action figures. Richard Branson's company, Virgin, competes in industries as diverse as transatlantic air travel, record shops, and financial services. The economic performance of all three of these firms suggests the potential benefits of corporate entrepreneurship.

> **Skunkworks** are independent units in larger organizations that are temporarily given autonomy to develop new ideas.

Structural isolation does not always require creating a separate business unit. Smaller, more informal *skunkworks* can be effective temporary environments for creative thinking and brainstorming. Whirlpool, for example, launched its first major brand in fifty years, Gladiator, from a skunkworks. Minnesota-based 3M, well known for its strong track record of new product development, often uses skunkworks. The firm has introduced more than 50,000 different products, including Scotch tape, optical films, insulation, drugs, and fuel cells. In an attempt to isolate innovative efforts from operations, 3M gives each engineer 15 percent of his or her time to explore new ideas. The hope is that this will stimulate creative juices and produce serendipitous discoveries.[48] Famously, the company's Post-it Notes were developed because of the "15 percent rule."

In addition to substantially different resource bases, corporate entrepreneurship and independent ventures differ in that corporate entrepreneurship can be (in fact, must be) supported by a much wider range of people up, down, and across the corporate hierarchy. For entrepreneurial initiatives to be successful in the corporate context, managers need to understand and embrace varied entrepreneurial roles. Figure 4.6 summaries key requirements in ten entrepreneurial roles.

The figure suggests that different kinds of entrepreneurial initiatives require different types of support. Initiatives that are intended to improve

Types of Entrepreneurial Initiatives

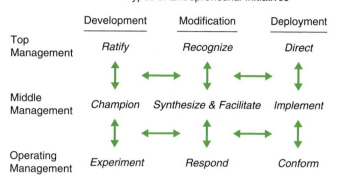

Figure 4.6 — Ten Managerial Roles in Corporate Entrepreneurship
Source: S. W. Floyd & P. J. Lane, Strategizing Throughout the Organization: Managing Role Conflict in Strategic Renewal, *Academy of Management Review* 25: 154–178.

the *deployment* of the organization's resources by improving processes or entering adjacent market niches, for example, require more conventional roles—in which top management directs, middle managers implement, and operating management conforms to the established game plan. The knowledge, skills, systems, and processes needed for these incremental innovations are close to what the organization already knows. These initiatives are vital to the profitability and protection of an organization's existing market, and in most organizations, initiatives of this type will predominate. Deployment initiatives do not produce whole new businesses. They reflect a rather minimal level of corporate entrepreneurship.

In more ambitious or radical corporate entrepreneurship efforts, the intent is to develop *new* competencies or capabilities. By definition, what the organization knows how to do, its current capabilities or competencies, have little relevance to the needs of a new entrepreneurial venture. (Remember the *Wall Street Journal's* interactive edition.) For such initiatives, top management tends to play a more passive role, articulating a broad vision and ratifying projects that come closest to achieving it. The direction behind the autonomous initiatives—the specific goals and work methods used—emerges from the bottom up. Operating managers experiment with new ideas; middle managers recognize some of these as having high potential, provide resources for pilot projects, and *champion* those that succeed for ratification on a corporate scale.[49]

Champions argue for an innovation's support in an organizational setting, stimulating allocation of capital and required cooperation.

In between radical initiatives that develop new competencies and incremental initiatives that improve existing competencies, there are also initiatives that significantly modify competencies without changing them altogether. When Amazon.com went from selling books to the "sell everything" strategy, for example, the shift in context was enough to require significant modification of its merchandising and logistical competencies. Though these changes were more than incremental improvements, they did not reflect a radical change in how Amazon competes. The initiatives associated with such change were developed partly as the result of top management's recognizing the need for such modification. That insight, however, was based on middle managers' synthesis of the situation—explaining what needed to be changed and what needed to stay the same in the shift from selling books to selling toys, for example. This synthesis, in turn, developed out of interactions between operating-level managers who were tasked with responding to the new situation and middle managers who facilitated these responses using problem-solving processes that helped figure out what needed to be done. If such a shift had occurred in a much smaller enterprise, many of these roles might have been performed by one or two managers at the very top of the organization. In a larger, more complex organization, entrepreneurial roles must be spread up and down the management hierarchy.

Figure 4.7 summarizes how entrepreneurship evolves in corporate settings: beginning with the identification of entrepreneurial opportunity, depending on the emergence of entrepreneurial initiative (focused on capability deployment, modification, or development), and leading to the renewal of organizational capability.

Worksheet 4.2:
Corporate
Resources—A
Tool for
Entrepreneurship
Planning
. . . .

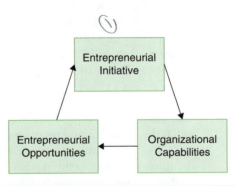

Figure 4.7 — Corporate Entrepreneurship

Source: Based on M. Jenkins & S. Floyd, Entrepreneurship, in M. Jenkins & V. Ambrosini (eds.), *Strategic Management: A Multiple Perspectives Approach* (London: Palgrave, 2002).

Dual strategy attempts to optimize current performance while simultaneously preparing for strategic changes that are expected to be necessary in the future.

IS AMBIDEXTERITY THE ANSWER?

Derek Abell suggests that strategists often must follow a *dual strategy*.[50] In other words, they must keep two business models in mind. The first and most sure must fit today's competitive environment, matching current resources with current customers' needs and interests. The second business model, which is less sure, especially in its timing, anticipates how the competitive environment is likely to evolve, how current customer needs might change, which new customers might become available, and how the resources of the firm (and its allies) will have to change to meet these circumstances.

Thinking in terms of dual strategies becomes more important if the expected future is quite different from the present. Many cautionary tales have been published about firms that believed the world would continue to reward their current model, and therefore went out of business.

From Harnesses to Automobile Shops to Rental Properties

In 1897, 17-year-old Bert Conn finished his apprenticeship in a harness-making shop outside Cleveland, Ohio, and set up his own business making harnesses for horse-drawn carriages. For more than a decade, Bert ran a thriving business in the growing Cleveland metropolis. Then, in 1908, Henry Ford introduced the low-priced, efficient Model T. With customers wishing to trade four legs for four wheels, demand for Bert's harness-making skills were in decline.

To survive, Bert applied his sewing and fabric-fitting skills to designing soft fabric tops for the new automobiles. The business gradually expanded to include a full range of automobile parts by 1920 and was renamed Lorain Autoparts. Bert's son Wayne took over the business in the 1940s and made it a National Auto Parts Association (NAPA) franchise. New branch stores were added in the 1960s.

The family business encountered competitive threats in the 1980s in the form of discount chains such as Autozone. Lorain Autoparts could not compete against these lower-priced products and was forced to close its stores. The next generation of the Conn family now rent the stores to other retailers.[51]

One obvious prescription from the many stories like this one is to pay attention to the environment and the firms that appear to be shaping it. The more radical, more risky, and potentially much more profitable prescription is to adopt a business model that attempts to make discontinuous change happen.

Gary Hamel and C. K. Prahalad call this "competing for the future."[52] They suggest that strategists should not worry about predicting the future, but instead work to create the future they desire. This requires psychological change from strategists, who must "forget" current recipes for success and be willing to endure major changes within the organization as old relationships as well as processes are dissolved. A few companies, such as Nokia (a company that moved from making rubber boots for fishermen to digital phones for the world), have been able to do this with spectacular success. We go into the details of several other examples in the second half of this book. It should be obvious, however, that there are no guarantees—developing a business model is risky because it is impossible to know how the world will evolve or whether a given firm can be adapted to these new circumstances.

Ambidextrous organizations manage the inconsistent demands of supporting current businesses while developing new entrepreneurial opportunities.

A few examples in this book suggest that it is possible to both maintain and improve the advantage of currently successful operations, and to consider new opportunities further afield. The ideal is to become an *ambidextrous* organization.[53] This is the ultimate challenge for the corporate entrepreneur: to anticipate and counter entrepreneurial attacks on the core business by developing new initiatives on its own, while also remaining alert to opportunities that are well beyond current success. It is not easy, but a number of companies have shown that it is possible.

CONCLUSIONS FOR THE STRATEGIST

Chapters 2, 3, and 4 draw together three ideas that we put at the heart of strategy. First, as described in Chapter 2, strategists must gather resources and use them effectively. They must also establish and maintain close connections with their customers and seek new ways to satisfy them, as discussed in Chapter 3.

This chapter suggests that an entrepreneurial mindset, within both new and established companies, is helpful for identifying the many different projects that might be developed by matching resources with opportunities to serve customers. However, choice among these strategic alternatives depends not only on capabilities within the company, as discussed in this chapter, but on the capabilities of competitors. This is such an important topic that we devote the next three chapters to its development. Chapter 5 considers the competition for profit. Chapter 6 describes the importance of specifying a business model. Chapter 7 describes the competitive advantages and disadvantages of being part of a diversified corporation.

Key Concepts

Entrepreneurs recognize opportunities, assess fit between the market and their organization, find and combine resources, develop innovative solutions, and strive to make a profit. The entrepreneur can be an individual working alone, but often **entrepreneurial teams** bring a pool of competencies to a new venture. In addition, organizations can be assessed as a whole for their ability to support entrepreneurial activity. **Serial entrepreneurs** start a number of entrepreneurial efforts over time.

Radical innovations are a significant departure from currently available product or service offerings. **Incremental innovations** contribute to the improvement of existing product or service offerings.

Timing is important. Often, the **first mover** in a new product or service category can define an innovation's characteristics in the minds of buyers, gaining valuable name recognition and brand loyalty. But the **second mover** in a new market also has potential advantages, especially the opportunity to learn from and improve on the efforts of first movers.

At each of these levels, the goal is **opportunity recognition**, or discovering an idea and forming it into a business concept. **Synchronicity** is the time-sensitive match between the entrepreneur's recognition of opportunity and occurrence of market need. **Feasibility analysis** evaluates the skills and readiness of the entrepreneur and determines the availability of and access to resources required for launching a new venture.

Entrepreneurship requires finding and utilizing resources. **Utilitarian resources** are required to produce a good or service. **Instrumental resources** are not directly required to produce a good or service, but are helpful for acquiring those resources. **Social capital** refers to the resources (both utilitarian and instrumental) available from relationships with others.

Entrepreneurship also involves the management of innovation. **Product innovations** are changes in the product or service offered to an existing or new market. **Process innovations** do not change the offering itself, but change the way in which the organization operates to produce a good or service. Either can be a **competence-destroying innovation** that makes existing product or service offerings obsolete. Resistance should therefore be anticipated, by both affected outsiders and managers of businesses losing ground within the entrepreneurial company itself.

The prototypic S-curve of technological innovation is due, in part, to the typical pattern of adoption within a social setting. **Innovators** are the first few percent of a new offering's users, who try a new offering because of its innovative qualities. **Early adopters** are the larger group of users who are drawn to an offering's innovative qualities, but tend to be more evaluative than innovators. They also tend to be opinion leaders in the social system adopting a new innovation. **Early majority users**, who fall in the first half of the total set of an innovation's users, are still ahead of average adopters in their social system. They tend to be less responsive to technological or innovative content and more responsive to practical features and credibility than innovators or early adopters. **Late majority users** are the large, conservative group in a community slower than all except the laggards. Finally, **laggards** are users in a community who are slowest to adopt a new product. **Lead users** are similar to the majority of an innovation's users, and are willing to help the producer improve its product or service to meet their needs.

Liability of newness is a new venture's comparative vulnerability due to a lack of experience, industry recognition, and customer familiarity. Often failures result from lack of capital. **Start-up capital** is the financial requirement for initiating a new venture. **Bootstrapping** is the use of an entrepreneurial individual's personal resources to finance a new business. **Venture capitalists** (VCs) are investors who search for and provide capital to entrepreneurs and can be critical as cash needs increase after start-up. An **angel investor** is a private individual who provides seed capital to early-stage ventures. An **initial public offering** (IPO) sells stock in a new venture to individual and institutional investors as an additional way to raise needed capital.

Franchising is an opportunity for entrepreneurial growth by offering exclusive rights to a brand and business model to other entrepreneurs in a specific locality in return for a royalty.

Corporate entrepreneurship is an effort by an enterprise with large, established businesses to discover new opportunities. Though corporations offer resources and many existing capabilities, organizational **inertia**, the tendency to remain in a current state, should be expected. More specifically, **core rigidities** are sources of current success that make new-venture development difficult.

In an effort to avoid problems from inertia and rigidity, corporations sometimes establish **skunkworks**—independent units that are temporarily given autonomy to develop new ideas. The chapter concludes with a brief discussion of **dual strategy**. This is an attempt to optimize current performance while simultaneously preparing for strategic changes that are expected to be necessary in the future. Recently, strategy theorists have suggested that it is important to become **ambidextrous** and manage the inconsistent demands of supporting current businesses while developing new entrepreneurial opportunities; both are necessary to sustain advantage over time in competitive environments.

Questions for Further Reflection

1. Research a new start-up in your community. How did the entrepreneur discover the opportunity for the venture? How were resources gathered? What has been the response of early adopters?

2. Identify a new venture established by a corporation—perhaps Amazon, L'Oréal, or another company mentioned in this text. Can you identify positive and negative aspects of the corporate parent for the new venture?

3. Consider the macro environment discussed in Chapter 1 for a company that interests you. What technological, political/legal, economic, demographic, and cultural trends present entrepreneurial opportunities for this organization?

Consider how a product or service has made gains in the market and its users.

Step 1: Identify a product or service that has made significant gains in the market.

Step 2: Think of who the first adopters were. Describe their characteristics and demands in column 1.

Step 3: Think of the characteristics and demands of more recent users. Put your ideas into column 2.

Step 4: Anticipate the characteristics and demands of late adopters in column 3.

Step 5: Consider the strategic changes required to respond to these customers.

S-Curve Analysis Worksheet 4.1	**Product or Service:** Time Frame:	
Analyst(s):	**Strategy Summary:**	
First Adopters	**More Recent Users**	**Demands of Late Adopters**
Strategic Response	**Strategic Response**	**Strategic Response**

Consider how a corporate parent could provide resources to a start-up.

Step 1: Identify a promising entrepreneurial start-up in your community.

Step 2: Think of several corporations that might be interested in acquiring such a company. Describe the resources that each corporate parent could bring to the start-up effort.

Corporate Resources Worksheet 4.2	Start-Up: Time Frame:
Analyst(s):	Strategy Summary:

Potential Corporate Acquirer	Resources That a Corporate Parent Could Bring to the Start-Up

NOTES

[1] Peterson, T. 2000. Moveable Feast. *Business Week* (July 11).

[2] Amazon to Offer Movie Downloading Service. 2006. CNN Money. (September 6). http://money.cnn.com/2006/09/06/technology/amazon-apple, accessed March 7, 2008.

[3] Dalrymple, J. 2006. Disney CEO Happy with Apple's Movie Strategy. Macworld.com (September 12). At http://www.macworld.com/news/2006/09/12/disney/index.php, accessed March 7, 2008.

[4] http://www.boingboing.net/2006/09/15/amazon_unbox_to_cust.html, accessed March 7, 2008.

[5] http://seattlepi.nwsource.com/business/158315_amazon28.html, accessed March 7, 2008.

[6]Sarason, Y., Dean, T., & Dillard, J. 2005. Entrepreneurship as the Nexus of Individual and Opportunity: A Structuration View. *Journal of Business Venturing* 21: 286–305.

[7]Douglas, E. J., & Shepherd, D. A. 2002. Self-Employment as a Career Choice: Attitudes, Entrepreneurial Intentions, and Utility Maximization. *Entrepreneurial Theory and Practice* 26(3): 81–90.

[8]O'Gorman, C., & Terjesen, S. 2006. Financing the Celtic Tigress: Venture Financing and Informal Investment in Ireland. *Venture Capital* 8(1): 69–88.

[9]Minniti, M., & Arenius, P. 2003. Women in Entrepreneurship. The Entrepreneurial Advantage of Nations: First Annual Global Entrepreneurship Symposium. April 29, New York, NY. http://www.gemconsortium.org, accessed March 7, 2008.

[10]Personal communication with Sally Edwards (December 9, 2003).

[11]Catmull, E. 2004. Speech to Edison Conference and Innovation Showcase, University of Utah (May 20), Salt Lake City, UT.

[12]Sahlman, W. A. 1997. How to Write a Great Business Plan. *Harvard Business Review* (July–August): 98–108.

[13]Covin, J. G., & Slevin, D. P. 1991. A Conceptual Model of Entrepreneurship as Firm Behavior. *Entrepreneurship: Theory and Practice* 16(1): 7–25.

[14]http://executiveeducation.wharton.upenn.edu/ebuzz/0611/thoughtleaders.html, accessed March 7, 2008.

[15]http://www.crocs.com/shop/customer_service/customer_service.jsp, accessed March 7, 2008; McLean, B. 2006. Crocophiles. *Fortune* (October 2): 57–58.

[16]http://radaronline.com/features/2006/09/clog_jam.php, accessed March 7, 2008.

[17]See financial details at http://moneycentral.msn.com/investor/research/profile.asp?Symbol=CROX, accessed March 7, 2008.

[18]Alsever, J. 2006. What a Croc! *Fast Company* (June): 76. http://www.fastcompany.com/magazine/106/croc.html, accessed March 7, 2008.

[19]Huget, J. 2006. Not Such a Croc: Might a Fad Shoe's Health Claims Stand? *Washington Post* (August 1). http://www.washingtonpost.com/wp-dyn/content/article/2006/07/31/AR2006073100890.html, accessed March 7, 2008.

[20]http://www.crocs.com/company/history.jsp, accessed March 7, 2008.

[21]Kim, W. C., & Mauborgne, R. 2004. Blue Ocean Strategy. *Harvard Business Review* (October): 76–84.

[22]It wasn't as easy as we thought it would be to find statistics on business failure rates. Some good advice appears to be offered by the MIT website at http://faq-libraries.mit.edu/recordDetail?id=8124&action=&library=mit_business&institution=mit, accessed May 13, 2007.

[23]Edelman, L. F., Brush, C. G., & Manolova, T. 2005. Co-Alignment in the Resource–Performance Relationship: Strategy as Mediator. *Journal of Business Venturing* 20: 359–383.

[24]Shay, J. 2004. The Entrepreneurial Process. Lecture, London School of Economics & Political Science. July, 29.

[25]Brush, C. G., Greene, P. G., & Hart, M. M. 2001. From Initial Idea to Unique Advantage: The Entrepreneurial Challenge of Constructing a Resource Base. *Academy of Management Executive* 15: 64–80.

[26]Florin, J., Lubatkin, M. H., & Schulze, W. S. 2003. A Social Capital Model of New Venture Performance. *Academy of Management Journal* 46: 374–385.

[27]http://en.wikipedia.org/wiki/Airbus_A380, accessed September 25, 2006.

[28]Rogers, E. 1983. *Diffusion of Innovations.* New York: Free Press.

[29] Mohr, J. 2001. *Marketing of High-Technology Products and Innovations*. Upper Saddle River, NJ: Prentice Hall.

[30] Rogers, E. 1983. *Diffusion of Innovations*. New York: Free Press.

[31] See von Hippel's home page at http://web.mit.edu/evhippel/www/index.html and http://outsideinnovation.blogs.com/pseybold/2006/09/best_practicest.html, accessed March 7, 2008.

[32] http://www.boeing.com/companyoffices/doingbiz/esd/index.htm, accessed March 7, 2008.

[33] U.S. Small Business Administration. 2001. The Small Business Economy. Washington, DC: U.S. Government Printing Office.

[34] There are many references to micro enterprise on the Web. See, for example, http://www.enterweb.org, accessed March 7, 2008; see also Acs, Z., O'Gorman, C., Szerb, L., & Terjesen, S. 2007. Could the Irish Miracle Be Repeated in Hungary? *Small Business Economics* (2/3): 123–142.

[35] Dimov, D., & Shepherd, D. 2005. Human Capital Theory and Venture Capital Firms: Exploring "Home Runs" and "Strike Outs." *Journal of Business Venturing* 20: 1–21.

[36] Higashide, H., & Birley, S. 2001. The Consequences of Conflict between the Venture Capitalist and the Entrepreneurial Team in the United Kingdom from the Perspective of the Venture Capitalist. *Journal of Business Venturing* 17: 59–81.

[37] Bygrave, W. & Zacharakis, A. 2003. *The Portable MBA in Entrepreneurship*. Hoboken: John Wiley & Sons.

[38] http://www.thebodyshop.com/bodyshop/company/index.jsp?cm_re=default-_-Footer-_-About_Us, accessed March 7, 2008.

[39] Chronicle of Philanthropy. 2007. Obituary: Anita Roddick, 64, Body Shop Founder. http://philanthropy.com/news/philanthropytoday/3008/obituary-anita-roddick-64-body-shop-founder, accessed January 21, 2008.

[40] Pitman, S. 2006. Body Shop Posts Increased Sales for 2005. Cosmeticsdesign.com (May 8). http://www.cosmeticsdesign.com/news/ng.asp?id=67539-the-body-shop-sales-l-oreal, accessed March 7, 2008.

[41] The quote from the *Evening Standard* is reported in Lyall, S. 2007. Anita Roddick, Body Shop Founder, Dies at 64. *New York Times* (September 12). http://www.nytimes.com/2007/09/12/world/europe/12roddick.html?_r=2&oref=slogin&oref=slogin, accessed January 21, 2008.

[42] Pinchot, G. 1985. *Intrapreneurship*. New York: Harper & Row.

[43] Pitman, Body Shop Posts Increased Sales.

[44] Andrew, J., & King, K. 2003. Boosting Innovation Productivity. Boston Consulting Group (April). http://www.bcg.com, accessed March 7, 2008.

[45] http://www.aka.tv/articles/article.asp?ArticleID=336, accessed March 7, 2008; information was also obtained from personal conversations with Diageo employees.

[46] Chandiramani, R. 2003. Diageo Shuts New Ventures Division. *Marketing* (July 10): 1; Diageo Closes Down Nightfly after Review. 2003. *Revolution* (June): 4.

[47] Leonard-Barton, D. 1992. Core Capabilities and Core Rigidities: A Paradox in Managing New Product Development. *Strategic Management Journal* 13: 111–125.

[48] Bowman, C., & Gleadle, P. 2003. Culture as a Dynamic Capability: The Case of 3M in the UK. Working paper presented at the Academy of Management, Seattle, WA.

[49] See Day, D. 1994. Raising Radicals: Different Processes for Championing Innovative Corporate Ventures. *Organization Science* 5: 148–152, for a discussion of the complexities of championing.

[50]Abell, D. F. 1993. *Managing with Dual Strategies.* New York: Free Press. See also Markides, C., & Charitou, C. D. 2004. Competing with Dual Business Models: A Contingency Approach. *Academy of Management Executive* 18: 22–36.

[51]Based on family history collected by Siri Terjesen.

[52]Hamel, G., & Prahalad, C. K. 1995. *Competing for the Future.* Boston: Harvard Business School Press.

[53]Tushan, M. L., & O'Reilly, C.A., III, 1996. Ambidextrous Organizations: Managing Evolutionary and Revolutionary Change. *California Management Review* 38(4): 8–31.

5 Competing with Rivals

→ → →

Anyone who wants a mobile phone has to choose among providers. Phone deals are changing so fast that it's hard to tell who has the best overall package. Do you have a mobile phone? Have you recently changed providers? Were you seeking more features, trying to lower your costs, or both? If you can respond to these questions, you have excellent experience to understand issues discussed in this chapter. You recognize relatively subtle differences among products and know that it's not just the product that attracts your attention, but an interconnected set of offerings from multiple providers. As a strategist you'll have to think about how profits are allocated among those players. It's not good to be part of a fabulous sales success if your company doesn't make any money.

In most markets, multiple firms compete for the same set of buyers with similar goods or services. Two broad categories of competitive environments characterize competition among these providers. *Oligopoly theory* describes relatively passive or benign competition among a limited number of firms. The theory of *hypercompetition*, in contrast, directs attention to more vicious contests, typically among larger groups of firms that reduce the potential for profit. Larger macro forces (technological, demographic, social, political/legal, and economic) influence both systems.

However, firms increasingly cooperate. *Collaborative strategies* provide a third framework for interacting with competitors that offer an expanding set of strategic opportunities. *Coopetition* describes a situation in which rivals compete fiercely in some markets while they cooperate in other areas.

· ·

To provide further detail we answer the following questions:

What distinguishes competitive environments?
What affects profit potential in different environments?
  Rivals
  Buyers
  Suppliers
  Substitutes
  New entrants
  Complements
  Strategic groups
How do macro forces affect the evolution of competitive conditions?
  Demographic environment
  Sociocultural environment
  Technological environment

We also discuss how competitive environments are often changed by innovations that begin with one or a few firms. A good example is GEMAYA, a term coined in a recent article by David Kirkpatrick in *Fortune* magazine.

NEXT-GENERATION COMPETITORS?

The Internet era has brought a new breed of global competitor: the integrated online commerce conglomerate. As early as 1999, Jeff Bezos claimed that Amazon offered "Earth's biggest selection" of goods, including books, greeting cards, and pet supplies. *Fortune* columnist David Kirkpatrick identified Amazon as one of six firms aspiring to provide a full suite of consumer goods and services with global reach—penetrating every market with an Internet connection at the end of 2005.[1] The GEMAYA firms (Google, eBay, MSN, Amazon, Yahoo, and AOL) have been acquiring key components to execute this strategy. For example, eBay acquired Skype for $2.6 billion in 2005, enabling it to compete with Google, MSN, and Yahoo's voice capabilities.

According to Kirkpatrick, each firm is building from its core strength. Amazon and eBay are leveraging their online commerce competencies, while Google is maximizing returns from its superior search engine technology and advertising systems. MSN builds on communications and news, while AOL relies on instant messaging and online content. Finally, Yahoo leverages its personalized portal for communications and shopping. Kirkpatrick has suggested that the next development may be that the GEMAYA firms develop into multifunctional consumer banks.

With their massive economies of scale and scope, the GEMAYA firms present a real challenge to local firms, and the Internet is enabling their further growth. For example, eBay has succeeded by building a huge market of both buyers and sellers of goods. How can smaller, local firms compete? Kirkpatrick suggests that in some industries big players may seek local partners, but it is highly unlikely that these will be marriages among equals. Furthermore, the current set of new competitors are all headquartered in the United States, an irksome prospect for commerce elsewhere in the world.

> However, at the end of 2007, two years after focusing attention on these giants as the drivers of the Internet, Kirkpatrick is reporting on new competitors: "The opportunities presented by the billions of people entering the world of digital communications are vast. Comscore's first-ever comprehensive study of the search industry, released last week, showed that China's Baidu is the world's third largest search site, behind just Google and Yahoo, and ahead of Microsoft, Ask, and everybody else."[2] Clearly, the game is still open.

WHAT DISTINGUISHES COMPETITIVE ENVIRONMENTS? ⚹

Competitive environments are sets of firms offering interconnected products, services, or experiences.

Industries are competitive settings where firms provide the same or similar sets of products and services.

GEMAYA is creating a *competitive environment.* Struggles among a few firms are affecting a much larger group of companies that surround them. The strategy field has spent a great deal of time thinking about these competitive contexts, especially in the more homogeneous settings commonly called an *industry.* In this chapter we will discuss how rivalry and its consequences require strategic responses that go beyond the considerations described in Chapters 2–4 (developing resources, connecting with buyers, and finding opportunities).

In near perfect competition, with similar firms able to imitate success almost immediately because market information is available to all players, there is little need for strategy. The only advantage available to firms is relative price, and price wars are the norm. Because there is almost no basis for competitive advantage, firms earn very little profit. This is an unappealing scenario, found primarily in the models of economists. Strategists in real firms continually search for advantages (such as new product features or faster delivery) that buyers will reward by paying higher prices than they would pay for the undifferentiated products of pure competition. Strategists also typically try to obscure their activities and the size of any profits made so that competitors cannot imitate their advantage. As they do so, strategic decision making becomes more interesting, more important, and more difficult.

Four descriptions of competetive environments suggest the broad range of settings that business firms might face: (1) monopoly, (2) oligopoly, (3) hypercompetition, and (4) pure competition.[3] Table 5.1 presents some of their important differences.

TABLE 5.1 FOUR TYPES OF COMPETITIVE ENVIRONMENTS ⚹ Mid

	Monopoly	Oligopoly	Hyper	Pure
Number of players	One	Few	Several	Many
Sustainability of advantage	Absolute	Long-term	Temporary	None
Profit potential	One big winner	Several big winners	Some winners, some losers	Very low

Strategists are oriented toward environments that allow them to affect outcomes in their favor—they seek competitive advantage. The monopoly environment is a special case that holds little interest in this competition-oriented chapter. The monopolist's obvious priority is to retain full control; as long as that is the case there are no direct competitors to worry about.[4] One example of a monopoly is the company once known as the Bell System. Until it was deregulated in the 1980s, it was the sole provider of both local and long distance services and telephone equipment, including the telephone itself. The Bell System was a regulated monopoly and literally had no competition. Pure competition, at the other end of the scale, is also of little interest for the strategist. Here, no firm can gain a competitive advantage, since by definition information about prices, markets, and production costs is shared equally among competitors. Imitation is virtually immediate. An example close to pure competition might include your local landscaping and lawn care industry.

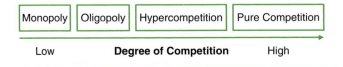

Figure 5.1 — Varied Levels of Competition

Very few companies, however, are located in a competitive environment that can be classified as either a monopoly or pure competition. Most firms find themselves in the two middle situations shown in Figure 5.1. They are either in an *oligopoly* with a limited number of producers acting in relatively predictable and coordinated ways to supply products and services, or in *hypercompetition*, in which competition is much more demanding and control more limited. Here the sources of advantage change quickly, and it is rare for any player to sustain above average profit.

Though they are an oversimplification of more complex reality, oligopoly and hypercompetition distinguish distinctly different environments that require different strategies to realize above-average returns. Situations like the one developing between Google, eBay, and other Internet conglomerates also emphasize that competitive struggles often influence many bystanders and are thus critical for strategists to study.

In the 1990s, when people focused on "new economy" conditions, Professor Richard D'Aveni of Tuck Business School coined the term *hypercompetition*. He and others argued that hypercompetition was becoming the prototypical environment that strategists would increasingly have to deal with.[5] Other scholars subsequently suggested that the trend is not so linear[6]—the level of competition should be expected to vary over time and across contexts.

Oligopoly exists when a few rivals compete for buyers in relatively predictable ways.

Hypercompetition exists when a significant number of rivals compete intensely and less predictably for competitive advantage.

We begin this chapter by describing oligopolies, competitive settings that have a limited number of significant players and fairly predictable interactions. This is the kind of environment most managers prefer. It is worth understanding the evidence that pushes firms toward creating this kind of environment when they can.

WHAT AFFECTS PROFIT POTENTIAL IN DIFFERENT ENVIRONMENTS?

The individual most identified with strategy under oligopolistic conditions is Professor Michael Porter of Harvard Business School. Two of his books, *Competitive Strategy* and *Competitive Advantage*, are fundamental reading for any strategist.[7] Porter was interested in answering two questions in these books:

1. What makes a competitive environment attractive to potential new entrants or to existing competitors? (What characterizes settings in which firms earn high profits?)

2. How does a firm compete? (What is the basis for higher-than-average returns within a given competitive environment?)

Figure 5.2 indicates that both corporate and business strategists are involved in answering these questions. In Chapter 7 we will describe how corporate strategists allocate resources across multiple industries and create a corporate strategy. In this chapter, we focus on how firms compete in a given competitive setting and create a business strategy.

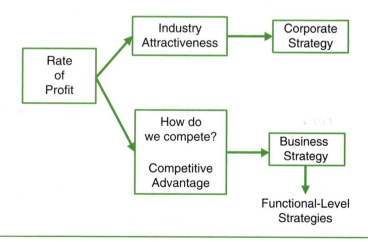

Figure 5.2 — Two Sources of Profit

Porter's work drew on *industrial organization (IO) economics*. This field of study investigates the relationship between the behavior of firms and market structure, what we call a competitive environment in this chapter. IO economists were traditionally concerned with how extraordinary profits could be reduced by government regulation. Porter and other academics realized that this large body of research could be turned on its head to ask how strategists could limit or avoid competition (and regulation) and thereby achieve above-average returns. Given that monopolies have largely been regulated to limit producer profitability, the possibility of profit generating competitive advantage focuses on oligopoly, which in Greek means "few sellers."

Porter began with the idea that an industry is much more than a set of direct competitors, some able to achieve more profit than others. He pointed out that powerful buyers can keep firms from making money, as can powerful suppliers. Profit is also reduced if an industry attracts new entrants or if attractive substitutes emerge. Andy Grove, CEO of Intel, also pointed out that attractive complements (i.e. system software providers) can also reduce a firm's profits. Today, analysts often add this sixth force to Porter's five to explain competition for profits made in an industry setting, as shown in Figure 5.3.

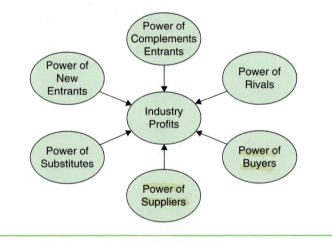

Figure 5.3 — Six Forces Affecting Profitability ✳

Porter's key insights are twofold: first, all of the actors that participate in an industry or competitive environment are in fact competitors for the profit that is available from providing customers with goods, services, and experiences . Second, a competitive setting will be especially attractive to a business strategist when these forces have relatively little power to capture available profit. Where any of these forces has power, the role of strategy is to mitigate, or if possible, defuse such power.

Rivals

At the core of the six forces model is the degree of rivalry among firms within the focal industry. The number of players, and their relative size, matters. The most stable and easy-to-anticipate structure is characterized by a few large companies with somewhat overlapping but distinct methods of operating. The overlap promotes shared interests and understanding, while distinct strategies reduce direct competition within the group. As we have already noted, economists call this situation *oligopoly*.

Smaller rivals can be an important and positive feature of oligopoly from the larger rivals' point of view. Smaller firms fill in product, service, or experience gaps that would be expensive for large firms to satisfy. Often smaller firms take the risk of developing new innovations in the hope of increasing profits, while larger firms have the resources to quickly adopt proven ideas.

These are conditions in which rivalry, though it exists, tends to be relatively inexpensive. Rivalry intensifies (and profits tend to go down) when industry growth is slow, there are high fixed costs in doing business, and the market lacks differentiated products. Overcapacity and high *barriers to exit* are also structural conditions that depress the potential profit in a competitive environment by maintaining the number of rivals who must battle for a slice of the smaller profit pie.

> **Barriers to exit** are conditions that increase the cost of leaving a competitive environment.

The Organization of Petroleum Exporting Countries (OPEC) and other producers in the oil and gas industry provide an example of oligopolistic conditions. Members maintain high profits by controlling the amount of oil made available. The small number of players in the retail gas market enjoy similar advantages. In the United States, a sequence of antitrust laws were passed to limit such behavior, responding to the power of the large, integrated holding companies established by Standard Oil and other companies in the late nineteenth century.[8]

Buyers

Buyers have the power to limit producer profits when they are few in number or large in size relative to those who are offering products or services. For example, automobile manufacturers typically have this advantage over parts suppliers. Buyers are less powerful if the input they are buying is important to their processes or if the cost of switching to other inputs is high. Thus, automobile manufacturers have less power over a tire company or a stereo company with a brand that customers desire than they do over suppliers that are unknown to the customer.

In general, buyers also will have less power if they are relatively fragmented, lack information about producers' costs, or are unable to coordinate activities among themselves. Consider the low power of end-consumers relative to mass-produced goods and services as a powerful example of this. For example, when gasoline prices rise, we, as buyers, may drive less often or search more carefully for the best available price, but we have virtually no ability to affect pump prices. Buyers can increase their power if they cooperate, however. One promised benefit of hospital mergers, for example, is better control over the costs of medical supplies.

It makes sense for producers to focus their efforts on connecting with "good" buyers that are willing to pay a premium for the products, services, or experiences on offer. Similarly, finding "good" suppliers that provide needed quality of inputs without high prices is a smart strategy.

Suppliers

Suppliers tend to be powerful (and thus retain a larger share of profit) when they are few in number. This is because buyers have little chance of bargaining—they must choose between relatively few alternatives. By the same logic, those who seek specialized inputs available from only one or a few suppliers are in a less powerful position.

Suppliers are also powerful if their buyers cannot produce needed inputs themselves or when there is little chance for the buyer to acquire a firm in the suppliers' industry. Suppliers are less willing to negotiate when a buyer's purchases are small relative to the supplier's overall market, and this, too, increases supplier power. Their bargaining power also will be high if buyers face high *switching costs*. You have experienced the influence of switching costs yourself if you belong to a frequent flyer program. Once you begin to accumulate miles within a program, flying on another airline imposes the costs of missing out on potential benefits.

Switching costs are incurred when a buyer changes suppliers.

Observation of many different competitive situations suggests that buyers try to limit the power of suppliers by themselves and are also likely to work with other buyers—that is, rivals producing the same goods or services. Individually or collectively, for example, buyers can spread their orders among suppliers to limit the size of supplying firms. Buying firms also can form consortia to group their orders. However, these and other strategies cannot be considered in isolation. To maintain their power and reduce costs in the face of powerful buyers, for example, suppliers may merge. Even in the face of such consolidation, however, buyers like Wal-Mart have the size and purchasing power to counteract supplier power.

Substitutes

Substitute products that satisfy a given set of buyer needs in a different way also tend to reduce the profits available to producing firms. The limitation on profitability imposed by substitutes is particularly high when they offer alternative goods and products that satisfy a similar set of needs at a significantly lower price. The power of substitutes also can be high if they offer equal or greater quality at a similar price. Both effects are conditioned on minimal buyer switching costs. Substitutes are more threatening if there is little possibility of industry participants producing the substitute product or service themselves.

By definition, firms offering substitutes come from outside the competitive environment being analyzed. The threat of substitute offerings therefore are harder for the strategist to recognize and predict. Typically, firms that produce substitutes have few commonalities with industry participants, and these outsiders are less likely to join in the tacit *collusion* that supports informal profit-protecting strategies. For example, with the invention and successful commercialization of digital photography, rolls of photographic film have been replaced by digital memory cards. Digital manufacturers are new to photography; they use unfamiliar technologies, have a different cost structure, and use suppliers that are not well known to established players in the photography (now called imaging) industry. As a result, it is unlikely that past strategies of firms in the photography industry will be successful competing against these substitutes.

The key thing to think about with respect to substitutes is the potential for disruption in the patters of industry rivalry. Who would have predicted that a cell phone would become a substitute for a watch? Watch manufacturers were already focusing on fashion, but the pressure to do so increased significantly with this substitute. There are often ripple effects. For example, there is only so much real estate on a wrist. What would you do if you sold bracelets, and found buyers attracted to collect watches?

New Entrants

Competitive settings are attractive to new entrants if they are (or appear to be) profitable. Strategists therefore try to erect *barriers to entry*. Ideally these barriers are significant enough that newcomers do not begin producing similar goods or services.

There are many types of barriers to entry. Researchers have paid attention to such things as economies of scale, brand identity, capital requirements, switching costs, proprietary technology, product differentiation, excess capacity, and access to distribution. Obviously, all these potential barriers to entry will not apply to any given situation. In different situations, different barriers help protect the profit of industry incumbents. If barriers are not in place, available profits will be diminished as new entrants become rivals. Sometimes current players try to make the industry setting appear unattractive by obscuring profits. In other cases, the barrier to entry is *retaliation* (or the perceived likelihood of retaliation) by those currently involved in a competitive setting. For example, firms facing a new entrant may reduce prices, setting off a price war. Price wars reduce the profits of all players, yet discourage entries. High-priced service warranties have a similar dynamic.

In short, to the extent that incumbents are powerful enough to maintain barriers to entry, profit in the competitive setting is expected to be

Collusion
exists when actors coordinate their activities to their mutual advantage. In many countries laws limit this activity, but tacit collusion (achieved without direct communication) can be difficult to prevent.

Barriers to entry
are conditions that increase the cost of competition for potential entrants.

Retaliation
is a willingness of current industry participants to use their resources to respond aggressively to competitive moves, including entry.

relatively high for the few firms that dominate an oligopolistic setting. To the extent that barriers do not exist, potential entrants have the power to reduce the profit that might otherwise have been shared among a small number of participants.

Complements

In many situations, complementary products or services enhance the value of the products or services provided by a group of rivals in a given competitive setting. In public health, for example, those who treat disease often try to enlist allied organizations that focus on diet and exercise. Hospitals, doctors and other medical providers are likely to be more successful when these additional services are available to their clients. In a for-profit environment, pharmaceutical firms desire relationships with doctors who prescribe pharmaceutical drugs, and thus medical practice is a complementary force that has a significant impact on the profitability of the pharmaceutical industry. Wireless internet connections from cell phones further expand the power of the computer.[9]

Like the five forces Porter discussed, complementary offerings in for-profit environments can appropriate value that would otherwise go to primary providers. As seen with suppliers and buyers, if organizations with complementary products are relatively concentrated (few in number), it may be difficult for primary providers in the industry to have much bargaining power. Similarly, if there are few substitutes for their supporting role, complements have power. This explains why Microsoft (the primary provider of PC operating systems) is highly profitable. Microsoft provides a valuable set of software complement to the offerings of hardware manufacturers that is difficult to get elsewhere.

Worksheet 5.1 provides a preliminary tool for exploring the power of complements and the other five forces Porter identified.

Worksheet 5.1:
Industry
Analysis—A Tool
for Analyzing
Industry Forces

Andrew Grove, one of the founders of Intel and its CEO for many years, emphasized the importance of complements in his book *Only the Paranoid Survive*.[10] His involvement in the computer industry gave him a good vantage point for understanding the "ecosystem" that attracts customers. Wireless Internet connections on cell phones have further expanded the power of the computer, for example. Compliments expand the size of profits available, but they also take a slice of those profits.

Industry analysis provides strategists and other stakeholders with an assessment of a specific competitive environment.

An important part of an organization's strategic agenda is to build strengths that counteract threats to profitability from all six forces in the competitive environment. The basic idea of *industry analysis*, as Porter defines it, is to understand how each of the competitive forces influences profitability. More recently, the term has come to have an additional financial focus, and is part of comparing firms on various measures of financial health. Various lists of these performance measures can be found on the Internet.[11]

A great deal of insight can be gained from industry analysis, and it continues to be widely used. There are potential problems with this framework, however. Perhaps most important, the boundaries of what constitutes an industry are increasingly difficult to identify. As we saw in the opening discussion of GEMAYA, firms searching for an advantage link their products and services in ways that complicate previous definitions industry boundaries. As industries metamorphose, the boundaries around the six forces we have just described blur. A competitive environment that was once defined as internet portals spills over to rivalry among search engines, for example.

Given these dynamics, industry analysis has been criticized for the static picture it provides. Further, the framework encourages an underlying assumption of a zero-sum game whereby a firm can only profit and grow at the expense of others' profit and growth. This may be shortsighted. As Toyota has shown, firms can expand their own profits by developing win-win relationships with suppliers. For example, the framework Porter proposed in 1980 pays too little attention to such possibilities, and we will remind you about the use of cooperative strategies at the end of the chapter.

Strategic Groups

Strategic groups are subsets of firms in a competitive setting that follow similar strategies.

Before leaving the description of industry structure it is important to consider *strategic groups* — collections of firms that follow the same basic strategy in areas such as pricing, degree of specialization (the inverse of product line breadth), geographic market coverage, degree of vertical integration, customer service, product quality, market image, R&D, technology position or other decisions of competitive strategy. Strategic groups can be found in many competitive settings. While some groups are more attractive than others in terms of profitability, often it is not easy for a firm to shift from a lower profit group into a higher profit group. For example, in the athletic shoe industry (which we briefly discussed in Chapter 3), firms can be grouped in terms of cost positioning and degree of vertical integration. Companies like Brooks, New Balance, and Mizuno spend little on advertising and lots on R&D in order to develop new technologies specific to running. Meanwhile, Puma, Adidas, and Reebok have huge advertising budgets, but tend to develop less tech-savvy products. The specialists do not have the revenues to support very high advertising budgets and thus cannot move into new buyer segments at will. But, money alone cannot buy the technical savvy and customer relations that the smaller niche players enjoy, and thus the larger firms are also constrained.

Strategic groups can significantly influence business strategy. First, as firms within a strategic group utilize similar strategies, they compete more directly inside the group than outside. The result is likely to be a distinctive competitive environment in terms of the six forces outlined earlier. One strategic group may struggle with the threat of supplier forward integration, for example, while another strategic group may enjoy higher than average returns in the industry, in part because it is more protected from supplier power.

A second important influence of strategic groups is cognitive; they affect how strategists think about their own firm in relation to others.[12] For example, it makes a difference if managers of a pizza restaurant see it as hangout for college students or a nice restaurant. The first strategic group competes with bars and even sports facilities, the second with other more upscale restaurants and cultural events.

HOW DO MACRO FORCES AFFECT THE EVOLUTION OF COMPETITIVE CONDITIONS?

As we briefly noted in Chapter 1, competitive environments exist within the context of a larger set of macro forces, as illustrated in Figure 5.4.

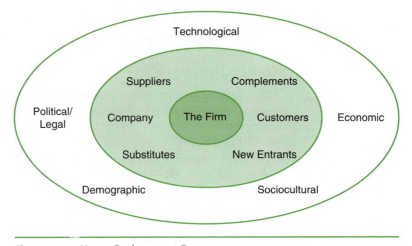

Figure 5.4 — Macro Environment Forces

Changes in the macro environment (in technology, consumer demand, regulation, or other factors) must be considered both as sources of competitive advantage (opportunities) and as potential source of erosion of competitive advantage (threats). As an example, consider Pirelli Tire's attempts to improve its competitive position.

Pirelli Reinvents the Wheel

Pirelli, one of the world's largest tire producers, introduced a dramatically different tire production process known as a *modular integrated robotized system* (MIRS) in 2000. Protected by patents, the Italian firm's process improved labor productivity by 80 percent and drastically shortened work-in-process cycle times from six days to seventy-two minutes!

In addition, the small, modular nature of Pirelli's new production process scientifically reduced its economies of scale. Conventional factories must produce more than 6 million tires annually to be effective. The new process made production of 1 million tires cost effective, thereby allowing smaller production sites. Units costing $42 million and taking up a mere 350 square meters could be installed almost anywhere, and could even be moved from one physical location to another. MIRS's flexibility allowed Pirelli to sign lucrative deals supplying tires to Ford and Dodge Ram. Industry observers even began talking about the possibility of supplying dealers with tires on a just-in-time inventory basis, further slashing costs and adding value at the same time.

It remains to be seen whether this new process will alter the fundamental balance among competitors within the worldwide tire industry. Pirelli has always been known for its high-end performance tires. Their new innovation made it possible to enter the less valuable but larger mass market as well. A particularly important question, from a strategic point of view, is how much of MIRS's possible advantage will Pirelli be able to realize, and how long will any advantage last before competitors meet or negate it?

Following its introduction, Pirelli constantly added new developments to the MIRS system, including a "continuous compound mixer" that improves the quality and flexibility of used rubber, an integrated computer-aided design (CAD) system that automatically adapts a facility for the production of different types of tires, and "spiral advanced technology," which allows MIRS to be used with larger tires. The latest product from Pirelli, a company that now describes its strategy as "continuous innovation," is a self-inflating motorcycle tire.

The company apparently transformed these technological advances into higher sales and profit. Though it planned to sell its truck tire production in the mid-1990s, for example, Pirelli later changed strategies to investing in tires these operations while preparing to sell its cable and telecom operations. Its advantage in production—as sales and income figures indicate—has not yet been matched by competitors. In fact, Pirelli now delivers know-how to other tire producers in Russia and India and has a strong desire to develop the Chinese market.[13]

Pirelli is an example of a company using technology strategically, and its competitors must worry about how this macro force will affect their situation. But this is just one of many macro forces that affect competition. It is relatively easy to generically characterize the largest forces and outline the kind of influence they might have on different industry forces, but specific influence in each area depends on the time and place of the strategist's analysis. These influences are so complex in practice that strategists often rely on industry associations and outside consultants for information. Still, strategists need to develop their own intuitions about key influences in the broader environment.

Demographic Environment

The demographic environment focuses on the human population. It makes sense to pay special attention to demographic characteristics of relevant groups, including their age, size, marital status, education, geographic distribution, ethnic mix, and income distribution. These data are often publicly available from the national census. They will suggest, for example, how soon retired people will demand different products and services than younger consumers in a particular market.

Sociocultural Environment

The sociocultural environment is created by a population's culture — its behaviors and values. These factors differ by geographic region and present unique business opportunities.

Ongoing changes in the sociocultural environment create new opportunities while reducing the appeal of others. Changes in eating habits provide just one example. As work and entertainment fill more time slots, our eating habits have changed. Fewer meals are cooked at home, for example, a social change that has increased opportunities for restaurants of all kinds and changed the kind of food purchased.[14] This has nutritional consequences, with many people eating less healthy diets, a worldwide trend that nonetheless has significant regional variations. The impact in America can be seen in opportunities such as vitamin supplements and health clubs.

Technological Environment

Opportunities available in the food industry are also influenced by technological changes. The way food is raised, preserved, and moved is changing dramatically. Farm scale has increased, in part because of increases in the efficient size of equipment. Decreases in transportation costs and other technological changes have also supported the creation of a global industry that makes fresh foods available year-round in many markets.

Technological advances have clearly been a deciding factor in many other strategic opportunities. Pirelli's new tire manufacturing system depends on scientific advances in miniaturization, robotics, and other areas, for example. These scientific advances are simultaneously affecting many competitive environments. Strategists are well advised to look to the impact of the technological environment on different kinds of firms when trying to predict evolution within their own setting.

Economic Environment

Strategists also must think about regional and national differences in economic growth rates, GDP, credit availability, foreign exchange rates, inflation rates, and trade balances. The impact of these and other factors on different sectors of the economy tend to differ. Increasingly available credit in developing economies, for example, is creating new competitors for companies in more developed economies. In the food industry alone, think of the strength of African flower growers or of farmed salmon from China. In the wine industry, there are serious competitors facing French and Californian wines from South America and other regions.

Political/Legal Environment

It also makes sense to pay attention to the political and legal environment. We have already discussed government antitrust regulations. Though standards are changing in an increasingly interconnected world, when Novell and Sun Microsystems complained to EU courts that Microsoft was using anticompetitive processes, the ultimate result was the largest penalties the EU had handed down to date.[15]

Continuing discussion about the food industry, think about the importance of health and safety regulation. Inspection of eating establishments is a key part of customer confidence in eating out. What we eat is also influenced by regulation of specific sectors, such as fishing. Concerns about genetically modified food are especially strong in the European Community, where significant legislation has been enacted.[16]

Once again, these are only a few examples of very broad macro-level influences. Strategists interested in innovation—that is to say, virtually all strategists—might note in particular that scientific advances are strongly supported by state and federal governments. Many locations also provide significant locational inducements to firms establishing headquarters and manufacturing facilities. Political instability makes other locations problematic.

We suggest that you use STEP analysis to consider sociocultural, technological, economic, and political/legal factors when establishing a viable strategy. Worksheet 5.2 provides a preliminary tool for exploring interconnections among these forces.

Perhaps you are wondering whether STEP analysis can be used with SWOT analysis, as described in Chapter 1. Figure 5.5 shows how they are hierarchically nested. Firm strengths and weaknesses can be defined only in a specific competitive environment, which can be understood only in terms of macro factors. In practice, the factors identified are also interrelated. As strategists understand their strengths and weaknesses, they can and should consider shifting the position of their firm into a more favorable environment, which will require revisiting prior assessments.

Worksheet 5.2:
Macro
Environment
(STEP)
Analysis—A
Tool for Linking
Strategy and
Context

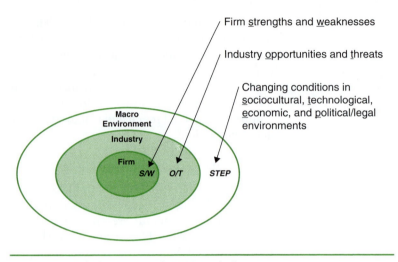

Figure 5.5 — Relating STEP and SWOT Analysis

The diagram as a whole is a target, with the "bull's-eye" the area of greatest strategic attention. The strategist's primary job is to develop strengths that are most likely to be profitable in a given competitive environment, as we will discuss in Chapter 6.

HOW DO ASYMMETRIES HELP EXPLAIN COMPETITIVE ADVANTAGE?

With the macro context as a background, we now want to consider some generic options for interacting with rivals. A key idea in devising strategy has to do with similarity among rivals. When pure competition exists, there are no *asymmetries*, or meaningful resource differences among competitors that lead to power differences and thus differences in profitability. Microeconomists often assume that all competitors are equal, which helps their ability to model interactions. In fact, every firm has a unique past and administrative heritage; ongoing learning and experimentation then accentuate the differences history has created. Some of these differences are asymmetries worth thinking about, because they offer a potential source of advantage over other players. Just remember that difference alone does not lead to above-average rates of return, as we pointed out in discussing the resource-based theory of the firm in Chapter 2.

Professor Richard Rumelt of UCLA argues that "a strategy that does not either create or exploit an asymmetry constituting an advantage must be rejected."[17] The trick, obviously, lies in determining which asymmetry is likely to constitute a competitive advantage. As we've already shown, in oligopolistic environments, the differences between actors that often make a difference include the following:

Asymmetries are differences among firms that explain difference in profitability.

- Size
- Access to information
- Ability to coordinate activities with similar actors (e.g., other suppliers)
- Ability to coordinate activities across the value chain (e.g., links with distributors)
- Ability to imitate

The nature of the difference that matters depends on the environment. Size is an advantage, for example, if it is associated with more resources and experience. But also consider the advantages of flexibility that smaller competitors often enjoy. Some firms gain advantage from not being tied to unprofitable contracts made in the past, others suffer. The key strategic question becomes, how can we make our unique features lead to results that different competitors cannot match?

Strategic positioning also makes a difference, because asymmetries that do not provide advantage in one competitive environment may be useful in others. Suppose, for example, that firm A possesses a unique source of raw materials and firm B has developed a unique manufacturing process in some competitive setting. It is possible that this resource difference reduces costs by exactly the same amount and therefore neither firm has an immediate advantage over the other. Yet their strategic options differ.

Strategists in firm A, with its unique raw materials, might look for other products in its home market for which the process advantages of firm B are not relevant and no other competitors have an advantage. Perhaps firm B has other options: it might take its manufacturing process to overseas markets where the raw-material advantage of firm A cannot be exploited because of distance. If no local competitors possess this advantage either, firm B now has a competitive advantage. The first firm therefore diversifies, while the second becomes a multinational, and both are profitable.

It is easy to understand, at least in abstract terms, that meaningful asymmetries like the one we just sketched out are likely to provoke additional strategic changes, furthering change in the competitive context. Figure 5.6 provides a schematic view of changes that lead to a different resource profile in competing firms.

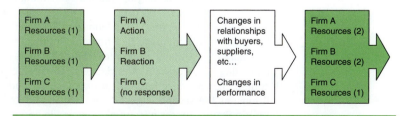

Figure 5.6 — Competitor Interaction and Changing Industry Structure

Competitive contexts change as a result of the kind of interaction shown (often including macro factors not diagrammed in the figure). Factors once at the center of strategic battles often come into balance, and competition moves to new ground where new asymmetries may make a difference.[18] When firms that were once rivals move apart, each firm is likely to become involved with new players in one or more areas identified by the six forces. These changes expose the firm to new risks and heighten the need for further strategizing. Consider the following example:

Carpet Makers Face Changing Customer Tastes

Carpet manufacturers in a number of Western countries face an uncomfortable reality—the homeowner's dream may have shifted from a desire for wall-to-wall carpeting to more "elegant" hardwood floors and other alternatives. For example, carpeting's share of overall spending on floor covering in the United States dropped from 80 percent in the 1980s to just 58 percent in twenty years' time.

To counter this gloomy trend and try to grow their businesses, the industry's two largest producers, Shaw Industries and Mohawk Industries, developed different strategies. Shaw chose to expand its involvement with carpeting by buying competitors and moving into the retail distribution of carpet. Mohawk also purchased competitors, but chose to branch out into other flooring options, emphasizing wood laminates and ceramic tile.

Historically, most carpet in the United States was sold through independent retail outlets. But starting in late 1995, Shaw bought several retail chains, including New York Carpet World and Carpetland USA, and opened its own stores. Within two years, Shaw controlled about 400 stores and was one of the nation's largest carpet retailers. It lacked knowledge about the intricacies of selling carpeting to individual consumers and was criticized by analysts for getting into an arena where it did not enjoy a competitive advantage. However, Shaw Industries, owned by Warren Buffett's Berkshire Hathaway Corporation, remains the number one seller of carpets in the world.[19]

Mohawk initially stayed out of retail sales, concentrating on differentiating into other floor coverings. Its strategy was to leverage its trucking and warehousing operations by sending more products through the same channels. "We're just as much a distribution company as a manufacturing company," said Mohawk CEO David Kolb, who called Mohawk "a growth company in a nongrowth industry."

Mohawk's strategy, perceived to be closer to its resource mix, involved exploiting resources and knowledge it already possessed, although, of course, Mohawk also had to learn about new products and processes.[20] It remains the second-largest carpet maker, and its Dal-Tile is one of the United States' largest makers of ceramic tile and stone flooring.[21]

This vignette suggests that changing social trends and new strategic moves affect multiple actors—not only rivals in direct competition, but also their suppliers, buyers, and substitutes. Must a firm wait until after the fact to predict the viability of competitive choices in such complex equations? Precise predictions are difficult, but estimates can be developed based on examining past competitive moves and their outcomes.

WHAT ARE GENERIC STRATEGIES FOR ACHIEVING COMPETITIVE ADVANTAGE?

Strategists who wish to enjoy the benefits of oligopoly must find a strategy that will protect their firm from powerful industry forces. This involves the development of a long-term, defensible source of competitive advantage. Porter's generic strategies framework, shown in Figure 5.7, was until recently seen as a guideline for developing that advantage. It still identifies competencies that are necessary to pursue these strategies, though few observers now think the framework is sufficient guidance on its own.

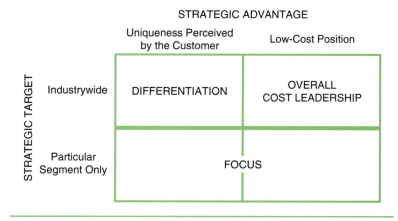

Figure 5.7 — Michael Porter's Generic Strategies Framework
Source: M. E. Porter, *Competitive Strategy* (New York: Free Press, 1980).

In this framework, the oligopolist's first choice (shown on the vertical dimension) concerns the marketplace. The business can attempt to serve the entire market or select a segment of buyers to address. The second choice (on the horizontal) is between taking either a low-cost position or developing uniqueness in buyers' eyes. Few firms have the resources to pursue multiple strategies at once, and Porter's significant contribution was to emphasize the importance of strategic clarity in making these one of decisions, which have implications for coordinating activities within the firm and for attracting the right customers.

Cost Leadership

The first strategic alternative attempts to achieve cost advantages relative to other producers so that the firm makes an above-average rate of return. A successful *cost leadership strategy* requires aggressive development of efficient-scale facilities and processes in order to produce a product or service at a lower cost than competitors must spend to provide the same benefit. Wal-Mart and Southwest Airlines both pursue this strategy with significant success.

Becoming the cost leader—the firm with the absolute lowest unit costs relative to all competitors in a given setting—is not, however, an easy strategy to implement, especially today, after many firms have developed quite sophisticated strategies for lowering cost. An especially important point, made by Professor John Kotter of Harvard Business School, among others, is that there is a distinct difference between being "cheap" and being the low-cost producer in a competitive setting. "Cheap is trying to get your prices down by nibbling costs off everything. If you're selling paper plates, you make them thinner. You hire people at minimum wage. Mindless stuff. But customers will eventually see the cheapness of it all. They'll notice that the paper plates don't work as well. They'll get tired of going into a grungy store with surly personnel, and they'll simply say to heck with it if they have an alternative."[22]

Successful low-cost producers recognize that they must succeed by being rigorously productive and efficient, which might mean spending more in some areas. For example, instead of buying used airplanes, Southwest Airlines has the newest and youngest fleet in the industry. That is expensive, but Southwest has traditionally bought only *one* type of aircraft, the Boeing 737, and this saves money on volume purchasing, pilot training, maintenance, spare parts inventory, and other activities.

Another company with a long-term cost leadership strategy is IKEA.

IKEA: Seating the World

Swedish retailer IKEA is known for its sleek, utilitarian flat-pack furniture. After IKEA designer Lars Engman's young daughter destroyed his high-priced Italian couch, he set about designing a more hard-wearing but still low-cost model with washable slip covers. The "Klippan" couch was first sold in 1980. Today, it retails for a little less than its original price. In the United States alone, over 1.5 million units were sold between 1998 and 2005.

The Klippan was initially manufactured entirely in Sweden, but later moved to lower-cost Poland, and now also sources from China. The Klippan frames are made of a mix of particleboard, fiberboard, and polyurethane foam. This composite is lighter than wood and has recently been developed so that it can be flat-packed. The flat packing saves 50 percent in shipping costs. IKEA continues to seek ways to save costs—such as centralizing slipcover production in four suppliers in Europe and China and cutting down the number of materials required to make the cushions. These changes have enabled IKEA to continue lowering the price of the Klippan.[23]

Differentiation

Differentiation strategies offer one or more unique attributes that buyers are willing to pay a price premium to receive.

Making your product or service stand out from the competition on the basis of features customers will pay more for is a very different strategy. *Differentiation* can come from many sources, including brand image, technology, features, customer service, dealer networks, and unique complementary support.[24] The objective is to provide a combination of attributes in the producing firm's product, service, or experience that will be recognized and valued by a specific set of buyers. Successful strategists will almost certainly spend more to provide this value, but they earn above-average industry profits because they can charge a price premium over cost.

Long-term success requires that the combination of factors used to achieve differentiation is difficult, if not impossible, to imitate by rivals. An offering can be differentiated many ways. Tangible features such as size, color, design, and weight are recognizable differences that can improve a product or service or make it more efficient. Other tangible differentiators include product complements such as pre-sales service (e.g., credit policies, accessories) and after-sales service (e.g., parts availability, upgrading options). Intangibles include distinctive qualities such as exclusivity, individuality, image, and security that the company is able to develop in the minds of buyers. Mercedes is an icon brand that has always relied on this strategy. It recently lost ground by extending its product line into lower priced and less differentiated products but is now paying increased attention to differentiation.

Mercedes-Benz: Driving Away the Brand?

Since 1902, Mercedes has built a reputation for premier, high-performance automobiles. By 2003, however, Mercedes-Benz had slumped to the bottom of the J. D. Power initial quality survey, in fourteenth place. One angry customer even set up a website, www.troublebenz.com, to document a host of quality problems in his new Mercedes-Benz, including broken door handles, faulty air-conditioning and heating, and early rust.

Mercedes was suffering from missteps at every stage of its value chain. First, engineers were dividing their attention between the high-end models and newer, less expensive models, such as the C-series. Second, Mercedes-Benz automobiles were among the most complicated to build, and even assembly line workers were regularly confused by the millions of customizable options on the shop floor. Finally, owners were also bewildered. The extensive manuals even documented how to flip down the sun visor! Mercedes-Benz needed a makeover.

In 2006, Mercedes-Benz introduced its latest in the S-class series of large luxury flagship sedans. To introduce the new model, Daimler-Chrysler CEO Dieter Zetsche donned a black leather jacket and rode into the Frankfurt auto show on a red American Jeep. Zetsche's bold statement was his first public signal for the makeover of Mercedes-Benz. He stated, "A brand is like a savings account, where you accumulate good experiences. We have pulled some assets out . . . and we expect to replace them with new products."

Zetsche initiated a company-wide quality-enhancing effort. Initiatives included eliminating more than 600 electronic functions in its cars that many owners didn't use, sharing a wider range of parts across the series of cars, upgrading components, and troubleshooting newly built cars. These efforts seem to be paying off, with Mercedes C-class and E-class cars tied for fifth place in the 2007 J. D. Power survey, even though there remain lingering problems with the dependability of older models.[24]

Focus

Focus strategies concentrate on achieving cost or differentiation advantages with a unique segment of the overall market.

The third generic strategy alternative relies on *focus*. This strategy targets a particular segment of the market. The firm's objective is to more efficiently and effectively meet the specific needs of this target group, thereby engendering buyer loyalty and above-average industry profits.

The trade-off for this strategy is usually a market share limited to the size of the specific buyer group. Within this limitation, profits can be significant. Consider the following differentiated-focus firm.

Orange County Choppers (OCC)

Paul Teutul started a steel fabrication business in the 1970s, but pursued his love of motorcycles by building them in his basement. In 1999, he introduced his first motorcycle, "True Blue," at the Daytona Biketo-berfest. In a few short years, he and his 28-year-old son Paul Jr. grew Orange County Choppers (OCC), which was recently voted a top twelve specialty maker in the United States by *American Iron Magazine,* a forum for Harley-Davidson's fans.

The motorcycle industry has seen its share of ups and downs: from 1.5 million new-unit sales in 1973 to only 480,000 in 1993. More recently, the industry has seen significant growth. There were 1.6 million units sold in 2002, mainly to an aging baby boomer population. After a peak in 2005, things started to slip again, decreasing dramatically by 2008 due to the slowdown in the American economy.

In this demanding industry, OCC follows a focused differentiation strategy based on quality and reputation; its specialty bikes cost as much as $200,000. To distinguish itself from other custom build firms, OCC features its business on the reality show *American Chopper*. Episodes aired over the last five years have followed the Teutuls as they seek inspiration for new bike designs, built them from scratch, and present them at bike shows. As a result of the show, the Teutuls and their business, located in Rock Tavern, New York, have gained celebrity status. Customers include musician Wyclef Jean and talk show host Jay Leno; orders are now coming in from all over the world.[25]

Combination Strategies

Porter argued in 1980 that firms not considering any of these three approaches, or firms attempting to pursue more than one of these strategies, would find themselves *stuck in the middle* and unable to realize profits above the industry average. Resource allocation choices would be muddled, thereby providing no real advantage to the firm in any of the three ways described. Externally, customers, suppliers, and others would be likely to receive confusing impressions.

Over time, however, strategists found that various combinations of these generic strategies were possible, and profitable. IKEA, with home furnishings stores around the globe, provides one good example. The firm focuses first on cost leadership, as we have just described, which is achieved though design, high volume, close connection with suppliers, and final assembly by the customer. But IKEA also offers distinctive, well-designed goods; it stands out from other low cost competitors at the bottom of the market for its quality and variety. Thus, one can see IKEA achieving advantage through cost leadership while pursuing a degree of differentiation at the same time. In part, this is a response to rivals who pursue differentiation as the basis of their advantage. By doing so, IKEA hopes that consumers will decide the premium price charged by more differentiated competitors is not worth the higher price.

Porter now describes successful combinations as seeking advantage on the basis of one strategy while pursuing parity on the other. Precisely because of competitor attention, all players attend to cost, differentiation, and focus. In some cases, however, this leads to homogenization of strategies within an industry, and this may trigger a state described as hypercompetition.

WHAT ARE THE CHARACTERISTICS OF HYPERCOMPETITION?

Keeping track of the competition is especially important in environments characterized by hypercompetition, which are quite different from the competitive environments we've just described. Here, rivals compete much more aggressively for market share, and their activities are deliberately difficult to anticipate. Other industry forces are likely to be apart of the picture. Suppliers may aggressively introduce new technologies. As barriers fall, potential entrants become a greater factor. Buyers are often informed but fickle. Complements, too, often want a greater piece of the action.

Two macro factors are especially implicated in creating this competitive landscape: new technology and globalization. Technological changes may erode many of the entry barriers that protect oligopolists. If new players find entry comparatively easy, and the profit picture looks good, competition can be expected to increase. In parallel, globalization eases access to many resources, including capital, and facilitates the entry of even more diverse, unpredictable players.

As we noted at the beginning of this chapter, Richard D'Aveni wrote *Hypercompetition: Managing the Dynamics of Strategic Maneuvering* in 1994. His description of competition is quite different from Porter's. D'Aveni suggested, "In hypercompetition the frequency, boldness, and aggressiveness of dynamic movement by the players accelerates to create a condition of constant disequilibrium and change. Market stability is threatened by short product life cycles, short product design cycles, new technologies, frequent entry by unexpected outsiders, repositioning by incumbents, and radical redefinitions of market boundaries as diverse industries merge. In other words, environments escalate toward higher and higher levels of uncertainty, dynamism, heterogeneity of the players, and hostility."[26]

The strategic advice offered by many observers of this kind of environment focuses on *attack*, not tacit collusion or *defense*. Cost and quality are still issues, but timing and know-how become more important as firms attempt to leapfrog each other.

Strategists have little time to enjoy profits from current success in this world; they often *cannibalize* current products to create new advantages. Nestlé's Nespresso machines, the result of significant investment, offer one example; the company hopes that upscale customers will buy its gourmet coffee capsules. Though it is a primarily a new market segment, it decreases the attraction of Nestlé's other coffee products.

It should be clear that descriptions of hypercompetition are quite different from Porter's 1980 description of oligopoly. The comparison of the two viewpoints in Table 5.2 emphasizes some of the most important differences.

Cannibalization strategies drop currently profitable offerings infavor of replacements that typically precede market demand.

TABLE 5.2 DIFFERENCES BETWEEN OLIGOPOLY & HYPERCOMPETITION

Element	Porter/Oligopoly	D'Aveni/ Hypercompetition
Sustainability of competitive advantage	Long-lasting	Temporary
Competition	Avoid	Embrace
Stability of marketplace	Stable; equilibrium	Disequilibrium; instability

(continued)

TABLE 5.2 (CONTINUED)

Element	Porter/Oligopoly	D'Aveni/ Hypercompetition
Focus	External (on markets)	Internal (on firms)
Strategy	Defend; cooperate	Attack; disrupt rivals
Source of competitive advantage	External to firm	Internal to firm

Table 5.2 shows that the two authors begin with fundamentally different assumptions about rivalry and the ability and speed of firms to adjust to one another's strategic initiatives. Porter assumes that once a competitive advantage has been created, it can be defended through the use of entry barriers discouraging rival firms from imitation over extended periods of time. D'Aveni refuses to embrace that fundamental assumption about the possibility of oligopoly, arguing that imitation is inevitable and rapid.

The point to recognize is that the approaches are incompatible. A strategist involved in a hypercompetitive environment who attempts to play an oligopoly game (erect entrance barriers, tacitly collude with rivals) is destined to fail. D'Aveni argues that in an oligopoly situation, if even one firm in the industry chooses to play by hypercompetitive rules, then all firms in the industry may be forced to play. He maintains that more and more industries are becoming hypercompetitive as technology and globalization increase overall levels of competition across industries.

But this transition may be reversible. Returning to the Pirelli example, the tire industry in the 1960s and 1970s represented a classic oligopoly. A few large, global players dominated markets and prices. However, as D'Aveni would predict, the movement from bias-ply to radial tire technology initiated a major change in the competitive environment. The longer-lasting radial design caused significant oversupply in the industry. Exit costs were high, however, and firms attempted to remain in the market even as profits evaporated and losses were counted in the hundreds of millions of dollars. Conditions associated with hypercompetition reigned for more than a decade.

Over time, however, consolidation among stronger firms, accompanied by the closure of older, less efficient factories, returned the industry to profitability and a more oligopolistic orientation. Many industries illustrate this movement between oligopoly and hypercompetition over time. The tire industry may be heading toward another tough period in which successful strategists will have to change their strategic logic once again.[27]

WHEN DO COMPETITORS COLLABORATE?

Much of the material we have reviewed in this chapter has a distinctly combatant tone. Perhaps you found this a little out of touch with the current times. We do too. Alliances are more and more central to organizations, a subject considered in more detail in upcoming chapters. The fall of Enron and other organizations has spurred executives and boards of directors to consider whether making a profit is their only goal. To effectively think about emerging competitive environments, new models are needed. In short, an important idea that needs to be added to the discussion so far involves *collaboration*, a word that comes from the Latin *collaborare*, "work together".[28]

Spontaneous Collaboration

Collaboration strategies involve working with others (including suppliers, buyers, complements, and competitors) to achieve mutually valued objectives.

We believe that people have an innate capacity for generosity without gain, and they naturally work with others—capabilities that strategists and those who study them have largely ignored as potential advantages in the last few decades focused almost exclusively on profit. Collaboration exists in many different forms in our day-to-day lives, but it is put into sharper focus when the day to day is disrupted.

Hurricane Katrina Creates the Opportunity to Serve Others

Uncertainty increases the pain of those struck by natural disaster. After Katrina hit New Orleans and surrounding areas, many volunteers responded. Some invented new ways to decrease the difficulties of families trying to reconnect with each other and find shelter.

On September 3, 2005, four days after the hurricane struck and the scope of the disaster had become increasingly evident, Texas-based nonprofit activist David Geilhufe realized the incredible inefficiency of Internet postings on the Red Cross website, Yahoo, and other locations by people trying to find loved ones. Using an automated process called "screen scraping," he organized a team of volunteers to create a centralized database that could systematically list name, location, age, and other descriptive information about missing people.

Geilhufe's PeopleFinder was quickly overloaded. A key problem was that those trying to make connection didn't have time, training, or equipment for standardized inputs. More than 3,000 additional volunteers got involved, enlisted primarily by bloggers. Eight days after the hurricane hit, more than 50,000 entries had been processed, and the number of entries to www.katrinalist.net continued to rise.

Meanwhile, in Utah, www.katrinahousing.org was started barely forty-eight hours after the storm. This site linked those evacuated with rooms across the country. Within two weeks, volunteers provided shelter for more than 5,000 people—another example among many others of not only generous but effective spontaneous response.

Of course, the communications links required to make PeopleFinder and the housing site helpful had been blown away. But other individuals and groups improvised wireless networks, brought computers, supplied voice over IP phones, and installed low-power radio stations on site. An estimated 2,600 pounds of equipment was shipped to the region within days.[29]

Writing about this cooperative effort in *Discover* magazine, Steven Johnson concludes, that "Grassroots efforts can replace certain government tasks when disaster strikes. We still need authorities to pull people out of toxic waters, repair levees, and keep order. But when it comes to good information, I suspect that . . . grassroots networkers will be as important [as government efforts], if not more so. . . . [T]hey are the true first responders."[30] We would draw an even larger conclusion. Information needs in for-profit organizations and nondisaster situations also benefit from the immediate inputs of informal and spontaneous networks. Virtually all formal systems need to improve their capacity for collaboration and must make room for informal collaboration as well.

Formal Collaboration

The achievements in lowering the cost of goods and services and in increasing their innovative content described in previous sections of this chapter often rely on closer relations with industry partners. For example:

- *Just-in-time manufacturing* cannot be carried out without close information links between the producer, the user, and any required intermediaries. As we discussed in Chapter 3, continuous and successful interaction is hard to maintain within an adversarial frame of mind. Many organizations have had to move away from a combative military mindset.
- *Research and development* is another high-cost, high-risk area in which firms are finding it advantageous to include areas of expertise they do not chose to control directly. Especially when they are following an exploration strategy, firms may even include competitors in their networks.

Clearly these activities involve gain, but their success depends on a different calculus than the strategies we have discussed so far. Although rivalry has to be kept in mind when interacting with competitors, important gains can be made through collaboration. For example, collaborators can help develop industry standards that maintain buyer confidence. Players also share the risk when moving into new markets. Finally, collaborations can help fortify barriers to entry. Perhaps the greatest challenge for today's business strategists is to consider how to collaborate with an organization that remains a competitor for industry profits. But this is exactly what strategists are learning to do in increasingly complex relationships.

Collaboration across Industries

Firms can also collaborate across industry borders. For example:

- *Community contributions* recognize that organizations are "citizens" with responsibilities at local, state, regional, national, and international levels. Companies expected to cooperate in time of disaster, as the response to Katrina helps illustrate.
- *Interest group participation* involves organizations banding together to influence government policy (including international organizations such as the World Trade Organization and the World Bank). These alliances can be formed within one industry or across players with similar interests.

We will give more attention to collaborative strategies in Chapter 7's discussion of corporate strategies. As an introduction, consider the many forms of collaboration shown in Table 5.3.

TABLE 5.3 EXAMPLES OF COLLABORATIVE ARRANGEMENTS

	Noncontractual Arrangements	Contractual Arrangements	Equity-Based Arrangements
Multilateral Arrangements	**Lobbying coalition** (e.g., European Roundtable of Industrialists) **Joint standard setting** (e.g., Linux coalition) **Learning communities** (e.g., Strategic Management Society)	**Research consortia** (e.g., Symbian in PDAs) **International marketing** (e.g., Star Alliance) **Export partnership** (e.g., Netherlands Export Combination)	**Shared payment system** (e.g., Visa) **Construction consortium** (e.g., Eurotunnel) **Joint reservation system** (e.g., Galileo)
Bilateral Arrangements	**Cross-selling deal** (e.g., between pharmaceutical firms) **R&D staff exchange** (e.g., between IT firms) **Market information sharing agreement** (e.g., between hardware and software makers)	**Licensing agreement** (e.g., Disney and Coca-Cola) **Co-development contract** (e.g., Disney and Pixar in movies) **Co-branding alliance** (e.g., Coca-Cola and McDonalds)	**New product joint venture** (e.g., Phillips and Nike in MP3 players) **Cross-border joint venture** (e.g., Eu-Man in training) **Local joint venture** (e.g., CNN Turk in Turkey)

Source: R. Meyer, *Mapping the Mind of the Strategist*, dissertation, Erasmus Research Institute of Management (Rotterdam, The Netherlands: Erasmus University, 2007), p. 146.

Most of these cooperative agreements are formed by competitors, and Meyer notes that "firms constantly struggle with the tension created by the need to work *together with others*, while simultaneously needing to pursue their *own interests.*"[31]

CONCLUSIONS FOR THE STRATEGIST

This chapter presents complex and basically incompatible views of rivalry. We can't apologize. Competition *is* a complex subject. In the oligopolistic world Michael Porter described in the 1980s, many strategists in the Western world hoped to create a competitive advantage that would generate a stream of profits over quite a long period of time. Eventual erosion had to be expected through imitation by rivals and claims to a larger share of the pie by other actors in the industry, but strategists could point to a variety of defensive and offensive moves that might be effective deterrents.

In the following years, sustained advantage often proved to be elusive. As the world economy globalizes and interactions among different kinds of economic systems increases, definitions of *industry* have often been blurred by complex activities of increasingly varied participants. In hypercompetitive environments, including the one that seems to be developing among Google, Microsoft, and other players, profits are more difficult to capture and sustain. The most effective strategy is to constantly create new sources of competitive advantage before your rivals can fully imitate your position. These activities may allow a firm to retain a high stream of profits, but innovation is risky and failure rates are high. That is why oligopoly is still so attractive and a major part of the industry evolution stories outlined in the next chapter.

Key Concepts

This chapter focuses on **competitive environments**—the conditions under which a company vies with other firms for profits and other desired outcomes. Though we recognize that boundaries are sometimes hard to identify, we also note that firms offering very similar products and services are called **industries**. Strategists often conduct an **industry analysis** to assess a specific competitive environment, including the financial health of firms in the industry.

Two kinds of competitive environments are particularly interesting. An **oligopoly** exists when a few rivals compete for buyers in relatively predictable ways. Firms operating in a **hypercompetitive** environment face more demanding conditions. This kind of environment exists when a significant number of rivals compete intensely and less predictably for competitive advantage.

Collusion takes place when actors coordinate their activities to their mutual advantage. While many countries restrict collusive behavior, **tacit collusion** is achieved without direct communication and can be difficult to prevent.

We spent significant time looking at six forces that compete for the profit made within an industry—suppliers, rivals, buyers, complements, substitutes, and new entrants. Rivalry is likely to be high among producing firms in less profitable industries when there are high **barriers to**

exit that increase the cost of leaving an industry. Suppliers are likely to capture a larger share of available profits if they dominate producers, which is likely to happen if buyers face high **switching costs** to change suppliers. The reverse logic holds when producing firms interact with their own buyers. These buyers are relatively powerful when they are larger, have more information, have low switching costs, and so on.

Rivals spend a good deal of time creating **barriers to entry** that increase the cost of competition for potential entrants and thus decrease the likelihood of sharing profits with additional players. One especially important barrier is **retaliation,** the willingness of current incumbents to reduce their profits in response to competitive moves, including entry. The chapter describes power inequalities that result from differences in size, access to information, ability to coordinate activities, ability to imitate, and other factors.

Strategic groups are subsets of firms in an industry that follow similar strategies. Within these groups and the larger industry, **asymmetries** are differences among firms that explain difference in profitability.

Generic strategies proposed by Michael Porter have had considerable influence on competition since 1980. A **cost leadership strategy** provides value to customers at lower cost than competitors' costs. A **differentiation** strategy offers one or more unique attributes that buyers are willing to pay a price premium to receive. A **focus** strategy concentrates on achieving cost or differentiation advantages with a unique subset of the overall market.

Porter argued that strategists will be **stuck in the middle** if they try to simultaneously implement more than one of these strategies, but over time some firms have had success doing so. In most industries today, all firms have to pay attention to basic principles of cost containment, product differentiation, and making differentiated offerings to at least some customers.

In conditions of hypercompetition, information about and analysis of rival firms that can be used to predict their activities becomes increasingly important. It is more likely that strategists will **cannibalize** currently profitable products by producing improvements ahead of market demand.

The chapter concludes, however, with a reminder that **collaboration** strategies that involve working with others to achieve mutually valued objectives—an increasingly important aspect of competitive environments.

Questions for Further Reflection

1. Identify an organization or unit of a larger operation that you would like to work for. Describe the "industry" within which it competes and the competitive advantage that the firm has or is trying to develop in this setting. What does this analysis suggest for the development of your own skills?

2. Identify the major competitors for an academic institution you have attended and describe its major competitors. How have

these organizations attempted to differentiate themselves? Can you identify additional strategies that might put your university or college in a better position?

3. Describe primary players in the personal computer market (Sony, HP, Dell, etc.). Pick at least two and consider how they are trying to create asymmetries between themselves and other producers. Are your two competitors differentially impacted by the increasing computing power of mobile telephones?

4. Reread the opening description of GEMAYA (Google, eBay, MSN, Amazon, Yahoo, and AOL). Analyze the power of one of these players over smaller firms. How do you characterize the current environment they helped establish (oligopoly, hyper-competition, or coopetition)? How do you expect this competitive environment to change in the next five years, and why?

WORKSHEET 5.1
Industry Analysis—A Tool for Analyzing Industry Forces

Consider how industry forces interact and have an impact on the competitive environment.

Step 1: Identify a firm that interests you.

Step 2: Identify the industry or industries within which this firm competes.

Step 3: Select one of these environments and describe the relative power of each industry force in column 1.

Step 4: Consider how much relative power your particular firm has with respect to each force in column 2.

Step 5: Consider the industry changes that might change industry structure in column 3, underlining those that would be most problematic for your firm.

Industry Forces Worksheet 5.1	Firm:
Analyst(s):	**Industries within Which the Firm Competes (underline the one to be analyzed):**

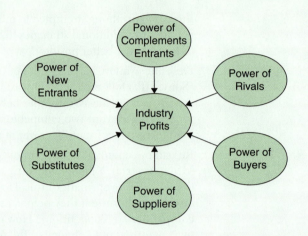

Industry Forces	Current Power within the Industry (Impact on Profits)	Power of Your Firm with Respect to Industry Force	Impact of Possible Change in the Macro Environment
Rivals			
Buyers			
Suppliers			
Substitutes			
New Entrants			
Complements			

This worksheet will help you use STEP analysis to consider how macro environment forces interact with and have an impact on the competitive environment.

Step 1: Identify an industry.

Step 2: Identify specific macro factors affecting your industry in column 1.

Step 3: Specify industry forces (buyers, suppliers, etc.) that have been most affected by each force in column 2.

Step 4: Anticipate future changes in either macro factor or affected industry force in column 3.

Macro Environment (STEP) Analysis Worksheet 5.2	Industry:
Analyst(s):	Summary:

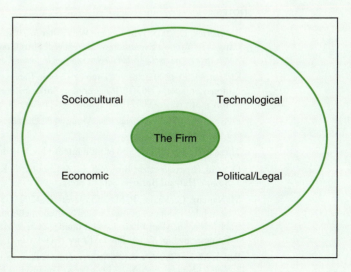

Macro Environment Force	Specific Factors Affecting the Industry	Impacts on Specific Industry Forces	Possible Future Changes in Environment or Industry Force
Sociocultural environment			
Technological environment			
Economic environment			
Political/legal environment			

NOTES

[1] Kirkpatrick, D. 2005. Why Google Will Falter in 2006: 8 Predictions for Tech, Including Why Yahoo's Expansion of Search Will Hurt Google. *Fortune* (December 19). *http://money.cnn.com/2005/12/19/technology/google_fortune/*, accessed January 21, 2008.

[2] Kirkpatrick, D. (2007). Tech's Time of Tumult. *Fortune* (October 19). http://money.cnn.com/2007/10/19/technology/kirkpatrick_global_tech.fortune/index.htm?postversion=2007101912, accessed January 21, 2008.

[3] D'Aveni, R. 1994. *Hypercompetition: Managing the Dynamics of Strategic Maneuvering.* New York: Free Press, p. 28.

[4] These environments are also of little interest because they have largely been privatized.

[5] D'Aveni, *Hypercompetition;* Brown, S. L., & Eisenhardt, K. M. 1998. *Competing on the Edge.* Boston: Harvard Business School Press.

[6] McNamara, G., Vaaler, P. M., and Devers, C. (2003). Same as It Ever Was: The Search for Evidence of Increasing Hypercompetition. *Strategic Management Journal* 24: 261–278. MacMillan, I., van Putten, A. G., & McGrath, R. G. 2003. Global Gamesmanship. *Harvard Business Review* (May): 62–71.

[7] Porter, M. E. 1980. *Competitive Strategy.* New York: Free Press; Porter, M. E. 1985. *Competitive Advantage.* New York: Free Press. The insights in these books have been broadly

applied, even in public and not-for-profit settings, though they require adjustment to the unique circumstances of missions that do not revolve around economic profit.

[8]http://en.wikipedia.org/wiki/Trust_%2819th_century%29, accessed May 20, 2007.

[9]Grove, A. 2000. Keynote address, Harvard International Conference on Internet and Society (June 2), Cambridge, MA. http://www.intel.com/pressroom/archive/speeches/ag060200.htm, accessed May 21, 2007.

[10]Grove, A. 1996. *Only the Paranoid Survive.* Boston: Harvard Business School Press. The preface is available at http://www.intel.com/pressroom/kits/bios/grove/paranoid.htm, accessed May 21, 2007.

[11]Many sites provide company and industry analyses, usually for a fee. There are also sites that provide analytic tools. See, for example, http://www.ventureline.com, accessed March 8, 2008.

[12]Reger, R. K., & Huff, A. S. 1993. Strategic Groups: A Cognitive Perspective. *Strategic Management Journal* 14: 103–124.

[13]Re-Inventing the Wheel. 2000. *The Economist* (April 22–28): 57–58; *European Rubber Journal*, various issues (April 2002, p. 28; July–August 2002, p. 30; May 2004, p. 7; June 2004, p. 6; September 2004, p. 11; November 2004, p. 12); *Tire Business*, various issues (vol. 20, no. 24, p. 4; vol. 22, no. 11, p. 24; vol. 22, no. 17, p. 3); http://www.pirelli.com/en_42/this_is_pirelli/company_overview/the_group/the_group.jhtml, accessed March 8, 2008.

[14]Frazao, E. (ed.). 1999. *America's Eating Habits: Changes and Consequences.* Economic Research Service, U.S. Department of Agriculture, p. 237.

[15]See discussion and associated links at http://en.wikipedia.org/wiki/European_Union_Microsoft_antitrust_case, accessed May 20, 2007.

[16]See http://ec.europa.eu/food/food/biotechnology/index_en.htm, accessed May 20, 2007.

[17]Rumelt, R. 1979. Evaluation of Strategy: Theory and Models. In D. E. Schendel & C. Hofer (eds.), *Strategic Management: A New View of Business Policy and Planning.* Boston: Little, Brown, pp. 196–217.

[18]Rumelt, Evaluation of Strategy, p. 203.

[19]http://www.hoovers.com/shaw-industries/--ID__11345--/free-co-profile.xhtml, accessed January 27, 2008.

[20]Hagerty, J. R. 1998. Carpet Makers Confront Era That Extols Wood Floors. *Wall Street Journal* (March 31).

[21]http://www.hoovers.com/shaw-industries/--ID__11345--/free-co-profile.xhtml, accessed January 27, 2008.

[22]Ballon, M. 1997. The Cheapest CEO in America. *Inc.* (October).

[23]What a Sweetheart of a Love Seat. 2005. *Business Week* (November 14). http://www.businessweek.com/magazine/content/05_46/b3959008.htm, accessed May 20, 2007. The story is widely told. See it, for example, in a newsletter from IKEA's Singapore store at http://www.ikea-friends.com/enewsletter/2007/eNewsletter_mar2007.pdf, accessed May 20, 2007.

[24]Taylor, A. 2005. Buffing Up a Faded Star: Mercedes Has Boosted the Quality of Its New Models, but Owners Are Still Mad about the Other Ones. Can the Brand Regain Its Luster? *Fortune* (October 19). http://www.whatcar.co.uk/news-special-report.aspx?NA=225557&EL=3196978, accessed May 20, 2007.

[25]http://dsc.discovery.com/fansites/amchopper/amchopper.html, accessed March 8, 2008. http://www.orangecountychoppers.com/occ/index.html, accessed May 6, 2008.

[26]D'Aveni, R. 2002. Competitive Pressure Systems: Mapping and Measuring Multi-Market Contact. *Sloan Management Review* 44(1): 39–49; Stalk, G., Jr., & Lachenauer, R.

2004. Hard Ball: Five Killer Strategies for Trouncing the Competition. *Harvard Business Review* (April): 62–71. For a study of rivalry in the airline industry, see Baum, J. A. C., & Korn, H. J. 1996. Competitive Dynamics of Interfirm Rivalry. *Academy of Management Journal* 39: 255–291. See also Chen, M.-J. 1996. Competitor Analysis and Interfirm Rivalry: Toward a Theoretical Integration. *Academy of Management Review* 21: 100–134.

[27] http://www.askoxford.com, accessed November 21, 2005.

[28] Johnson, S. B. 2005. Emerging Technology: Ordinary People Can Solve Communication Problems Much Quicker Than Clueless Government Officials When Catastrophes Like Hurricane Katrina Strike. *Discover* (January 12). http://discovermagazine.com/2005/dec/emerging-technology, May 21, 2007.

[29] Johnson, Emerging Technology.

[30] Meyer, R. 2007. *Mapping the Mind of the Strategist*. Dissertation, Erasmus Research Institute of Management. Rotterdam, The Netherlands: Erasmus University, p. 147.

6

Specifying a Business Model

→ → →

A a student of strategy, you probably think about how to maximize your performance in many different areas of life. We are not just talking about doing well in sports, of course. Personal strategists consider many areas of activity. You almost certainly compare your success and lack of success to how well people around you are doing—perhaps that's also caused your goals to change. This chapter provides a similar overview of how strategists focus on business performance and compare it with performance by other firms.

In previous chapters we have established the need to consider organizational resources, customer needs and interests, entrepreneurial opportunities, and rivals. Now we emphasize synthesizing these concerns in a business model that defines how sufficient profits will be made to survive and hopefully prosper. Business models can be crucial for obtaining external funding and are equally helpful in coordinating employee, supplier, buyer, and stakeholder activities. Many not-for-profit organizations also use business model logic to establish their economic viability.

. . . .

Those who study strategy have identified a number of business models with remarkable resilience, though of course strategists must update models that worked well in the past. The following pages expand on these observations by considering the following questions:

What are common business models?
  Subscription model
  Razor-and-blades model
  Broker, advertising, community, and other models
  First mover, second mover, reinventor
How can value chain analysis contribute to strategic change?
  Linking value chain activities
  Deconstructing the value chain
How can the life cycle be used as a source of business model ideas?
  Stage 1: birth of a new offering
  Stage 2: systems
  Stage 3: solutions
  Stage 4: relationships

What can be learned from competitors, customers, and others?
   Franchise model
   Promising practices
   Open innovation
How do business plans differ from business models?

A common observation is that over time competition in profitable markets tends to increase, weaker companies are pushed out, and profits accrue to a smaller number of large firms with niche players around them. Many competitive environments could be used as illustration. We begin with a brief example about increasing competition in the video game industry.

CONSOLES: A FIERCELY COMPETITIVE GAME

Although it was once considered a hobby market, the computer and video gaming industry generated almost $18 billion in revenues in 2007, up 43 percent from 2006—stronger growth than perhaps any other entertainment sector. The game console market emerged in the early 1980s with the release of consoles by Nintendo and Atari and is now dominated by Sony, Microsoft, and Nintendo. Firms compete on their technology. The current console war for primacy and market saturation is the most hotly contested in recent console history. All three firms have announced new consoles in the last few years, using varying strategies.

Sony has dominated the market. Its strong consumer base is complemented by countless third-party developers of new software. The PlayStation 2 can play DVDs and is backward compatible, providing a back catalog of games even before it was released. The firm's strategy with PlayStation 3 continues to draw on its deep strength in gaming technology. The new model was launched in November 2006; 7.6 million units were sold in 2007.

Since 2003, newcomer Microsoft has established a recognizable fan base around the world. Luckily its entry into the console industry was subsidized by other business lines; Microsoft consoles lost money for the first two years. Microsoft's Xbox 360 was named so that consumers would think of it as a third-generation system. It was announced two weeks before Sony's and Nintendo's latest models at a televised MTV event—the kind of pre-emptive strike for which the firm is well known. In 2007 the system outsold the PlayStation 3 at 8.2 million units.

For some time Nintendo has been described as struggling with a conflicting brand image because its family-friendly image from the 1990s is not as cool as that of other players. Still, Nintendo has sold more than 22 million GameCube consoles, a system that plays newly released games but also enables users to download nearly thirty years of games, satisfying "old-school" gamers. However, its new console, Wii (pronounced "we" for readers who are oblivious to this industry), is the 2007 winner. Wii has three-dimensional motion-sensing controllers and the ability to receive messages from the Internet in standby mode.

The Wii was released in November 2006; Nintendo sold 1.1 million units by the end of the year. In 2007 more than 16 million units were sold.

Who has the winning approach? Popular games for all three machines made 2007 a banner year and illustrate the power of the "razor-and-blades" business model described shortly. Prediction for success is difficult, however, because the demographics of gaming are changing. Hard-core game players are getting older; more women are becoming involved. "Social games" are becoming popular. The route to long-term profits is not clearly marked.[1]

WHAT ARE COMMON BUSINESS MODELS?

Business models summarize how strategic decisions are expected to make a profit.

We emphasize *business models* in this book because many companies develop promising strategies but do not survive. They may begin with a terrific idea and have the resources to develop a working prototype, for example, but find they cannot produce it at the scale the market requires. Or they jump both of these hurdles but cannot generate sufficient sales to cover their costs. There are many possible scenarios for failure and a smaller number of winning propositions. Sony, Microsoft, and Nintendo have different strategies, for example, but the business model that will support longer-term survival is not yet clear.

A business model is a simplification of the primary elements of strategy, as represented by the interlocking puzzle pieces in Figure 6.1. It should describe how revenues will exceed the costs of being in a competitive environment.

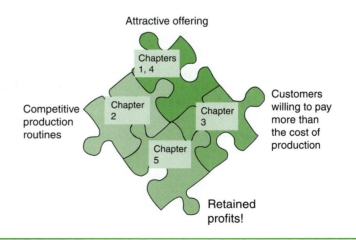

Figure 6.1 — Business Model Basics

Profit is not necessarily an organization's only objective, as we have tried to make clear throughout this book. Interestingly, however, even organizations that intend to contribute to the social good must think about where the resources to stay alive will come from. A business model accounts for how incoming resources will exceed costs incurred, despite the activities of rivals—which almost all organizations have. As briefly discussed at the end of the chapter, the business model must be distinguished from a *business plan*, which is a more formal and complete document meant to reassure strategists that key issues have been considered, and in turn attract partners and financing.

> **Business plans are a more complete overview of company activities, followed by detailed financial analysis.**

Novel business models are relatively rare. Even a company established around a new invention, such as Napster, typically follows patterns of activity made familiar by previous companies. Napster.com currently charges a monthly fee for downloads; it is using a subscription model.

Subscription Model

The subscription model was developed more than a century ago by companies selling magazines and newspapers. The basic idea is that customers pay a periodic fee for access to a specified good, service, or experience. Book clubs, cable television, cell phone providers, fitness clubs, and many other firms follow the money-making logic of this model, as does your landlord and utility company. The attractive feature of this model is that strategists can calculate costs based on a known number of buyers and set rates accordingly. That can be a major advantage compared to the uncertainties of engaging customers for a single purchase.

A second advantage comes to sellers who offer upgraded services for a price (such as extra movie channels from television services). The company can target buyers much more easily than the firm trying to make onetime "cold" contacts because a relationship has already been established.

Customers can win as well. They often value the convenience of an established contact (think about having to reconsider housing every month!). The customer loses, however, if a paid-for offering is not used (time-share resorts come to mind as a possible example). In some cases the subscription model allows customers to afford goods they might not be able to buy outright (leased cars provide a well-known example, but we didn't realize until we were working on this chapter that it is possible to lease fancy handbags for important occasions as well).[2] Netflix is another example of a subscription that many readers are likely to have tried.

Netflix Improves on an Established Business Model

Netflix offered a variety of monthly subscription rates to almost 8 million subscribers in 2007. The rate determines how many DVDs (TV shows or independent films) the user may keep at one time. As soon as one DVD is returned, the next in a user-determined list is dispatched by mail. It is a big operation. In mid-2007 Netflix shipped approximately 1.6 million DVDs a day and announced that it had posted more than a billion DVDs to subscribers to date. Not bad for a 9-year-old company.

That's the kind of business that invites imitators and can change industry practice. Wal-Mart tried the idea in 2002, but bowed out in favor of a cross-promotional deal with Netflix. Blockbuster, a company that prospered for years by renting tapes for short periods and collecting late fees from those who did get them back in time, began offering a flat-rate subscription by mail in 2004. Other video rental stores, such as Hollywood Video, also moved to a flat-rate scheme for the walk-in trade. It is nice to have the movie in hand when you want it, but these stores (like brick-and-mortar bookstores) can maintain an inventory that is only a fraction of the vast stock Netflix offers.

Though it follows a well-known subscription model, Netflix's processes are innovative enough that the firm has been awarded business model patents on its "dynamic queuing" system and its methods of communication and delivery. Those patents are the basis of a lawsuit filed against Blockbuster, which has not been resolved as we write this short description.[3]

Netflix's profit, as with all subscription models, requires attention to inventory and logistics. But frequent users definitely cost more than the price of subscription. The company gives priority shipping to customers who use their service least often. The "throttling" of frequent users through slower returns led to a court case in 2004 that was ultimately settled without Netflix admitting wrongdoing.

The company faces new competitors Redbox (the company delivering recent DVDs in retail outlets like McDonalds) and on–demand movies from Amazon and iTunes. The business model is still unique, however. Netflix has been praised for its contribution to the distribution of independent films. In fact, it is a good example of making a profit from what Chris Anderson calls "the Long Tail."[4] In brief, Anderson observes that the bulk of many markets revolve around a small number of products (this month's movie hits, for example), but the total market is much larger. Increased choice, which Netflix can provide from centralized locations, significantly expands the number of customers it serves. These buyers/subscribers have specialized interests that a brick-and-mortar store cannot afford to serve. Netflix does so without significantly increasing its costs. It is a basic idea behind many Internet businesses and a logic well worth developing.[5]

Razor-and-Blades Model

Another well-known business model is named after the Gillette company's idea of selling razor handles relatively cheaply at the beginning of the 1900s. The profit was made from the disposable razor—a repeat purchase for a relatively small price that produced significant income for the company for many years.

You are a contributor to profit from this business model if you buy a game console: anticipated profits come primarily from premium games sold by the manufacturer, even though other vendors increase the attraction. You are involved in the same game if you buy a printer and then purchase ink cartridges. The cell phone you bought is relatively cheap, because of the airtime contract you signed. The phone plus contract is a good example of combining a subscription model with the razor-and-blades idea. TV dishes are sold following the same logic. Once again, the business model explains how a company intends to make a profit.

Broker, Advertising, Community, and Other Models

In the past, businesses were often categorized as manufacturing or service organizations. We all know that this line is blurring. Many manufacturers are bundling services into their products. Instead of simply shipping goods, they are supporting customer use of their products. New product-service combinations require new business models facilitated by the latest information and communication technology. Business models must also change when companies focus on customer experience.

There is a propensity to think that the Internet is accelerating this trend and generating many new models for doing business. Often, however, old models are merely being recycled and revised as markets evolve. Google, for example, is a very new idea, but it makes money by combining a brokerage model with an advertising model.

Brokers are paid to bring people and organizations together. Travel agents and real estate agents are brokers. So are eBay and PayPal. The Internet has undercut the viability of some older broker models (many travel agents have gone out of business, for example) while creating a landscape where other brokers have emerged (www.kayak.com. and other sites quickly search for the lowest airfare available among many sites, while "consolidators" such as www.airgorilla.com make a limited number of airplane seats from established carriers available at a discount).[6] Often revenues are increased by including advertising on the site. For another example, consider Joost.

> ### Choosing an Advertising Model over a Subscription Model
>
> Joost was formed by Niklas Zennstrom and Janus Friis, digital entrepreneurs who had previous experience in the communications industry. They founded the free Internet phone service Skype, which eBay picked up for $2.6 billion in 2005. Before that, they created Kazaa, a firm reviled for the way it encouraged the unprofitable sharing of music files over the Internet. (It was shut down by court order.)
>
> In 2006 they moved to free TV, and commercial interests were paramount. They are trying to merge familiar TV format and content with

familiar Internet tools such as instant messaging and chat that will allow people to share the TV experience. How will the company survive? Executive vice president of content strategy and acquisition Yvette Alberdingk Thijm said Joost will run traditional thirty-second TV spots, in addition to unique ads, including one advertising unit she described as a "hand raiser," in which the ad drifts across the screen.

Thijm also said that Joost plans to bank on ad revenue to build its business, and—like broadcast TV—won't charge subscription fees for content. "We have no plans to do a subscription [service]. We really thought long and hard about the business model, and we believe that there is a huge market for long-form, free-to-the-user video; professionally produced storytelling."[7]

That confidence had lost some luster by the beginning of 2008. The devotion to full-length programs and respecting copyrights brought notable partners, including CBS, but critics complain that alternatives such as YouTube are more convenient. Content quality is also a concern: AOL's Hulu offers *Heroes, Survivor, The Simpsons,* and other popular shows.

Some question how many people want to watch full-length shows on their computers, and many complain that they are not able to interact as they expected on Joost—for example, users cannot develop their own programming sequences.

Equally problematic, a growing number of competitors are offering alternatives. The most promising seem to come from P2P sites in China, where Joost has also made an entry. Clearly the winning business model has not yet been proven.[8]

The Joost story suggests that selecting a business model and winning much more difficult. Yet many approaches are similar to ideas developed before the Internet, as can be seen in Michael Rappa's taxonomy of business options in Table 6.1.

TABLE 6.1 INTERNET BUSINESS MODELS

Business Model	Description	Examples
Brokerage	Brokers are market makers who bring buyers and sellers together and facilitate exchanges	ebay.com, carsdirect.com
Advertising	An extension of the classic media model: provides free content mingled with advertising	google.com, yahoo.com, buy.com
Infomediary	Provides a valuable product or service in exchange for detailed buying information	nytimes.com
Merchant	"E-tailers"—classic wholesalers and retailers	amazon.com, walmart.com

(continued)

TABLE 6.1 (CONTINUED)

Business Model	Description	Examples
Manufacturer	Producers circumvent wholesalers and retailers by approaching buyers directly through the Internet	dell.com
Affiliate	Sites provide click-through to merchant sites, receiving a share of the revenue in exchange	yahoo.com, cnn.com
Community	Loyal users return frequently for information or services	npr.com
Subscription	Users pay a fee to access the site for information or products	wsj.com
Utility	Metered usage or pay-as-you-go	authentica.com

Source: M. Rappa, Business Models on the Web (October 15, 2000), http://digitalenterprise.org/models/models.html, April 7, 2008.

It is worth highlighting community models as a relatively novel business idea because they do not focus on profit. The development of Linux is one well-known example; Habitat for Humanity is another. The gain may be the satisfaction of doing something for others or the pleasure of interacting with like-minded individuals. Those who contribute may also be motivated by the challenge of the tasks involved or reputation gained from contribution.

Additional models can be found for Internet businesses. For example, auctions have been revitalized via the Internet, which provides increased liquidity to the bidding process. As a result, companies like eBay have generated many new business opportunities. In addition to the possibilities for selling goods, consider the opportunities of a business model that offers complementary services. For example, money can be made by firms that facilitate the process of valuing goods, verifying their condition, handing payments, packing, and shipping. The cost advantages include relatively low costs (eBay provides helpful tools), but it is necessary to attract customers when so many purchasing options are available and to price shipping and handling in a way that is competitive but still leaves a profit. Amazon and many other sites offer reselling, as well as affiliate programs, with similar trade-offs.

First-mover advantages reap the benefits of early entry into an emerging market.

First Mover, Second Mover, Reinventor

We discussed *first-mover* advantages in Chapter 5, but the idea is worth another look as a business model. The basic logic is simple: the company that innovates has an opportunity to shape a new market, build reputation, learn from its early activities, and become more efficient than latecomers. A good example is IKEA, a firm that initiated many new ideas about making and selling furniture.

IKEA's First-Mover Advantage

IKEA offered its first furniture catalog in 1951, pioneering the idea of selling furniture in flatbox packages to be assembled by the customer. The company, owned by a nonprofit foundation, now operates in Europe, North America, the Middle East, and Asia. Though noted for Scandinavian design, styles are diversifying to accommodate international tastes.

The target market for IKEA is young, primarily white-collar customers, often with young families. They are interested in reliable quality and low-priced goods. The firm stresses design and showcases its products in full-scale room displays so that customers can imagine how they might be combined. Furniture and other household goods are generally priced at least 25 percent below products from similar stores; IKEA further distinguishes itself by offering a fun, stress-free shopping experience, with ample parking, play areas, and a restaurant. An extensive in-store inventory enables IKEA to fulfill most orders immediately. Costs are lower because customers take items from storage shelves and carry them home for assembly. In addition, IKEA enjoys scale economies from operating more than 230 stores.[9]

Decreasing costs are often a key factor in the first mover's competitive advantage, as IKEA illustrates, but that advantage is achieved only with focused attention. The benefit that might be obtained can be shown statistically in an *experience curve*. In many different product categories, research has shown that costs fall exponentially as cumulative output increases. Figure 6.2 shows how price has declined in disk drives as a result of capturing these dynamics.[10]

Experience curves graph the relationship between cost and units produced.

First generalized by the Boston Consulting Group, the benefits of accumulated experience can be traced to learning that is translated into improved product design, process technologies, capacity utilization, and other efficiencies. First movers can gain these advantages if they move down the experience curve more quickly than their competitors. Though there is a strong incentive to maximize market share to capture these volume-based economies, market share does not in itself ensure profitability; the advantages of scale have to be deliberately captured.[11]

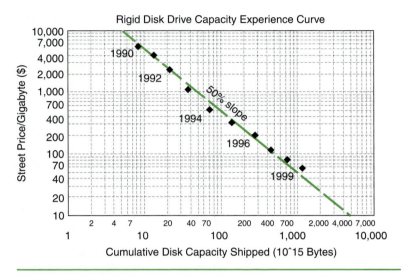

Figure 6.2 — Example Experience Curve for Computer Disk Drives

Source: R. E. Albright, What Can Past Technology Forecasts Tell Us about the Future?, *Technological Forecasting and Social Change* (June 2000): 443–464.

The first company to enter a market is not necessarily successful; in fact, many quickly fail. Early dot-com disasters cast doubt on the first-mover model. Many investments were made based on the idea that the first company in a market would win. A more sophisticated model is to enter a market while expectations are fluid, then be the first to establish a dominate design, or *product standard.*

Product standards are the set of attributes that customers expect in a given market.

That is not the end of opportunity. Once a product standard is set, competitors have a clearer idea of *what* to produce; more is known about customer demands and how efficiency can be gained in meeting those expectations. Typically buyers are less diverse than those encountered by first movers, which makes delivery more cost effective. Basically, successful second movers improve on the business models of first movers while avoiding the dead ends they encountered.

As we first discussed in Chapter 5, large companies in oligopolistic markets often leapfrog smaller competitors' early advantage relatively easily. Microsoft, a latecomer to the video gaming industry, typically chooses to be a second mover. In the 1990s, for example, its Internet Explorer eclipsed first mover Netscape, though it is possible that the battle is not over.

The Browser Wars

Launched in 1994, Netscape Communications—a Web browser based in part on University of Illinois technology developed to facilitate communication among academics—quickly gained a 90 percent market share. Microsoft saw Netscape as a threat to its Windows operating system and wanted to play a role in establishing Internet standards. It purchased similar Mosaic technology from a University of Illinois spin-off and created Internet Explorer, setting off the "browser wars."

Web browsers handle many different elements used for Web design and use. Both Netscape and Internet Explorer were praised for their ability to support user navigation, multimedia files, security, bookmarking, and other features that quickly became standard. By 1998, however, Internet Explorer enjoyed a significantly greater market share than Netscape, which had just been acquired by AOL. Microsoft's second-mover advantage as a much larger company included the fact that Internet Explorer is integrated with all other Microsoft office products, which are often preinstalled on new computers.

By September 2005, Microsoft's advantages supported a dominant market share, estimated to be 85 percent or even higher.[12] Netscape continues to be used by a much smaller portion of the market, but interestingly the company's philosophy lives on. Using a lizardlike icon developed in Netscape's early days, the Mozilla organization was founded in 1998 to create a new suite of tools. The name is a contraction of *Mosaic* and *killer* and was no doubt attractive because of its similarity to the name of the monster Godzilla.

Mozilla was registered as a nonprofit organization in 2003 with significant funding from AOL and then transformed into a foundation in 2005. The foundation describes itself as an open-source community of developers and testers who support the Firefox web browser, Thunderbird e-mail, and other software. Firefox was praised for features that Internet Explorer does not have and for being more secure from hackers. Users have paid attention, and the new browser has slowly gained market share.

By the middle of 2007 Mozilla claimed 25 percent market share worldwide (higher in Europe) to Internet Explorer's 66 percent. More conservative estimates agreed with the pattern of slow growth, but put the figures at 17 percent versus 76 percent. The big news, however, was the June 2007 announcement from Apple's Steve Jobs that Apple was releasing a PC version of Safari. The company indicated that it hoped some PC owners trying the free browser software would be more likely to download iTunes and perhaps move to a Mac. The move was also meant to lure developers to the iPhone. Apple said its market share rose to 4.03 percent over the next six months; other observers put its overall market share well above 5 percent. Clearly the browser wars are not over.[13]

Perhaps the biggest lesson to be learned from the study of market advantage is that it cannot be expected to last forever. As profit increases, more players are attracted to the market. Dominance also creates enemies. In the area of operating systems, many programmers develop free improvements driven in part by the desire to change the model that Microsoft has imposed. In fact, the open-source idea is a very interesting emerging business model. Think of Wikipedia.

Timing is important in predicting and explaining winners and losers, but it would be a mistake to imply that the business strategist has a choice between two positive models. It is not easy to develop a model and it is not easy copy and improve on a rewarded model, even a well-documented one.

Some strategists want far more. Steve Jobs has led Apple to significant success by what he describes as "reinvention." Apple enthusiasts point to the Mac, iPod, iPhone, and Apple TV. The idea at the center of this "business model" is that the company provides an offering that is so attractive it not only captures of a current model, it generates a new market.

HOW CAN VALUE CHAIN ANALYSIS CONTRIBUTE TO STRATEGIC CHANGE?

Value chains identify the primary and supporting activities used by an organization to create value for customers.

We now turn to another source of business model ideas: reorganizing the relationship among value-producing activities. The *value chain*, popularized by Michael Porter, provides an excellent means of generating and analyzing strategic alternatives.[14]

The basic framework Porter proposed is shown in Figure 6.3. Five primary activities are necessary in most business models to create a product, service, or experience. Common activities include the following:

1. *Inbound logistics:* all activities involved in the receipt and storage of raw materials necessary for the production of the firm's goods or services, including transportation, warehousing, and inventory.

2. *Operations:* the actual creation of the product or service of the firm, including manufacturing, work in progress, and machinery.

3. *Outbound logistics:* activities involved in getting the product or service to the final customer, including warehousing, shipping, and stocking.

4. *Marketing and sales:* all activities involved in the promotion of the product or service, including advertising, direct sales, and point-of-purchase displays.

5. *Service:* after-sales service, including warranties and service technicians.

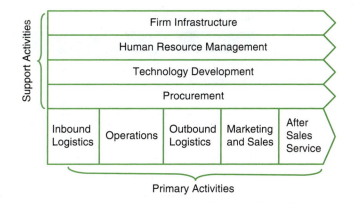

Figure 6.3 — Value Chain Analysis

At the top of this figure are four support activities that affect all primary activities. Although they facilitate primary activities, they create overhead costs for the firm that must be added to the cost of production. In many firms these supporting activities include the following:

1. *Firm infrastructure:* including general management responsible for the overall direction of the firm.

2. *Human resource management:* hiring, training, personnel development, evaluation, benefits, reward structures, and related activities.

3. *Technology development:* acquisition and application of technology across the organization. Information technology and the use of the Internet are the most visible of these activities.

4. *Procurement:* acquisition of materials necessary for the creation of the product or service of the firm.

Although it may be useful for a firm to develop a value chain that more uniquely relates to its business model, it is useful to check a more specific model against these basic activities. Value chain analysis using the categories shown in Figure 6.3 can describe existing processes and help identify potential new processes, or combinations of processes, that might improve profits. In areas where significant revenue enhancing expertise cannot be found within the firm, outsourcing is an attractive alternative to paying for support activities with the firm. This and other recent changes in business models can be found in Table 6.2.

TABLE 6.2 NEW BUSINESS MODELS FOR VALUE CHAIN ACTIVITIES

Activity Area	New Business Model Developments
Human resource management	Outsourcing recruitment, payroll, etc.
Finance	Outsourcing accounting services such as accounts payable and accounts receivable to offshore locations
Inbound logistics	Supply chain management, relationship marketing, and creative value through networks
Information technology	Collection of customer data via the Internet
Production	Mass customization processes
Marketing	Guerrilla marketing, network marketing
Outbound logistics	Hub-and-spoke delivery systems

The basic idea is that firms should adapt their value chains to become more effective competitors. For example, in the early 1990s Compaq Computer built personal computers for inventory. As a new entrant in this market, Dell altered this standard approach by building to customer orders. With this business model, Dell reduced its inventory costs and eliminated unwanted and slow-moving computers in comparison to Compaq and other competitors. The success of Dell's new approach ultimately resulted in more sophisticated approaches to assembly by all firms in order to remain cost effective.

As a second example of a revised value chain, consider how Canon created a new mix of activities to compete against Xerox.

Canon Destroys the Xerox Business Model

Xerox gradually built a sophisticated technician network to provide excellent after-sales service for its office copiers. Xerox repair technicians provided twenty-four-hour support and made regular on-site service calls. The barriers to entry were enormous. Xerox had accumulated experience and tacit knowledge, while customers expected the high level of service the company provided.

In an effort to enter the copier market, Canon was confronted with either developing a similar repair network, which was terribly expensive, or changing its approach to the market. The company chose to concentrate on operations—modularizing copier components and thereby eliminating the need for a complex technician network. Canon users were offered the possibility of diagnosing their own problems and replacing a defective module themselves. The new mix of primary activities proved to be more cost efficient and customer friendly. Gradually, the new business model moved Xerox out of the low end of the market.

> Then Canon began moving upscale into more sophisticated prod-
> ucts. In the top tier of the market, copiers with the fastest speed and
> volume (more than seventy copies a minute), Canon moved from 0 per-
> cent market share in 2000 to 23 percent in 2002. The company recently
> announced that it was increasing the manufacture of high-end copiers in
> its facility near Tokyo and doubling production of ink-jet printers. By this
> point Xerox was struggling to find an effective competitive response as
> a second mover in a market that it had initially dominated.[15]

Linking Value Chain Activities

The Canon example is important for a number of reasons. Although additional revenue can be attained through the redefinition of a single activity,
the more desirable approach is to link activities together. This creates a complex process that is more difficult to imitate, even by those with experience in
the market. If some activities can be eliminated altogether, the cost savings
can be used in other areas or used to lower the price of the product or service
for the final buyer. Sophisticated models that take value chains into account
also consider whether necessary activities should be carried out within the organization. Dell outsourced its after-sales service to an outside vendor, while
they concentrated on internal operations—its primary source of advantage.
Had Dell been forced to develop a technical service group, it might have
drained valuable resources away from its operations activity.

The most successful models link the seller's value chain to the user's value chain of activities. One example is provided by a chocolate manufacturer
that realized bakers were spending money melting the bars it sold. The firm
saved money by leaving the product in a liquid state after processing. More
important, its buyers saved money when they were able to drop a step in their
processes. Canon's success can be similarly traced to its insight that waiting
for repair is costly for users, no matter how expert that service ultimately is.

Support activities that are not directly involved in the creation of the
firm's goods or services may seem to be easy targets for streamlining in
the quest for profits. However, support activities can provide an invaluable source of competitive advantage to the firm, particularly if they can
be linked with primary activities. The worldwide shortage of technology workers, for example, means that human resource management is
an important function assisting technology development. Consider how
Trilogy Softwear makes this link.

Tough Tactics Win in a Tough Market

Trilogy, a Texas-based sales management software development firm,
has always been known as a rebel in the software industry. Founder
Joe Liemandt dropped out of Stanford to start his own computer-related
company in 1989. Within two years, Trilogy landed a $3.5 million deal

with Hewlett-Packard. Joe has always emphasized a unique corporate culture of innovation and support for risk taking. The company runs its own Trilogy University to indoctrinate new hires into the entrepreneurial culture that supports this behavior among all its employees.

Faced with stiff competition for technology graduates from the top universities, Trilogy developed a unique and unorthodox means of attracting the best and brightest technology graduates through career fairs, parties, late-night phone calls, and visits to its Austin, Texas, headquarters—all with the intention of landing the most talented software engineers coming out of college.

Recruitment is followed by the Trilogy University "boot camp"—where new hires are subjected to relentless pressure to develop real-time software projects. Liemandt often takes part in the instruction, using the "camp" as a means of continuing a needed entrepreneurial spirit even as the firm continues to grow.

Interestingly, the company tried to make money from its business model in the late 1990s by spinning off a number of Internet start-ups, including CollegeHire.com, a direct spin off of its high-tech recruitment process. Unfortunately this and other efforts were part of the .com crash. Despite contracts with companies like Amazon, the company closed in 2001.[16]

The Trilogy case illustrates important integration across three support activities: firm infrastructure (founder Joe Liemandt), human resource management (the recruitment process Trilogy pioneered), and the direct activity of operations (the unique corporate culture that rewards risk takers). This linkage across activities creates a competitive advantage that is fundamental to Trilogy's success. The social complexity of the linkage makes imitating Trilogy's approach difficult.

Deconstructing the Value Chain

We have talked a good deal about how new information technologies have forced firms to re-examine how they can create additional value within their chain of activities. Consider car retailing. In most places car dealerships are a one-stop shop—providing information about cars, holding inventory, and brokering financing alternatives. Often the dealership also sells used cars and offers maintenance and repair services. As a source of competitive advantage, these companies have a number of assets: location, scale, cost, sales force management, and service.

In the information technology age, newcomers to the retail car industry are creating a different, cost-saving, customer-serving value chain. Firms specializing in selling used cars on the Internet provide large selections. Auto manufacturers increasingly provide online product information about new cars. Brokers can list a large number of new-car choices on a single site. Individuals may be able to request that a car be brought to their home or office so that they can take it on a test drive. Consumers can also put their financing requirements out for bid on the

Internet. As a result of these and other developments, we expect that there will be fewer car dealerships with massive showrooms.

Technology is not the only factor driving these developments. Customers want new things. Their personal value chain activities are shifting, and car dealers have to find new ways to connect with their activities. Companies that offer business-to-business services have found that it is very useful to map their customer's value chain with as much detail as their own, as we illustrated with Canon's activities in the copier market. Business-to-consumer offerings are making similar gains.

Innovative companies are a source of evolution. Dell, for example, first attempted to distribute its product through national retail outlets, including ComputerLand. However, with little room left on the shelves, Dell was refused access to the established distribution chain. As a result, the company developed an innovative direct marketing approach to the consumer PC market. Direct selling was not a new concept, but it had never been applied to selling PCs before. The eventual success of this model forced all competitors in the industry to adjust their strategies to include direct marketing. Dell continues to change its basic business approach with its pioneering work in the build-to-order sales model supported strongly by its Internet presence. This idea has now become a basic business model. Consider the following incarnation.

BYOB: Build Your Own Barbie

Since her debut at the American International Toy Show in 1959, Mattel's Barbie doll has become one of the most popular brands in toy history, with sales in more than 150 countries around the world. It is estimated that the average American girl between ages 3 and 11 owns ten Barbie dolls.

In the late 1990s customers could order a Barbie doll tailored to their personal preferences. They could decide what color hair, eyes, and skin Barbie would have and choose her hairstyle, clothing, and accessories. Barbies ordered at the Barbie.com website were shipped within six to eight weeks at a cost of $39.95. Mattel ultimately closed that site, with some observers suggesting that the most important "customization" in a child's mind is the selection of a doll's name—which requires little facilitation. But five years later Mattel created a custom car factory at FAO Schwarz that allowed customers to make a range of choices, watch a short video on how custom cars were made, and receive their own custom car (selected from a stock of all possible choice combinations) that was laser printed with the owner's name and unique registration number.

Neither option is available in 2008 from Mattel, but customized toys live on. If you are interested in customizing a doll, go to www.mytwinn. com. And the Build-a-Bear Workshop offers in-store and online possibilities to customize teddy bears and other stuffed animals.[17]

By urging you as a strategist to pay attention to your company's value chain and how it interacts (or might interact) with the value chain of customers (even children), we are suggesting a tool for more fine-grained understanding of business models and their evolution. A tool for trying the needed analysis on your own can be found in Worksheet 6.1.

Worksheet 6.1:
Value Chain
Analysis—A Tool
for Increasing
Profitability
....

HOW CAN THE LIFE CYCLE BE USED AS A SOURCE OF BUSINESS MODEL IDEAS?

The strategy field has an interesting problem. On the one hand, as social scientists we look for patterns that repeat in an organized fashion. On the other hand, strategists recognize the need for uniqueness. The very existence of regularity acts against competitive advantage as more and more firms adopt similar approaches to a situation. Imitation eliminates the rarity strategists seek in order to attract above-average returns, and thus strategy evolves away from established patterns.

Richard Rumelt describes the formulation of organizational strategy as "problem solving of the most unstructured sort."[18] An ill-structured problem offers two remedies: (1) classify it and apply standard procedures to it, or (2) seek some way of structuring the problem that is meaningful so that current knowledge and experience can be used to develop a more distinctive solution.[19] Rumelt identifies theoretical schemes that distinguish the critical from the noncritical in strategy as *frame theories*,[20] including Porter's five forces, generic strategies, and something we have not yet discussed, life cycle models.

Frame theories
help the strategist
identify critical
aspects of a
problematic
situation.

The *life cycle* model is a potential tool for developing a business model that focuses on stages of development. A simplified product life cycle is outlined in Figure 6.4; we think it can still be seen in many markets, even though cycles are shortening because of increased competition in a globalizing environment.

The life cycle
outlines a
generalized
progression
of growth and
decline.

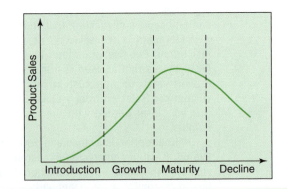

Figure 6.4 — Traditional Product/Market Life Cycle

An example of successive product life cycles is illustrated in. Figure 6.5, from a recent analyst report. It documents the sales of Sony game consoles from 1995 to 2006, as described at the beginning of this chapter.

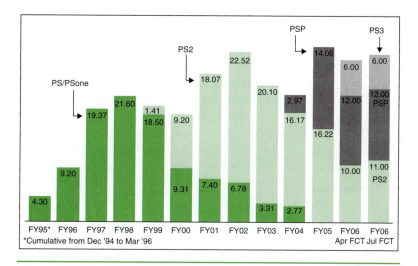

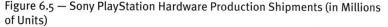

Figure 6.5 — Sony PlayStation Hardware Production Shipments (in Millions of Units)

Source: Sony, First Quarter Analyst Report, 2006. http://www.sony.net/SonyInfo/IR/financial/fr/06g1_sonypre.pdf, accessed March 10, 2008.

Rumelt notes that the "product/market life cycle concept provides a powerful frame theory that has yet to be fully developed."[21] He notes that "rivalry is the fundamental concept that drives strategy" and thus calls for a sharper focus on the nature of rivalry in each phase of the model. The key idea for strategic analysis is that the basis of rivalry and activities of rival firms change as organizations transition from one stage to the next.

The idiosyncratic learning that occurs through participation in a specific competitive environment is an important barrier to new entrants. Firms must be involved in the immediate industry of interest or in a related competitive environment in order to learn which factors are critical for movement to the next stage of development. Rumelt's description of the life cycle at the industry (or competitive environment) level has four stages.

Stage 1: Birth of a New Offering

As a new product, service, or experience is identified, firms experiment with different options regarding product attributes and different variations of the product. Components of the product or service tend to evolve separately from one another as new firms enter this emerging competitive environment. The size of the new market is initially small, and typically stage 1 participants are also small and unable to control the entire production and distribution process. Alternative technologies support differing product or service offerings. This limits the growth of the competitive environment as a whole. Competing designs mean that the market is fragmented.[22] Firms' offerings are rarely interchangeable, which may lead to buyer frustration and reluctance to commit serious resources.

If the product, service, or experience does find a market, experience accumulates, learning must occur as activities are repeated, and larger resource allocations that support product or service developments become imperative. As strategists make choices that unite manufacturing, distribution, and support activities (such as warranty options), business models become clearer. The more successful product ideas are likely to be copied and become the industry standard. The *standardization* that characterizes the end of this stage may signal good news for the development of the competitive environment as a whole, but bad news for individual firms. Firms that previously made compatible resource allocation choices succeed, less fortunate firms fail. *Economies of scale* begin to be important at this point, and firms may merge in order to achieve more optimal levels of production and operations, as shown in Table 6.3.

Standardization occurs when every product or service is produced to specified requirements.

Economies of scale are cost savings enjoyed through more efficient production of larger volumes of a product or service.

TABLE 6.3 CHARACTERISTICS OF STAGE 1 OF THE INDUSTRY LIFE CYCLE

Rivals	Small entrepreneurial firms dominate.
Sales	Sales figures are low and initially grow slowly.
Entrants	New entrants may be numerous.
Buyers	Most potential users are unsophisticated; but early adopters may be very sophisticated.
Offerings	A wide variety of product or service offerings exist.
Evolution	Movement to the next stage occurs when standards evolve.

Stage 2: Systems

As a dominant design evolves, providers begin to package their offerings into more complete *systems* based on the final end user's needs. The product, service, or experience package is no longer viewed as isolated components; opportunities to enhance interconnections are recognized and exploited. For example, computers are now often bundled with software, printers, CD drives, and Internet connectivity to provide an ever-increasing level of utility to the end user.

Systems are packages of goods or services that meet an end user's needs.

User needs also shift as users learn more about the product or service and its applications. They understand more about how their needs interact and seek solutions that work together to provide more utility. Producers both react to and anticipate these changes, as higher "value packages" become possible. Prices usually drop as firms move along the learning curve and economies of scale reduce costs. Less successful firms continue to drop out of the market, but the cost of entry has increased, and a few fast-growing firms begin to dominate with name brands.

The existence of standards requires that firms attempt to differentiate their products or services on nonstandardized aspects of the system, including delivery, service, and brand. Intel recognized this in the early days of its development and used the profits from early success in the microprocessor market to create brand recognition for "Intel Inside"—the world's largest cooperative, ingredient-brand marketing program. Intel managed to convey a difference between its chips and those of its competitor (primarily Advanced Micro Devices [AMD]) in the mind of consumers, even though the actual differences may have been small.

The increasing emphasis on systems may be an opportunity for older, more established firms, or it may require new firms to enter the market. Over time, competition typically moves away from differentiation and more and more toward price as the primary form of advantage. This creates its own dynamic. For example, Intel recognized that basic memory chips would lose their value as more and more firms entered production and chose to shift its emphasis to microprocessors. This move provided more value to the end user and supported Intel's charging a higher price.

Although firms in stage 2 of the generic life cycle we are describing initially enjoy high revenue growth (in comparison to stage 1), the signal of the end of the period occurs when average growth levels taper off. As prices drop because of increased competition, firms either drop out or merge in order to support economies of scale for production and distribution purposes. Many firms that appeared to have a "good strategy" in the past merely enjoyed the high growth of the market. Overcapacity occurs as revenue growth shrinks, and competition turns to price in order to attract buyers, as shown in Table 6.4. To see how some of these ideas fit the evolution of the game console market, see details in Wikipedia's history of this industry.[23]

TABLE 6.4 CHARACTERISTICS OF STAGE 2 OF THE INDUSTRY LIFE CYCLE

Rivals	Larger firms dominate.
Sales	Sales figures grow rapidly.
Entrants	New entrants are much less likely than in Stage 1.
Buyers	Users become more sophisticated.
Offerings	A standardized line of product or service offerings exists and usage becomes easier.
Evolution	Movement to the next stage occurs as growth rates drop and firms move to more customized options.

Stage 3: Solutions

Customized offerings make or alter a product, services, experience combination to meet individual or personal specifications.

As firms move from standardized systems into more *customized offerings*, they typically address the more idiosyncratic needs of the final user. This is likely to include a larger service component than was originally offered by firms, though service may be provided by firms other than the primary provider or manufacturer. More recently, attention to user experience has also distinguished firm offerings.

As users become more sophisticated, they require a greater degree of dependability and value from a specific product or service. At the same time, they may desire variety. Stage 2, the systems stage, allows providers to tailor generic offerings into more customized packages. In stage 3, the solutions stage, market segmentation and even mass customization techniques are developed. Although standards still exist, firms rush to offer product, service, or experience options that meet the more specific needs of their buyers. Instead of the product or service driving the solution, the solution dictates the nature of what is provided. Table 6.5 illustrates stage 3.

Bundling is the practice of grouping a set of offerings together as a package.

The practice of *bundling* offers end users greater value at reduced prices. In addition, however, firms start to offer start-to-finish alternatives that may enable movement from lower-margin options to higher-value alternatives. Basically, firms seek to enter additional avenues of revenue generation associated with their offering at this stage. For example, General Electric builds jet engines and added a unit that provides spare parts to engine maintenance firms. When GE chose to view jet engines as a service, air miles became the focus, and the company expanded its activities to include maintenance and repair services to upgrade their capabilities.

Table 6.5 Characteristics of Stage 3 of the Industry Life Cycle

Rivals	Firms tend to merge as the market consolidates.
Sales	Sales figures stagnate, but movement to higher-margin offerings can provide profits.
Entrants	New entrants are few or nonexistent.
Buyers	Users demand more value.
Offerings	Mass customization is attractive.
Evolution	Movement to the next stage occurs when customer information systems develop.

Stage 4: Relationships

As firms engage in closer exchanges with their customers, the seller is better able to anticipate the needs of the buyer. Many grocery chains, for example, offer shoppers a card that provides them with weekly discounts on selected items and opportunities for prizes. Similar to frequent-flyer cards issued by airlines, these cards collect massive amounts of information about buyers, including shopping habits, sensitivity to coupons, average size of purchase, and other valuable insights. The card hopefully binds buyers to the chain (or airline) and discourages them from shopping elsewhere.

Although overall industry revenue growth may be small or nonexistent in stage 4, close relationships with users allow some firms to stay ahead of their competition by identifying market niches. Firms capable of identifying areas of profit and providing valued services to these attractive markets will experience above-average returns. Because the market is becoming more complex and larger firms may be trapped in less effective ways of doing things, some of these profitable players may be newer, smaller firms.

The development of the Internet is particularly important for allowing firms to collect better real-time information on their buyers. The knowledge gained by allowing buyers to interact more closely with the firm serves as a basis for next-generation services. *Relationship technology* helps firms collect and analyze data about customers. Airlines use this kind of information to determine which frequent flyers are high-value customers. Sophisticated grocers use loyalty cards to collect information that is used to tailor additional offerings to a customer's past buying behavior. (There is a good description of the loyalty business model on Wikipedia.[24])

> **Relationship technology helps organizations collect and analyze data about users.**

Similarly, banks use the relationship approach to offer customers specific banking products, either with a live teller or automatically as the individual accesses an ATM. Again, the information system targets products and services for specific clients. Insurance companies, communications firms, and other firms are following suit. The result is customized service at a mass production cost,[25] as shown in Table 6.6.

TABLE 6.6 CHARACTERISTICS OF STAGE 4 OF THE INDUSTRY LIFE CYCLE

Rivals	A mixture of large and small firms.
Sales	Profitable niches in otherwise competitive markets.
Entrants	New entrants occur.
Buyers	Knowledgeable users are very demanding about their requirements.
Offerings	A service and experience orientation dominates.
Evolution	A new industry cycle is likely to evolve.

Of course, the history of a particular company or market is unlikely to advance as smoothly as this description. The economy and other macro forces affect consumption. (Think, for example, how slowly many alternative-energy products have grown in the last few decades despite concern for the environment.) Discontinuities can occur from major innovations. Hypercompetitive environments compress life cycles. Despite these and other real-world complexities, the dynamics outlined

Worksheet 6.2:
Life Cycle
Analysis—A Tool
for Anticipating
Evolutionary
Change

here are well worth thinking about, which we encourage you to do in Worksheet 6.2. The focus is on predicting how profit advantages of a business model might change. Though the overall expectation is for increased competition, and thus decreased profit, changing conditions also create new opportunities.

WHAT CAN BE LEARNED FROM COMPETITORS, CUSTOMERS, AND OTHERS?

As a competitive environment matures, strategists have more and more chances to learn from others. One model that has come to have world-wide impact through observation and imitation by others has been developed for more than 150 years, but is particularly well illustrated by Ray Kroc, the founder of McDonald's.[26]

Franchise Model

In 1955 Ray Kroc was the catalyst for a major change in the chain of activities that established restaurants had been carrying out for a long time. The model has now been adapted to many different competitive environments.

The McDonald's Fast-Food Franchising Model

McDonald's reconfigured the fast-food industry when it used assembly line manufacturing processes in food preparation. The company developed highly codified standards and emphasized a simplified menu; the double decision allowed it to achieve tremendous cost advantages over other restaurants. Its in-store operations, from food preparation to customer service, supported a consistently high-quality product and service experience. These activities were so clearly defined that they could be replicated by others, and the company gradually added processes to control more and more relevant operations, including very sophisticated models for site selection. All McDonald's restaurants looked and felt alike, which consumers appreciated and rewarded with high return rates. Competitors, such as Burger King and Taco Bell imitated the style and approach of McDonald's.

The International Franchise Association (IFA) contends that franchising represents 50 percent of all McDonald's retail sales in the United States, a figure close to $1 trillion. The economic impact of the model is much bigger than these figures, of course, because the franchising model has been widely adopted as a means of national and international expansion in many other industries. In the United States, the IFA estimates that 1 out of every 12 retail businesses is a franchise and that a new franchise opens every eight minutes. Internationally, the IFA estimates that there are about 15,000 franchising companies around the world, in about seventy-five different businesses. Records show a growth rate of between 5 and 10 percent for franchising in the United States, 15 percent growth in Europe, and 20 to 25 percent in South America.

A second major trend within franchising is a movement beyond goods and into services. These include residential cleaning, commercial cleaning, home improvement, medical and health services, and wholesale distribution—all areas rather far afield from the food industry in which McDonald's developed so many franchising ideas.[27]

Franchises are a major form of new business start-ups around the world. The franchisor provides a proven formula for success, training, and a trademark supported by a much larger advertising budget than individual franchisees could afford. Often the franchisor helps in site selection and negotiation of leases; in addition to initial training, it typically provides organizational systems and ongoing mentoring. These are substantial benefits that directly address three things that can lead to start-up failure: lack of business know-how, insufficient start-up capital, and inadequate cash flow.[28] A franchisee can generally get a business off the ground much more quickly than if a new concept had to be developed from scratch. Consumers can also benefit from receiving a consistent product in many locations.

In return for these benefits, the franchisee pays a substantial start-up fee and must closely follow the franchise model. Signage, store layout, uniforms, hours, local advertising, and many other details must be adhered to. Ongoing royalties, contributions to national and international advertising costs, and a proportion of profits to the franchisor are part of the contract. In other words, there is a significant loss of control.

It is often claimed that fewer franchises fail than other new business, though one academic study found that "young franchise startups exhibit both higher rates of firm discontinuance and lower mean profitability than cohort independent business startups."[29] There is also a significant amount of legal action over nonperformance.

Several specific risks for franchisees can be identified. Supplies often have to be purchased from the franchisor, with some franchisees claiming they have unwittingly participated in a razor-and-blades model used by the franchisor. Legal advisors also suggest paying particularly attention to exclusivity, because as franchisors try to grow they may add sites in close proximity.[30] In addition, most contracts are written to cover a significant period of time, and royalties are required whether or not the business is succeeding.[31]

There are also risks for those establishing a franchise. The skills that lead to business success may not be the skills that lead to franchisor success. Some communities are restricting "formula businesses."[32] An incompetent franchisee can jeopardize brand image. In fact, a significant number of businesses that attempt to expand through franchising fail.

Promising Practices

Of course, it is not necessary to be a franchisee to learn from the success of other companies. McDonald's success may be traced to many things, including resource choices, accumulated management experience, superior learning ability, and even pure luck. Once success was demonstrated, however, participants in the food industry, and then companies more and more removed from this sector, experimented with similar approaches to their products, service, and experience offerings.

Attention to success, or *best practice*, is a critical force driving evolution in many different competitive environments. Strategists often *benchmark* their activities against their strongest competitors, or even consider standards set in other settings. For example, Southwest Airlines benchmarks its refueling and service practices against NASCAR pit stops.[33]

Chapter 5's discussion of strategic groups shows how groups of firms can mimic entire strategies, not just a specific process or product. However, as we already mentioned at the beginning of our discussion of frame theories, too much copying can be self-defeating. As practices are copied, there are fewer opportunities to differentiate offerings within the current business model, and incumbents are left to compete only on price. A more fruitful response is to understand best practice and then improve on it with a unique business model.

The idea of identifying and learning from best practice has been used around the world in the public sector and among nonprofits, with significant government expenditure focused on ensuring that agencies communicate their own best practices and draw on the most promising experiences of other agencies. One interesting development has been the recognition that the diffusion of successful ideas is more difficult than many advocates expected. Thus there has been a shift of attention away from thinking about best practices to thinking about *promising practices*.[34] This move recognizes that every situation is different and thus will require some unique responses. Second, many individuals, especially in the Western world, are more easily motivated by participation in solution finding than by replication of solutions. Most important, competitive advantage depends on rising above common practice. A change in vocabulary to collecting "promising practices" is meant to encourage strategists to aspire to the highest standards demonstrated by others, then adapt them.

One way to look at a competitive environment is to see it as a vast collection of promising practices available for further development. We just noted the broad diffusion of McDonald's production and franchising ideas. Here is another example of how the strategies of a major

---

Best practice describes a procedure that has been particularly successful for a specific firm.

Benchmarking refers to the practice of comparing a unit's performance, usually on specific evaluative criteria, to the best performance of similar units in other companies.

Promising practices are a pool of ideas from other firms that strategists can adapt to their own unique situation.

airline influenced train service in Great Britain, which is interesting in part because after privatization the UK government offered franchise contracts for specified routes.

Virgin Rail: Sir Richard Branson Borrows a Trick from the Airline Industry

After privatization in the 1980s, the British rail system came under increasing pressure from customers complaining about poor service and interrupted schedules. In part, the system suffers from outdated infrastructures and poorly coordinated service. With experts predicting an increase in passenger traffic approaching 50 percent within a few years, the situation was seen as untenable by many observers, yet a useful change of practices had not been identified.

Successfully bidding for two routes, the Virgin Rail Group borrowed tricks developed in the postderegulation American airline industry. Rather than the point-to-point system that the British rail system depended on, Virgin decided to change to a hub-and-spoke approach, with Birmingham as its hub. Passengers were asked to change trains more often, but in return they received more frequent and varied service options. A hub-and-spoke system saves money because it is much cheaper to operate than a point-to-point method, which requires unused capacity to continue to the end of the line.

At the same time, Virgin Rail provided more customer services. For example, it improved lounges and offered meals that are more reminiscent of old-time service on the airlines than the rolling cart with a few cans of soft drinks and some sandwiches now found on most trains and planes.

A recent update of this story underscores an important point about learning from others; however, the applicability of even the most promising practice has to be carefully considered. Virgin and other incumbents lost contracts in 2007. The winners, including a consortia that included the Hong Kong Underground, promised more seats and higher prices.[35]

Open Innovation

Open innovation is the practice of drawing innovative ideas from multiple sources outside formal R&D departments.

Although "borrowed experience"[36] is one source of innovation, there are many others. In Chapter 3 we described the many ways that companies could learn from their customers and emphasized that employee knowledge of and attention to customers is critical. The idea of *open innovation* pushes this general idea even further.[37]

It is clear that innovation is important to organizations; research has demonstrated in particular how new products not only facilitate the survival of firms but contribute to broader social welfare.[38] Many argue, however, that organizations do not focus enough on future oriented activities. As Peter Drucker said, "Today no one needs to be convinced that innovation is important—intense competition, along with fast changing markets and technologies, has made sure of that. How to innovate is the key question."[39]

"Democratizing innovation"[40] has recently been proposed as the answer to this key question. This new model is a radical departure from past practices of centralized research and development in which innovation is sought in separate organizational units, project management designs, and incentive systems. An important drawback of the centralized approach is that breakthrough innovations do not always originate in the R&D unit of an organization.[41] Examples include the development of the ulcer medication Losec, which corporate innovation managers at the pharmaceutical giant Astra (today AstraZeneca) tried to stop,[42] but which grew and became the world's most widely sold prescribed medication.

This incident suggests that management is part of the reason why innovative ideas from the periphery are often not recognized in the core of an organization. When innovation is expected to happen in an officially designated place, the signal is that only a tiny fraction of the organization is meant to be inventive, and few outside innovations occur or survive.[43] Furthermore, when corporate innovation systems are centralized, the practices, values, and incentive systems that might pick up dispersed innovations are not in place. As markets become more global and competitive, the loss is increasingly important because more diverse ideas are needed.

A second critical issue is that centralized innovation practices often focus on product innovations. But successful products are increasingly embedded in complementary services and customer experiences, which are supported by a variety of activities. As we said in Chapter 3, service quality and innovation relies on employee involvement.[44] As customers are rapidly coming to expect attention to the experience of engaging with a product or service,[45] the points of required innovation and contact are even more widely dispersed. Centralized innovation management practices cannot develop the necessary reach. The people closest to this growing complexity are important sources of information and breakthrough.

Several scholars have recently highlighted the benefits of opening up the innovation process.[46] The central insight is that by encouraging and considering the ideas and solution knowledge of a large number of individuals, new creativity can be brought into the organization. The practical benefits of this overall approach can be seen in the success of open-source software such as Linux. We believe, with others, that a dominant capability of open-source software development systems is to incorporate the "wisdom of the periphery,"[47] and that many other companies can learn from this experience.

However, some companies enthused about innovation have also discovered that it does not bring benefits automatically. Innovation is not a business model in itself, ensuring a path to profitability. Rather, innovation is the beginning of what may become a viable model, if it leads to an attractive offering that engages customers, and can be produced reliably and defended from others.

HOW DO BUSINESS PLANS DIFFER FROM BUSINESS MODELS?

A business plan formalizes the business model. It defines the firm's strategy but also provides feasibility analyses that support financial decisions. Well-developed plans enable entrepreneurs to map their future, set realistic goals, and communicate clearly with would-be financiers and other stakeholders.

There are three types of business plans: summary, full, and operational. A summary business plan is approximately ten pages long and is meant to elicit an initial response from others. Full business plans tend to be ten to forty pages long and are written to seek financing as well as business partners. An operational business plan tends to be even longer; it provides detailed guidance for a going concern and is especially important when growth brings many newcomers into an organization.

A key part of the business plan is the financial projections, which are often communicated with proforma financial statements. A business plan can seem very similar to a firm's strategic plan or business model, except for its detail and an increased focus on financing.

A typical business plan has several sections. The first section usually provides a description of the business: the product, service, or experience to be created; markets; locations; competition; management; personnel; and the type and use of financing sought. A second section typically focuses on financing: sales forecasts, income statement, balance sheet, cash flow, sources and uses of funds, break-even analysis, assumptions, and financial ratios. A third section includes supporting documents, much like an appendix. You can find a broad outline typical for many business plans, and several examples, at www.sba.gov/starting_business/planning/writingplan.html. Many university courses and government agencies also provide help to those interested in expressing their ideas in this widely used format.

CONCLUSIONS FOR THE STRATEGIST

We hope that you have drawn three important conclusions from the discussion so far:

1. Competitive environments are always changing (more slowly in some settings, more rapidly in others) as participants try to achieve new advantages.

2. Though the idiosyncratic details of specific evolutionary paths are fascinating, most of these efforts have an identifiable pattern.

3. Value chain analysis can help outline details of operations for further collaborative and competitive strategies.

4. Useful prescriptions also can be made by considering life cycle changes.

The obvious implication of these observations is that strategists can anticipate some events likely to occur in their future. The problem of course, is that even if the predictions are correct, anticipating their exact timing is more difficult that merely expecting certain relationships to unfold at some point in the future. Without a concrete time frame, however, strategic response is difficult.

New business models drive the evolution of competitive environments and require responsive adaptation by all participants; over time the most successful are copied and adapted in many different settings. Making a life cycle analysis of a product (or an interrelated set of products) can suggest important issues for the timing of new moves.

Although these themes are fascinating, we must end this chapter on a cautionary note. As industries evolve, their profit potential tends to decline. Increasing competition tends to drive down prices and thus profit potential for all players. Innovation is an obvious escape from these difficulties, and around the world governments are making investments to improve the innovative capacity of workers and industries located within their boundaries. We are particularly excited about the possibilities of open innovation, even though it poses new management challenges.

As a business strategist you may benefit from investment in innovations, but first look closely at the external environment and at internal capabilities. These are the two subjects we address in the next sections of this book.

Key Terms

In this chapter we considered competitors as a major evolutionary force in the business environment. A **business model** summarizes how key strategic decisions are expected to make a profit. A **business plan** is a more complete overview of company activities, followed by detailed financial analysis.

The **experience curve** graphs the relationship between cost and units produced. In many different industries, costs fall exponentially as output increases as a result of learning and related process and product improvements. **First movers** often have the advantage of progressing down this curve more quickly than their competitors. But a second-mover strategy also has some advantages, especially in a setting where **product standards** (the capabilities required in order to attract customers in a market) are important.

Frame theories help the strategist identify critical aspects of a problematic situation that might be addressed in a business model. This chapter discusses two specific contributions. The **life cycle** model describes industry changes from initial innovation, growth if markets are found, and eventual decline. The terms used to describe four different stages include the following:

- **Standardization**—when every product or service is produced to specified requirements.
- **Economies of scale**—cost savings enjoyed through more efficient production of larger volumes of a product or service.
- **Systems**—packages of goods or services that meet an end user's needs.
- **Customized offerings**—products or services that are altered to meet individual or personal specifications.
- **Bundling**—grouping a set of products or services together as a package.
- **Relationship technology**—technology that helps organizations collect and analyze data about users.

The other frame theory, **value chain** analysis, identifies the primary activities used within an organization to create value for customers.

Competitors often learn about successful business models by observing each other. **Best practice** describes an idea or procedure that has been particularly successful. **Benchmarking** refers to the practice of comparing a company unit's performance, usually on specific evaluative criteria, to the best performance of other companies in that area. **Promising practices** are ideas that others have used successfully to meet a set of similar conditions; the set is proposed as a pool of ideas that practitioners can use to tailor a response to their own unique situation. **Open innovation** is the practice of drawing innovation ideas from multiple sources, including those that are outside formal R&D departments.

Questions for Further Reflection

1. Specify your most important career objectives. What models for achieving those objectives can you derive from observing, interviewing, or reading about those who have succeeded in achieving this objective?

2. Find an example of a single business firm that has changed its business model in the last few years. (Dell is an example.) How did the firm modify the primary and support activities in its value chain? How does this change relate to business models used by competitors?

3. Visit websites that discuss business models (for example, www. digitalenterprise.org/models/models.html, which discusses Internet models). Identify two strong competitors following a similar model. Should one or both pursue a dual strategy in anticipation of market evolution, in your opinion?

WORKSHEET 6.1
Value Chain Analysis—A Tool for Increasing Profitability

Identify a firm's basic activities and the functions that support them, and then link these activities to customer value chains.

Step 1: Select a firm and a customer whose value chains you can identify.

Step 2: Make a list of the firm's value chain activities in column 1.

Step 3: Now identify one of the firm's major customers, and list their major value chain activities in column 2.

Step 4: Consider how the firm and customer value chain activities are currently linked in column 3.

Step 5: Consider additional links that would add value to the customer in column 4.

Step 6: Add links that would increase profitability or add other value to your firm in column 5.

Value Chain Linking to Customers Worksheet 6.2	Firm:
Analyst(s):	**Summary:**

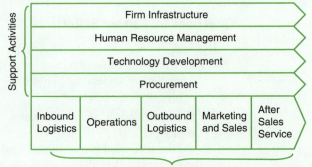

Value Chain Activity	Firm Activity	Customer Activity	Current Links between Activities	Additional Links Adding Value for Customer	Additional Links Adding Value for Your Firm
Firm infrastructure					
Human resource management					
Technology development					
Procurement					
Inbound logistics					
Operations					
Outbound logistics					
Marketing and sales					
After-sales service					

Draw the life cycle of a specific product, predict its future evolution, and suggest a promising business model for a specific competitor.

Step 1: Select a product that has gone through at least two life cycle changes.

Step 2: Draw the life cycle of the product in the empty box.

Step 3: Consider the characteristics of the stages in the life cycle through which the product has evolved. Put your ideas in the relevant boxes in column 1.

Step 4: Predict the future evolution of the product. Put your ideas in the relevant boxes in column 2.

Step 5: Suggest a promising business model for a specific competitor. Put your ideas in the relevant boxes in column 3.

Life Cycle Analysis Worksheet 6.1	**Product:**
Analyst(s):	**Summary:**

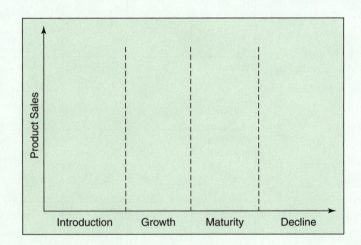

Stage	Characteristics	Business Model
Introduction		
Growth		
Maturity		
Decline		

NOTES

[1] Davies, C. 2008. Video Game Sales Reach Record Highs in 2007. Daily Vidette Online. http://media.www.dailyvidette.com/media/storage/paper420/news/2008/01/24/News/Video.Game.Sales.Reach.Record.Highs.In.2007-3165787.shtml, accessed January 28, 2008; McCormack, K. & Montevirgen, C. 2007. Who's Winning the Console Wars? *Business Week* (January 22). http://www.businessweek.com/print/investor/content/jan2007/pi20070122_415523.htm, accessed May 14, 2007; Hafer, M. 2005. Elitism in Gaming (and the Business Model That Supports It). Games First! http://www.gamesfirst.com/index.php?id=27, accessed March 10, 2008; History of Video Game Consoles: Seventh Generation. http://www.wikipedia.org, accessed March 10, 2008. See also http://www.vgchartz.com/forum/thread.php?id=15493&start=0, accessed January 28, 2008.

[2] See, for example, http://www.begborroworsteal.com/ui/welcome?adTrackId=8481&sourceCode=8481, accessed May 20, 2007.

[3] Netflix, Inc. 2008. Q4 2007 Earnings Call Transcript. http://seekingalpha.com/article/61343-netflix-inc-q4-2007-earnings-call-transcript?page=1, accessed January 28, 2008; Bylund, A. 2006. Netflix Awarded Business Model Patent, Immediately Sues Blockbuster. Ars Technica (April 15). http://arstechnica.com/news.ars/post/20060405-6528.html, accessed May 14, 2007.

[4] Anderson, C. 2006. *The Long Tail.* New York: Hyperion; see also http://longtail.typepad.com and http://www.wired.com/wired/archive/12.10/tail.html, accessed May 14, 2007.

[5] Wesienthal, J. (2008). DVD Kiosk Operator Redbox to file for IPO. Paidcontents (May 2). http://www.paidcontent.org/entry/419-dvd-kiosk-operator- redbox-to-file-for-ipo/, accessed May 4, 2008.

[6] See http://www.google.com/Top/Recreation/Travel/Consolidators/, accessed May 20, 2007.

[7] http://www.joost.com/about.html, accessed January 28, 2008; Donohue, S. 2007. After YouTube: Getting Joost Up. Multichannel News (May 7). http://www.multichannel. com/article/CA6439443.html, accessed May 14, 2007.

[8] Not Too Juiced by Joost: Who Really Wants to See Full-Length TV Shows on the Web? 2007. *Business Week* (June 1), http://www.businessweek.com/magazine/content/07_24/ b4038023.htm, accessed January 28, 2008; Roettgers, J. 2008. Five Ways to Save Joost. New TeeVee (January 19). http://newteevee.com/2008/01/19/five-ways-to-save-joost/, accessed January 28, 2008.

[9] http://www.ikea.com/ms/en_US/about_ikea/timeline/full_story.html; http://www.ikea. com/ms/en_US/about_ikea_new/facts_figures/index.html and http://www.hoovers. com/IKEA/-ID__42925-/free-co-factsheet.xhtml, accessed March 10, 2008.

[10] Ghemawat, P. 1985. Building Strategy on the Experience Curve. *Harvard Business Review* (March–April).

[11] Wensley, R. 1982. PIMS and BCG: New Horizons or False Dawn? *Strategic Management Journal* 3: 147–158.

[12] http://www.e-janco.com/browser.htm, accessed March 10, 2008.

[13] http://www.microsoft.com/windows/ie/default.mspx, http://www.mozilla.org, http:// www.blooberry.com/indexdot/history/netscape.htm, http://www.forbes.com/ infoimaging/2004/02/04/cx_ah_0204tentech.html, http://en.wikipedia.org/wiki/ Mozilla, and http://mozillalinks.org/wp/2007/06/w3counter-firefox-holds-25-of-browser-market/, accessed March 10, 2008. Mendelson, E. (2008). The Next Browser War. PC Magazine (April, 23). http://www.pcmag.com/article2/0,2817,2286276,00. asp, accessed May 3, 2008.

[14] Porter, M. E. 1995. *Competitive Advantage*. New York: Free Press.

[15] Holstein, W. J. 2002. Canon Takes Aim at Xerox. *Fortune* (September 19).

[16] Based on Schermerhorn, R. 2006. Trilogy Software: High Performance Company of the Future? http://www.wiley.com/college/man/schermerhorn332879/site/tour/ic/page00 .htm, http://www.trilogy.com, accessed March 10, 2008. http://www.ecommercetimes .com/story/1277.html?welcome=1209839858, and http://www.ebituaries.whirlycott .com/viewsit.php?site=109, accessed May 3, 2008.

[17] Martin, S., & Revah, S. 1998. Build Your Own Barbie Online. CNET News.com (November 4). http://www.canada.cnet.com/news/0-1007-200-334987.html, accessed March 10, 2008; Mattel website, http://www.mattel.com/branded/barbie/, accessed March 10, 2008. See also Piller, F. 2006. Pimp Your Play. http://mass-customization.blogs.com/mass_ customization_open_i/2006/03/pimp_your_play_.html, accessed January 29, 2008.

[18] Rumelt, R. 1979. "Evaluating Competitive Strategies," in Schendel, D. E. and Hofer, C. (eds.), *Strategic Management: A New View of Business Policy and Planning*. Boston: Little, Brown, and Co.

[19] Rumelt, R. 1979.

[20] Rumelt, R. 1979.

[21] Rumelt, R. 1979.

[22] Teece, D. 1987. *The Competitive Challenge: Strategies for Industrial Innovation and Renewal* (ed.) (New York: Harper & Row, Ballinger Division.)

[23] http://en.wikipedia.org/wiki/Video_game_console, accessed May 21, 2007.

[24] http://en.wikipedia.org/wiki/Loyalty_program, accessed May 20, 2007.

[25] Richardson, M. 2005. Internet Transforms Banking in Asia. *International Herald Tribune* (October 25): 25.

[26] http://en.wikipedia.org/wiki/Franchising, accessed May 20, 2007.

[27] Franchising's Increasingly Adaptable Business Model. 2000. *International Herald Tribune* (November 16): 14.

[28] Counsel, J. 2002. What You Should Know *before* You Buy a Franchise. The Profit Clinic (April 25). http://www.profitclinic.com/SmallBiz/ResInfo/DntGo/Frnchs.html, accessed May 20, 2007. See also MFV. Franchising in Canada—The Pros and Cons of Buying a Franchise. http://www.betheboss.ca/general.cfm?page=bf2.cfm, accessed May 20, 2007.

[29] Bates, T. 1995. Analysis of Survival Rates among Franchise and Independent Small Business Startups. *Journal of Small Business Management.* (April). http://findarticles.com/p/articles/mi_hb177/is_199504/ai_hibm1G117355572, accessed May 20, 2007.

[30] Hidden Risks in Franchise Deals. 2004. *Swindon Advertiser* (January 7). http://archive.thisiswiltshire.co.uk/2004/1/7/128688.html, accessed May 20, 2007.

[31] See http://www.insun.us/financial-risk.php, accessed March 10, 2008, for a discussion of these and other risks.

[32] See Formula Business Restrictions, http://www.newrules.org/retail/formula.html, accessed May 20, 2007.

[33] Blanchard, D. 2005. Logistically Speaking: The Trouble with Benchmarking. *Logistics Today* (June). http://www.logisticstoday.com/displayStory.asp?sNO=7206, accessed December 26, 2007.

[34] See, for example, http://www.promising-practices.org and http://www.promisingpractices.net, accessed March 10, 2008.

[35] Poole, R., Jr., & Butler, V. 1999. Airline Deregulation: The Unfinished Revolution. http://www.rppi.org/ps255.html#_Toc444592613, accessed March 10, 2008. Milmo, D. (2007). Virgin Trains loses Cross Country Rail Franchise. The Guardian (July 10). http://www.guardian.co.uk/business/2007/jul/10/transportintheuk, accessed May 4, 2008.

[36] Huff, A. S. 1982. Industry Influences on Strategy Reformulation. *Strategic Management Journal*, 3(2): 119–131.

[37] This section draws on research being developed at the IOM chair at the Technical University of Munich.

[38] Debruyne M., Moenaert, R., Griffin, A., Hart, S., Hultink, E. J., & Robben, H. 2002. The Impact of New Product Launch Strategies on Competitive Reaction in Industrial Markets. *Journal of Product Innovation Management* 19(2): 159–170.

[39] Drucker, P. F. 1998. The Discipline of Innovation. *Harvard Business Review*, 76(2): 149–157.

[40] von Hippel, E. 2005. *Democratizing Innovation.* MIT Press: Boston, MA.

[41] Johnson, G., & Huff, A. S. (1998). "Everyday Innovation/Everyday Strategy" in Hamel, G., Prahalad, C. K., & Thomas, H., *Strategic Flexibility: Managing in a Turbulent Economy.* John Wiley & Sons: Chicester, UK.

[42] Östholm I., & Eliasson, G. 1996. Nya skapelser: Losec-entreprenörens recept. Stockholm: Fischer & Co.

[43] Chesbrough, H. 2003. *Open Innovation: The new imperative for creating and profiting from technology,* Harvard Business School Press: Boston, MA.

[44] White, B. & Schneider, B. 2004 *Service Quality: Research Perspectives,* Thousand Oaks, CA: Sage.

[45] Cagan J., & Vogel, C. M. *Creating Breakthrough Products: Innovation from Product Planning to Program Approval.* Upper Saddle River, N.J.: Financial Times Prentice Hall.

[46] Chesbrough, 2003; Gassmann & Enkel, 2004; Piller, 2005; von Hippel, 2005

7

Considering Corporate Strategy

Imagine that you own a sporting goods store: Are you in the sports equipment business? Tennis, golf, or general sports? Do you want to sell sports fashion wear as well as equipment? Answering these and other questions requires judgments about the most effective boundaries of your firm. If it's a small operation, you'll be defining your business, but if you grow and try different solutions in different places, you will be considering questions of corporate strategy.

Corporate strategists decide what businesses they want their organization to be in. Managing external boundaries often involves corporate oversight of very fine-grained decisions about parts of the value chain. For example, should the golf equipment store affiliate with a golf course? Hire a golfing pro and offer unique instructional videos?

In addition to making boundary decisions, the management of multiple businesses by the corporate center may be seen as a "parenting" responsibility. Good corporate parents help establish objectives and monitor business units' financial performance. They facilitate sharing insights and skills across units in different divisions. They often provide systems that improve business unit operations. They can assign individuals to different units over time to expand their management skills and strategic insights.

· ·

This chapter addresses these issues by answering the following questions:

How do corporate strategists pursue growth?

How are economic transactions among firms facilitated?
   Spot market exchange
   Long-term contracts
   Alliances
   Networks
   Equity joint ventures
   Transaction cost analysis

Can diversification leverage core competence?
   Diversification and core competencies
   Corporate parenting
   Why managers diversify beyond current competence

When is learning an outcome of alliance?
   Barriers to learning in an alliance
   Overcoming barriers to learning

Decisions made at the top of a multibusiness firm must be strategic. Sony's experience demonstrates the importance and range of alternatives facing strategists in a major corporation.

final

SONY: FROM TOKYO TELECOMMUNICATIONS TO GLOBAL CONGLOMERATE

The world's largest consumer electronics company was founded in 1946 as Tokyo Telecommunications Engineering. The company built the first Japanese tape recorder in 1950, and seven years later it renamed itself Sony for *sonus* (the Latin word for "sound") and *sonny* ("little man"). Over the next two decades, Sony built the first color TV, home video recorder, and personal audio player (the Walkman). In the late 1980s, however, increasing global competition in consumer electronics led Sony to diversify its product and geographic scope. The firm embarked on a journey of growth through acquisitions and alliances that continues to the present day. Although Sony's corporate ventures have met with varying degrees of success, the firm continues to be one of the most recognized consumer brands.[1]

It is highly unlikely that Sony's growth could have been achieved through internal development alone. In fact, Sony provides a good example of how participation in an increasingly varied set of industries can be used to build value. Sony's first major diversified acquisitions were CBS Records in 1988 at a price of $2 billion and Columbia Pictures in the following year for $4.9 billion. In the early 1990s, Sony formed an alliance with Nintendo to produce a video game console. After Nintendo left the venture, Sony released its own PlayStation, which in 2003 accounted for 70 percent of the worldwide market. The company also became involved with music distribution as part of an alliance with BMG, one of its biggest rivals in the recorded music industry.[2]

Other diversification efforts focused on the growing computer market. In the early 1990s an alliance between Sony and Apple Computer led to one of the world's first personal digital assistants, the Newton. In 1994, Sony signed another important alliance with Intel to pursue the joint development of a personal computer that blended Intel's leading chip technology with Sony's unmatched expertise in designing innovative electronic devices. Another joint venture involved manufacturing liquid crystal displays with Samsung electronics. Sony also joined NTT DoCoMo to develop personal identification chips, Brightstor to design electronic storage solutions, and RealNetworks to create digital audio solutions.

Many of these ventures were not long-term winners. The Newton was eclipsed by other products. Then Sony ended a disappointing mobile-phone manufacturing alliance with Ericsson. Sometimes, however, one venture leads to another. SonyEricsson now sells music phones that challenge Apple's iPod—the music system that quickly replaced the Walkman after it was announced in 2001.[3]

In order to manage an increasingly complex mix of businesses, Sony simplified its organization structure, beginning with the consolidation of all electronics products into a single group. In addition, the company standardized and reduced the number of manufactured parts across all businesses. But these moves did not keep the company from losing money as it faced increasing competition in key areas. In March 2005, with its shares selling at less than half their price in 2001, the company named a non-Japanese CEO, Howard Stringer. A veteran of only eight years at Sony, Stringer announced that he would close eleven factories and cut 10,000 jobs (6.6 percent of the workforce) by March 2008.[4] In an early interview, he noted:

> Because Sony has such a broad range of products, [we] get picked off by competitors along the way. You don't get necessarily beaten, but you get seriously challenged. Kodak is back in the camera game and Canon is back in it. And you get HP and Dell in the computer side, and then you get more people than ever in the electronic side, including the Chinese, who have taken a real dent out of the high-end marketplace. But in terms of the variety of products, Sony is still unbeatable. The question is how much variety is too much variety.[5]

Stringer faced a challenge faced by all corporate strategists. His decisions not only shape the activities of the businesses he controls, but also influence the opportunities available to their supply chain partners, their competitors, and those selling complementary offerings. Thus, corporate strategy is important to understand even by strategists in single-business firms.

How Do Strategists Pursue Growth?

Corporate strategy determines the industries where the corporation will operate and what activities will be undertaken by firms within the corporation.

Corporate strategy is about defining and managing the boundaries of an organization. The driver of these decisions is often growth. Sony is a good example of a typical pattern: the company first grew through internal innovation. Some observers would still describe consumer electronics as Sony's core business, and the company certainly continues to protect and develop important resources in this area. However, Sony's later growth involved acquisitions of other businesses, such as Columbia Motion Pictures. Its corporate vision is to connect creative units in ways that make it more competitive. For example, Sony transformed the storyline of Columbia Pictures movie *Zathura* into software for the PlayStation product line.

Given its significant resources, Sony might have entered the motion picture business or developed the Newton using internal resources, following the way it grew in consumer electronics in the first decades of its existence. Why, one might ask, did this company buy its way into motion pictures, rather than start a movie studio from scratch? Why did it decide to join with Apple in a product development venture? A short answer to these questions is that starting a new business and learning how to be successful in a new industry takes time and requires enormous resources. Rather than develop a competence internally, corporate strategists often decide that it will be much quicker and more efficient to buy it from another firm, which means that envisioned promise can be more fully assessed before purchase. They can make a direct *acquisition* of a competence by purchasing a controlling interest in a company. Alternatively, they can form a *strategic alliance* with one or more companies that already have the needed competence.

To simplify the logic behind expanding boundaries in these ways, consider the decisions facing the owner of a snowboard shop. Selling snowboards can be an exciting business, but one of the problems is that snowboarding is a seasonal activity. What happens in spring and summer when the world is green and almost no one is thinking about hitting the slopes? One obvious answer for the business strategist is to diversify the product mix to include other kinds of sporting equipment—such as skateboards. The technical competencies for expansion into skateboards would appear to be available or easy to develop for a snowboard firm. And there is another attraction to this expansion: if winter brings little snow, skateboard sales may provide needed income.

By offsetting the natural seasonality and variance of the original snowboard business, expansion potentially enhances firm performance in three ways:

- *Financial growth*: increasing the overall stream of revenues flowing into the business
- *Financial stability*: leveling out or smoothing the revenues, profits and cash flow of the business
- *Shared costs*: spreading the costs of rent, employee salaries, advertising, accounting services, and other business activities across higher unit sales volume

Taken together, these three benefits reduce the overall level of financial risk, a concept we defined in Chapter 2 as uncertainty about future revenues, costs and profits.

It is easy to imagine that other diversification efforts would be attractive to our hypothetical snowboard company—such as further broadening the types of equipment sold (skis, in-line skates) and selling holiday packages (sports-oriented winter and summer options). Worksheet 7.1 in this chapter provides a questionnaire that you can use to assess growth and diversification opportunities within a single business that interests you.

Even superficial brainstorming reveals that as the products and services added in the understandable pursuit of growth and lower risk become more diverse, strategic opportunities involve increasingly disparate

Acquisition is a strategy in which one firm buys a controlling or 100 percent interest in another firm.

Strategic alliance is a strategy in which two or more firms form a relationship in order to pursue mutual interests that have implications for the long-term strategy of at least one of the partner firms.

Worksheet 7.1: Options for Growth and Diversification—A Tool for Profiling Company Capabilities

technologies and a widening mix of buyers. At some point the issues facing the strategist can no longer be approached from the perspective of business level or competitive strategy. The *scope* of activity undertaken suggests a need for strategic decision making at the corporate level and the likely development of a new business unit that can focus on new resource needs, customers, opportunities, and rivals.

Corporate strategists can also become involved as business *scale* increases, because it becomes increasingly attractive to involve others in risk-spreading activities. Purchasing a company in the music industry allowed Sony to quickly gain additional revenue from the revolution launched by its Walkman personal cassette player; sharing costs with Apple helped Sony reduce the financial risks associated with developing a radically new, high-tech product such as the Newton.

If one were to follow the logic of reducing financial risk to its extreme, *diversification* would eventually take a firm with sufficient resources into businesses across all sectors of the economy. From the shareholder's perspective, holding stock in this superdiversified firm would be like holding stock in a mutual fund. In fact, some strategists think of their business as a portfolio of financial assets. Berkshire Hathaway, which is run by Warren Buffett, is such a business. Buffett has been enormously successful, but he does not invest in just any business. Instead, he is widely praised as a "stock picker"—an astute analyst of which companies are the best investments. If you had purchased $10,000 worth of stock in Berkshire Hathaway in 1975, for example, it would have been worth more than $9.8 million at the end of 1998. Reflecting that impressive record, the stock price of this firm has moved from about $12 per share in 1936 to more than $137,980 per share in December 2007.

However, research shows that most corporations that operate on the portfolio principle don't do nearly as well. For example, a recent study by the consulting firm Marakon Associates found that the aggregate value of most conglomerates when considered as independent businesses was greater than the market value of the corporation as a whole.[6] Thus, the potential reduction in financial risk that arises as the result of combining a diverse set of businesses may *increase* risk faced by strategists and stockholders.

This chapter focuses on the logic behind multibusiness, multipartner decisions. When we use the term *business* or *business unit*, we are talking about subsidiaries in a multidivisional organization. Their businesses are more than financial assets in a holding company, and corporate strategy is not just about picking business investments. Though assessing the promise of each business is important, our next vignette shows that corporate strategy focuses on supporting activities *within* businesses and creating and managing relationships *across* businesses.

Scope
is the range of activities within a single firm or corporation.

Scale
refers to the overall size of a business, usually measured by annual revenues, unit volumes, or total assets.

Diversification
is an external growth strategy in which the firm expands its scope to include businesses competing in different markets.

> ## UTC Benefits from Unrelated Business Units
>
> A major source of financial risk facing managers at United Technologies Corporation (UTC) has to do with the level of defense spending in the United States. In the early 1990s, when the cold war ended, UTC's revenues would have been in jeopardy if Pratt & Whitney (jet engines) and Sikorsky (helicopters) were its only businesses, because both of these divisions were highly dependent on orders from the U.S. military. Fortunately for UTC, however, the downturn in these businesses in the 1990s was partially offset by growth in elevators (Otis) and air-conditioning equipment (Carrier). In the next decade, the global economy suffered a setback in response to terrorist activities, and revenue in these commercial areas diminished but was in turn offset by increased revenues from defense-related businesses. Thus, the key to reducing financial risk at UTC is the fact that downturns in some of its businesses tend to be balanced by upturns in others.
>
> UTC's George David was named CEO of the Year by *Business Week* in 2003. The magazine noted that UTC "has quietly outperformed rival General Electric Co. in total shareholder return and averaged double-digit earnings growth." Employee relations may well be part of this story of productivity, as UTC provides more than $60 million a year in its Employee Scholar Program (ESP) toward associate, bachelor, master, or doctoral degrees in any field. Students are also given three weeks of paid leave to study and $5,000 to $10,000 in UTC stock immediate after acquiring a degree.[7]
>
> Over the following five years stock prices rose steadily. At the beginning of 2008, Otis Elevator controlled more than 75 percent of the China market, Pratt & Whitney's sales were benefiting from a strong demand for jets around the world, Carrier was supporting strong global infrastructure growth, and Sikorsky had just won the largest contract in its history—a $7.4 billion deal to supply helicopters for the U.S. Army and Navy. *Business Week* called UTC "a glimmer of sunlight into an otherwise gloomy fourth-quarter earnings season."[8]

At a company like UTC, corporate strategy represents the basis for deciding the following:

- How to invest the company's financial resources across multiple business units
- How to link and support business activities
- Whether to acquire or form alliances with other businesses
- When to divest part or all of its businesses
- When to modify network relationships
- How to set a corporate-wide benefit package

The decisions made reflect corporate experience and skills. The goal in each decision is to increase the value of the corporation.

In overview, corporate strategists ask: What businesses should we be in? And which businesses should we avoid? Put simply, the focus of corporate strategy is on determining the scope and boundaries of the diversified firm. As we will see, the question of where to draw firm boundaries can be usefully transformed into questions about how to design economic transactions. Because profit is assumed to be the primary objective of the firm, economic analysis takes priority. However, toward the end of the chapter we will show how uncertainty about future events requires a non-economic analysis of firm boundaries as well.

HOW ARE ECONOMIC TRANSACTIONS AMONG FIRMS FACILITATED?

Business organizations are vehicles for facilitating economic transactions, and the boundaries of most corporations are therefore designed to make the economic transactions of their businesses efficient. Economic transactions are typically thought of as interactions "at arm's length," governed by legal or contractual terms between two people or two firms with distinct boundaries. However, one can also observe buyer-seller relationships between functions or divisions *within* corporations. For example, the Center for Leadership Effectiveness—a unit within GE Capital—sells training and development programs to many of GE Capital's operating divisions.[9]

Why has GE Capital decided to produce these products and services and sell them in an internal market rather than buy them in an external market? Or, to put the question differently, why did it decide to draw the boundaries of its firm so that it carries out development activities itself, rather than rely on outside suppliers? To use language first used in manufacturing businesses: Why did GE Capital decide to make rather than buy these products and services? In order to answer this question, it is necessary to define the alternative ways corporate strategists can organize economic transactions.

Figure 7.1 depicts the choices available to corporate strategists who are designing an economic relationship. On one extreme, they might find a desired product or service in a pure market situation—what economists would call a spot market—where people come together to transact an exchange and then go their way, without committing themselves to future exchanges. This is the kind of relationship individual consumers

Figure 7.1 — Continuum of Choices for Structuring Economic Relationships

have with a local grocer or gasoline retailer; corporate strategists act in a similar way when they purchase most commodities.

At the other extreme of choices shown in Figure 7.1, corporate strategists acquire a company that performs a desired activity and integrate it with existing businesses. This choice is labeled *pure hierarchy*, which means they will use the corporation's hierarchical control mechanisms to organize the economic relationship. This is the choice AOL made when it acquired Time Warner with business units to produce content (movies, e-books, news magazines) for online distribution. By owning the activities that produce the content, AOL gained privileged access to that content. Typically, the rules for setting transfer prices between two business units of the same corporation are set by managers in the corporate headquarters—that is, by the corporate hierarchy. But price advantages are not the only reason to bring an activity into the corporation—speed of access, confidentiality, and other attributes of such close relationships may also be financially attractive.

The two ends of the continuum represent two fundamentally different choices for structuring an economic exchange, whether the transaction involves tangible products, intangible services, or even information. In addition to these two extremes, there are three other common arrangements. These in-between alternatives combine features of both markets and hierarchies:

Spot Market Exchange

Currencies are exchanged in a spot market. Gold, crude oil, and other commodities are also purchased in a spot market. Two key features are that the exchange is in cash and the transaction is immediate: the exchange takes place at the point of sale.

Long-Term Contracts

Transactions between businesses may not be onetime events (as in spot markets). Rather, they may occur repeatedly over a period of time, and in such situations, managers often execute formal, *long-term contracts* that detail the terms of the exchange, including such things as quantities, prices, product specifications, and delivery dates. A pharmaceutical manufacturer's purchasing arrangements with the firm that produces its packaging materials, for instance, might be covered by a long-term, formal agreement.

Franchise agreements, like those between McDonald's Corporation and its independent franchisees, are another type of long-term contract. In effect, franchise agreements sell an independent entrepreneur the knowledge required to compete in a particular industry in exchange for a royalty. The McDonald's franchise agreement thus details such things as standards for operating the restaurant (cleanliness, product quality, and service), joint advertising arrangements, and hours of operation. The company provides training in these and other areas and charges

Long-term contracts are formal relationships between companies that detail the provision of quantities, prices, specifications, and delivery of products or services over time.

royalty fees for using its expertise. As long as the franchisee lives up to the contract, s/he may continue to use the McDonald's brand name, benefiting not only from the corporation's advertising but also from the years of experience and accumulated knowledge of McDonald's corporate management.

Alliances and Networks

Economic exchanges that are organized as an alliance are used with increasing frequency by corporate strategists. We have already defined *alliances* as informal relationships between two or more firms formed to pursue mutual interests. What distinguishes an alliance from a contractual relationship is its informal character. Though some parts of the relationship may be in written form, in an alliance the trustworthiness of the parties involved is a substitute for a formal contract. Though trust may not be binding, concerns about corporate reputation usually prevent firms from blatant violations of the alliance agreement. Just as in interpersonal relationships, once a company develops a reputation for being untrustworthy, few will want to do business in the future. As one research team put it, the implicit contract covering an alliance is "socially—not legally—binding."[10]

If there are multiple partners with multiple relationships involved, alliances may become *networks*—comprised of companies that focus on a specific set of activities and are linked by a common agenda. Thus, McDonald's relies on a carefully chosen network of partners to produce, install, and service hundreds of pieces of equipment (such as fryers, griddles, ice makers, and signs) used in more than 10,000 restaurants worldwide. Suppliers don't get long-term contracts, but instead are expected to judge from experience how many of their products will be required in a given year. They develop close working relationships, and McDonald's trusts them to allocate manufacturing capacity and schedule deliveries.

Equity Joint Ventures

A more formal arrangement is an *equity joint venture*, in which two or more firms create a new business for the purpose of carrying out some kind of mutually beneficial activity. A joint equity venture is likely to include negotiated agreements about share of ownership and management control. But operational details are often left open—to be decided informally by managers within the joint venture itself. Equity joint ventures can be considered a type of strategic alliance in which the partners organize their cooperative activity within a new and separate venture. This suits situations in which there is too much uncertainty to write down every expectation in advance (as one would do in a formal contract). Joint ownership increases the likelihood that the partners will cooperate when unanticipated circumstances arise. Equity joint ventures

Alliances are frequent but informal relationships between parties based on trust and reputation.

Networks are alliances between multiple companies that focus on a particular set of activities that are linked by a common agenda.

An equity joint venture is a formal relationship between two or more firms to create a new business or carry out some kind of mutually beneficial activity.

are often used in high-technology industries to manage the uncertainty and share the risks in large, costly research and development projects.

Many real-world economic relationships between firms blend elements of long-term contracts, alliances, and equity joint ventures. For example, some long-term contracts leave much of the relationship underspecified. This produces an arrangement that is more like an alliance than an arm's-length relationship. Or an equity joint venture may be contractually circumscribed as to the kinds of activities that the new entity is allowed to pursue. The venture may even be subject to a *sunset clause* defining the date on which it ceases to exist.

The number of alternatives for structuring an economic relationship may be confusing at first. Fortunately, analytical approaches can help narrow down the choices for strategists. Indeed, strategists use two types of analysis to determine how to structure an economic relationship: one focusing on the costs of the transaction, and the other focusing on leveraging and developing core competencies. We begin with the former, which is known as transaction cost analysis (TCA).

Transaction Cost Analysis

Transaction cost analysis examines the efficiency of creating and monitoring economic relationships.

As its name suggests, *transaction cost analysis* (TCA) focuses on the efficiency of creating and monitoring economic relationships. The analysis focuses more on the *indirect* costs of governing (or managing) the transaction than on the *direct* costs of producing a product or service.[11] TCA emphasizes that indirect costs rise as the level of uncertainty (or risk) increases in a situation, including the risk that one of the parties will take advantage of another. According to TCA, this risk is ever-present. TCA assumes that people will do what is in their economic self-interest and that this will often lead to *opportunism*—one party taking advantage of the other party by neglecting or shirking their obligation (either explicit or implicit) in the arrangement. Opportunism may be unintentional, as when a key scientist in a high-tech research and development joint venture decides to take a job with a competitor, or it may be deliberate and malicious, as when an individual job seeker gains employment in order to steal intellectual property.

Recalling the two extremes of the continuum outlined in Figure 7.1, TCA allows us to compare the costs of a transaction carried out in a market context versus a transaction that occurs within a hierarchical firm. In markets, direct costs are captured in the price charged by the seller, while indirect costs are due to the costs of creating and monitoring the contract (if any). In hierarchies, it is easy to assume that the direct costs will always be lower than in a market, because the seller's profit has been eliminated from the costs of production. However, if the market seller is more efficient at producing the product or service, its direct costs may actually be lower than production within the diversified firm.

In addition, indirect costs are likely to be higher in a hierarchical arrangement than a more market oriented one. In a simple market transaction, any needed controls are part of the negotiation. Firms tend to use more control systems, formal procedures, and managerial time to manage internal transactions; all are aspects of bureaucracy. At Sharp Corporation, for example, 4 to 5 percent of all employees work at corporate headquarters. Their job is to manage complex relationships between the manufacturing and marketing divisions of the company. This involves an elaborate system of planning and coordination as well as overseeing the negotiation of transfer prices between divisions. Transfer pricing is a method of accounting for internal transactions. To set the transfer price for a given year and to plan output requires intensive negotiation and dozens of meetings. The company even has a committee to keep up with all the committees! The reason that all this bureaucracy is worth it is that after internal negotiation, Sharp's manufacturing and marketing divisions can make and distribute products such as liquid crystal displays that are higher quality than similar products available on the open market.

Increasingly, however, corporate headquarters are shrinking.[12] Traditional back-office activities, such as basic accounting and payroll, are often transferred out of corporate headquarters and into regional headquarters or shared service centers, which operate as a profit-and-loss unit that charges other business units for its services. Increasingly, firms have outsourced service operations once they have a clearer picture of their costs as described in Chapter 6.[13] When boundaries are redrawn, by either centralization or outsourcing, staff time and energies in corporate headquarters can be focused on the core work of corporate management. Berkshire Hathaway, with just eleven and a half people on corporate staff (Warren Buffett's secretary is a half-time employee), represents a rather extreme example of this approach.

Thus, an important part of the TCA equation has to do with the benefits of markets and hierarchies. Markets offer powerful incentives to sellers in the form of lower prices and higher profit than many corporate arrangements. This pay-for-performance gives people a good reason to live up to their responsibilities. A major benefit of corporate hierarchies, on the other hand, is the ability to coordinate relationship activities. Business units and subsidiaries are free to be innovative. Good ideas flow back to corporate headquarters more easily, and corporate strategists can act as intermediaries diffusing innovations to the rest of the firm.[14]

As the need for innovation and coordination increases, corporate strategists tend to favor hierarchy. It is usually better to perform an activity within the firm if the work to be done has to be combined with other work in order to be useful. (Sharp's liquid crystal displays must be combined with calculators, computers, and other devices to be useful, for example.) On the other hand, if the work can be performed independently and if it produces a distinct output, a market arrangement is likely to be better. Markets avoid coordination costs such as layers of management that are inherent to internal arrangements; they also give both sides of the relationship more autonomy. Autonomy can be especially important if the work to be done is creative, is technology based, or involves professional expertise.

Figure 7.2 summarizes this discussion of the costs and benefits of markets and hierarchies.

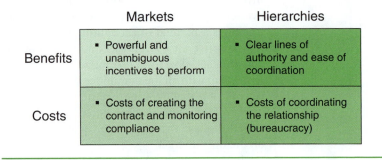

	Markets	Hierarchies
Benefits	• Powerful and unambiguous incentives to perform	• Clear lines of authority and ease of coordination
Costs	• Costs of creating the contract and monitoring compliance	• Costs of coordinating the relationship (bureaucracy)

Figure 7.2 — Costs and Benefits of Markets and Hierarchies

A series of three strategic choices made by managers at America Online (AOL) show how transaction cost analysis works.

Evaluating AOL's Strategy with Transaction Cost Analysis

Back in 1997, Amazon and AOL agreed to a contract that made Amazon the exclusive bookstore on the AOL home page.[15] For providing Amazon with access to more than 22 million AOL subscribers, AOL took a percentage of the revenues generated by the link. There was no need to coordinate with Amazon, however, because the bookseller handles all the e-commerce on its own. Rather than build an expensive joint venture to manage this relatively simple interaction, AOL and Amazon kept their relationship more marketlike by using a long-term contract. Eventually, however, AOL added other booksellers, including Barnesandnoble.com.[16] As one analyst put it, "If you were AOL, why wouldn't you [sign both deals]? Malls don't have just one bookstore."[17]

AOL also entered into a failed joint venture with Enron Corporation and IBM to sell utility services over the Internet through a company called NewEnergy, which was owned 60 percent by Enron and 20 percent each by IBM and AOL. AOL agreed to provide Web distribution, IBM handled billing and customer service, and Enron secured the power. It is easy to see the need for coordination among these three sets of activities, and the joint venture was created as a way to govern necessary interactions. Although the creation of the joint venture increased transaction costs (in the form of management), NewEnergy hoped to repay the investment with substantial profits to its partners. Note that it is highly unlikely that AOL would choose to merge with IBM and Enron to accomplish this goal. Such an arrangement would divert management's attention from its distinctive competencies as a media company. The joint venture facilitated exploration of a new and potentially profitable area of interest without diluting the company's strategic focus. Some distance turned out to be a good thing, because the joint venture failed miserably and members of the former NewEnergy management team became the target of a number of lawsuits for improper use of investors' money.

AOL's arrangement with Time Warner provides an example of a third strategic choice. Like AOL, Time Warner is in the media business, and AOL was willing to spend $183 billion to acquire it. The goal was to become the leader in interactive television, music, and other services that can be distributed over the Web. Essentially, AOL wanted to create a business that integrated the production and delivery of media content, including music, movies, books, and games. It saw the merger with Time Warner as a way to enhance AOL's competitive advantage on the Internet. Moreover, AOL strategists felt that the merger might "change the rules of the game" in the media industry, giving them a sustainable lead over their rivals. When integration of this kind is the goal, only a hierarchical arrangement will suffice. There is too much uncertainty about how technology will develop for a long-term contract and too many potential connections between AOL and Time Warner to allow for a joint venture. Transaction cost analysis shows why an acquisition (use of hierarchy) is a more attractive choice.[18]

CAN DIVERSIFICATION LEVERAGE CORE COMPETENCE?

Now that the range of corporate boundary choices has been laid out, we want to step back to discuss the logic behind corporate relationships. The decision to form a relationship with a particular business is part of a corporation's *diversification strategy*—the logic for external growth and corporate-level resource allocation across multiple business units. As suggested earlier, diversification strategy is easiest to describe in terms of the similarity or relatedness of the industries where a corporation competes. Relatedness can range from very high (when all the corporation's units are competing in the same industry) to very low (when all the corporation's units are competing in different industries.) McDonald's Corporation provides an example of high relatedness; its several business units all compete in the restaurant industry. General Electric (GE), by contrast, has dozens of business units competing in industries as diverse as electric light bulbs, plastics, consumer appliances, jet engines, financial services, and even power generation equipment. GE pursues a strategy of unrelated diversification. Unlike Berkshire Hathaway,

Diversification strategy defines the logic for external growth and corporate-level resource allocation across multiple business units.

however, GE tries to add value to its individual businesses with management controls and training.

Based on the idea of relatedness, we can identify four types of diversification strategy, ordered in Figure 7.3 from most related to least related.

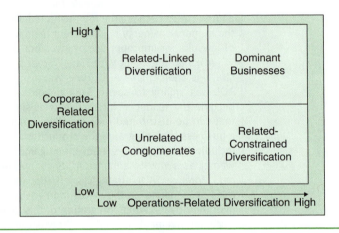

Figure 7.3 — Diversification Strategies

- *Dominant businesses* are companies in which most or all of the firm's revenues come from one industry. In its early days, Kodak was a clear example, because it competed exclusively in the film manufacturing and processing industry.
- *Related-constrained diversifiers* are corporations that compete in a set of industries in which a common pool of competencies enhances economic performance. Sony, for example, competes in industries in which competencies in creativity and innovation are necessary. Another example would be Honda and its line of cars, motorcycles, and lawn mowers.
- *Related-linked diversifiers* are corporations that compete in industries that are linked to one another in some way, often along the chain of production (raw material–manufacturing–distribution). Sony's game business can be linked to its motion picture business in this way, as movies provide the raw creative material for games. Thus, Sony is simultaneously pursuing both related-constrained and related-linked diversification strategies. In another example, Disney has migrated from theme parks to movies and TV shows to broadcasting companies.
- *Unrelated diversifiers (conglomerates)* are corporations in which most of the businesses in the company's portfolio are in unrelated industries, not linked along a value chain and not related by a common set of competencies. These firms are known as

conglomerates. Sony does not pursue unrelated diversification, but if it were to begin competing in automotive manufacturing, financial services, or retailing, we would almost certainly describe it as a conglomerate. A classic example is Japan's Mitsubishi Group, with portfolio companies in the energy, machinery, chemicals, metals, food, and general merchandise industries.

Although it is easy to differentiate between dominant businesses and conglomerates, the difference between related-constrained and related-linked diversification is more subtle. Figures 7.4 and 7.5 explore the differences involved.

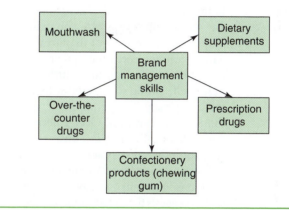

Figure 7.4 — Related-Constrained Diversification by a Pharmaceutical Company

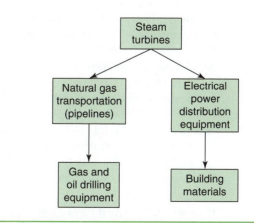

Figure 7.5 — Related-Linked Diversification by a Manufacturer of Steam Turbines

The essence of related-constrained diversification is that management chooses where to compete based on the firm's resource pool—its competencies. For example, the company in Figure 7.4 competes in a diverse set of industries. Although chewing gum might seem to have little in common with prescription drugs, dietary supplements, over-the-counter drugs, and mouthwash, all of these products need strong brand management competencies. One can imagine corporate management increasing competency in individual businesses' brand management by shared training, rotation of staff, and diffusion of successful practices.

In the related-linked choice illustrated in Figure 7.5, managers built their diversification strategy by looking for businesses that could be more directly connected to what they were already doing. This took them into businesses that are linked in a value chain—from raw material inputs to production processes to distribution of products. This strategy is also known as *vertical integration.* The manufacturing company used as an example in Figure 7.5 got its start as a manufacturer of steam turbines. These turbines were used in natural gas pipelines, and the company saw an opportunity to sell more turbines by getting into the pipeline business itself. Doing so exposed it to companies in the business of manufacturing gas-drilling equipment, and it saw this as an obvious link to the pipeline business. Over a period of time, the corporation not only competed in the pipeline business, it added businesses that manufacture equipment to extract natural gas out of the ground and compress it before it is transported in the pipeline.

Consistent with the resource-based view of economic performance, research suggests that related-constrained diversification strategies yield stronger returns than related-linked or conglomerate forms of diversification.[19] Overall performance is higher, it has been argued, because constrained diversification leverages competencies accumulated at the corporate level within business units and therefore contributes to the unit's competitive advantage. That is, related-constrained diversification extends the scope of the corporation's activities to businesses that can benefit from leveraging the competencies of the corporation, and it avoids expansion into businesses in which the corporation's competencies offer no advantage.

Diversification strategy need not require that the corporation own businesses in all of the industries in which it competes. In the case of Cisco Systems, for example, independent firms produce a whole range of products for the Internet, but do most of the manufacturing under Cisco's name. The strategic alliance between Cisco and its manufacturing partners provides links like those in Figure 7.5, but the relationships between units go beyond Cisco's formal boundaries.

Diversification and Core Competencies

From a resource-based perspective, corporate strategists should expand the scope of the firm to the extent that the decision to acquire a new

A core competence represents the skills or knowledge used by a corporation to add value across multiple business units.

business leverages the firm's core competencies. The concept of *core competence* is like the concept of distinctive competence from Chapter 2, except that it functions on the level of corporate strategy. Core competencies represent the skills or knowledge used by a corporation to add value across multiple business units. For example, strategists at United Technologies Corporation (UTC) identify the ability to develop and manufacture unusually strong but lightweight materials as one of the corporation's core competencies. It deploys this particular core competence in the design and manufacturing of high-tech carbon fiber materials for use in helicopters, jet engines, and elevators. The management of UTC believes that each of its business units enjoys a competitive advantage as the result of its access to this core competence. Similarly, access to the same core competence was a factor in GE's decision to form a product development alliance with UTC for a new lightweight jet engine. GE determined that this project was beyond its scope because it lacked one of the key competencies needed to be successful. But GE also brought capital and experience into the alliance that was attractive to UTC. Together UTC and GE expect to develop a superior engine at a lower cost than either would have been able to develop alone.

Divestment is a strategic choice to contract corporate boundaries.

The logic of core competence also can be applied to questions of corporate *divestment*—the decision to reduce the firm's boundaries by selling a business unit. Kodak illustrates the benefits of thinking about both the businesses to be in and the businesses *not* to be in.

Kodak Takes a Picture of Itself

CEO Kay Whitmore and other Kodak management were motivated to examine their core competencies after experiencing a period of very poor financial performance in the 1980s. Their bad numbers were attributed to a diversification strategy that had run amok. Starting out in photography, Kodak had entered pharmaceuticals, floppy disk manufacturing, software, and several other businesses. By the late 1980s it became clear that most of this diversification had been a mistake. Strategists working at Kodak during this time had expanded the scope of the business into industries and activities in which the firm's resources, skills, and core competencies produced no advantage. Following a core competence analysis, the company divested itself of many businesses that were deemed peripheral.

The analysis also guided additional investment. By 1989, Kodak executives had defined six specific core competencies underlying success in its imaging business (one of three sectors in which Kodak would still compete). Identifying core competencies in this focused way opened up new avenues for growth. For example, the Kodak Photo CD System was conceived as an opportunity to combine Kodak's competence in electronics with its competence in silver halide photography.

With a new century, the company is focusing on a transition to digital. The company has a number one position in commercial printing and a strong presence in radiology. Home printing has promise, via alliances with Lexmark and others, but this market has not been as strong as many anticipated. Meanwhile, the move away from film in Asia and other international markets has been more rapid than expected. Kodak announced approximately $3 billion in restructuring charges from 2004 through 2006, but one negative analyst noted, "When nonrecurring charges happen every quarter, they're recurring, that's your business model." The analyst wondered whether the company could integrate commercial printing or expand beyond its radiology niche given that much larger companies, including GE, are also targeting medical opportunities.[20]

The company is still trying to transform itself into a digital imaging company. In 2007 it announced 3,000 layoffs in addition to the more than 25,000 announced since 2004, along with the sale of its health-imaging unit, which Chief Executive Antonio Perez said was the last of the restructuring decisions. The Kodak name, one of the most widely recognized in the world, continues to be a major asset, but it is still difficult to tell whether the strategy will succeed.[21]

Notice that while transaction cost analysis focuses on the indirect costs of organizing an economic exchange (the costs of hierarchies or contracts), core competence analysis focuses on the direct costs of producing a good or service (efficiency or effectiveness of competing). Thus, Kodak blundered when it extended itself into pharmaceuticals because it lacked needed core competencies and could not be an efficient producer, not because acquisition was a poor way of organizing the associated transactions.

Corporate Parenting

In addition to using transaction cost analysis and core competence logic for thinking about acquisition decisions, one can compare the job of managing a diversified group of business units to the job of parenting.[22] The metaphor is compelling:

- Good corporate parents add value to the businesses that they own.
- Bad corporate parents impose systems that cause business units to perform below what they would if they were on their own.

Unlike most parents, however, corporate parents choose their children. The key to becoming a good corporate parent, therefore, is assessing the fit between the skills of a corporate parent and the needs of a potential new business. To do this, corporate strategists should start by identifying the set of factors that are critical to the business's success. Then, they should look for fit between their own skills and opportunities for improving the businesses they acquire.

Defining Corporate Skills at Cooper Industries

Robert Cizik, CEO of Houston-based Cooper Industries, a global manufacturer of electrical products, faced a parenting decision in 1989 when he considered whether to acquire Champion International. Champion owned a well-known brand in spark plugs and other automotive parts, but had accumulated a bloated bureaucracy and allowed its manufacturing processes to become woefully inefficient. Champion's products, however, fit within Cooper's scope of activities. More important to Cizik, Champion seemed to be a company that could benefit from what Cooper did best—instilling financial discipline and improving manufacturing operations. Using a process that Cizik referred to as "Cooperization," the corporation transformed dozens of underperforming manufacturers into profit centers for its shareholders. In choosing to acquire Champion, therefore, Cizik and his management team decided that their parenting skills could provide the kind of help that was needed to make Champion a success.

Cizik was CEO from 1975 to 1996, followed by John Riley, Jr., from 1996 to 2005. When Riley announced his successor, Kirk Hachingian, he noted that Cooper's strategy had become even more focused:

> A new Cooper Industries has evolved over the past several years. During this time, we've become a stronger, more focused global company. In my view, tomorrow's winners and losers will be separated by the ability to maintain leading market position, financial strength, and consistently generate profitable growth, both here and abroad, in all markets.[23]

Several different situations create parenting opportunities like those Cooper recognized in Champion:

1. *Size and age:* For business units that are old and large and have accumulated too much bureaucracy, a corporate parent may improve the situation by offering corporate services that relieve the business unit of excessive overhead. For units that are young and small and lack needed skills, a corporate parent may be able to help by providing needed competencies.

2. *Management:* A business unit may suffer from poor quality management relative to its competitors. A significant opportunity may exist for the corporate parent to insert management talent into the business.

3. *Business definition:* The business unit may not have done a good job of defining the scope of its activity. Target markets may

be too narrow or too broad, or there may be too much or too little vertical integration. Corporate strategies may be able to refocus or restructure the business to maximize its competitive advantage.

4. *Predictable errors:* The business unit may have fallen into dysfunctional patterns of decision making, attaching itself to strategies that seem foolish from a more objective viewpoint. By taking a fresh look at business strategy, corporate parents may also help the business unit discover alternatives that would otherwise remain unrecognized.

5. *Linkages:* As we noted earlier, a linked diversification strategy may give business units the opportunity to gain more efficient access to raw materials or channels of distribution within the corporation.

6. *Common capabilities:* Business units may bring capabilities that could be shared with other businesses in their parent's portfolio. Here, the parenting opportunity is to foster synergy with existing business units or future acquisitions.

7. *Special expertise:* Just as Cooper's expertise in manufacturing helped Champion, sometimes a business unit can benefit from the parent's specialized knowledge base.

8. *External relations:* Many business units have established relationships with other businesses in the form of strategic alliances or supply networks. Corporate parents may be able to manage these better or provide access to new and valuable relationships.

9. *Major boundary decisions:* When a business is facing an acquisition of its own, downsizing, or considering other generic strategies, the corporate parent may be able to offer knowledge about facing such decisions wisely from its past experience.

10. *Strategic changes:* Major changes are always risky. When change is needed but the business lacks experience changing direction or market position, a corporate parent may be able to help.

Each of these situations represents an opportunity for a corporate parent to help business units succeed. Parenting skills are more general than the notion of core competency, however. Providing access to a corporate core competency makes the business unit better off; ideally corporate parenting further contributes to its competitive advantage. Worksheet 7.1, suggested at the beginning of this chapter, provides a preliminary tool for carrying out the needed analysis.

Why Managers Diversify beyond Current Competence

Given the logic of core competence and good parenting, why do corporate strategists acquire businesses in which they have neither the opportunity to leverage a core competence nor the chance to use parenting skills? The answer may lie in the mistaken idea that "bigger is always better." Empirical research shows that most managers prefer strategies that favor growth and expansion.[24] An important and obvious driver is the fact that bigger businesses typically mean bigger salaries and more career opportunities for managers.[25] Other possible explanations for expansive behavior range from seeking new challenges to responding to serendipitous opportunities.

The understandable desire for growth, however, tends to lead managers into increasingly unrelated diversification as they exhaust opportunities that draw on a given set of competencies or parenting skills. Figure 7.6 offers an example of the result. As the figure shows, Disney's animated film and theme park businesses are closely related because they share the company's core competence in developing unique family entertainment. Motion pictures and TV programs are also logical because they draw on similar competencies and are likely to benefit from the parenting opportunities just listed. The quest for growth, however, also led Disney into businesses, such as real estate development, that are more peripherally related to its core competencies. Interestingly, responding to poor financial performance, in early 2004 Disney announced that it was divesting key parts of its real estate business.

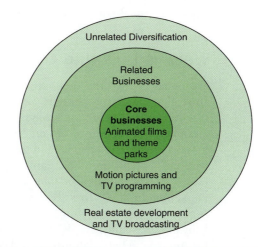

Figure 7.6 — Diversification and Expansion of Business Scope at Disney

Although the argument so far has emphasized the need to carefully define core competencies and constrain diversification strategy, what happens when a corporation has reached the limits of core competencies? Does this mean it can grow no further? With technologies always changing, shouldn't diversified companies expect to enter new markets and develop new competencies? Doesn't a robust economy require that firms develop new skills and capabilities? In short, how does the need to learn square with the idea of leveraging core competencies?

These questions take us back to an issue we addressed in Chapter 2 — the challenges associated with accumulating new resources and learning new competencies. Firms that diversify beyond their existing core competencies assume the strategic risks associated with resource accumulation. Deciding whether these risks are necessary to adaptation or overly threaten corporate profits is at the crux of diversification decisions. That question has to be settled on a case-by-case basis by comparing existing core competencies with the competencies needed to compete in the area of an acquisition.

Every acquisition assumes some risk, but stretching firm boundaries into an unrelated business increases the chance that management in the acquiring firm will be unable to contribute to the acquired firm. Even if we assume that the acquired firm brings its own advantage, diversification that is too far from corporate experience makes it likely that managers in the acquiring firm—without experience in what makes the new business successful—will fail to sustain the advantage they purchased. As they ignore or shed unrecognized assets or invest in the wrong resources the potential benefits of acquisition are lost. On balance, research suggests that stretching too far away from existing competencies is likely to lead to lower financial performance.[26] As we will see next, the risk of learning through acquisitions is one reason that corporations enter into strategic alliances as an alternative strategy for learning new competencies.

WHEN IS LEARNING AN OUTCOME OF ALLIANCE?

We noted in the brief description of AOL's alliance with Enron and IBM that attractive partners usually have different competencies. Although alliances are not always successful, ventures like this provide an opportunity to learn from different experiences. Good alliances internalize new competencies and then deploy them, with or without the partner's participation. For example, Toys "R" Us, like many other retailers, sought out Amazon.com as a partner with expertise in Internet marketing. In 2000, Toys "R" Us signed a ten-year agreement to make Amazon its exclusive online retailer for Toys "R" Us toys, games, and baby products and Toys "R" Us the exclusive provider of such products for Amazon. That relationship worked for a few years, but then Toys "R" Us executives were annoyed when Amazon signed agreements with rivals such as Target and zShops. The relationship ended unhappily in 2006 with a court order to sever the partnership, but each partner is using what it learned to sell more toys on the Web.[27]

If partners are not current or potential competitors, learning alliances between firms can result in win-win outcomes. That's the intent behind recent R&D alliances between telecommunications companies seeking to develop equipment for third-generation wireless technologies. Motorola, a telephone equipment manufacturer, partners with Cisco, a switch maker. Both firms stand to gain advantage-producing knowledge, and because they don't compete with each other, both have an interest in sharing as much information as possible. The potential for learning new competencies and building competitive advantage in strategic alliances has become so important that one researcher has referred to the current period of time as "the age of alliance capitalism."[28]

Some kinds of relationships, however, do not provide access to a partner's skills and knowledge. Buyers and sellers in a spot market, for example, rarely interact on a level that is sufficient to transfer knowledge. Research shows that alliances and equity joint ventures are more effective as learning vehicles than contract-based relationships.[29] In industries in which technology and innovation are the basis of competitive advantage, these forms of interaction have become key elements of competitive strategy, but also highly risky ones.

Learning from Toyota

The automobile industry is one of the most global industries in the world and the setting of especially complicated interfirm arrangements. A long-term joint venture between General Motors (GM) and Toyota, called New United Motor Manufacturing Inc. (NUMMI) is a good example[30]. Among the reasons GM gave for entering this agreement was the potential for valuable learning. Today, NUMMI plays a role in the development and training of most senior-level managers at GM. Topics include manufacturing and engineering processes, and NUMMI is also a source of knowledge about continuous improvement, quality, and human resource systems. GM managers from around the world are sent to visit NUMMI with the explicit objective of improving their own unit's strategy. When managers of a new plant for GM's Opel subsidiary visited NUMMI, for instance, the goal was simple: "to build a plant like NUMMI."[31]

GM has been trying to learn from NUMMI for almost twenty years, and the company has no doubt gained a significant amount of knowledge. But Toyota continues to erode the American firm's market share in North America. Part of the reason may be that matching Toyota's quality and cost position is a moving target. Rather than resting on its laurels, the Japanese partner has moved even more quickly than GM to acquire new knowledge and skills from this and other alliance relationships.

Barriers to Learning in an Alliance

Learning is not automatic in an alliance or joint venture. In fact, research suggests that the process can be difficult and frustrating.[32] Two major barriers to acquiring valuable knowledge in an alliance are concerns about knowledge spillovers and the tacitness of the knowledge shared.

Can Knowledge Spill Over?   There are many reasons for a company to be wary in a learning alliance. Although it may be willing to share some things, there are likely to be other technologies or trade secrets that it wants to protect. However, it is not easy to control what a partner learns. Once access to company information and people are provided, there is really no way to strictly delimit what lessons the partner takes away. Because industrial espionage rarely makes the news, a good example of *knowledge spillover* comes from the diplomatic front. During the Clinton administration, the United States entered into an agreement to share nuclear power generation technology with the People's Republic of China. Although there is no proof of their accusations, Republicans in Congress later asserted that China's nuclear weapons program was the real beneficiary. This example makes an important point about spillover. No matter how circumspect the arrangements for deciding what to share, it is virtually impossible to specify how the knowledge will ultimately be used.

Concerns about spillover result in a number of constraints on a learning relationship. Engineers may be limited in their access to documentation. Long lists may be made of specific ideas, patents, or designs that may not be shared, or even discussed. Physical location and movement of personnel may be constricted. In many cases, the joint venture's headquarters may be oceans away from either partner's facilities. Although these arrangements may prevent leakage of sensitive information, they also undermine trust and deter sharing of information. A scientist in a drug company alliance, for example, might have to reread the list of restricted information before every meeting with managers from the partnering firm. Situations like this are not conducive to the open information sharing required for learning.

How Tacit Is the Knowledge to Be Shared?   *Tacit knowledge* is the kind of knowledge that is difficult or impossible to articulate in words or write down on paper. Athletic performance relies on tacit knowledge, for example. Riding a bike could never be learned simply by reading a manual. Tacit knowledge is acquired from experience and learning by doing. In contrast, explicit knowledge is easier to share and takes the form of formulas, engineering drawings, books, and manuals. Transferring tacit knowledge is much more difficult. (That's why good coaches are so valuable!)

> **Knowledge spillover** is the risk that the knowledge of one firm will inadvertently transfer to others.

> **Tacit knowledge** is know-how that is difficult to codify and transfer.

Indeed, tacit knowledge may be one of the reasons that GM has failed to learn as much as it hoped from NUMMI. The process of continuous improvement relies on a high level of participation from production workers. In Japan, employees and managers have shared joint responsibility for the manufacturing process for decades. This experience has led to communication skills and routines that produce a high level of involvement. Experiences in labor-management relationships in the U.S. automobile industry, however, are epitomized by detailed union contracts containing clearly delineated roles and responsibilities. A much different, more protective style of communication between management and labor developed from this experience. In short, the unstated, tacit assumptions about how employees and managers communicate in the two countries are quite different. Formal training programs simply do not provide a sufficient amount or quality of experience for U.S. managers to learn to communicate in the way that managers at Toyota connect. Research shows that barriers to the transfer of tacit knowledge have plagued other strategic alliances as well.[33]

Ironically, the greater a relationship's potential to increase competitive advantage, the more likely it is to suffer from the problems of spillover and tacit knowledge. After all, spillover worries would not even exist if the knowledge weren't worth protecting. And the fact that tacit knowledge is difficult to transfer means that it is less imitable. As we learned in Chapter 2, inimitability is a critical feature of the knowledge underlying competitive advantage. Thus, diminishing these barriers is an important strategic priority.

Overcoming Barriers to Learning

Three principles are important to more effective learning in strategic alliances.

1. *The relationship must have a sufficient number of connections between the partners.* This may seem obvious, but too many strategic alliances share information without sharing people. If transferring tacit knowledge is the goal, personnel transfer may be required because this is the only way that an individual can experience what is needed to acquire tacit knowledge. Even long visits may be insufficient, unless employees are coached in advance about what to expect, what to pay attention to, and what to take away from their experience. In addition to personnel transfers, there must be deliberate, ongoing interactions between managers and employees at multiple levels. To improve communication skills, not only managers but also employees and perhaps employee-manager teams may need to experience the partner's work environment.

2. *The knowledge goals of the relationship should be related to what an organization already knows.* Research shows that the capacity of both people and firms to absorb new knowledge is a function of the relationship between target knowledge and prior experience.[34] Without the *absorptive capacity* that comes from prior experience in a particular area of expertise, an organization enters into a strategic alliance lacking necessary preparation. Not only will employees not understand what they are supposed to learn, but they will not even know what they do not know. Thus, acquiring valuable knowledge from a technology joint venture may require up-front investments in internal research. Once people in the organization have gained some experience with the technology, they are in a much better position to learn new things from a partner. Because chemistry constitutes the knowledge base of many large pharmaceutical firms, for example, their ability to learn from biotech joint ventures has depended to some degree on their willingness and ability to make up-front investments in biology and related scientific specializations.

> **Absorptive capacity**
> is the ability to learn from external sources.

3. *The organizational cultures of potential partners must be aligned.* In fact, differences in the values and norms of two partners may be the ultimate, but often hidden, barrier to knowledge transfer.[35] Cultural differences may be most stark when the national cultures of two firms are different. Thus, international joint ventures like NUMMI are attractive for their learning potential, but often such learning is frustrated by simple things, such as lack of a common language and cultural differences between different partners.

Learning is also difficult when organizational cultures clash. Apple Computer, for example, has tried to partner with IBM on a number of occasions. Each time, however, cultural differences have made the relationship stormy. Both firms are based in the United States, but one can hardly imagine two computer firms that are more different in their corporate cultures. Everything from how people dress to what they value in new technology differs, and this makes it very difficult for them to communicate. Research in the pharmaceutical industry similarly confirms that learning between firms decreases when organizational cultures are different.[36]

Pursuing learning in relationships blocked by cultural differences can waste management's time and shareholder resources. But the more alike two organizational cultures are, the less the two firms may have to learn from each other. The reason Apple and IBM have chosen to partner over the years is because they have different, but complementary, skills. If strategists limit themselves to strategic alliances in which cultures are aligned, they may forgo valuable learning opportunities.

In sum, relationships with other firms, especially alliances and joint ventures, have become an important vehicle for organizational learning. Sometimes firms cooperate in order to compete with one another, as we noted in Chapter 3. In other cases, firms with complementary products join in an alliance, and the learning becomes mutually beneficial. Spillover concerns and the tacit nature of knowledge often erect barriers to learning. These may be overcome if the alliance is designed with sufficient connections, if the partners start out with sufficient absorptive capacity, and if the cultures of the partners are aligned. As examples like the GM-Toyota and Apple-IBM alliances suggest, however, firms don't limit their alliance strategies to others like themselves. The potential benefits of learning from differences are simply too attractive. Worksheet 7.2 provides a tool for documenting the potential learning in an alliance.

Worksheet 7.2:
Strategic Alliance Analysis—A Tool for Assessing Learning across Firm Boundaries

CONCLUSIONS FOR THE STRATEGIST

As corporate strategists make the boundary decisions we have discussed in this chapter, they are collectively blurring industry boundaries. That means that corporate strategy is especially important and interesting. In the long term, society changes as business activities become linked in the complicated ways that corporations are devising. These linkages not only connect aspects of life that were previously considered to be separate, but provide goods and services that did not exist in the past. Companies have to change their boundaries in response, and of course there is a reciprocal relationship—corporations also cause environmental shifts.

People tend to think of something they buy, such as a Sony PlayStation, in terms of product features, company reputation, and alternative products available on the market. This chapter's discussion of corporate strategy outlines a more complicated picture behind the attributes that engage consumers. When video games were first introduced, for example, they were arcadelike games of skill. As the technology developed, they became more complex. Less predictably, gaming metamorphosed into a much richer experience based on strong storylines that cross into other media. For example, the game Tomb Raider (1996) spawned numerous comic books, two movies (2001, 2003), and a series of original novels.[37] This cross-pollination is more understandable once one knows that Sony, the market leader in gaming, is deliberately seeking creative connections among its business units, which include a major motion picture studio.

Smaller, individually owned businesses play a part in this evolution. Corporations influence them as owners and partners; the activities of large corporations also create niche opportunities for independent smaller players. Overall, the connections among organizations are increasingly intricate, and their ongoing evolution is important for the business strategist to understand.

Key Concepts

Corporate strategy defines and manages boundaries; more specifically it determines the industries in which the corporation will operate and what activities will be undertaken. Two choices given particular attention in this chapter are **acquisition,** in which a controlling interest is obtained in another firm, and **strategic alliance,** in which an ongoing but less formal relationship is established with one or more firms to pursue mutual interests. These relationships allow the corporation to expand its **scope,** or range of activities. They tend to be growth strategies in which the **scale,** or overall size of the organization, expands as well.

Business organizations are vehicles to facilitate economic transactions, and the boundaries of most corporations are therefore designed to make economic transactions efficient. Two forms of analysis are often used to evaluate possible options. The first, **transaction cost analysis,** examines the cost of creating and monitoring different kinds of economic relationships established by businesses. The possible form of these relationships includes **long-term contracts,** which are formal relationships between companies that detail the quantities, prices, specifications, and delivery of products or services over time. **Alliances** are ongoing but more informal relationships between firms based on trust and reputation that have implications for at least one partner's strategy. **Networks** are alliances among multiple companies that focus on a particular set of activities linked by a common agenda. An **equity joint venture** is a formal relationship between two or more firms to create a new business or carry out some other kind of mutually beneficial activity.

The other form of analysis looks at the costs and benefits of relationships within and between businesses. Four different **diversification strategies,** or logics for achieving external growth and determining resource allocation, are briefly outlined. They vary in the links they seek to establish within and between businesses. Diversification around a **dominant business** strives for benefits from relationships along both dimensions. **Related-constrained diversifiers** search for operational links across businesses. **Related-linked diversifiers** primarily seek buyer-seller relationships across business units. **Unrelated diversifiers (conglomerates)** do not look for synergies in either area but make acquisition decisions strictly in terms of financial criteria. In firms following the dominant business or related-constrained kinds of diversification, the role of the **corporate parent** is to seek **core competence,** or skills and knowledge that can add value across multiple business units. Good corporate parents add value to their business units. When corporate parents cannot add value, **divestment** may become the best option. Beyond gaining access to resources without having to own them, strategic alliances also offer an opportunity for the corporation to learn new competencies. This can require transferring **tacit knowledge**, which is difficult and often costly. Firms must consider how to increase their **absorptive capacity** before they can learn from an alliance that involves unfamiliar knowledge. One downside of some alliances is that they expose partners to the risk of **knowledge spillover** that will enable new or stronger competitors.

Questions for Further Reflection

1. Read Ian Wylie's short article "Harry Potter's Corporate Parent" in *Fast Company* (August 2001) at http://www.fastcompany.com (search for "corporate parent"). Summarize the rules for managing a diverse portfolio that the article suggests and consider how relevant they are in businesses other than publishing. Then consider how one runaway success (such as the Harry Potter series) affects corporate strategy.

2. Obtain information on Kodak, UTC, Cooper, or another corporation with which you are familiar. What corporate strategies has the firm pursued? How successful has it been? What strategy would you advise over the next few years, and why?

3. Choose an industry that interests you (entertainment, mobile phone, oil and gas, automotive, alternative energy, and so on). Find an example of a strategic alliance or joint venture that took place between two or more companies at least three years ago by searching on one of these terms and the industry that interests you. Research news coverage of the relationship that interests you. What happened to the relationship? What were the major outcomes for each partner?

WORKSHEET 7.1
Options for Growth and Diversification—A Tool for Profiling Company Capabilities

Analyze a firm's options for growth and diversification of its single business.

Step 1: Talk to the owner of a relatively small but successful company in your community. Identify the firm's distinctive competencies and resources in column 1 of the worksheet.

Step 2: Consider how these competencies might help the firm grow. Put your answers in column 2.

Step 3: Could these competencies be leveraged in related product lines? Identify a product in column 3 with your reasons.

Step 4: Suggest a promising growth strategy. Put your ideas in the box at the bottom of the worksheet. How do you think your informant would respond to these suggestions? Have a second conversation with your informant if possible.

Options for Growth and Diversification Worksheet 7.1	Product Line:
Analyst(s):	Summary:

Competence	Projected Future Growth	Diversification Options

Identified Future Strategy:

WORKSHEET 7.2
Strategic Alliance Analysis—A Tool for Assessing Learning across Firm Boundaries

This worksheet provides a set of questions for analyzing how well an economic unit is learning from alliance partners.

Step 1: Select a unit or a firm which has a strategic alliance with another unit or firm.

Step 2: Using the Internet and other resources, identify the key components of the strategic alliance. Put your ideas in column 1.

Step 3: Consider how the first unit or firm might learn from this alliance. Put your answers in column 2.

Step 4: Compare how another partner might learn from this alliance. Put your answers in column 3.

Step 5: Analyze what has actually been learned from available information. Put your answers in column 4.

Strategic Alliance Analysis Worksheet 7.2		Strategic Alliance: Unit/Firm One: Unit/Firm Two:	
Analyst(s):		Summary:	

Strategic Alliance Key Component	Partner A Learning Potential	Partner B Learning Potential	Actual Learning

NOTES

[1] http://www.harrisinteractive.com/harris_poll/index.asp?PID=590 and http://bwnt. businessweek.com/brand/2006/, accessed March 13, 2008.

[2]Approved in 2004, the merger was annulled in 2006 by the EU courts. Reuters (June 26, 2007). www.reuters.com/article/IndustryNews/idUSBFA00004192006027, accessed March 24, 2008.

[3]Ewing, J. 2006. Music Phones Tackle the iPod. Business Week Online (July 11). http://yahoo.businessweek.com/globalbiz/content/jul2006/gb20060711_026111.htm, accessed March 13, 2008.

[4]Edwards, C. 2006. Hitting the Right Notes at Sony. Business Week Online (January 9). http://www.businessweek.com/technology/content/jan2006/tc20060109_265301.htm, accessed March 13, 2008.

[5]Schlender, B. 2005. "If You Don't Act, You Will Kill the Company." Interview: New Sony Chief Howard Stringer on What It Will Take to Rally His Struggling Company. *Fortune* (April 4). http://money.cnn.com/magazines/fortune/fortune_archive/2005/04/04/8255922/index.htm, accessed March 13, 2008. Stahl, L. 2006. *60 Minutes* (January 8). http://www.cbsnews.com/stories/2006/01/06/60minutes/main1183023_page3.shtml, accessed March 13, 2008.

[6]http://www.marakon.com/ideas_pdf/id_030830_kaye.pdf, accessed March 13, 2008.

[7]The Best and Worst Managers of 2003. 2004. *Business Week* (January 12). http://www.businessweek.com/magazine/content/04_02/b3865709.htm, accessed March 13, 2008; personal conversation with Michael Shimkus, Sikorsky/UTC employee and MBA student at Texas Christian University.

[8]Steverman, B. 2008. United Technologies: Global Growth Holds Up. *Business Week* (January 23). http://www.businessweek.com/print/investor/content/jan2008/pi20080123_121078.htm, accessed January 30, 2008.

[9]http://www.gecapital.com, accessed March 13, 2008.

[10]Jones, C., Hesterly, W. S., & Borgatti, S. P. 1997. A General Theory of Network Governance: Exchange Conditions and Social Mechanisms. *Academy of Management Review* 22: 911–945.

[11]Williamson, O. E. 1985. *The Economic Institutions of Capitalism*. New York: Free Press.

[12]Birkinshaw, J., Braunerhjelm, P., Holm, U., & Terjesen, S. 2006. Why Do Some Multinational Corporations Relocate Their Corporate Headquarters Overseas? *Strategic Management Journal* 27(7): 681–700.

[13]Terjesen, S. 2006. Outsourcing and Offshoring of Finance Activities. In H. Kehal & V. Singh (eds.), *Outsourcing and Offshoring in the 21st Century*. Hershey, PA: Idea Group.

[14]Birkinshaw, J. 2001. Unleash Innovation in Foreign Subsidiaries. *Harvard Business Review* 79(3): 131–137.

[15]Kirsner, S. 1997. AOL Wins Easy Money in Booksellers' Battle. *Wired* (December 18). http://www.wired.com/news/business/0,1367,9271,00.html, accessed March 13, 2008.

[16]Prior, M. 2001. Amazon's Agreement with AOL Reveals E-Tailer's New Strategy. *DSN Retailing Today* (August 6).

[17]Miles, S., & Ricciuti, M. 1997. AOL Books on Barnes & Noble. CNET News.com (December 17).

[18]Johnson, C. A. 2001. Amazon + AOL = Trouble for Retailers and Portals. Forrester Research (July 25). http://www.forrester.com/ER/Research/Brief/Excerpt/0,1317,13104,00.html, accessed March 13, 2008.

[19]Palich, L. E., Cardinal, L. B., & Miller, C. C. 2000. Curvilinearity in the Diversification-Performance Lineage: An Examination of Over Three Decades of Research. *Strategic Management Journal* 10: 271–284; Markides, C., & Williamson, P. J. 1994. Related Diversification, Core Competencies and Corporate Performance. *Strategic Management Journal* 15(5): 149–166. See also Rumelt, R. P. 1974. *Strategy, Structure and Economic Performance*. Cambridge, MA: Harvard University Press.

[20]Boorstin, J. 2005. Bill Miller's Kodak Moment: The Visionary Fund Manager Is Sticking with the Photo Giant Despite Its Long Slide. *Fortune* (November 14). http://money.cnn.com/magazines/fortune/fortune_archive/2005/11/14/8360701/index.htm, accessed March 13, 2008.

[21]Kodak Cutting up to 3,000 More Jobs. 2007. *USA Today* (February 8). http://www.usatoday.com/money/industries/manufacturing/2007-02-08-kodak_x.htm, accessed January 31, 2008. See also The 100 Top Brands. 2006. *Business Week*. http://bwnt.businessweek.com/brand/2006/, accessed January 31, 2008.

[22]Campbell, A., Goold, M., & Alexander, M. 1995. Corporate Strategy: The Quest for Parenting Advantage. *Harvard Business Review* (March–April): 121–132; Goold, M., & Campbell, A. 1989. *Strategies and Styles: The Role of the Centre in Managing Diversified Corporations.* London: Blackwell.

[23]Cooper Industries Names Hachigian as CEO. 2005. Electrical Manufacturers Association. http://www.nema.org/media/ind/20050428b.cfm, accessed January 31, 2008.

[24]Gray, S. R., & Cannella, A. A., Jr. 1997. The Role of Risk in Executive Compensation. Journal of *Management* 23: 517–540.

[25]Lubatkin, M. H., & Lane, P. J. 1996. The Merger Mavens Still Have It Wrong! *Academy of Management Executive* 10(1): 21–39; Lubakin, M. H. (1988). Value-Creating Mergers: Fact or Folklore? *Academy of Management Executive* 2(4): 295–302.

[26]Wade, M. R., & Gravill, J. I. 2003. Diversification and Performance of Japanese IT Subsidiaries: A Resource-Based View. *Information and Management* 40(4): 305–316; Markides & Williamson, Related Diversification, 149–166.

[27]D'Innocenzio, A. Once Partners, Amazon.com and Toysrus.com Become Rivals. *USA Today* (October 5, 2006) http://www.usatoday.com/tech/news/2006-10-05-amazon-toysrus_x.htm, accessed March 24, 2008.

[28]Dunning, J. 1995. Reappraising the Eclectic Paradigm in an Age of Alliance Capitalism. *Journal of International Business Studies* 26: 461–492.

[29]Mowery, D. C., Oxley, J. E., & Silverman, B. S. 1996. Strategic Alliances and Interfirm Knowledge Transfer. *Strategic Management Journal* 17: 77–92.

[30]http://www.nummi.com, accessed March 13, 2008.

[31]Inkpen, A. C. 1998. Learning and Knowledge Acquisition through International Strategic Alliances. *Academy of Management Executive* 12: 69–80.

[32]Inkpen, A. C. 1996. Creating Knowledge through Collaboration. *California Management Review* 39(1): 123–140; Inkpen, A. C., & Crossan, M. M. 1995. Believing Is Seeing: Joint Ventures and Organizational Learning. *Journal of Management Studies* 32: 595–618.

[33]Yan, A., & Gray, B. 1994. Bargaining Power, Management Control and Performance in United States–China Joint Ventures: A Comparative Case Study. *Academy of Management Journal* 37: 1478–1517.

[34]Cohen, W. M., & Levinthal, D. A. 1990. Absorptive Capacity: A New Perspective on Learning and Innovation. *Administrative Science Quarterly* 35: 128–152.

[35]Lyles, M. A., & Salk, J. E. 1996. Knowledge Acquisition from Foreign Parents in International Joint Ventures. *Journal of International Business Studies* 27: 877–904; Lane, P. J., Lyles, M. A., & Salk, J. E. 1998. Relative Absorptive Capacity, Trust, and Interorganizational Learning in International Joint Ventures. In M. A. Hitt, J. E. Ricart, & R. D. Nixon (eds.)., *Managing Strategically in an Interconnected World* (pp. 374–397). New York: Wiley.

[36]Lane, P. J., & Lubatkin, M. 1998. Relative Absorptive Capacity and Interorganizational Learning. *Strategic Management Journal* 19: 461–477.

[37]http://en.wikipedia.org/wiki/Tomb_Raider_series#Original_novels, accessed March 13, 2008.

8

Thinking Globally

→ → →

You use many products—sold by firms such as Sony, MTV, Nokia, Nestlé, Disney, and McDonald's—that indicate that the world is moving toward a more integrated, global economy. You also know of many changes in the macro environment that facilitate global operations. Media and travel increase the market for international products. Information and transportation technologies are reducing the cost of managing geographically dispersed operations. Barriers to cross-border trade and investment are in general going down. This chapter discusses the resulting opportunities for small and large firms, while recognizing that there are impediments and risks to globalization as well.

In today's competitive environment, firms that confine themselves to a domestic market may put themselves at a significant competitive disadvantage. Firms conducting international activities can exploit opportunities to increase market demand, reduce costs, and learn from global partners. In an increasingly competitive environment, firms are entering domains they once would have ignored.

· ·

Those who choose to operate in more than one country must understand the basic alternatives for where and how to position activities in a globalizing environment. In this chapter we answer the following questions:

What are the advantages and disadvantages of international diversification?

How can competitive advantage be increased through international expansion?

Exploit economies of scale
Exploit economies of scope
Exploit national differences

What are alternative strategies for international expansion?

What are alternative entry modes?

Export
License
Franchise
Joint venture
Wholly owned subsidiary

What are significant cross-cultural differences?

Whirlpool's international expansion sets the stage for the discussion.

· ·

WHIRLPOOL'S "WORLD WASHER" STRATEGY

Americans have long known Whirlpool for its washing machines, dryers, dishwashers, and other kitchen appliances. Whirlpool also manufactured most of the major appliances sold under Sears' Kenmore brand. In North America, however, the appliance industry has been very competitive for some time. By the late 1980s, facing fierce rivals like General Electric, Whirlpool began looking for new growth prospects.

At that time, Whirlpool's major European competitors—Electrolux (Sweden), Thompson (France), and Philips (the Netherlands)—were all pursuing a multidomestic strategy. These competitors saw the situation as one in which the need for local responsiveness was paramount. Thus, they operated independent subsidiaries for each country, each with its own manufacturing and marketing resources. This approach made sense because there are significant technical differences in producing washing machines and other appliances across countries, including different electrical standards and safety codes.

Furthermore, customers from different cultures had come to expect different things from domestic appliances. In the United Kingdom, for example, washing machines were relatively small, loaded from the front, and installed under the kitchen counter. In Germany, the spin cycle ran at speeds three or four times faster than in the United States, and water temperatures were much hotter, while the French believed that speed and temperature ruined expensive fabrics. Countries also differed in where people expect the controls to be—top, side, or front. Furthermore, by the late 1980s each major country in Europe already had an established brand name and an entrenched set of competitors.

Executives at Whirlpool believed that an alternative strategy could be successful. They looked to global integration for an advantage, believing that they could leverage their industry-leading competence in low-cost manufacturing. The CEO at the time, David Whitwam, launched an initiative he called "the world washer." The frame and motor of the washer were manufactured in a low-cost country (Brazil) and then assembled to local standards by European-based affiliates. A global Whirlpool brand was used, rather than regional or country brands.

This strategy was a major success, allowing Whirlpool to grow and geographically diversify its sales, becoming the number one selling appliance brand in the world. Whirlpool is a now truly global enterprise, with more than $18 billion in net sales in 2007. The company has forty-seven manufacturing centers and twenty-six research centers located throughout the world and markets its products in more than 170 countries. Its ambitious goals are still reflected in a vision statement adopted in the 1980s, calling for Whirlpool products to be in every home, everywhere.[1]

WHAT ARE THE ADVANTAGES AND DISADVANTAGES OF INTERNATIONAL DIVERSIFICATION?

The possibility of selling around the world has had an extraordinary impact on the size and location of economic activity. Every year *Fortune* magazine lists the 2,000 largest corporations in the world. A snapshot of the top 25 firms by revenues is shown in Table 8.1.

TABLE 8.1 TOP 25 FIRMS IN THE WORLD BY MARKET VALUE

Rank	Company	Headquarters Location	Revenues ($ Millions)	Profits ($ Millions)
1	Wal-Mart Stores	United States	$351,139.0	$11,284.0
2	Exxon Mobil	United States	347,254.0	39,500.0
3	Royal Dutch Shell	Netherlands	318,845.0	25,442.0
4	BP	Britain	274,316.0	22,000.0
5	General Motors	United States	207,349.0	−1,978.0
6	Toyota Motor	Japan	204,746.4	14,055.8
7	Chevron	United States	200,567.0	17,138.0
8	DaimlerChrysler	Germany	190,191.4	4,048.8
9	ConocoPhillips	United States	172,451.0	15,550.0
10	Total	France	168,356.7	14,764.7
11	General Electric	United States	168,307.0	20,829.0
12	Ford Motor	United States	160,126.0	−12,613.0
13	ING Group	Netherlands	158,274.3	9,650.8
14	Citigroup	United States	146,777.0	21,538.0
15	AXA	France	139,738.1	6,379.9
16	Volkswagen	Germany	132,323.1	3,449.0
17	Sinopec	China	131,636.0	3,703.1
18	Crédit Agricole	France	128,481.3	8,975.8
19	Allianz	Germany	125,346.0	8,808.9
20	Fortis	Brussels	121,201.8	5,459.0
21	Bank of America Corp.	United States	117,017.0	21,133.0
22	HSBC Holdings	Britain	115,361.0	15,789.0
23	American Intl. Group	United States	113,194.0	14,048.0
24	China National Petroleum	China	110,520.2	13,265.3
25	BNP Paribas	France	109,213.6	9,169.0

Source: Fortune (November 2007).

Globalization is the trend toward a more integrated and interdependent world economy.

The overall list is an immediate indicator of the *globalization* of products and brands. It includes companies with home bases in forty-six countries, $18 trillion in combined revenue, 63 million employees, and profits of $492 billion. The United States is headquarters for 776 of these companies; Japan (the second-largest economy in the world) is home to 331 firms.

International expansion may allow firms to earn greater returns on their existing skills and competencies. Firms may reduce financial risk by increasing revenue, smoothing cash flow, and spreading costs. Increasingly, and controversially, firms have also used an international strategy as a way of strengthening bargaining power with labor, suppliers, and host governments.

However, geographic expansion does have its disadvantages. Markets differ in ways that cannot always be anticipated. Increasing operations around the world can reduce the effectiveness of corporate managers because they face increased coordination and control costs. In fact, many firms have not obtained the hoped-for financial returns of selling in other countries. The Chinese market has immense potential, for example, yet many firms have suffered years of losses trying to establish profitable operations in this market.

Another disadvantage for firms that operate at great distances from their major markets is the loss of flexibility and responsiveness to shifting consumer tastes. As an example, U.S. clothing and toy firms often have to place orders with their Chinese manufacturing suppliers months ahead of the big "back to school" and Christmas selling seasons. These firms have to make sales predictions with little feedback from consumers about what will sell. If a particular toy takes off in terms of consumer demand at the beginning of the Christmas season, the firm is often unable to get any significant new inventory into the retail stores until after the end of December.

While recognizing these and other problems, we still believe that the internationalizing context of most markets must be recognized and given serious consideration by almost all strategists. Economic ties and opportunities are increasingly international. Tastes are increasingly influenced by other cultures. Global differences in labor costs alone mean that even small companies trying to serve one market must think about the international strategies of suppliers and competitors.

HOW CAN COMPETITIVE ADVANTAGE BE INCREASED THROUGH INTERNATIONAL EXPANSION?

Christopher Bartlett, Sumantra Ghoshal, and Julian Birkinshaw, in their book *Transnational Management*, identify three ways for firms to use international diversification to build competitive advantage: exploit national differences in sourcing and market potential across countries, exploit economies of scale, and exploit economies of scope.[2] The second and third strategies use concepts familiar from Chapter 5 and will be discussed first. Exploiting national differences is then given a bit more attention.

Exploit Economies of Scale

Economies of scale
are unit cost reductions achieved by producing products at the most efficient volume.

Economies of scale refer to reduction in per unit cost as production volume is increased. A firm establishes a competitive cost advantage when it reaches a level of output at which it can take advantage of all scale effects. International expansion has been attractive in the past because higher levels of production volume allowed firms to reduce costs as they learned the most efficient ways to produce a particular good.

While economies of scale are coming down in many industries, as we saw in Chapter 4's discussion of the tire industry, they remain an important consideration in others. One source of economies of scale is the ability of the firm to spread fixed costs over a larger volume. For example, the costs to set up production or to develop a new product can be substantial. The larger volume resulting from international operations can make an important difference in meeting these fixed costs. Benefiting from these basic but powerful concepts, Korean electronics firms were able to build plants that operated at the same (efficient) scale of more experienced Japanese firms, but they were unfortunately unable to match the Japanese process-related efficiencies learned over decades of operating global-scale plants.

Exploit Economies of Scope   *↳ source of cost*

Scope is a second potential source of cost reduction that can be as important as scale economies in motivating firms to internationalize their activities. *Economies of scope* arise when firms that have pursued related diversification can share production, development, marketing, or distribution costs across several related products or businesses. The result is that the costs are less than if the products were produced or distributed separately.

Economies of scope
result from spreading activities across multiple products or businesses.

In the case of personal-care consumer products such as shampoo, toothpaste, and deodorant, firms like Unilever and Procter & Gamble have internationalized their activities so that they can obtain substantial economies of scope across many product lines. They use common consumer research, marketing programs, and sales forces (selling to the same multinational retailers) for these different products. In a similar vein, Coca-Cola captures economies of scope by maintaining a single brand name across the globe.

Exploit National Differences

Many firms first enter international markets to exploit location advantages such as reduced labor and material costs. In recent years the

Factor endowments are resources that firms can draw on in a given country to produce goods and services.

quality of a country's education system and management know-how have become more important *factor endowments* than natural resources and materials. As the combination of skills sought becomes more complex, the attraction of this kind of expansion can be expected to increase.

Strategists can gain cost or differential advantages by configuring their value chain across national locations to take advantage of different national factor endowments. For example, General Electric's lighting division recently relocated its R&D facility to Hungary to take advantage of an available supply of highly qualified, relatively low-paid scientists. Other firms locate facilities in Taiwan, India, and Israel to take advantage of high-skilled, relatively low-cost software designers. Some companies locate manufacturing operations in one low-cost region, such as Southeast Asia, and assembly operations in another location, such as Mexico, to take advantage of varied costs and skills in the global labor market. Following a similar logic, firms from around the world locate offices in Silicon Valley, despite its high costs, because of the advantage of drawing on the concentrated set of resources that are available there.

Traditionally, it has been assumed that the comparative advantage of different nations in hosting various economic activities would change relatively slowly over time. Over the past few decades the comparative advantage of nations has shifted more rapidly, greatly complicating the strategist's job. Governments now compete for international companies' business and have become much more actively engaged in developing industrial policies to attract foreign corporate investment into their respective countries. Wage rates, currency exchange fluctuations, interest rates, and inflation all impact the relative cost and advantage of operating in different countries. The result can be a rapid change in the strategic location of a firm's activities. Major portions of the textile industry, for example, have shifted from Spain or Brazil to Taiwan or Korea and then to China, Malaysia, or Sri Lanka in search of a reliable low-cost workforce.

Michael Porter, who developed the framework for industry analysis we described in Chapter 4, provides a second influential framework for analyzing the comparative advantage of different industry locations shown in Figure 8.1. This framework resulted from his research, which attempted to determine why some nations succeed and others fail in international competition. Porter's model can be used to analyze the advantages of different countries when a firm is deciding where to locate its wholly owned facilities or outsource particular parts of its value chain. Figure 8.1 directs attention to four particularly important issues.

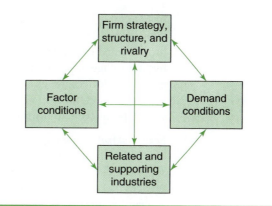

Figure 8.1 — Determinants of National Advantage

Source: M. E. Porter, *The Comparative Advantage of Nations* (New York: Free Press, 1990), p. 72.

1. *Factor conditions* can be defined at a country level as the resources needed for production in different industries. There is an important distinction between *basic factors*, such as natural resources, and *advanced factors*, such as communication and transportation infrastructure and a skilled labor force. The advanced factors are becoming increasingly important determinants of a country's comparative advantage. An example is Japan, which has very little natural factor endowment but a highly skilled and dedicated workforce.

2. *Firm strategy, structure, and rivalry* describe the competitive environment in a particular location. Porter contends that firms in certain countries tend to emphasize similar strategies. For example, German firms emphasize improving manufacturing processes and product design, and hence many of Germany's CEOs have an engineering background. Over time, they provide a particularly attractive resource for international firms that need these inputs.

In addition to explaining international differences in attracting firms to locate their activities within a given country, a second key idea in this model is that the level and sophistication of domestic rivalry can create pressures on domestic firms to be more innovative and efficient so that when they enter other international markets they will be strong competitors.

3. *Demand conditions* encompass the size, structure, and needs of a company's home market. Most firms are more sensitive to the needs and tastes of people in the country where they are

headquartered. If consumer demand is more sophisticated and knowledgeable in a particular country for a particular product, firms located in that country can be expected to gain a competitive advantage. Japan is known for having sophisticated buyers of electronic devices, for example, which has helped firms that have a home market in Japan be more innovative and develop higher-quality products than firms with less sophisticated consumers.

4. *Related and supporting industries* constitute an important fourth aspect of national advantage. If related industries that are an industry's suppliers, distributors, and complements can provide products or services that are internationally competitive, this too can help the strategist achieve a competitive locational advantage. The presence of world-leading semiconductor firms has helped U.S. firms that manufacture personal computers, for example. One indication of the force of this factor is that successful industries within a particular country tend to be grouped into clusters of related companies. One example is the German textile sector, which includes high-quality wool, synthetic fibers, and a wide range of textile machinery. A second is Motorsport Valley in England, home of major contenders in the Grand Prix.

The diamond framework found in Figure 8.1 is an immediately useful tool. Strategists in a firm like McDonald's thinking about whether they should enter Russia, for example, would see that although they would face little rivalry (the focus on analysis in the uppermost box of the diamond), they would have significant challenges in finding and training people (supply conditions) and pricing products so that they were affordable to local consumers (demand conditions). Furthermore, it would be difficult to identify firms in related industries such as meat processing and kitchen equipment manufacturing, with the necessary sophistication to become partners in the company's efforts to build new stores. McDonald's Canada succeeded in working out these details — but it took fourteen years![3]

In addition to helping a company like McDonald's understand the challenges of expanding geographically, the diamond model helps strategists understand the importance of national origin of products in determining the nature of their competitors' core competencies. It is no coincidence that the Swiss make good watches, the Germans make good machinery, the Dutch grow beautiful flowers, and the Americans create motion pictures seen around the world. In large part, the specific advantages of individual firms in these and many other industries must be related to supporting conditions among buyers, suppliers, and complementary goods. Current interest is now turning to the potential advantage of competitors from less developed countries, as discussed in a recent issue of *Business Week Online*.

Emerging Economies

The next generation of global firms is emerging from developing countries such as Mexico (Cemex), India (Ranbaxy), and Russia (Lukoil). Based on data collected from 3,000 firms in twelve developing countries, the consulting firm Boston Consulting Group (BCG) identified 100 emerging multinational firms positioned to "radically transform industries and markets around the world." Taken together in 2005, these firms had $715 billion in revenue, $145 billion in operating profits, and half a trillion dollars in assets. On average, the firms grew 24 percent annually between 2001 and 2006.

BCG investigated the factors that enabled these third-world multinationals to become global players, finding key advantages linked to access to dynamic, growth markets, high levels of innovation, and low cost resources, including human capital and raw materials. According to *Business Week*, "the best of the pack are proving as innovative and expertly run as any in the business, astutely absorbing global consumer trends and technologies and getting new products to market faster than their rivals."

U.S. corporations have a long history of defending territory against foreign rivals. The 1980s were dominated by turf wars with major Japanese players, including Sony and Toyota. By the 1990s, the newest competitors came from the "dragon" economies of South Korea (Hyundai) and Taiwan. The latest competitors are different in that their home countries are relatively poor, with per capita incomes of just $620 and $1,300 per year in India and China, respectively. Third-world multinationals thus face a market characterized by little capital, low-income consumers, extensive consumer regulations, and underdeveloped infrastructure. These nations are also more likely to have corrupt governments and business-unfriendly rules and regulations. Faced with this environment, the new multinationals have had to develop extremely reliable, low-cost, easy-to-use-and-understand goods and services. These strengths, particularly in development and marketing, are useful in the real-world market.

These multinationals emerged in the late 1990s after the Asian financial crisis. Following the devaluation of Asian firms, Western firms decided to pull out of many developing nations and sold their assets cheaply to local players. These local players began to explore opportunities in local and foreign markets. Developing countries began to invest in each other's economies, increasing these FDI flows threefold between 1995 and 2003 to $60 billion. In December 2007, the World Bank estimated that production from developing nations accounts for 40 percent of global output.[4]

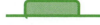

Worksheet 8.1:
The Diamond
Model—A Tool
for Exploring
Locational
Differences

The clear lesson to be learned is that competitive advantage depends more and more on understanding relationships among countries. Worksheet 8.1 is a useful tool.

WHAT ARE ALTERNATIVE STRATEGIES FOR INTERNATIONAL EXPANSION?

Firms that decide to compete internationally face two different types of competitive pressure—the need to be responsive to different national markets and the need to be cost efficient. These pressures place conflicting demands on firms. To minimize costs, a firm needs to standardize the products it offers and integrate its international operations so that it can achieve the lowest unit cost. However, this reduces the firm's ability to offer different products that meet the tastes and preferences that arise from national differences. Developing differentiated products and marketing strategies for each country raises costs.

	Competitive Forces for Local Responsiveness	
	Low	**High**
High (Competitive Forces for Low Cost)	**Global Strategy** The firm develops a standardized product that it sells to all customers throughout the world.	**Transnational Strategy** The firm attempts to combine the benefits of global integration to achieve low cost with the benefits of being locally responsive.
Low (Competitive Forces for Low Cost)	**International Strategy** The firm uses the competitive approach it developed in its home market to enter international markets.	**Multidomestic Strategy** The firm develops separate operating subsidiaries, each of which develops products to meet the specific needs of the international market it serves.

Figure 8.2 — Alternative International Strategies

Source: C. Bartlett, S. Ghoshal, & J. Birkinshaw, *Transnational Management* (Boston: McGraw-Hill, 2004).

International strategies utilize domestic resources and capabilities to expand sales and operations across more than one country boundary.

Multidomestic strategies develop products, services, and experiences that respond to national differences.

As shown in Figure 8.2, when a firm faces international markets where the pressures for low cost and local responsiveness are low, it can pursue an *international strategy.*

As the firm grows it may determine that certain international markets have indigenous competitors that lack the capabilities it possesses. The firm can then begin to sell into those international markets with its existing products. Most firms pursuing this strategy maintain R&D functions in their home country and maintain tight control over marketing and product strategies. This strategy is usually possible in markets where the pressures for low cost and local responsiveness are low. An example is Toys "R" Us. It uses the marketing and logistics approaches it developed for the U.S. market in all of its international efforts.

When a firm tailors its products or services to meet different national cultural tastes, it often follows a *multidomestic strategy*.

Selecting a multidomestic strategy takes into account differing consumer tastes and preferences across regions and nations. But in addition, the demands or regulations of the host country's government may require the international firm to customize its products or services for the local country before it is allowed to conduct operations in that country. For example, governments may require that a certain percentage of the value of the product be manufactured locally. Firms following a multidomestic strategy delegate considerable autonomy to each subsidiary, allowing these units to respond effectively to local conditions. Many, if not all, of the activities in the firm's value chain will be produced in each country. Competitive moves are made without consideration for their impact on operations based in other countries.

Nestlé is an example of an international firm that uses different national strategies. It has developed a wide assortment of chocolate candies to suit the tastes of different countries. The firm tailors its marketing strategies to meet the competitive conditions within each market. The disadvantage of this strategic approach is that firms incur higher costs, because many of their value chain activities are reproduced in each subsidiary's home country.

Many of the major personal-care manufacturers have also used a multidomestic strategy. They too set up relatively independent subsidiary organizations in each of the countries in which they operate. The subsidiary manager normally has profit-and-loss responsibility for his or her country operations. Additionally, the subsidiary manager can develop products and marketing strategies that he or she believes best meet the competitive conditions of the country. L'Oréal is an example of a company that has been highly successful with this strategy.

In recent years, personal-care firms have increasingly attempted to globally integrate at least some activities, especially R&D. For example, Kao (a Japanese competitor in this market) and Procter & Gamble use networked research facilities located in Asia, the United States, and Europe that work together to develop new offerings such as environmentally friendly products. Both companies then allow local subsidiary managers to adopt or adapt these products to fit their respective markets.

As international markets evolve, firms struggle to find the correct balance between local and global responses. In some highly competitive markets, strategists have found it necessary to aggressively pursue both local adaptation and the efficiencies gained from global presence simultaneously, leading to a third alternative, *transnational strategy*, which balances the efficiencies of integrated strategy with local responsiveness.

Transnational strategy emphasizes responsiveness to local needs and global efficiency simultaneously.

Transnational companies respond to local needs while also taking part in the global economy. This strategic approach is worth considering by small businesses as well as by large international firms, though it is difficult to pursue two different and sometimes conflicting objectives simultaneously.

Although the balance is challenging, many competitors in the pharmaceutical industry appear to be successfully implementing a transnational strategy. As a result of the high costs of research and development, firms are more and more likely to coordinate R&D across all of their national markets. At the same time, they must be responsive to local government requirements with regard to pricing and regulations affecting testing, advertising, and distribution that vary from country to country.

Changing markets appear to be increasing the need to respond to local conditions. Chris Anderson, editor in chief of *Wired* magazine, argues that the twenty-first century will be dominated by niche markets.[5] In the past, record companies promoted blockbuster hits that might sell millions of copies, but this strategy has recently found less success. Consumers have increasingly heterogeneous interests, and thus a larger number of offerings are needed. Anderson argues that low or decreasing unit costs of these offerings in many industries allows companies to make money in this changing environment.

In markets where consumer tastes are very similar or economies of scale are significant, firms may be able to achieve greater efficiencies with a *global strategy*.

Global strategies integrate international operations to achieve cost and differentiation advantages in multiple economies.

The need to incur the costs of multidomestic strategies may be diminishing. Theodore Levitt, a Harvard marketing professor, has argued for some time that as a result of new communication and transportation technologies, the tastes and preferences of consumers around the world are becoming similar.[6] He points to emergence of global brands such as Coca-Cola, McDonald's, and Levi Strauss as examples of the globalization of demand. In addition to the apparent convergence of consumer tastes, two other economic drivers are pressuring firms to adopt a global strategy for their international operations: the need to amortize the huge R&D costs incurred by developing new products, and achieving scale economies.

Firms pursuing a global strategy view all of their national markets as parts of an integrated market whole, so that competitive moves made in any particular country are undertaken only after analysis of their impact on other markets. Firms configure their value chains to maximize locational advantages and economies of scale. Generally, their marketing strategies are uniformly implemented worldwide to develop brand names that have global recognition. The result of these and other integrated decisions is that firms manufacture products on a global scale in a few efficient plants strategically located in different parts of the world. Many international Japanese firms (including Toyota, Canon, and Matsushita) have used this approach to gain significant market share in international markets. They concentrate on achieving the best-quality/low-cost position for their products.

Implementing a global strategy requires that companies achieve a high level of coordination among various worldwide operations, which means that there will be a relatively high level of centralization and control at corporate headquarters. Most of the strategic decisions are made at the parent company level, and the subsidiary manager implements centrally designed strategies. This allows competitive moves to be made simultaneously across countries, including actions in multiple markets in the hope of draining competitor resources, as we will discuss at the end of this chapter.

The power of global advertising is a particularly important aspect of global success. Royal Philips provides one example.[7]

Make Simplicity King at Royal Philips

When Gerard Kleisterlee took the helm of Royal Philips Electronics in 2001, the Dutch conglomerate's empire included TVs, lighting, medical devices, and semiconductors. The missing key component: a coherent brand. "We had to choose whether Philips was a company built around its core technologies or one built around its core brand," says Kleisterlee, who presided over a healthy 14 percent gain in global brand value last year.

He wisely chose the latter. In doing so, Kleisterlee had to shake up the way Philips thought about customers and communication without alienating the engineering and science units critical to innovation. In 2004 Philips launched its global "Sense and Simplicity" campaign as a "health-care, lifestyle, and technology" company offering easy-to-use products designed around the consumer. To fast-track these efforts, Kleisterlee created an internal think tank, the Simplicity Advisory Board, composed entirely of Philips outsiders. The first members included a British fashion designer, a Chinese architect, an American radiologist, and an American professor at the Massachusetts Institute of Technology.

The advisory board looked at overarching questions such as, How can simplicity be executed? The board's strategic advice led to a series of new, user-friendly products. It wasn't enough to design a small defibrillator that could be stashed in public spaces such as airports and workplaces. Consumers dictated that it be the size of a laptop and simple enough that the untrained could spark a heart back to life in seconds using built-in audio instructions.

Philips installed new test centers around the world where products are extensively critiqued by consumers. That saved the company from flubbing the launch of its WACS7000 Wireless Music Center and Station, which it postponed when the software was rewritten because of complaints of overcomplexity.

Brand value hasn't come cheaply for Philips. Analysts say the company spent $170 million in 2005 and invested around the same amount the next year on the new campaign. But Kleisterlee knew that the company's future valuation depended on the strength of the brand: "Everything we do, from our products to the way we work with our suppliers and customers, has to live up to the simplicity promise."

In January 2008, the company reported 5 percent sales growth in 2007 and 7.7 percent earnings before interest and taxes. Kleisterlee indicated that the 2004–2007 strategic plan had been successfully implemented and announced "Vision 2010" to further simplify management in its three core businesses and achieve higher levels of operating profitability.[8]

There are two important disadvantages of the global strategy. The first is that global firms can lose flexibility by maintaining just a few manufacturing locations. A disruption in the production of a critical component, for example, will be very costly. Government intervention from a national location could similarly increase costs. A second risk is that centralizing activities such as R&D increases the likelihood that the firm will be slower to identify innovations that occur in countries where it is active only in sales and distribution. The reason for changing sales levels may be difficult to decipher far away from the market; spotting new trends can be even more difficult.

Glocal strategies have emerged to deal with some of these problems. We have mentioned IKEA several times in this book, but it is worth going into a bit more detail because the firm provides such a good example.

> **Glocal strategy** attends to differences in local markets but also carries out some activities on a global basis.

Adding Local Dimensions to Global Design

IKEA is owned by a private foundation and does not reveal operating statistics. Mattias Karlkjell of ABG Sundal Collier in Stockholm conservatively estimates, however, that its pretax operating profits of around $1.7 billion in 2005 were based on a 10 percent margin. That is an impressive statistic for retailing. In the United States, competitor Pier 1 Imports has a 5 percent margin; Target does a little better at 7.7 percent.

Business Week's recent article on the company describes a global middle class with similar buying habits as the source of IKEA's success.[9] Even spending per customer is comparable. In Russia, the average buyer spends about $85 per trip, according to IKEA, which is precisely the amount spent by the average customer in the company's Swedish home market.

Helpful factor conditions in Sweden include egalitarianism, frugality, and an appreciation for clean design. The company is also obsessed by cost control. Twelve full-time designers at the company's headquarters work with eighty freelancers to translate distinctive designs (including many prize winners) into low-cost production.

A global strategy directs operations that are remarkably similar in the company's 226 locations in Europe, Asia, Australia, and the United States. Each IKEA store is a large yellow and blue building that averages 300,000 square feet (about five football fields) and displays approximately 7,000 items. A child-care facility is available at the entrance, which encourages longer stays by parents, as does the restaurant in the center of the facility. Shoppers are directed in a circle route of wide aisles past room displays that invite browsing but do not impede one-way traffic.

Business Week suggests that "IKEA is far more than a furniture merchant. It sells a lifestyle that customers around the world embrace as a signal that they've arrived, that they have good taste and recognize value"; it is "the quintessential global cult brand." That success is supporting approximately twenty new store openings per year, which is about the maximum that the company believes its supply chain can support. Currently IKEA uses 1,300 suppliers from fifty-three countries. If IKEA maintains its historic growth rate, it will need to source twice as much material by 2010 as it does in 2007!

Growth has required adaptation to local markets. The company is about to re-enter the Japanese market after failing miserably thirty years ago by not recognizing Japanese quality standards. In the 1990s it was similarly insensitive to U.S. consumers, who wanted higher quality and found the company's offerings undersized. IKEA's performance has now improved. It changed measurements in centimeters to American standards, increased comfort, and expanded furniture designs to fit U.S. homes. IKEA also offers goods to appeal to the growing Latino market. Local concessions are critical to the company's expansion plans. By the end of 2007, IKEA had 260 stores, but 82 percent of its sales were from Europe. There is obviously huge potential (and risk) to expand the 15 percent from North America and the 3 percent from Asia and Australia.[10]

WHAT ARE ALTERNATIVE ENTRY MODES?

Once international strategists have decided which markets they want to enter, the next major decision is how to enter those markets—which entry mode to choose. In Chapter 5, we examined different economic relationships within and across firm boundaries. Now we will look at these ways of operating again in terms of a firm that is trying to move into a new international market. The choices for international entry include exporting, licensing, franchising, joint ventures, and wholly owned subsidiaries. Each of these entry modes has advantages and disadvantages in terms of potential return and risk, as summarized in Figure 8.3.

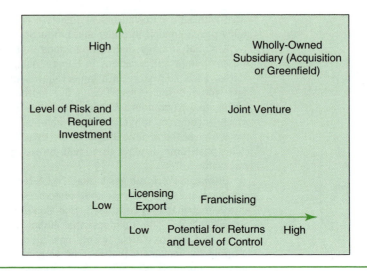

Figure 8.3 — Entry Mode Characteristics

Export

Most firms begin international diversification by exporting. This approach has several advantages. First, it requires little international experience. Second, it requires a relatively small level of financial investment. Both characteristics lower financial risk. Small firms with little capital to risk often choose to export to learn more about a potential market before committing additional resources. The disadvantage of this approach is that the firm is also likely to realize lower returns, due to high transportation costs and tariffs.

License

Licensing is an agreement in which a company, as licensor, agrees to make its intellectual property available to a company in another country. The agreement can include patents, processes, designs, copyrights (for literary, musical, or artistic compositions as well as technical ideas), trademarks, and trade and brand names. In exchange, the licensee agrees to pay the licensor a royalty.

Licensing has two major advantages for the licensor. It too is a low-risk mode of entry because it requires little financial investment. The licensee puts up most of the immediate investment capital, but it benefits because it does not have to pay for development costs. An example of successful use of this strategy comes from the Canadian brewer Molson. The company decided it was much cheaper to license its beer to Miller for distribution in the United States rather than enter the United States on its own. It would have cost Molson more than $100 million just to begin to gain market share in the United States.

Instead, through the licensing agreement, Molson quickly gained share and a new revenue stream.

The financial disadvantage of this entry mode is that it often generates relatively low profit returns. In addition, the licensor loses some control over the use of its products or processes, which could hurt the firm's brand reputation. However, a company can take precautions by requiring checks to ensure the quality of the products and marketing practices used by its licensee over time.

A third disadvantage, which we have already discussed as a generic attribute of alliance, is that the licensee may gain knowledge from the licensor that enables it to develop its own skills and competencies so that it ultimately becomes a competitor. This is what happened to RCA, which licensed its color television technology to Sony and Matsushita. The two foreign companies quickly improved on RCA's technology and then entered the U.S. market on their own, achieving larger U.S. market shares than any American brand.

Changing strategies can also jeopardize a once-appealing agreement. At the end of 2005, Miller Brewing Company sued to end its licensing agreement with Molson to sell Miller brands in Canada. It claimed that Molson's merger with Coors Brewing Company would allow Coors access to Miller's business secrets.[11]

Franchise

Franchising is a specialized form of licensing, usually involving agreements between service firms. Franchising has increased dramatically in recent years. The franchise is defined as a transfer of technology, standardized business systems, brand name, or trademark to an independent company or person that is the franchisee. The franchisee agrees to follow specific rules about how it will conduct its business. In return, the franchisor receives a royalty based on sales volume. Sometimes the franchisee is required to purchase key ingredients or equipment from the franchisor.

There are many examples of this form of international expansion, including hotels (Marriott, Holiday Inn, Hilton, Forte) and fast-food restaurants (McDonald's, Burger King, Kentucky Fried Chicken). In the case of Marriott, franchisees currently pay an application fee an ongoing percentage of their revenues as royalties, and a percentage of Marriott's marketing costs.[12]

As with licensing, the main advantage is that franchising is an inexpensive way of exploiting a foreign market opportunity. It is a fast and relatively easy method for a firm to leverage its brand name and standardized business systems internationally. The franchisee benefits from lower start-up costs and access to a proven business model.

Franchising has disadvantages as well, but these are usually less severe than in other forms of licensing. The most important issue for the franchisor is potential loss of control over the brand and product quality, damaging its reputation. This was a major issue for McDonald's in Russia. Although franchises account for 80 percent of all stores in the United States and 50 percent in Europe, the Russians are not yet using this strategy. Internal and external analysts agree that "regional restaurant franchises [in Russia] can really vary in the quality and service that they offer." Further, the legal situation for franchising is not yet clear.[13]

Joint Venture

A joint venture has already been defined as a firm that is owned by two or more partners; in this chapter we are interested in partners that are headquartered in different countries. The founding firms share ownership and usually contribute managers who jointly supervise the new venture. In many joint ventures the partners each own an equal percent of the venture; however, one firm may retain majority ownership share so that it can exert tighter control. More complex arrangements are also possible. For example, many firms from various European countries are partners in Airbus, the aircraft manufacturing firm, and each partner owns a different number of shares.

As we discussed in the last chapter, joint ventures have two important advantages. First, shared ownership reduces the financial investment and risk involved in developing a new market. Second, firms can benefit from the skills of other partners. A particularly common example for international strategists is a venture in which one partner provides technological or other expertise to the joint venture while the other provides local knowledge of culture and business methods.

Despite these important advantages, international joint ventures have several disadvantages. First, as with licensing, one or more firms in the venture may give up control of their technology or other proprietary knowledge. These firms may ultimately create a new competitor.

Second, partners may have different, even opposing, goals that might not be obvious, or seem threatening, at the start of the venture. One firm may want to coordinate the activities of its joint venture as part of its global strategy, for example, which means less decision-making involvement for other partners. Or one firm may want to gain experience or location advantages, while its partners are interested only in maximizing return on the investment they have made in the joint venture.

A third problem is that the objectives of partners often change over time. This is one explanation of why most joint venture partnerships are dissolved within five years of formation.[14] Partners are likely to have learned or gained what they needed from their partners in a relatively short period of time; after that, the relationship is no longer attractive.

Wholly Owned Subsidiary

Many large international corporations entering strategically important markets establish a wholly owned subsidiary, in which they own 100 percent of the stock. The parent can either acquire an existing firm in the targeted country or build an entirely new operation. *Greenfield ventures* can be more expensive and take more time than acquiring existing facilities. They also are considered more risky because the revenues and profits are more uncertain for a newly created venture. However, greenfield sites afford greater freedom to design the operations—plant layout, location, and corporate culture—exactly as the parent desires.

Throughout the 1990s, companies in the United States used acquisition to facilitate their efforts to consolidate and reorganize to meet the demands of a more competitive global economy. Over the past decade, 50 to 80 percent of all foreign direct investment has resulted from merger and acquisition activity.[15] By the beginning of this century, acquisition was spreading to major international markets, as described in the following example.

> **Greenfield ventures** are new operations created "from the ground up" as a wholly owned subsidiary.

Growth of Mergers and Acquisitions in China and India

Even though China offers a relatively difficult political and legal environment, it is experiencing a dramatic increase in cross-border and domestic joint ventures and acquisitions. For example, Nissan Motor Company paid $1.03 billion for a 50 percent stake in China's Dongfeng Motor Company, and brewer Anheuser-Busch paid $182 million to increase its stake in China's Tsingtao Brewery.

The market in China has changed since the late 1990s, when the stock of some of China's biggest state-owned firms was sold to the public. The Chinese government encouraged several of China's primary domestic industries to consolidate and reorganize to become more efficient. Partnerships are an important means of achieving this goal.

Through the early 2000s, the Chinese government made its domestic markets more accessible by agreeing to adhere to the practices of the World Trade Organization. This has greatly encouraged multinational companies to buy stakes in Chinese ventures. Meanwhile, cross-border mergers and acquisitions from Asian companies have grown significantly. One source reported 2,359 acquisitions in Asia, Europe, and North America with a dollar value of $67.4 billion in 2006.[16]

One of the most important advantages of acquisition versus greenfield development is that the acquiring firm can move very quickly into major markets. In China and other desirable developing markets, strategists are attracted by the opportunity of more easily establishing first-mover advantages, a topic we discussed in Chapter 5. Acquisition is also attractive as a means for quickly establishing scale to reduce the advantage that a competitor has in a particular market.

A second advantage of acquisition or greenfield development, because the firm owns 100 percent of its subsidiary, is that the firm has complete control over strategic decisions. For a global corporation, this means organizing activities in ways that maximize returns from a network of subsidiaries. More generally, the wholly owned subsidiary, if successful, offers better profit potential than any other entry mode, because the firm does not have to share its profits with any partners.

But full ownership also requires the greatest financial investment and thus entails the greatest risk. The empirical evidence suggests that most acquisitions and mergers have not delivered promised shareholder returns. We discussed the problem of incompatible corporate cultures in Chapter 7, and the subsequent difficulty of realizing possible strategic synergies. Many U.S. acquiring and acquired firms have very different corporate values and approaches to getting things done than their international partners. One negative result can be that employee morale plummets and there is a high turnover of talented employees. This is the most frequent explanation for early problems with Daimler's merger with Chrysler.

The End of a Marriage That Once Seemed to Be Made in Heaven

In 1998 the DaimlerChrysler merger created the world's largest commercial auto manufacturer. When the merger took place, Daimler CEO Jürgen Schrempp claimed that by merging a luxury automaker with a mass-market brand, he would create the most profitable auto manufacturer in the world. The merged firm was expected to develop new economies of scale and scope, increasing the results possible from either firm on its own.

Chrysler was known to be a flexible manufacturer that had successfully identified major new product niches such as the minivan and four-wheel-drive SUVs. Daimler had manufacturing expertise at the high end of the automobile market and a worldwide distribution network that could immediately expand the distribution of Chrysler products. It was hoped that the combination of these strengths would help the new firm challenge increasingly strong Asian competitors, especially Toyota and Honda.

However, at the end of 2003, the market capitalization of Daimler-Chrysler was about $38 billion, significantly lower than $47 billion in 1998 before the merger. In *the* 1998–2003 period, Daimler lost billions of dollars from its investment in Chrysler. Many analysts believed that if it were not for Daimler, Chrysler would have gone bankrupt. Although some production costs were cut, anticipated synergies were not easily found. In addition, Japanese and other competitors had successfully followed Chrysler's lead, introducing minivans, pickup trucks, and SUVs that eroded Chrysler's formerly attractive market share.

Making matters worse, Daimler's mostly German management had an approach that did not go over well with Chrysler managers. Difficulties were in part the result of differences required to manufacture luxury cars versus mass-market cars, but they were increased by the very different national cultures of the two firms. Whatever the cause, most of the top executive team of Chrysler had left the firm by early 2003.[17]

By 2006 a number of these problems had been addressed and the picture looked more positive. The Chrysler Group provided one-third of the company's earnings in the first half of 2005 as quality and portfolio issues beset other divisions.[18] Market capitalization reached $54 billion by August,[19] worldwide sales were up 9 percent for newly launched Mercedes vehicles, and "commonalization" was being planned.[20]

Still, the American market proved to be difficult. The three producers that have dominated the U.S. market saw their sales decrease significantly in the first half of 2006 with Chrysler and Ford losing more than 30 percent market share, while many rivals owned by international firms saw sales gain. Toyota (up 16 percent) and Honda (up 10 percent) were particularly important and led an effort to increase sales in the upscale market that DaimlerChrysler had hoped to dominate.[21]

In the summer of 2006, DaimlerChrysler sought to make a positive out of a negative in its U.S. television advertisements, with the German CEO presented as an amusing cultural misfit to America. The company still faced the high labor and health care costs that are central to the difficulties of GM and Ford, and the models that brought them success were less in favor as fuel prices soared.

By April 2007 the company confirmed that buyers were being sought as German investors declared that "this marriage made in heaven turned out to be a complete failure"—in fact, some discontents suggested that Daimler could itself become a takeover target if it did not sell Chrysler.[22] By May, the company in effect paid Cerberus Capital Management, a private equity investment firm, $650 million to end its exposure to health care and other costs as well as ongoing operational losses.[23]

Worksheet 8.2: Entry Mode Alternatives—A Tool for Comparing Advantages and Disadvantages

Many more examples of international expansion could be offered. Worksheet 8.2 is a useful tool for comparing their advantages and disadvantages.

WHAT ARE SIGNIFICANT CROSS-CULTURAL DIFFERENCES?

The DaimlerChrysler story highlights the need for sensitivity when dealing with other cultures. As we discussed in Chapter 1, strategists must try to satisfy both external (customers, governments) and internal (employee) stakeholders. This becomes much more complicated when the firm operates in more than one country. There are many examples of unanticipated product requirements in other countries that keep firms from successfully internationalizing. But this is not the only significant barrier to international operation; strategists are likely to find that even more important management problems come from vast differences in work culture as well as management culture across activity sites.

An example of important cross-cultural differences in understanding the purpose of management can be found in international response to the following statement: "The main reason for hierarchical structures is so that everybody knows who has authority over whom." Andre Laurent studied research from twelve countries and detected the differences shown in Figure 8.4. As indicated, Indonesians appear more comfortable with a hierarchical structure of authority (86 percent) than do Americans (18 percent) and Germans (24 percent).

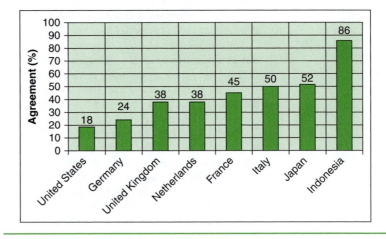

Figure 8.4 — Agreement on the Use of Hierarchy

Source: Adapted from A. Laurent, (1983) "The cultural diversity of Western conceptions of management," *International Studies of Management and Organization*, 13: 1–2. pp. 75–96.

On the employee side, Geert Hofstede has made significant contributions to understanding the impact of international culture on employees. Working with Michael Bond, Hofstede has tried to make sense of cultural differences by clustering countries that share similar attitudes toward work goals, needs and values, as illustrated in Figure 8.5.

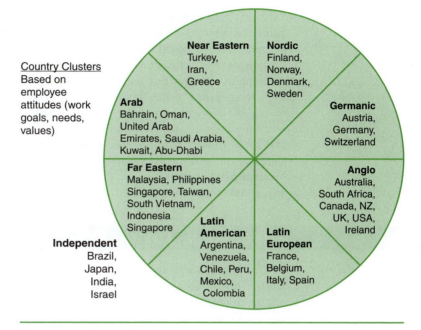

Country Clusters Based on employee attitudes (work goals, needs, values)

Near Eastern Turkey, Iran, Greece

Nordic Finland, Norway, Denmark, Sweden

Arab Bahrain, Oman, United Arab Emirates, Saudi Arabia, Kuwait, Abu-Dhabi

Germanic Austria, Germany, Switzerland

Far Eastern Malaysia, Philippines Singapore, Taiwan, South Vietnam, Indonesia Singapore

Anglo Australia, South Africa, Canada, NZ, UK, USA, Ireland

Independent Brazil, Japan, India, Israel

Latin American Argentina, Venezuela, Chile, Peru, Mexico, Colombia

Latin European France, Belgium, Italy, Spain

Figure 8.5 — Country Clusters

Source: G. Hofstede & M. Bond, The Confucius Connection: From Cultural Roots to Economic Growth, *Organizational Dynamics* 16(4): 5–21.

Hofstede is a Dutch researcher who has spent his career trying to understand the nature of these differences. His website suggests the following:

> For those who work in international business, it is sometimes amazing how different people in other cultures behave. We tend to have a human instinct that "deep inside" all people are the same—but they are not. Therefore, if we go into another country and make decisions based on how we operate in our own home country—the chances are we'll make some very bad decisions.[24]

Many other resources are also available. It is important to try to understand new economic powerhouses—not only China and India, but countries such as Brazil, Russia, Mexico, and Indonesia.[25] It also makes sense for us and many of our readers to become more informed about the nature of Islamic culture.

Of course, problems deriving from cultural differences are just one type of risk encountered in the international environment. Additional risks include political and economic factors. Political risks concern the likelihood that political forces can affect a country's business environment and adversely affects the profit of the firm. Forces can take the form of social unrest, unstable governments, war, or terrorist activities. Unfortunately, today we are experiencing an increase in social unrest, especially in countries where there is more than one ethnic group. Economic risks are related to the likelihood that the government's management of the economy will affect the country's business environment—for example, resulting in currency fluctuations and changes in the inflation rate. An even more serious risk is the possibility of nationalization of industries or firms. These risks are highly related to political risks. If a country's economy is mismanaged, it can lead to demonstrations, labor strikes, and social unrest. Though these factors affecting international expansion are worthy of book-length exploration,[26] the most important point for strategists to remember is that the increasingly connected world presents a universe of opportunities and threats.

CONCLUSIONS FOR THE STRATEGIST

In this chapter we've argued that it makes sense for all strategists in all kinds of organizations to be aware of the global environment, even if operating in one location. The decision to expand operations internationally is an important strategic option, though of course not for everyone. However, many strategists can enhance their firm's competitive position by exploiting differences between national markets, taking advantage of economies of scale and locational differences when they configure their value chain.

The choice of international strategies is based primarily on strategists' assessment of two major competitive pressures—pressure to be locally responsive and pressure to provide a more integrated, and frequently lower-cost, multinational position. It is difficult to find the right balance between these pressures and unlikely that the firm will choose to be totally responsive or completely global. Although a position on the transnational continuum between these two extremes is attractive, it is also the most difficult to implement.

This choice must be put in a dynamic context, and it is a subject that will increasingly occupy our attention in this book. The forces shaping international markets are changing relatively rapidly because of changes in consumers' tastes and competitive actions. Therefore strategists are well advised to monitor and learn from their customers and partners and frequently reassess whether their international strategy is still effective.

Key Concepts

Most observers believe that **globalization,** the trend toward a more integrated and interdependent world economy, will continue to gain strength in the next decades. A **global strategy** focuses on developing one strategy for markets in many countries, but this is not the only choice for operating in more than one country. An **international strategy** oversees the production and sale of goods and services in more than one national market but does not attempt an integrated strategy.

International strategies are often attractive because they increase profitability through **economies of scale** (unit cost reductions achieved by producing at efficient product volumes) and **economies of scope** (cost reductions achieved from spreading value chain activities across multiple products or businesses).

International strategies are facilitated by **factor endowments** or resources available in the countries that produce goods and services. Important factor conditions involve rivalry, demand, supporting industries, and factors affecting commercial activity, such as natural resources, communication, transportation, and labor skills.

Firms can choose from three different categories of international strategies. One alternative to the global strategy is a **multidomestic strategy** that requires firms to tailor their products and services to meet the specific requirements of local markets. A **transnational strategy** emphasizes responsiveness to local needs and global efficiency simultaneously. This is sometimes called **glocal strategy**.

Strategists can enter an international market in several ways, including exporting, licensing, franchising, joint venture, and wholly owned subsidiaries. The highest level of control and potential return is associated with a **greenfield venture**—a new, wholly owned subsidiary. Acquisition is another alternative that leads to wholly owned subsidiaries, but firms must be careful to recognize and respond to cross-cultural differences when managing acquisions.

Questions for Further Reflection

1. For the last several years Ross Dawson, CEO of the consulting firm Advanced Human Technologies, has developed a map summarizing trends affecting society. The 2008 map is based on the five lines of the Shanghai subway (labeled Society, Politics, Demographics, Economy, and Technology) with Globalization as a central intersection. It's available under an Attribution-ShareAlike Creative Commons license. That makes it possible to ask, How would you modify the many stops listed? The map can be downloaded at http://www.rossdawsonblog.com/weblog/archives/2008/01/see_our_latest.html.

2. Keep a log of the products you buy for a week. Which ones are produced by an international company? Can you cluster the firms on the basis of similar strategies?

3. Choose a foreign company that operates in your home market. How, if at all, does this firm combat a "liability of foreignness"?

Compare locational advantages of three operational locations in a specific industry.

Step 1: Select an industry that interests you.

Step 2: Identify three locations (countries or regions) where the industry is present in columns 1, 2, and 3 of the worksheet.

Step 3: Compare locations by describing the factors listed in Porter's diamond model.

The Diamond Model Worksheet 8.1	Industry:
Analyst(s):	Summary:

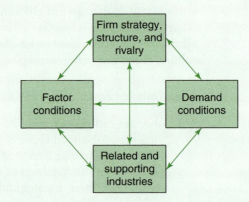

	Location One	Location Two	Location Three
Factor Conditions			
Demand Conditions			

Related and Supporting Industries			
Firm Strategy, Structure, and Rivalry			

Entry Mode Alternatives—A Tool for Comparing Advantages and Disadvantages

Compare advantages and disadvantages of international entry modes.

Step 1: Select a firm currently operating in just one country that you believe has the potential to become international.

Step 2: Consider the advantages and disadvantages of exporting. Put your answers in row 1.

Step 3: Consider the advantages and disadvantages of licensing. Put your answers in row 2.

Step 4: What are the advantages and disadvantages of franchising? Put your answers in row 3.

Step 5: Consider the advantages and disadvantages of a joint venture. Put your answers in row 4.

Step 6: What are the advantages and disadvantages of a wholly owned subsidiary? Put your answers in row 5.

Step 7: Based on your analysis, what method(s) of expansions would you recommend to the firm? Put your answers in the last box.

Entry Mode Alternatives Worksheet 8.2	Firm and Industry:
Analyst(s):	**Product Summary:**

	Advantages	Disadvantages
Export		
License		
Franchise		
Joint Venture		
Wholly Owned Subsidiary		

Recommendation:

NOTES

[1] Whirlpool Corporation. 2006. http://www.whirlpool.com, accessed March 14, 2008.

[2] Bartlett, C., Ghoshal, S., & Birkinshaw, J. 2004. *Transnational Management.* Boston: McGraw-Hill.

[3] http://www.mcdonalds.com/countries/russia.html, accessed October 9, 2006.

[4] Engardio, P., et al., 2006. Emerging Giants: Multinationals from China, India, Brazil, Russia, and Even Egypt Are Coming On Strong. They're Hungry—and Want Your Customers. They're Changing the Global Game. Business Week Online (July 31); ICP. 2007. News Release: 2005 International Comparison Program: Preliminary Global Report Compares Size of Economies (December). http://siteresources.worldbank.org/ICPINT/Resources/finalICPrelease.doc, accessed February 2, 2008.

[5] Anderson, C. 2006. *The Long Tail.* New York: Hyperion.

[6] Levitt, T. 1983. The Globalization of Markets. *Harvard Business Review* (May–June): 92–107.

[7] Kiley, D., et al. 2006 . Best Global Brands: How the BusinessWeek/Interbrand Top 100 Companies Are Using Their Brands to Fuel Expansion. Business Week Online (December 20).

[8] Philips Annual Results. 2007. http://www.newscenter.philips.com/about/news/press/20080121_q4_results.page?, accessed February 2, 2008.

[9] IKEA: How the Swedish Retailer Became a Global Cult Brand. 2005. Business Week Online (November 14).

[10] IKEA Group in Figures. 2008. http://www.ikea-group.ikea.com/?ID=10, accessed February 2, 2008.

[11] Daykin, T. 2005. Miller Sues to End Deal with Molson after Coors Merger. *Milwaukee Journal Sentinel* (December 20). http://www.jsonline.com/story/index.aspx?id=379295, accessed March 14, 2008.

[12] *Pacific Business News*, (December 20, 2002). www.mariott.com/development/north-america-documents/default.mi, accessed March 24, 2008.

[13] McDonald's Set for 20% Increase in Russia. 2005. *St. Petersburg (Russia) Times* (June 10). http://www.sptimes.ru/story/3805, accessed March 14, 2008.

[14] Inkpen, A., & Beamish, P. 1997. Knowledge, Bargaining Power and the Instability of International Joint Ventures. *Academy of Management Review* 22: 177–202.

[15] United Nations. 2004. World Investment Report, 2004. New York: United Nations.

[16] Webb, S. 2003. Investment Banks Look to China, with Eyes on Lucrative Deals. *Wall Street Journal*, eastern edition (March 5): B11; Norton Rose Group. 2007. Cross-Border Mergers and Acquisitions: The Asian Perspective. http://www.nortonrose.com/knowledge/publications/2007/pub11909.aspx?page=071016105532&lang=en-gb, accessed February 2, 2008.

[17] Edmondson, G., & Kerwin, K. 2003. DaimlerChrysler; Stalled. *Business Week* (September 29).

[18] Dark Days at Daimler. 2005. Business Week Online (August 15).

[19] Full Year 2006 Annual Report. http://www.daimler.com, accessed March 24, 2008.

[20] Full Year 2006 Annual Report. http://www.daimler.com, accessed March 24, 2008.

[21] Crane, M. 2006. Toyota, Honda Surge in US Auto Market. Forbes.com (August 3).

[22] Daimler Confirms Talks on Selling Chrysler. 2007. *New York Times* (April 14). http://www.nytimes.com/2007/04/04/business/04cnd-daimler.html?_r=1&hp&oref=slogin, accessed January 7, 2008.

[23] Isidore, C. 2007. Daimler Pays to Dump Chrysler: German Automaker Will End Up Actually Paying $650 Million to Unload Chrysler to End Its Exposure to Billions in Ongoing Losses, Health Care Costs. CNN Money.com (May 14). http://money.cnn.com/2007/05/14/news/companies/chrysler_sale/index.htm, accessed January 7, 2008.

[24] http://www.geert-hofstede.com, accessed January 7, 2008.

[25] For an introduction to emerging markets, see http://en.wikipedia.org/wiki/Emerging_markets, accessed January 7, 2008.

[26] Peng, M. 2006. *Global Strategy*. Mason, OH: Thompson/South-Western; Yip, G. S. 1992. *Total Global Strategy*. Englewood Cliffs, NJ: Prentice Hall.

9 Acting Responsibly

Are you among the many people around the world who are concerned about the current and future quality of the environment? Are you bothered by charges of leaders' wrongdoing? Do you want to build a career but also do something that goes beyond your individual interests? This chapter addresses these large, important interests from an organizational perspective.

Throughout this book, we have discussed globalizing markets, new technology, and other macroeconomic changes. We now focus on how these factors are increasing interdependencies among firms, employees, customers, providers of capital, and the communities they affect. Corporate managers, especially at the level of the board of directors, are more frequently setting boundaries for their firms and holding them accountable for the communication of ethical standards and the development of organization controls that result in ethical decisions and behavior. The managers within these firms also must be held accountable for development and support of organization culture and other controls that result in ethical decisions and behavior.

Unfortunately, in recent years it seems that systems of corporate governance, which include the board of directors, shareholders, and top management, need to be reformed. Many boards of directors have not adequately controlled and monitored the decisions of the firm's top managers. The WorldCom and Enron bankruptcies illustrate the failures that have led to reform. However, employees of failed companies not only lose their jobs, they receive no severance packages and often lose their pension funds. Bankruptcies also impact other firms, including suppliers and holders of firm debt, as well as local communities.

. . . .

Clearly, there is a pressing need to restore the public's confidence in the corporate world. This need can be met only by recognizing and listening to concerns within firms as well as the larger group of stakeholders that are affected by their behavior. In this chapter we review the stakeholder model of the corporation first described in Chapter 1, and use it as an initial framework to consider the following questions:

What is sustainable strategy?

How are standards for corporate governance changing?
Separation of ownership and managerial control
More diverse boards of directors
More active institutional investors
Corporate governance reform in the United States: the Sarbanes-Oxley act

What are internal forces for social responsibility?
Business ethics
Corporate codes of ethics

What intensifies ethical dilemmas?
Multinational operations
Multistakeholder judgments

Though many readers will be familiar with the story, it is worthwhile reiterating events in a single company that put corporate reform on the public agenda.

ENRON: WRONGDOING THAT CAPTURED WORLD ATTENTION

Enron was once America's seventh-largest firm, with more than $101 billion in reported revenues and 25,000 employees worldwide. The company was listed as one of the best companies to work for on three different occasions, received six environmental awards, and was named for six years in a row as "Most Innovative Company in America" by *Fortune* magazine.[1] It had also developed strong policies on human rights and put together a corporate statement of values emphasizing "communication, respect, and integrity."[2]

Behind the scenes, Enron was engaged in a number of aggressive and questionable accounting practices, but they were insufficient to keep the operation afloat. In October 2001, the company announced huge losses, and on December 2, 2001, the energy trader filed for bankruptcy. Observers are still debating how it all happened.

Enron was led by bright strategists. CEO Ken Lay had a Ph.D. in economics, once worked as an energy economist in the U.S. Department of the Interior, and had been Enron's CEO since 1986. CFO Jeff Skilling was a Harvard Business School MBA and former McKinsey consultant. Under their leadership in the mid-1990s, Enron pursued a dual strategy of investing in physical assets and developing a market for trading energy futures.

To manage the strained balance sheet that resulted from these activities, strategists established a number of special-purpose entities (SPEs) to move certain liabilities (and assets) off the balance sheet. SPEs often created extraordinary profits and personal gains for the top managers who engineered the deals. They also made the firm appear more financially robust than it was.

Arthur Andersen LLP, the largest accounting firm in the United States, had served as Enron's auditors since 1985. Some Andersen accountants working at Enron expressed doubt about the accounting of Enron's off-balance sheets, but they still signed off on financial statements that hid billions of dollars in debt and losses. Andersen earned $25 million in audit fees and $26 million in consulting fees in 2000 alone.

After Enron's filing, Andersen was brought to trial in Houston, Texas (where Enron was headquartered) to face allegations that employees had illegally destroyed thousands of documents and computer records relating to the company. David Duncan, lead client manager from Andersen, and other top Andersen managers argued that this was "routine house-keeping" that involved drafts and not final documents, but jurors found them guilty of obstructing justice by destroying evidence that the Securities and Exchange Commission had requested for its Enron inquiry.

The U.S. Supreme Court unanimously overturned that decision in May 2005, finding that instructions to jurors were unclear.[3] However, the charges destroyed Andersen's reputation for solid accounting. Many clients left Andersen once charges were made, and even before the trial was concluded in June 2002, the firm voluntarily surrendered its licenses to practice as certified public accountants in the United States,[4] leaving almost 30,000 employees without benefits.[5]

Meanwhile, Enron's Jeffrey Skilling and Kenneth Lay were found guilty of conspiracy and fraud in May 2006. In a separate case Lay was also found guilty of bank fraud. It was the end of several cases brought against Enron employees, including former CFO Andrew Fastow, who pleaded guilty to criminal charges and agreed to a ten-year jail term in 2004.[6] Lay died of a heart attack before being sentenced, and Skilling's lawyers are planning appeals of his conviction. Their activities continue to raise questions about business and accounting practices carried out by many different firms around the world.

What Is Sustainable Strategy?

Clearly, Enron's SPEs and accounting strategies did not pass the test of time. We begin this chapter with a topic that deserves a book of its own—the growing attention to sustainable strategy. A basic meaning of the term *sustainable* is "capable of being maintained over time." That idea alone is worth attention by strategists. Sustainable strategy requires that strategists develop specific resources or competencies that their competitors will not erode. Although an important message of this and previous chapters is that a firm that makes these commitments reduces its flexibility, we hope you also remember the advantages of competitive advantage.

However, advantage is not the sole criterion for strategy. An expanded and more contemporary definition of *sustainable strategy* is that it can be carried out over time with minimal negative impacts on the environment or society. In fact, an increasing number of stakeholders want firm activities to make positive contributions to the broader environment, rather than merely minimize the harm they cause.

Stakeholder concerns are adding up. A *Business Week* poll of 2,000 people reported that 95 percent agreed with the following claim: "U.S. corporations should have more than one purpose. They also owe something to their workers and the communities in which they operate, and they should sometimes sacrifice some profit for the sake of making things

Sustainable strategies not only minimize harm, but make positive contributions to the environment and society as well as their firm survival.

better for their workers and communities." In contrast, just 4 percent agreed with this statement: "U.S. corporations should have only one purpose—to make the most profit for their shareholders—and their pursuit of that goal will be best for America in the long run." Approximately 45 percent of the *Fortune* global top 250 companies issue environmental, social, or sustainability reports in addition to their financial reports.[7]

✳ The *triple bottom line* is also known as "people, planet, profit" and captures an expanded spectrum of economic, environmental, and social values and criteria for measuring an organization's success.[8]

HOW ARE STANDARDS FOR CORPORATE GOVERNANCE CHANGING?

Events at other companies have increased concern about business practice. Recently:

- Citigroup was involved in the Enron and other financial scandals and was charged with predatory lending practices through a recently acquired subsidiary.
- Merrill Lynch executives were indicted for allegedly assisting Enron in a year-end 1999 deal involving the "parking" of Enron assets with Merrill Lynch. That arrangement allowed Enron to illegally inflate the year-end 1999 financial position that it presented in its annual report, which also was used to pay its executives unwarranted bonuses.
- Fannie Mae executives were found to have manipulated earning projections to assure their bonuses.
- Bayer pled guilty to defrauding the federal government out of hundreds of millions of dollars in Medicare payments. Bayer was charged with knowingly providing Medicaid with incorrect data regarding pricing of prescription drugs.
- Boeing leased tanker planes to the Pentagon to refuel fighter planes in midair. It would have been much cheaper for the Pentagon to purchase the planes. As a result of media attention, the Pentagon canceled the $27.6 billion contract.

Corporate governance is the system that monitors the strategic direction and performance of a firm consistent with the interests of shareholders.

Other scandals at WorldCom, Tyco, Global Crossing, ImClone, Adelphia Communications, and other companies increased scrutiny of corporations and boards of directors by investors, regulators, and legislators. Pressure continues to be placed on corporations to improve their corporate governance system so that effective and ethical strategic decision making is ensured.

An effective *corporate governance* system can provide an important competitive advantage. Corporate governance concerns the shared responsibility of directing a firm consistent with the interests of shareholders. The

Final #12

primary participants are in governance shareholders, the executive team, and the board of directors. The *board of directors* is the group of individuals who monitor the behavior of the top management team. Members can be either "inside" directors who hold management positions in the firm or "outside" directors who do not hold another position in the firm. In public corporations, board members are elected by voting shareholders.

Corporate governance abuses are also exemplified by Dennis Kozlowski's activities as the former CEO of Tyco.

Dennis Kozlowski Claims Expenses

In 2002, the Securities and Exchange Commission (SEC) sued Dennis Kozlowski, CEO of Tyco International, and CFO Mark Swartz for looting more than $600 million from the company. At one time Kozlowski was one of the highest-paid executives in the world. He was accused of running his company like a "private bank," taking out hundreds of millions of dollars in unauthorized personal loans and paying for exorbitant gifts for himself and his executives with company funds.

Some observers argue that Kozlowski deserved to be well compensated, given the increase in the firm's stock price from $4.50 per share in 1991 to about $60 at the end of 2001. Kozlowski earned $5.65 million in total compensation in 2001, plus $30.4 million in restricted stock awards. But few people approved of the loans and gifts that he purchased with company funds. For instance, Kozlowski used about $2.1 million in company funds to throw his wife a birthday party on the Italian island of Sardinia. The Roman-themed party featured Jimmy Buffett singing for a one-night fee of $250,000, an ice sculpture of Michelangelo's *David* peeing vodka, and a birthday cake shaped like a woman with sparklers on her breasts. The evening ended with a laser show forming and re-forming his wife's name in the sky.

In another incident, Kozlowski was accused of improperly using at least $5.7 million (not including artwork) in Tyco funds to furnish his $18 million luxury apartment. His purchases included a Regency mahogany bookcase, circa 1810 ($105,000), a George I walnut arabesque tall case clock ($113,750), a custom queen bed skirt ($4,995), a custom pillow ($2,665), an Ascherberg grand piano, circa 1895 ($77,000), a chandelier, painted iron, circa 1930 ($32,500), and a flower basket ($2,600).[9]

It is clear that Tyco did not have an effective governance system. Kozlowski went to enormous lengths to keep Tyco's outside directors in the dark. He personally controlled all information that went to the board. Many of the directors were benefiting from their relationship with Kozlowski and Tyco. Director Joshua M. Berman, for example, was paid $360,000 annually for providing "legal services," according to SEC filings. Even worse, the lead director, Frank E. Walsh, Jr., received a $20 million fee for his services in assisting Tyco's disastrous acquisition of commercial-finance company CIT Group. Tyco's board should have insisted on meeting directly with the internal auditors, but given their relationship with Kozlowski, it is not surprising that they were satisfied with hearing only from Kozlowski or his CFO.[10]

In the last few years legislators, academic theorists, business leaders, and even the general public have given a great deal of attention to rules and formal structures that might prevent abuses like those found at Tyco. In the United States, the location of most of the abuses we have just cited, the attention has focused on role separation. Given the prominence of U.S.-based firms in globalization, as well as the central role played by U.S. stock markets, this principle also has an important effect on corporate behavior in other countries.

Separation of Ownership and Managerial Control

Before the 1920s, most firms were managed by their founders and descendants. When the owner of the firm is also the manager, the manager can be expected to act in a way that is consistent with the firm owner's best interests. But as organizations grow and operations become much more complex and difficult to manage, professional managers are often hired. If managers are to be effective, owners must become less directly involved in the daily decision making of the firm. In 1932, Adolf Berle and Gardiner Means wrote a seminal book titled *The Modern Corporation and Private Property* in which they discussed the implications of this separation of corporate ownership from managerial control. They recognized that as professional managers take over the decision-making responsibility, there is potential for conflict between the goals of the owners and the goals of the managers who run the firm. This is called the *agency problem*.

Agency theory addresses the goal conflict that can exist between principals (owners) and their agents.

The key idea of *agency theory* is that one party (the principal) delegates work to another party (the agent). Agency theory addresses the issue that there may be goal conflict between the principal and the agent. In the case of corporate governance, the theory defines the relationship between the shareholder (the principal) and the manager (the agent). The behavior of managers is influenced or controlled by incentives from and oversight of the board of directors, but observation suggests that managers can act in ways that are not consistent with the interests of their shareholders. In theory, stock options can counter agency conflicts by vesting the manager as a shareholder.

Some observers of business behavior point to executive behavior as an indicator of agency problems. Total direct compensation for CEOs at major U.S. corporations jumped 15 percent to a median of $3,022,505 in 2002 (not counting bonuses, stock options, and other perks). Corporate CEOs of sixty-nine firms received median cash bonuses of $605,000.[11] CEO compensation continues to rise significantly, despite complaints from the public and government that executives are being excessively compensated.

Let's look at the specific example of Michael Eisner, Walt Disney's CEO, who was under pressure to resign from several of his largest shareholders in spring 2004. If he resigned or quit, he could have walked away with more than $370 million in compensation. Eisner's contract entitled him to receive $1 million a year salary through the end of his contract in 2006 and a $6 million bonus for each of the next four years, in addition to $4.2 million in pension. But the big money came from the 21 million stock options he received in 1996. If Disney stock were to rise an average of 8 percent a year, those options would be worth $337 million when they expired in 2008 and 2011.[12]

So why have shareholders not been able to elect boards of directors who will properly monitor managers' compensation and other activities? Stock ownership has become widely dispersed among thousands of individuals. These investors have a small stake in the firm relative to the total number of shares issued. If they want to force existing management to consider alternative strategic agendas, they have to engage in a mass communication program among thousands of poorly informed individual shareholders. Unless discontented stockholders have a substantial investment in such firms, it is unlikely they will spend the time and money necessary to engage in a proxy contest with the management of the firm. They are more likely to simply sell their stock positions and move their investments elsewhere. The result is that effective control of the firm has passed to the firm's managers. Managers can act in accordance with their own objectives and perceptions, which may or may not be in the best interest of shareholders.

final #12

More Diverse Boards of Directors

In theory, a firm's management is accountable for its performance to its shareholders. Shareholders elect boards of directors, and boards elect CEOs. Directors act as representatives of the legal owners of a firm, the stockholders. The board represents the key corporate governance mechanism, whose function is to prevent agency problems. All publicly held corporations are required to have boards of directors to represent the firm's shareholders.

Boards of directors have three primary responsibilities. The first, assigned by law, is to monitor executives to ensure that they are acting responsibly and consistently with regard to shareholder interests. Courts hold directors accountable for making decisions consistent with the business judgment rule. This rule has been interpreted to mean that directors demonstrate loyalty to the interests of shareholders and exercise due diligence in making decisions; that is, directors must discover as much information as possible on an issue and consider all reasonable alternatives.

As part of the monitoring function, board members are responsible for selecting, evaluating, and, if necessary, replacing the CEO. In addition, the board determines management compensation and reviews systems and processes to ensure that the firm is complying with all applicable laws and regulations.

The second role of the board is to monitor and approve the firm's major strategic initiatives. These decisions usually include approval of major new product development programs, divestitures, acquisitions, and mergers.

The third function is to provide the firm with connections to the external environment to help the firm acquire needed resources. An effective board will be composed of directors who each have different career experiences and contacts. For large corporations, board members will typically have worked with government, law firms, consumer groups, customer or supplier firms, and financial institutions.[13] This provides executives with the ability to contact important advisors and potential providers of financial as well as human capital.

Most boards are composed of twelve to fifteen members and meet quarterly. Much of the board's work is carried out in standing committees. Boards generally have an executive committee, which works closely with the firm's executive team and can make decisions as representatives of the entire board if necessary. Other standing committees include an audit committee, which is responsible for fiduciary oversight of the company; the compensation committee, which develops and approves compensation plans for the executives of the firm; the finance committee, which oversees the investing of company funds and reviews capital needs; and the nominating committee, which selects candidates to sit on the board.

Recent reformers have been trying to address two key issues regarding the board: CEO duality and director selection. The first issue is perhaps the most important agency problem in corporate governance. *CEO duality* occurs when the CEO is also the chair of the board of directors. Estimates are that about 75 percent of corporate CEOs are also chairs of their respective boards of directors. As we have discussed, the board is responsible for evaluating the CEO's performance. This puts the CEO in the enviable position of having a say in his or her own annual performance evaluation. In most firms the board chair controls the solicitation and voting of proxies. Board meetings usually follow an agenda compiled by the board chair, though other directors can ask for items to be included. The agenda and relevant material are typically sent to directors a few days before the meeting. Directors can never know as much about the organization as the management and depend on being supplied with necessary, accurate, timely information. Unfortunately we have seen many recent examples of boards that knew too little too late.

CEO duality exists when the CEO of a firm is also chair of the board.

The second issue is the selection of directors. The board chair can nominate all committee chairpersons and assign duties to board members. A recent study by Korn/Ferry, an international human resource consulting firm, found that most board vacancies were filled from the board chair's recommendations. The chair could stack the board with personal allies. Under these circumstances, the firm's executives may possess substantial discretion to pursue their own strategies and increase their own power and security. A related issue involves the ratio of inside board members to outside members. Inside board members are those who have some relationship with the firm, such as being current or former employees of the firm or relatives of an employee. It is argued that inside board members may be more likely to favor management over the interests of shareholders. Outside directors, not currently or previously employees or related to employees, are assumed to be more independent of management and more likely to act in accordance with shareholder interests.

Of course, some outside directors are more independent and objective than others. Some outside directors may serve the firm as lawyers, bankers, consultants, or major customers or suppliers. These directors can be expected to side with the incumbent management when the board faces a critical governance issue. So having a large number of outside board members does not ensure that shareholders' interests will be foremost.

Still, shareholders are best served by a board composed of a high percentage of independent, outside members, especially directors without a vested interest. TIAA-CREF, one of America's largest public pension funds (teachers and university professors), has gone on record saying that it will invest only in corporations that have a majority of directors who are outsiders.

Many experts recommend that boards increase the diversity of board members' backgrounds to bring a breadth of experience to organizations. Key aspects of board diversity include geography, human capital (education, work experience, previous board experience), social capital (networks), age, and gender. Some boards have limited diversity; for example, there are few women on boards of directors of publicly traded companies in the United States, the United Kingdom, and elsewhere in the world.[14]

Worksheet 9.1 can be used to help analyze a company's board of directors.

More Active Institutional Investors

One of the most important trends in corporate governance is the increasing activism of *institutional investors*. Large institutional investors, most importantly the public pension funds, are demanding a far more active role in the management of many large corporations.

Worksheet 9.1: Corporate Governance Structure—A Tool for Analyzing a Corporate Board of Directors

Institutional investors include pension funds, mutual funds, insurance companies, foundations, and trusts investing in public firms.

In his 1976 book, *The Unseen Revolution: How Pension Fund Socialism Came to America*, Peter Drucker identified the growing importance of a new player in corporate governance: the institutional investor. Institutional investors accounted for about 12 percent of all shares on the New York Stock Exchange in 1950; in 2007, they controlled more than 50 percent of all corporate stock in the United States and 60 percent of all the shares in the 1,000 largest U.S. corporations.

Institutional investors represent perhaps the most important source of long-term capital and well-informed shareholders. Institutional investors hold a significantly higher number of shares than individual investors. The owner of any large block of stock, particularly the well-informed institutional investor, has greater incentives to monitor a firm's managers than the less-informed individual investor. The sheer size of holdings that institutions have generally prevents them from selling their stock in response to a short-term drop in earnings. When institutions do sell, share prices can drop dramatically, forcing institutions to take substantial capital losses on such transactions. Recognizing this dilemma, institutions have been using their voting power to influence or change firm management rather than simply selling their stock holdings.

In addition, when a firm's stock ownership is highly concentrated in the hands of institutional investors, the costs of opposing the firm's management are greatly reduced. A few discontented shareholders can meet with a small number of educated, well-informed, professional institutional portfolio managers. The largest public pension fund in the United States, with more than $200 billion in assets, is the California Public Employees Retirement System (CalPERS), which has been very effective in organizing institutional investors. In 2003, CalPERS formed the Council for Institutional Investors to find ways to work together to increase accountability of corporate managers to their shareholders. The council has been a major force in improving the independence of directors and has lobbied state and federal officials to reduce regulations, which in the past have prevented institutional investors from taking a more active role in the governance process. An example of institutional activism occurred at Walt Disney's annual shareholders' meeting in 2004.

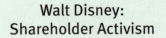

Walt Disney:
Shareholder Activism

Disney's stock price lost 23 percent of its value over the period 1998–2003, which was significantly more than the average for the Standard & Poor's 500. Disney's institutional investors had become increasingly frustrated with CEO Michael Eisner's inability and unwillingness to address their concerns. They accused the board of being insular and blindly loyal to Eisner.[15]

> At the last minute Eisner did try to meet with these large institutional investors, especially the two largest: CalPERS (which owned more than 9 million shares) and the California State Teachers Retirement System (8 million shares). Eisner tried to convince them that he had a strategic vision and would be able to obtain 30 percent growth in earnings in 2004 and double-digit increases through 2007. Despite this last-minute effort, 43 percent of Disney's shareholders voted that they had no confidence in Michael Eisner. As a result of the vote, hoping to reduce criticism from institutional investors, the board agreed to take the board chair's title away from Eisner. An outside board member, former U.S. senator George Mitchell, was named the new chairman. The institutional investors then formed a shareholder committee to review Mitchell's actions and to maintain pressure on the board to remain independent from Eisner.
>
> As you probably know, things have moved on at Disney. Robert Iger replaced Eisner as CEO. A second important change came with the purchase of Pixar Animation Studios, which made Steve Jobs (Pixar's chairman, CEO, and 50.6 percent owner) the largest shareholder of Disney and a member of its board of directors.

As an aside, it is interesting that Jobs drew SEC attention for allegedly suggesting backdating of options at Apple in 2007. Apple admitted that stock option grants were backdated and then improperly reported. The company took an $84 million charge to fix the error. At the time of this writing it has been reported that Jobs has been subpoenaed with respect to the SEC investigation but is not under investigation. External observers have explicitly indicated that the incident is not comparable to cases of executive wrongdoing at Enron and other high-profile cases.

Corporate Governance Reform in the United States: The Sarbanes-Oxley Act

After the seemingly endless wave of accounting scandals that shook corporate America, the U.S. Congress passed a bill in July 2002 called the Sarbanes-Oxley Act (SOA) or "Sar-Box." The purpose of the bill is "to promote corporate responsibility, enhance public disclosure, improve the quality and transparency of financial reporting and auditing, create a Public Company Accounting Oversight Board, protect the objectivity of research analysts, and strengthen penalties for securities law violations."[16] According to PricewaterhouseCoopers, SOA is "the single most important piece of legislation affecting corporate governance, financial disclosure and the practice of public accounting since the U.S. securities laws of the 1930s."[17]

The four most important provisions address accountability in financial reporting, independence of the audit committee members, executive compensation, and the establishment of a corporate code of conduct. First, the act requires that the CEO and CFO personally certify all reports filed with the Securities and Exchange Commission. The executives are required to disclose any additional information related to the company's financial operations, such as off–balance sheet transactions (which were prevalent in the Enron scandal). The act establishes severe criminal charges if these provisions are not followed. The penalties for inaccurate certification "range from up to ten years and $1 million for a knowing violation to up to twenty years and $5 million for a willful violation."[18]

Second, SOA has provisions that protect the independence of the board's auditing committee members and objectivity of research analysts. Third, it contains several provisions that restrict some of the executive compensation abuses exposed in recent scandals such as Enron and Tyco. These include prohibiting executives and directors from taking personal loans from the corporation and restricting increases in compensation due to extraordinary events or financial restatements.

Code of Conduct ✳Fourth, SOA requires companies to develop codes of conduct for their senior executives. The code of ethics is intended to extend personal responsibility for the company's performance to the firm's attorneys and even regular employees. The attorneys are required to report any violations of securities laws to the company's executives, and if the latter fail to respond appropriately, the attorney must bring the issue in front of the audit committee.

Overall, the SOA is moving corporate governance from a system of mostly voluntary compliance to mandating accountability and ethical corporate practices. In the future, directors of boards will most likely become much more proactive in executing their board oversight responsibilities. In 2002, of the 17,000 public companies in the United States, 330 restated their earnings, up 22 percent from 2001.[19]

We should note that the Sarbanes-Oxley Act has raised a number of concerns on the part of corporate America. This is a very complex law and it is claimed to be much more burdensome than necessary. (The first installment of regulations is more than 3,000 pages!)[20] Some people also believe that no matter how many rules we develop, they will never be enough to stop executives who want to lie and steal. Instead, they argue, we need an increased awareness of and commitment to personal values and ethics from managers.[21] Furthermore, the cost of SOA compliance is a great burden of time and expense, especially for small firms.

Mainly as a result of the Sarbanes-Oxley Act, many firms have revised guidelines for their boards of directors and have tried to improve the ability of the board to provide independent oversight of the corporation's management. The most important provisions concern the role of independent directors, developing a process for board self-evaluation, ensuring that board members have access to needed information, and addressing compensation issues of the executives and board members.

Some provisions of Microsoft's guidelines provide examples.

Microsoft Corporation Corporate Governance Guidelines

Board Composition and Selection; Independent Directors

Board Membership Criteria. . . . In evaluating the suitability of individual Board members, the Board takes into account many factors, including general understanding of marketing, finance, and other disciplines relevant to the success of a large publicly traded company in today's business environment; understanding of [Microsoft's] business and technology; [and] educational and professional background. . . . The Board evaluates each individual in the context of the Board as a whole, with the objective of recommending a group that can best perpetuate the success of the . . . business and represent shareholder interests through the exercise of sound judgment, using its diversity of experience. . . .

Board Composition–Mix of Management and Independent Directors. The Board intends that, except during periods of temporary vacancies, a substantial majority of its directors will be independent. . . . [In] determining the independence of a director, [the Board will apply] the definition of "independent director" in the listing standards of the Nasdaq Stock Market, and applicable laws and regulations. . . .

Board Meetings; Involvement of Senior Management

Access to Employees. The Board should have access to Company employees in order to ensure that directors can ask all questions and glean all information necessary to fulfill their duties. The Board may specify a protocol for making such inquiries. Management is encouraged to invite Company personnel to any Board meeting at which their presence and expertise would help the Board have a full understanding of matters being considered.

Executive Sessions of Independent Directors. The independent directors of the Company will meet regularly in executive session, i.e., without management present—at least quarterly each fiscal year. Executive sessions of the independent directors will be called and chaired by the Chairman of the Board, if the Chairman is an independent director, or otherwise by the Chairman of the Governance and Nominating Committee. . . . These executive session discussions may include such topics as the independent directors determine.

Performance Evaluation

Annual CEO Evaluation. The Chairman of the Board, . . . or otherwise the Chairman of the Governance and Nominating Committee . . . , leads the [committee] in conducting a review of the performance of the CEO at least annually. The evaluation results . . . are communicated to the CEO. The [committee] establish[es] the evaluation process and determine[s] the criteria on which the performance of the CEO is evaluated.

Board Self-Evaluation. The Governance and Nominating Committee is responsible for conducting an annual evaluation of the performance of the Board, and . . . [evaluation] results are reported to the Board.

The Governance and Nominating Committee's report should generally include an assessment of the Board's compliance with the principles set forth in these guidelines, as well as identification of areas in which the Board could improve its performance. . . .

Compensation

Board Compensation Review. . . . Company management should report to the Board on an annual basis how the Company's director compensation practices compare with those of other large public corporations. The Board should make changes in its director compensation practices only upon the recommendation of the Compensation Committee, and following discussion and unanimous concurrence by the Board.

    Director Stock Ownership. The Board believes that, in order to align the interests of directors and shareholders, directors should have a significant financial stake in the Company. Each director should own shares equal in value to a minimum of three times the base annual retainer payable to a director. . . . The Board will evaluate whether exceptions should be made for any director on whom this requirement would impose a financial hardship.[22]

Though sometimes criticized as overly increasing the burdens of both serving as a director and reporting to the government, Sarbanes-Oxley has had a monumental effect—not only in the United States but on international companies that wish to operate in the United Sates. Other governments considering governance issues have also been strongly influenced by the approach taken. Not surprisingly, there have been some changes over time, most notably an effort to reduce the reporting burden on smaller companies.[23] We expect ongoing efforts by world governments to legislate governance reform.

WHAT ARE INTERNAL FORCES FOR SOCIAL RESPONSIBILITY?

It is unlikely that external monitoring can create the kind of world that we want to live in. Internal judgments about right and wrong are much more influential. *Corporate social responsibility* is an obligation of the organization to act in ways that serve both its own interests and the interests of its many stakeholders.[24] There are four levels of corporate social responsibility: (1) economic responsibility to be productive and profitable, (2) legal obligation to abide by written laws and government regulations, (3) ethical responsibility to abide by standards of acceptable behavior as judged by the firm's stakeholders, and (4) philanthropic responsibility, which is giving back to society to improve the quality of life.[25]

Corporate social responsibility is an obligation of the organization to act in ways that serve both its own interests and the interests of its many stakeholders.

There has been general acceptance of the idea that the firm's first priority is to maximize shareholder return. The established practice in the United States is that firms are allowed to behave in any way that does not substantially hurt consumers or society and does not substantially reduce competition.[26] However, over time, businesses have shown that they cannot be trusted to do what is right in areas such as consumer safety and environmental protection.[27] Governments create laws and regulations to establish minimum standards for responsible behavior. Laws have been passed to address specific problems such as regulating competition, consumer protection, employee equality, and safety.

In recent years, public policy has shifted toward mandating ethical behavior from firms instead of relying on voluntary compliance. The most important laws in this area are the Federal Sentencing Guidelines for Organizations and the Sarbanes-Oxley Act. The Federal Sentencing Guidelines for Organizations require firms to establish codes of ethical conduct and compliance programs to ensure that employees behave in legal and ethical ways. As we discussed earlier, the Sarbanes-Oxley Act established a system of federal oversight over corporate accounting procedures.

Corporate philanthropic activities aimed at improving the quality of life of the community in which the corporation exists are voluntary. There are benefits to the corporation, such as attracting and retaining employees and creating positive publicity for the corporation's brand name. The most common corporate activity is providing donations to local and national charitable organizations. Many corporations actively participate in United Way campaigns, raising money for local community nonprofit organizations. In 2002, U.S. corporations gave more than $12 billion to environmental and social causes.[28]

In addition, in recent years, many corporations have become concerned about the quality of education in the United States. Corporations believe that the current labor pool lacks many basic work skills. As a result, corporations such as Hewlett-Packard, American Express, and Apple Computer have donated equipment, money, and employee time to help improve schools in their communities and throughout the nation.[29]

Business Ethics

Business ethics are the set of defined standards and moral principles that guide behavior in a business environment.[30] Each business decision has a moral component, which managers must consider. Ethics is usually defined as a code of moral behavior that sets standards of right or wrong.[31]

Most ethical problems in the workplace arise when people are asked to do something that they think is not consistent with their own personal

Business ethics are defined standards and moral principles that guide behavior in a business environment.

values. Values are underlying beliefs and attitudes that help determine individual behavior.[32] There is no universal code of ethics. Even within an organization that has a published ethics code, strategic managers can find themselves faced with decisions that have ambiguous but potentially serious ethical implications. Because many people have different values, we can expect that they will have different interpretations of what are ethical and unethical behaviors.

For example, when does gathering competitor intelligence cross over into being unethical and become an act of corporate espionage? Ethics also may change meaning in different countries. Bribery may be part of doing business in some countries, but illegal in other countries.

Leaders of all organizations can have a tremendous influence on individual behavior within the context of the firm if they can establish a social context within which ethical behavior becomes the accepted norm.[33] Archie Carroll, in his article "In Search of the Moral Manager," describes most middle managers as well intentioned but failing to take into account ethical considerations when they make decisions.[34] Carroll contends that an individual's ethical standards depend largely on what the group believes rather than his or her personal values.

It is not easy to develop values across a corporation. Studies suggest that most adults have not developed a set of values of their own, much less internalized a company's ethics.[35] Nor is it easy to teach values. Many of the top managers at Enron and Andersen held advanced business degrees, which likely included a business ethics course. But nothing guaranteed that the managers benefited from such a course.

Establishing and adhering to business ethics affects every aspect of internal and external operations, as wide ranging as half truths, false advertising, health and safety, handling AIDS in the workplace, conflicts of interest, and discrimination by race, gender, age, or sexual orientation.

Accenture: Does Corporate Location Make a Difference?

Following the split from Arthur Andersen in 2000, management consulting firm Accenture incorporated in Bermuda, where the firm has only three employees and pays a maximum annual Bermuda government fee of $27,825. In an article in the *Wall Street Journal*, an Accenture company official indicated "doubt" that the Bermuda courts "would recognize or enforce judgments of U.S. courts against us or our officers or directors based on the civil liabilities provisions of the federal or state securities laws of the U.S. or would hear actions against us or those persons based on those laws."[36]

Meanwhile, $684 million of Accenture's $11.4 billion in revenues comes from consulting contracts with U.S. federal, state, and local government agencies, including the contract to manage the website of the Internal Revenue Service. Accenture also owns a holding company in Luxembourg, a European tax haven. There are some legal attempts to put an end to these questionable practices. For example, the state of California is threatening not to invest in American companies that relocate their headquarters to avoid taxes. Congress is considering legislation to prohibit offshore companies from bidding on government contracts. However, Accenture has tried to be a good corporate citizen in other respects, such as giving free consultant time to nongovernment organizations and making donations to a number of charities such as United Way.

Corporate Codes of Ethics

One common approach that firms are using to establish ethical behavior throughout their organization is the development of a code of ethics. Seattle-based Brooks Sports's code of conduct makes explicit the company's policy against forced labor, child labor, discrimination, harassment, and abuse. Furthermore, Brooks guarantees that all employees will work the hours required by their country and be fairly compensated for this work.

final 13.

Brooks Sports Code of Conduct

Brooks Sports Inc. creates high-performance running shoes, apparel and accessories in more than 80 countries worldwide. Brooks' purpose is to inspire people around the world to run and be active. And our mission is to be the leader in performance running and one of the most admired companies in the industry.

Respect and integrity are operating values that we hold dear at our company. We expect all employees and partners to conduct themselves legally, ethically and in the most respectful manner each and every day. Brooks' Code of Conduct has been developed for our factories to ensure that they uphold and maintain these values as their employees produce quality Brooks products.

Forced Labor: There shall not be any use of forced labor, whether in the form of prison labor, indentured labor, bonded labor or otherwise.

Child Labor: No person shall be employed at an age younger than 15 or younger than the age for completing compulsory education in the country of manufacture where such age is higher than 15.

Harassment or Abuse: Every employee shall be treated with respect and dignity. No employee shall be subject to any physical, sexual, psychological or verbal harassment or abuse.

Nondiscrimination: No person shall be subject to any discrimination in employment, including hiring, salary, benefits, advancement, discipline, termination or retirement, on the basis of gender, race, religion, age, disability, sexual orientation, nationality, political opinion, or social or ethnic origin.

Health and Safety: Employers shall provide a safe and healthy working environment to prevent accidents and injury to health arising out of, linked with, or occurring in the course of work or as a result of the operation of employer facilities.

Freedom of Association and Collective Bargaining: Employers shall recognize and respect the right of employees to freedom of association and collective bargaining.

Wages and Benefits: Employers recognize that wages are essential to meeting employees' basic needs. Employers shall pay employees, as a floor, at least the minimum wage required by local law and shall provide legally mandated benefits.

Hours of Work: Employees shall not be required to work more than the limits on regular and overtime hours allowed by the law of the country of manufacture.

Overtime Compensation: In addition to their compensation for regular hours of work, employees shall be compensated for overtime hours at such premium rate as is legally required in the country of manufacture or, in those countries where such laws do not exist, at a rate at least equal to their regular hourly compensation rate.

Environmental Stewardship: All factories producing goods under the Brooks brand must adhere to all environmental standards, rules and regulations on the local, state and national levels.[37]

Worksheet 9.2: Code of Ethics—A Tool for Analyzing a Corporate Values Statement

Worksheet 9.2 gives you a framework for analyzing a company's Code of Ethics statement.

Although approximately three out of every four firms have written a code of ethical conduct,[38] considerable evidence suggests that these codes do not guarantee good moral conduct. For example, Figure 9.1 shows part of the first of six pages of Enron's Code of Ethics sent to all employees in an interoffice memo from CEO Ken Lay on July 1, 2000, seventeen months before the firm went bankrupt due to the alleged illegal activities of Lay and other top managers.

We should not be surprised to see bad behavior even when a document like this exists. It is not enough to publish corporate documents or to have executives make speeches about the importance of ethical conduct. Boards of directors and firm executives may be sincere when they declare their commitment toward codes of conduct, but this message has to be translated through many layers of the hierarchy and often across national borders and in different languages. Managers can

```
                                                                    INTEROFFICE
                                                                    MEMORANDUM

        [ENRON logo]



    To:     All Employees

    From:   Ken                                    Department:   Office of the Chairman

    Subject:  Code of Ethics                             Date:   July 1, 2000
```

As officers and employees of Enron Corp., its subsidiaries, and its affiliated companies ("Enron" or collectively the "Company"), we are responsible for conducting the business affairs of the Company in accordance with all applicable laws and in a moral and honest manner.

To make certain that we understand what is expected of us, Enron has adopted certain policies, with the approval of the Board of Directors, all of which are set forth in the enclosed booklet revised July 2000. *Please note that Enron has added the Principles of Human Rights; provided further description of our Business Ethics policy with respect to our legal contracts, the selection of outside counsel, and the making of disparaging remarks, oral or written, about Enron by employees; provided further clarification of Enron's policy with respect to Confidential Information and Trade Secrets; decreased the number of days passwords are valid under Enron's Communication Services and Equipment Policy, provided additional information with respect to the criminal penalties and civil fines assessed by the US government under the Foreign Corrupt Practices Act: and clarified Enron's policy with respect to Conflicts of Interests, Investments, and Outside Business Interests of Employees.*

The Code of Ethics contains commonsense rules of conduct with which the great majority of Enron employees routinely confirm. However, I ask that you read them carefully and completely and that, as you do, you reflect on your past actions to make certain that you have complied with the policies. It is absolutely essential that you fully comply with these policies in the future. If you have any questions, talk them over with your supervisor, manager, or Enron legal counsel.

Figure 9.1 — Memo on Enron's Code of Ethics

Source: http://www.thesmokinggun.com/enron/enronethics2.html, accessed March 14, 2008.

be overwhelmed by the pressures to meet short-term sales and profit objectives.

Therefore, more important than codes of conduct, strategic leaders have a responsibility to create and sustain an ethical culture within which employees act ethically as a matter of everyday behavior.[39] They need to serve as role models, exhibiting ethical behavior that clearly demonstrates that they value how business goals are obtained as much as reaching those goals.

Employees are exceptionally keen observers of their leaders' actions, and they will quickly identify any discrepancies between the leaders' values and their actual behavior. Many employees who observe questionable behavior adjust their behavior by lowering their personal ethical standards to fit in.[40]

WHAT INTENSIFIES ETHICAL DILEMMAS?

As we have discussed, values and ethical standards vary from person to person and organization to organization. As firms engage in complex activities, the variance increases. It is instructive to look at ethical issues that arise from international activities, but complex judgments can also arise with respect to standards in one country.

Multinational Operations

Every nation has a distinctive culture and often has several distinct sub-cultures. Each of these cultures has its own beliefs as to what constitutes ethical behavior. Cultures differ based on religions, language, technology, and social organization. This greatly complicates the ability of multinational corporations (MNCs) to establish uniform ethical standards across all of its operations.

We also contend that because of their sheer size and consequentially their impact on the economy and society, MNCs have an even more critical need to carefully consider the impact of their behavior. In many situations, MNCs possess more knowledge, more resources, and consequently more power than the host governments of countries in which the firm operates. As a result, MNCs have been subject to increasing scrutiny and criticism. MNCs have been accused of exploiting natural and human resources, unduly influencing host governments, and using unfair competitive practices in dealing with local firms, especially in less developed countries.

International government and nonprofit organizations have attempted to establish a universal set of ethical standards.[41] These standards include values such as respect, fairness, equality, and integrity. But, there is no general agreement on a universal standard of ethical conduct. One problem is that even if there is agreement on the values, different cultures interpret those values differently and therefore interpret their implementation differently.

So the challenge for MNCs is to accommodate cultural differences in ethics and regulations between countries and also to develop a code of conduct that the firm wants to adhere to worldwide. Many MNCs have agreed to abide by the *Sullivan Principles*, which define social responsibilities that firms will follow around the world. Other MNCs have signed the UN Global Compact, which requires firms to support free-trade unions, abolish child labor, and protect the environment. In his book *Competing with Integrity in International Business*, Richard De George highlights seven standards for MNCs that provide a basis for evaluating and responding to charges of unethical behavior, particularly when operating in countries with inadequate background institutions:

1. Multinationals should do no intentional harm.
2. Multinationals should produce more good than harm for the host country.
3. Multinationals should contribute by their activity to the host country's development.
4. Multinationals should respect the human rights of their employees.

5. To the extent that local culture does not violate ethical norms, multinationals should respect the local culture and work with and not against it.

6. Multinationals should pay their fair share of taxes.

7. Multinationals should cooperate with the local government in developing and enforcing just background institutions.[42]

The following case demonstrates the difficulties faced by MNCs that want to operate in every country around the world.

Pepsi: Operations in Burma/Myanmar

In November 1991, Pepsi, the U.S.-based soft drink manufacturer, built a bottling plant in Burma, a small country in the Asian subcontinent. Burma has a long history of social and political instability. In 1962 the military took over, creating the State Law & Order Restoration Council (SLORC), which jailed democracy supporters, turned a blind eye to child labor, imposed martial law, and even renamed the country Myanmar. In the 1990 election, the military junta received just 2 percent of the vote; 82 percent voted for the National League for Democracy (NLD). SLORC did not accept the outcome and remained in power.

One year later, when Pepsi entered Burma by building a bottling plant, it did so through a joint venture with a businessman named Thein Tun (Tun), who was close to SLORC officials. By 1996, Pepsi Burma had more than 240 employees, $14 million in revenues, and a 90 percent market share because the Burmese army prevented any other soft drink manufacturer from entering the country. All of Pepsi's taxes went directly to SLORC, which supported the military rule.

At the time, Burmese democracy demonstrators, led by Aung San Suu Kyi (Suu Kyi), urged Pepsi and other MNCs to leave the country. Petro-Canada left in 1992, followed by Levi Strauss in May 1993. Pepsi remained but took a hit at home; in April 1996, Harvard University canceled its Pepsi contract. Other universities and municipalities followed suit. In May 1996, Pepsi declared that it would leave Burma except for meeting its contractual obligations with the local franchise bottler. Protesters were furious that Pepsi continued to operate much as before. In June 1996, Pepsi's joint venture partner Tun attended an SLORC-sponsored antidemocracy rally and reportedly said that business in Burma should stop all prodemocracy activities. This move infuriated the "Boycott Pepsi" movement, which increased its efforts against Pepsi. By 1997, Pepsi buckled under the pressure and withdrew completely from Burma.[43]

Multistakeholder Judgments

Wal-Mart's story is a good place to end this chapter. It shows that company actions are likely to be interpreted in multiple ways. In part this is due to multiple stakeholders, each with their own ethical criteria. More important, company activities (like individual activities) have varied impacts even from one point of view. It is often impossible to act without some negative effect, and the most difficult ethical decisions involve choosing among alternatives that each have some problematic consequences. "The law of large numbers" magnifies these consequences for large firms like Wal-Mart.

America's Largest Retailer Cannot Help but Have an Impact

Wal-Mart's website proudly notes that an "independently certified study found that Wal-Mart saves the average household more than $2,300 per year." Wal-Mart also claims that "every year we create tens of thousands of jobs—many of them in neighborhoods that desperately need jobs."[44] Increasingly, however, company activities have generated negative reactions. A number of fault-finding websites have been established (including www.walmartwatch.com and blog. wakeupwalmart.com), and a highly critical film, *Wal-Mart: The High Cost of Low Price*, was released in 2005. Critics' concerns include the following:

- *Low wages:* Even after recent pay increases, $9.68/hour paid to the average Wal-Mart associate puts a family of four below the poverty line—and far below the standard set by competitor Costco, where the average pay is $17/hour.[45]
- *Poor health care benefits: The New York Times* reported that 46 percent of associates' children are either on Medicaid or uninsured.[46]
- *Reliance on part-time workers:* The wage and health situation is more problematic because the company hires many part-time workers, who receive fewer benefits than full-time employees.
- *Discrimination against female employees:* Wal-Mart was recently named in the "largest civil rights class action ever certified against a private employer"—it includes more than 1.6 million current and former female employees.[47]
- *Resistance to unions:* Wal-Mart claims that "there has never been a need for a Wal-Mart union due to the familiar, special relationship between Wal-Mart associates and their managers."[48] The unrepresented unions note that "in twenty-five U.S. states, the company has had to face legal complaints about violations of workers' rights."[49]

Treatment of individual workers (both positive and negative) obviously has community effects, but critics also point to macro impacts on the national and international economy. Two especially contentious issues involve the following:

- *Closure of smaller businesses:* Between 1983 and 1993, "the state of Iowa lost 553 grocery stores, 298 hardware stores, 293 building supply stores, 161 variety stores, 158 women's apparel stores, 153 shoe stores, 116 drug stores, and 111 men's and boys apparel [stores]. With few large-scale retail stores in 1983 and many in 1993, many attribute the collapse of so many stores to big box incursion into the state."[50]
- *Loss of American jobs:* Wal-Mart is said to have imported only 6 percent of its total merchandise in 1994, following a well-publicized campaign by Sam Walton for suppliers to "Bring it home to America." By 2004, however, the company imported 60 percent of its total merchandise.[51] That year a PBS special noted that "some economists credit Wal-Mart's single-minded focus on low costs with helping contain U.S. inflation, [but] others charge that the company is the main force driving the massive overseas shift to China in the production of American consumer goods, resulting in hundreds of thousands of lost jobs and a lower standard of living [in the U.S.][52]."

For many years the company had a policy of not publicly responding to such criticisms. At the beginning of 2005, however, Wal-Mart established a new website (www.walmartfacts.com) and a "war room" staffed by political consultants savvy about influencing public opinion.[53] These efforts made the public more aware of community-oriented campaigns, including a partnership with America's Second Harvest, a food bank network, to match up to $5 million raised for those in need.[54] Wal-Mart was also widely praised in August 2005 for using its logistics capabilities after Hurricane Katrina to "immediately [send] 1,900 truckloads of water and other emergency supplies to the afflicted."[55] The company was among the most active corporate contributors—giving $18 million to the hurricane relief effort, providing $14.5 million to associates affected by the hurricane, donating merchandise, and collecting contributions at its stores.[56]

A few years before Katrina, company leaders had begun to take environmental issues seriously. CEO Lee Scott admits that their environmental efforts were initially a "defensive strategy," but he has "a passion" for guiding Wal-Mart's efforts today.[57] A recent article in *Fortune* reports that Katrina "deepened Scott's resolve." Scott said: "We stepped back . . . and asked one simple question: How can Wal-Mart be that company—the one we were during Katrina—all the time?"

Skeptics were amazed by the specificity of the goals broadcast to all Wal-Mart facilities in November 2005, which included increasing vehicle efficiency by 25 percent in three years and doubling efficiency in ten; reducing store energy use by 30 percent; and reducing solid waste from U.S. stores by 25 percent within three years.[58] The scale of the company (for example, Wal-Mart has the second-largest fleet of trucks in the nation) makes that commitment very significant. It is also consistent with Wal-Mart's strategy to save customers money.

In January 2008, Scott announced that Wal-Mart would expand this initiative. Areas of additional emphasis include more energy-saving products, making high-energy-use products more efficient, working with other retailers to improve standards for global suppliers, and reducing the cost of prescriptions.[59]

Over time, ethical evaluation becomes even more complicated as new ideas shift understanding of ethical behavior. Consider, for example, the move from early pleas to recycle (once a major focus by those urging greater care for the environment) to more complex suggestions that companies and individuals should "reduce, reuse, and then recycle." This focus of attention further transformed into a concern for sustainability, but that idea is also being eclipsed. In their book *Cradle to Cradle*, William McDonough and Michael Braungart argue that conscientious action should consider the impact of the entire process of production, consumption, and disposal.[60] Their company is working with large companies, such as Ford to find ways that conscientious activity can also be affordable. Wal-Mart has identified similar synergies, which is one reason why environmentalists are positive about their continuing commitment.

We don't want to imply, however, that responsibility is just a corporate issue. Individual actors must consider their own values and act on them as well. The results can have widespread impact, as Valerie Casey discovered.

Guidelines for Green Design

Valerie Casey, the global head of software/digital experiences at IDEO, was happy with her job but frustrated about uneven involvement of her company and their clients in environmental issues. She wrote what she called a "Kyoto Treaty" of design in response.

In a little over a year, the document became a set of formal principles called the "Designers Accord" signed by thousands of designers. A six-member advisory board helps increase its impact.

Although the voluntary principles reflect practices already in place in some companies, a *Business Week* article suggests that the accord "marks a paradigm shift." Not only have major professional associations endorsed it, but it establishes the ground for further conversation around the globe. That's a very impressive result from one individual acting on her frustration![61]

CONCLUSIONS FOR THE STRATEGIST

One of the critical tasks of firm strategists is to manage the various stakeholders who impact the firm. The firm's executives have a responsibility to safeguard the welfare of the corporation, which requires them to balance the multiple and often conflicting claims of the firm's stakeholders. Shareholders want higher returns, customers want a better product at a lower cost, employees want higher wages, and the community wants help to provide a better quality of life for the members of its community.

Executives need to include major stakeholders within their strategic framework of analysis and decision making. If the firm is able to establish collaborative relationships with its many stakeholders, reduced risks and increased shareholder wealth can result.

The corporate governance system, composed most importantly of shareholders, the board of directors, and the firm's top managers, needs to shape the stakeholder management process to ensure that the corporation is behaving in a socially responsible and ethical manner.

Key Concepts

Sustainable strategies not only minimize harm, but make positive contributions to the environment and society as well as their firm's survival. **Corporate governance** is the system that monitors the strategic direction and performance of a firm consistent with the interests of shareholders and sometimes other stakeholders. The **board of directors** has legal responsibility for firm behavior. **CEO duality** exists when the CEO is also chair of the board.

Agency theory addresses the goal conflict that can exist between principals (owners) and agents (managers). **Institutional investors,** including pension funds, mutual funds, insurance companies, and foundations and trusts, are particularly influential owners.

Corporate social responsibility refers to the economic, legal, ethical, and philanthropic duties of a firm to act in ways that serve its own and other stakeholders' interests. Values are underlying philosophies that guide behavior and decisions. **Business ethics** are the set of standards and conduct that an organization uses when dealing within the organization and in the external environment.

Questions for Further Reflection

1. One of your colleagues tells you that she has interviewed with and accepted another job at a competitor, to start in three months. A few days later, you meet with your manager about the opportunity to manage a neat project that you are very excited about, but your manager tells you that you won't get to work on that project because your colleague has been assigned as the project's manager. What would you do, and why?

2. Find a case in which a company's management modified corporate governance practices to improve profitability. Find an example in which governance changes could reduce profitability.

3. Many legitimate corporations use unsolicited e-mail pop-ups as a key advertising strategy. Is this unethical? Why and when? Defend your argument with examples and facts.

WORKSHEET 9.1
Corporate Governance Structure—A Tool for Analyzing a Corporate Board of Directors

---

Boards of directors take responsibility for firm strategy and are held accountable for the firm's actions. This worksheet will help you find and analyze a company's board of directors.

Step 1: Identify a company and list the members of its board of directors in column 1 of the worksheet.

Step 2: Fill in column 2 with board of director attributes, including insider or outsider status and career background.

Step 3: Think of the resources these directors may provide for corporate governance as well as company strategies. Complete column 3 with these ideas.

Step 4: Identify potential issues with standards for governance, such as CEO duality or an overly high proportion of inside directors, in column 4.

ALTERNATIVES
- Analyze the members of a specific committee, such as compensation or nomination. Based on the profiles of these directors, what decisions might you anticipate the firm to make regarding executive compensation or the short list for an open director's seat?
- Analyze the backgrounds of the members of a specific committee. Based on the profiles of these directors, what type of competence or group of stakeholders is highly represented? Is there a set of skills that you believe is missing?

Corporate Governance Structure Worksheet 9.1	Organization: Time Frame:
Analyst(s):	**Strategy Summary:**

Members of Board of Directors	Attributes	Potential Contributions to Strategy and Governance	Corporate Governance Issues

Find and analyze a company's code of ethics.

Step 1: Find the code of ethics for a company that interests you.

Step 2: Fill in column 1 of the table with key attributes from the code of ethics.

Step 3: Brainstorm possible scenarios that firm employees, at any level, might encounter with respect to the attributes. Complete column 2.

Step 4: Does the code offer enough guidance with respect to these situations? Think of how an employee might interpret this code. Complete column 3 with these ideas.

ALTERNATIVES

- Use the Internet and other resources to identify any potential ethics challenge with which the firm has recently been involved. Is this in contrast to the code of ethics? What does the code of ethics suggest about how managers should behave?

Code of Ethics Worksheet 9.2	Organization: Time Frame:
Analyst(s):	Summary:

Key Attributes	Possible Scenarios	Quality of Guidance Available

NOTES

[1] Enron website. February 6, 2001. Cited in Propaganda Examples from Enron Corporation. http://www.propagandacritic.com/articles/examples.enron.html, accessed August 20, 2006.

[2] Waddock, S. 2002. Comment: Fluff Is Not Enough—Managing Responsibility for Corporate Citizenship Ethical Corporation (March 18). http://www.ethicalcorp.com/content.asp?ContentID=47, accessed March 26, 2008.

[3] PBS Online. 2005. Supreme Court Watch (May 31). http://www.pbs.org/newshour/bb/law/jan-june05/scotus_5-31.html, accessed March 14, 2008.

[4] http://en.wikipedia.org/wiki/Arthur_Andersen, accessed August 20, 2006.

[5] PBS Online, Supreme Court Watch, May 31, 2005.

[6] Enron's Lay and Skilling Guilty. 2006. BBC News (May 25). http://news.bbc.co.uk/2/hi/business/5017298.stm, accessed March 14, 2008; http://money.cnn.com/2006/05/25/news/newsmakers/enron_verdict/index.htm?cnn=yes, accessed March 14, 2008.

[7] http://www.businessethics.ca/3bl/triple-bottom-line.pdf, accessed March 14, 2008.

[8] Enterprise³: Your Business and the Triple Bottom Line Guide. Economic, Environmental, Social Performance. http://www.mfe.govt.nz/publications/sus-dev/enterprise3-triple-bottom-line-guide-jun03.pdf, accessed March 14, 2008; http://en.wikipedia.org/wiki/Triple_bottom_line, accessed March 14, 2008.

[9] Jury to Glimpse Kozlowski Lavish Lifestyle. http://www.redorbit.com/news/general/24534/jury_to_glimpse_kozlowski_lavish_lifestyle/index.html, accessed March 14, 2008.

[10] Symonds, W. C. 2002. Tyco, How Did They Miss a Scam So Big? *Business Week* (September 30): 40; DeBaise, C., & Maremont, M. 2003. Jurors Examine Costs of Décor Chez Kozlowski. *Wall Street Journal*, eastern edition (December 16): B1.

[11] Lubin, J. S. 2003 Executive Pay Keeps Rising, Despite Outcry. *Wall Street Journal* (October 3).

[12] Lavelle, L., & Sager, I. 2004. No Mickey Mouse Payoff for Eisner. *Business Week* (March 22).

[13] Hillman, A. J., Cannella, A. A., Jr., & Paetzold, R. L. 2000. The Resource Dependence Role of Corporate Directors: Strategic Adaptation of Board Composition in Response to Environmental Changes. *Journal of Management Studies* 37(2): 235–255; Singh, V., Terjesen, S., & Vinnicombe, S. 2008. Newly Appointed Directors in the Boardroom: How Do Women and Men Differ? *European Management Journal*. Forthcoming.

[14] Terjesen, S., & Singh, V. Female Presence on Corporate Boards. *Journal of Business Ethics* (forthcoming).

[15] Grover, R., & Borrus, A. 2004. Can Michael Eisner Hold the Fort? Having Fired the First Volley, Disney Stockholders Are in No Mood to Back Off. *Business Week* (March 22).

[16] Vlahakis, P., Wintner, J. M., & Cammaker, J. R. 2002. Understanding the Sarbanes-Oxley Act of 2002. *Corporate Governance Advisor* (September–October).

[17] Belmonte, S. J. 2003. Shining Light on Little-Known New Law. *Lodging Hospitality* 59(14): 26.

[18] Armstrong Teasdale. 2003. Corporate Governance Developments Post Sarbanes-Oxley. September. http://www.armstrongteasdale.com/ClientAlerts/Sarbanes Update_September2003.pdf, accessed March 14, 2008.

[19] McHugh, D. 2003. Post Enron Restatements Hit Record. MSNBC (January 21).

[20]Ferrell, O., Fraedrich, J., & Ferrell, L. 2005. *Business Ethics: Ethical Decision Making*. Boston: Houghton Mifflin.

[21]McHugh, D. 2003. Business Wants to Restore Public Trust. America Online (January 28).

[22]Microsoft Corporate Guidelines. http://www.microsoft.com/about/companyinformation/corporategovernance/guidelines.mspx, accessed March 14, 2008.

[23]SEC Commissioners Endorse Improved Sarbanes-Oxley Implementation to Ease Smaller Company Burdens, Focusing Effort on "What Truly Matters." http://www.sec.gov/news/press/2007/2007-62.htm, accessed January 17, 2008.

[24]Miles, R. 1987. *Managing the Corporate Social Environment*. Englewood Cliffs, NJ: Prentice Hall.

[25]Carroll, A. B. 1991. The Pyramid of Corporate Social Responsibility: Toward the Moral Management of Organizational Stakeholders. *Business Horizons* 34: 42.

[26]Ferrell, Fraedrich, & Ferrell, *Business Ethics*.

[27]For example, see Terjesen, S. 2003. Norsk Hydro: Utkal Project. In P. Gooderham & O. Nordhaug (eds.), *International Management*. Malden, MA: Blackwell.

[28]American Association of Fundraising Counsel. 2003. Charity Holds Its Own in Tough Times. Press release (June 23), http://www.aafrc.org/press_releases/trustreleases/charityholds.html, accessed March 14, 2008.

[29]Ferrell, Fraedrich, & Ferrell, *Business Ethics*.

[30]Ferrell, Fraedrich, & Ferrell, *Business Ethics*.

[31]Trevino, L., & Nelson, K. 1995. *Managing Business Ethics*. New York: Wiley.

[32]Schermerhorn, J. 2005. *Management* (8th ed.). New York: Wiley.

[33]Thomas, T., Schermerhorn, J., & Dienhart, J. 2004. Strategic Leadership of Ethical Behavior in Business. *Academy of Management Executive* 18 (2): 56–66.

[34]Carroll, A. 2001. In Search of the Moral Manager. *Business Horizons* (March–April): 7–15.

[35]Kohlberg, L. 1973. Stages and Aging in Moral Development: Some Speculations. *Gerontologist* 13(4): 497–502.

[36]Accenture's U.S. SEC filings; Simpson, G. 2002. The Economy: Consultants Accenture, Monday Take Steps That May Reduce Taxes. *Wall Street Journal* (July 3): A2.

[37]Brooks Sports Code of Conduct. http://www.runhappy.com.au/corporate/conduct.html, accessed March 14, 2008.

[38]According to a 1998 survey by SHRM and the Ethics Resource Center, 74 percent of respondents reported that their firm had written stands of ethical conduct in business.

[39]Thomas, Schermerhorn, & Dienhart, *Strategic Leadership*, 56–66. See also Bowen, F., & Sharma, S. 2005. Resourcing Corporate Environmental Strategy: Behavioral and Resource-Based Perspectives. *Academy of Management Best Paper Perspectives*, pp. A1–A6; Ferrell, O. C. 2004. Customer Stakeholders and Business Ethics. *Academy of Management Executive* 18: 126–129.

[40]Bandura, A. 1977. *Social Learning Theory*. Englewood Cliffs, N J: Prentice Hall.

[41]Ferrell, Fraedrich, & Ferrell, *Business Ethics*.

[42]De George, R. T. 1999. *Competing with Integrity in International Business* (5th ed.). Upper Saddle River, NJ: Prentice Hall.

[43]Burma Is the Last Straw for Pepsi. 1997. *The Independent* (January 29): 13; Myanmar: To Drink or Not to Drink: Human Rights Activists Want to Choke Off the Generals.

1996. *Asiaweek* (May 11); Vatikiotis, M. 1995. Sarong Executives. *Far Eastern Economic Review* 158(8): 58–59.

[44] http://www.walmartfacts.com/featuredtopics/?id=2, accessed March 14, 2008.

[45] Greenhouse, S. 2005. How Costco Became the Anti-Wal-Mart. *New York Times* (July 17). http://www.nytimes.com/2005/07/17/business/yourmoney/17costco.html?pagewanted=1&ei=5088&en=8b31033c5b6a6d68&ex=1279252800&partner=rssnyt&emc=rss, accessed March 14, 2008.

[46] http://walmartwatch.com/home/pages/key_quotes_from_the_secret_wal_mart_memo, accessed March 14, 2008.

[47] http://www.walmartclass.com/walmartclass_forthepress.html, accessed March 14, 2008.

[48] http://www.walmartfacts.com/wal-mart-union.aspx, accessed March 14, 2008.

[49] http://www.union-network.org/unisite/Sectors/Commerce/Multinationals/Wal-Mart_union_busting_operator_named_for_threatening_workers.htm, accessed March 14, 2008.

[50] http://www.pbs.org/wgbh/pages/frontline/shows/walmart/interviews/gereffi.html, accessed March 26, 2008.

[51] http://www.wakeupwalmart.com/press/20060711.html, accessed March 14, 2008.

[52] http://www.pbs.org/wgbh/pages/frontline/teach/walmart/, accessed March 14, 2008.

[53] Barbaro, M. 2005. A New Weapon for Wal-Mart: A War Room. *New York Times* (November 1). http://select.nytimes.com/gst/abstract.html?res=F60A13F6345B0C728CDDA80994DD404482, accessed March 14, 2008.

[54] http://www.secondharvest.org/news_room/2006_News_Releases/030206.html, accessed March 14, 2008.

[55] Featherstone, L. 2005. Wal-Mart to the Rescue! *The Nation* (September 13). http://www.thenation.com/doc/20050926/featherstone, accessed March 14, 2008.

[56] http:// www.pbs.org/wgbh/pages/frontline/shows/walmart/interviews/gereffi.html, accessed March 26, 2008.

[57] http:// walmartwatch.com/img/documents/21st_Century_Leadership.pdf

[58] http:// walmartwatch.com/img/documents/21st_Century_Leadership.pdf

[59] Wal-Mart to Expand Environmental Program. 2008. http://money.cnn.com/2008/01/23/news/companies/walmart_goals.ap/index.htm, accessed January 31, 2008.

[60] McDonough, W., & Braungart, M. 2002. *Cradle to Cradle: Remaking the Way We Make Things.* New York: North Point Press; http://www.mcdonough.com/cradle_to_cradle.htm, accessed March 14, 2008.

[61] Scanlon, J. 2008. A New Model for Green Design. *Business Week* (January 18). http://www.businessweek.com/innovate/content/jan2008/id20080118_434274.htm, accessed January 31, 2008.

10

Ensuring Execution

⮕ ⮕ ⮕

We've all had a great idea, but failed to put it into practice. One of the authors of this book still feels guilty about spending a lot of time planning a perfect Mother's Day event, complete with flowers and a surprise lunch, which somehow never happened. Organizational strategists also fail to translate many promising ideas into practice, but interestingly, ideas about what is required are changing significantly.

At one time carrying out a strategy was considered much less important than identifying the "right" strategy in the first place. In today's world, developing and executing strategy blend together. Most people believe that the main challenge of execution is how to empower employees to be adaptive and innovative while also coordinating their activities toward common objectives. We praised this kind of ambidexterity in Chapter 4, which emphasized that employees need to have the flexibility to deliver on a company's strategy in the face of unanticipated events and with very little oversight. Now we describe the organizational mechanisms that both align employees' actions with strategy and facilitate responsiveness when strategy needs to change.

· ·

The chapter is devoted to answering the following questions:

How can strategy execution support the increasing need for flexibility?
Focus on strategic flexibility
Align organizational activity with emerging strategy
Align people to strategy and strategy to people
Align structure to strategy

How is strategic planning changing?
Formality and timing of strategic planning
Planning and the resource allocation process

How is individual and unit performance improved?
Financial control systems
The Balanced Scorecard
Linking data, decision making, and reward

A big part of the problem is that employees and other stakeholders do not even understand what the strategy is, or the role they are expected to play in making it happen. Two Harvard faculty members, Robert Kaplan and David Norton, found that only 5 percent of the workforce understands their company's strategy, only 25 percent of managers have incentives that are linked to strategy, 85 percent of executive teams spend less than one hour per month discussing strategy, and 60 percent of organizations don't make even basic links between expense budgets and strategy.[1] If people in the organization do not understand strategy or the organization does not consistently reward efforts to make it happen, it should not be surprising when good intentions fail. Successful organizations have to avoid these traps, as illustrated by Trader Joe's.

HOW TO MAKE GROCERY SHOPPING FUN

In the mid-1960s, Joe Coulombe was vacationing on a beach but worrying about the increasing competition facing his three small Pronto Markets from the expansion of 7-Eleven convenience stores. Following the kind of advice found in Chapter 5 of this book, he decided to differentiate his stores by seeking out unusual gourmet foods available at low cost as producer closeouts. The renamed Trader Joe's was born with an island theme from that vision of appealing offerings at a reasonable price.

Over time, executives have brought a number of important ideas together to achieve high volume sales in a market dominated by larger, less profitable stores.

1. Trader Joe's stores have a distinct image. Employees (known as "crew") wear Hawaiian shirts meant to express a worldwide search for "cool items to bring to customers" and help everyone "relax and have some fun." The informal atmosphere is reinforced by hand-lettered signs on blackboards created by "store sign artists" who are told to create "unique, fun, and informative signs to promote our products" and make "sure that our Customers have a truly terrific shopping adventure!"

2. The stores are much smaller than major U.S. grocery stores like Safeway or Kroger, and they carry many fewer items. At least 80 percent of all sales come from *appealing in-store brands* developed over decades from unique sources. All are sourced from non–genetically modified ingredients.

3. Management has learned *tight cost control,* in part from Aldi, the low-cost grocer largely responsible for Wal-Mart's lack of success in Germany. Trader Joe's is privately held by a family trust established by one of Aldi's owners, hence the absence of publicly available operating statistics, though the store is widely assumed to be much more profitable than most competitors. Like Aldi it pays a great deal of attention to controlling labor costs, a primary expense in grocery retailing.

4. While employees work hard in their Hawaiian shirts, *compensation and bonuses significantly higher than industry average* include health insurance (medical, dental, and vision) for workers and dependents (including crew members working approximately half-time or more), life and accident insurance, paid time off, and a 15.4 percent contribution to a company-funded retirement fund.

5. There are clear career paths at Trader Joe's and *strong ongoing training programs* to help crew members follow them. The result

is a high number of applicants for vacancies and low employee turnover. The company has been praised for giving clear directions to hourly workers, making sure they have the right equipment to carry out their jobs, and providing frequent feedback. For full-time workers, TJ's Leadership Development Program offers specific courses for every stage of professional development.

6. Trader Joe's managers say they pay more and do more training because they expect more. Crew members exemplify *clearly expressed values,* which include "a passion for food" and "a passion for customer service."

7. Most of these decisions run counter to U.S. practices in general and grocery retail practices in particular. Perhaps the most startling departure is Trader Joe's commitment to *employee involvement in decision making at all levels.* Although cost-control standards are clearly specified, there is a great deal of autonomy for store-level decisions about product mix and display. Inputs are sought even from young, part-time workers.

These ideas result in a culture that almost all employees and shoppers enjoy, and by the end of 2007 the company had expanded to 294 stores in twenty-two states. If you search for negative comments on the Internet, you will find that lack of parking is one of the few complaints made by customers, and most report that they hike the extra distance that may be required because they appreciate Trader Joe's unique combination of food, wine, and ambience. You can get a feel for this unique approach on the company website (www.traderjoes.com), though you'll find the following advice:

> The 100% best, guaranteed fastest, absolute premium, we're talking first rate way to get your questions answered is by talking directly to the good folks at your neighborhood Trader Joe's. They're snazzy dressers, they really know their stuff . . . and did we mention, they're snazzy dressers.[2]

HOW CAN STRATEGY EXECUTION SUPPORT THE INCREASING NEED FOR FLEXIBILITY?

Strategy implementation refers to the second stage of a linear process that involves first formulating strategy and then building the structures and control systems to make the strategy a reality.

To understand how companies like Trader Joe's succeed, it is useful to look back at how ideas about *strategy implementation* have changed over the last twenty-five years. Before the 1980s—when networked computers and globalization began to dominate economic activity—many large organizations faced relatively stable and less competitive environments. Top executives were seen as responsible for developing firm strategy and providing detailed marching orders to organization members. Often the most important strategic objective was ensuring that the firm used its resources efficiently. Implementation was based on the three Cs: command, control, and coordination. Executives and managers determined what needed to be done in a strategic plan and then built organizational structures and control systems to put the strategy into place.

Unfortunately, many companies stumbled in the process of putting their ideas into practice. In their book *Execution: The Discipline of Getting Things Done*,[3] Larry Bossidy, former CEO of Honeywell, and Ram Charan chronicle the challenges involved.

Larry Bossidy Recognizes a Problem at Honeywell

After spending thirty-four years at General Electric, Larry Bossidy was appointed the CEO of AlliedSignal (which became Honeywell) in 1991. When Bossidy walked into his new job, he was shocked to discover how poor the firm was at execution. Although AlliedSignal had bright people who were working hard, they were not managing the details of the business and did not understand what needed to be done to implement strategy.

People in the company knew they had a problem and had spent a lot of time working on improving their processes. Bossidy thought little of it was useful. For example, business unit strategic plans were typically six-inch-thick books full of data about products, but they had little to do with strategy. AlliedSignal's operating plan was just a numbers exercise, with many plants being run by accountants, not production people. There were no specific action plans, and people were not being held accountable for outcomes. AlliedSignal had no company-wide measures for real productivity growth or quality.

Bossidy reflected on his experiences with GE's three core processes: one for people, one for strategy, and one for budgeting/operations. At GE, the three core processes were interlinked, with people selected and promoted in light of strategic and operational objectives and plans, and operational plans linked to strategic goals and human capacities. Bossidy adapted these ideas to AlliedSignal, contending that the real job of a CEO is to actively run the processes that put strategy into practice. (In contrast, the CEO before Bossidy believed his job was to concentrate on issues of corporate strategy, especially buying and selling businesses; he thought strategy implementation was a job for those lower in the hierarchy.)

Honeywell's website recognizes Bossidy's accomplishments with this impressive summary:

> Throughout the 90s, Lawrence A. Bossidy led a growth and productivity transformation that quintupled the market value of AlliedSignal shares and significantly outperformed the Dow Jones Industrial Average and the S&P 500.[4]

As the globalizing environment becomes more complex, customers become more sophisticated, and companies are more involved with numerous alliances, we agree with Bossidy and Charan's emphasis on execution. Conceptualizing strategy is important, but putting it into action and learning from that process is even more important.

In the new competitive landscape, Trader Joe's, Honeywell, and many other firms are encountering perpetual change. Time frames for strategic action are drastically shorter than they were in the past. There is often too little time for developing a formal plan, much less formal implementation. Revising how employees understand the link between strategy and action is particularly important when firms must innovate. Dartmouth professors Vijay Govindarajan and Chris Trimble observe that when a firm innovates such as developing a new business model, no matter how much research is done there will always be uncertainty. They recommend that you must experiment, learn, and adapt as you proceed with implementation of any new innovation.

Organizations still need to align organizational structure with strategic intent. Such alignment, however, must not be so tight as to undermine the organization's ability to respond to the unexpected. Not just the structure but culture and people have to be able to bend. The language of *strategy execution* has been developed to deal with this critical need.

> **Strategy execution** is an interactive process of experimenting with structures and routines that will refine strategic direction.

Focus on Strategic Flexibility

Strategic flexibility means the ability to respond to the unexpected. Organizations need the capacity to go beyond current plans and to stretch what the organization "knows how to do." The term means more than responsiveness, it also means being proactive. Competitive advantage must be continuously renewed and sustained: thus strategy itself is a project in ongoing development.[6]

> **Strategic flexibility** is the ability to respond to unanticipated situations in ways that are compatible with the organization's strategic vision.

In today's competitive environments, this almost always means organizing people in teams around specific *strategic initiatives*. These initiatives may be focused on developing new markets, creating new products, pursuing process innovations, or launching new corporate ventures. By creating and managing a portfolio of such initiatives, organizations can match the level of uncertainty in the external environment with the degree of internal variety represented in their portfolio of initiatives. Thus, for example, if executives in charge of new product development at Honeywell face high uncertainty about which of five different technologies will best meet the needs of its customers for a given electronic device, they may decide to launch five parallel initiatives. Under these circumstances, Honeywell will commit resources to different initiatives in stages over time, continuously reviewing progress, and regularly reconsidering whether the initiative continues to make sense in the external market. As uncertainty decreases over time, resources are re-allocated to reflect the latest market and technical information, and at the point when large-scale product development is warranted, the organization's new product strategy is more likely to be successful.

> **Strategic initiatives** are teams of people organized to develop new markets, create new products, pursue process innovations, or launch new corporate ventures.

Eric Beinhocker, a senior advisor to McKinsey & Company, suggests that this kind of strategy should be described as a "portfolio of experiments."[7] The use of many small initiatives is an important way to execute this idea. Initiatives create *strategic options*, which in aggregate yield the flexibility to respond to a range of uncertain futures.

New initiatives typically challenge the organization and its established ways of doing things. GE's former CEO Jack Welch was a master at creating this environment.

> **Strategic options** are promising directions for new strategy that are explored with relatively small investments until further information is available.

GE Adopts "Destroy Your Business" as a Strategy

Jack Welch won fame for shaking up General Electric in the early 1980s by demanding that each business become number one or number two in its respective industry. Even though GE was achieving substantial growth in its return to shareholders, every couple of years Welch launched a major new initiative. For several years each GE unit had a full-time "destroyyourbusiness.com" team charged with reinventing the unit's basic way of managing, operating, and even thinking about its business.[8]

Welch used this initiative, for example, to force businesses to rethink their relationship to the Internet. He recognized that he and his team were not in a position to direct specific responses from the top down. There was simply too much uncertainty. Thus, "destroyyourbusiness.com" was a global corporate initiative involving hundreds of project teams and hundreds of millions of dollars, but most of the specifics — which products to develop, how to enter new markets, and what kind of new technologies to use — were defined by people in project teams at middle and lower levels of the organization.

Welch's approach to executing strategy had an enormous influence on many other firms, not only GE competitors, but other companies that were also struggling with how to respond to a changing environment. CEOs like Jim McNernew at 3M and Robert Nardelli at Home Depot[9] were hired because of their experience in the GE environment. Many smaller entrepreneurial firms, including eBay, hired strategists with experience in tough large competitive environments to build their capacity to put strategy into action.

Agility, or strategic flexibility, still requires top-level attention, but it is increasingly recognized that important ideas emerge from middle and lower levels in the organization. In other words, managing strategic flexibility, or execution, requires autonomy, spontaneity, and improvisation at all levels of the organization.

However, as we have noted from the very first chapter of this book, strategists must also develop resources and competencies that competitors find difficult to imitate. This requires consistent investments of both money and time. After making such commitments, change becomes more expensive, difficult, and unlikely. A familiar but compelling example of the dilemma between maintaining flexibility and committing resources is highlighted by IBM's experience in personal computers.

Half Magic at IBM

IBM funded a separate effort to develop what was only beginning to be known as the "personal computer" in Boca Raton, Florida, in 1980. Because the company was far behind Apple and other competitors in developing a machine for this emerging market, the development team made the strategic decision not to source hardware internally but instead to purchase microprocessors from Intel and the operating system from Microsoft.

The product introduced in 1981 enjoyed initial success. The IBM name was trusted, and corporate purchasers in particular were eager buyers. As customers became more knowledgeable and confident, however, hundreds of rivals began to compete successfully with "clones" of IBM products. Cloning was made easier by the company's decision to create an open architecture that encouraged inputs from outsiders, but as a result of the entry of many lower-cost rivals, the PC industry became a low-margin, commodity business.

Looking back, it is difficult to say what IBM should have done differently. Lacking the necessary competencies to execute a more protected strategy, finding outside suppliers for key components seems a wise decision. IBM saw its role as designing, assembling, and marketing the final product, and it made substantial investments to develop superiority along these lines. Unfortunately, the resource commitments to execute IBM's strategy were too easy for rivals to imitate, and intense competition eroded most of the profit from this strategy. Intel's and Microsoft's contributions created most of the value, and those companies made most of the profit.

By the time these disadvantages were clear, IBM had tightly aligned its organization around a nonsustainable strategy. The company was too inflexible to change course in time to defend its position against rivals. In 2004, after more than twenty years, IBM sold its personal computer division to Lenovo, China's largest computer manufacturer.[10]

Align Organizational Activity with Emerging Strategy

Firms must be able to harness the discretionary power of individual employees. It takes the combined intelligence and hard work of people throughout the organization, working together, to develop effective solutions to strategic threats and opportunities. The person who is "on the front line" is typically in a better position to manage the continuous adaptation necessary for success in a fast-changing environment than higher-level managers who are further from the action. In most large organizations, executives do not have the time or information necessary to make the critical decisions. They rely heavily on members at middle and lower levels to formulate and implement actions in a way that aligns with strategy. This requires that people share an understanding of the logic behind the strategy so that they can adjust their behavior in a way that is consistent with the intent behind a strategy without having to be told the specifics.

Dell Computer's "Winning" Formula

Michael Dell argues that Dell's success is due to consistent execution "embedded in Dell DNA." "Maintaining a low-cost position is extremely difficult; it is more difficult for Dell because it is constantly improving its product and service offerings. This effort requires countless detailed decisions and constant monitoring of key outcome variables such as inventory reduction and speed of delivery.

Dell's "Winning Culture" initiative plays a critical role in the firm's ability to execute its strategy. The culture is described as "focus on the customer, be open and direct in communications, be a good global citizen, have fun in winning." The values that are critical to the success of the firm are understood by all—being customer-centric, emphasizing the importance of quality, reducing cycle time, and maintaining no inventory. Information is considered the most important management tool, and Dell employees are held accountable for responding to information. If the number of customer calls is down, for example, employees respond by doing more advertising or making more sales calls, without having to get permission from upper management. Until very recently this company with a culture described as maintaining a sense of urgency was one of the most admired companies in the world.

However, beginning in 2005 Dell began to report that it would not meet forecasted earnings. By the August 2006 stockholders' meeting, shares were at the lowest point in five years.[12] Many observers believe that Michael Dell's 2004 decision to withdraw from daily operations was a key part of the problem. Paul Saffo, a Silicon Valley technology consultant, advises: "Dell needs to get back to its roots, and to do that it needs Mike. Mike is a powerful spokesman. [His return] would resonate both with consumers and with the folks on Wall Street."[13]

Back on board at the beginning of 2007, Michael Dell is helping to revive his company's winning formula. A *Business Week* article reports that strategists realized the "DNA of cost-cutting" had gotten in the way of customer service. Too many customers were having problems with their machines and spending too much time being passed from technician to technician looking for solutions. Service spending was increased by 35 percent when Dell got involved again, outsourcing partners were reduced in number, and technicians were no longer evaluated in terms of their short "handling time" of incoming calls. The company has established wikis that customer edit together, with Michael Dell enthusiastically saying: "A company this size is not going to be about a couple of people coming up with ideas. It's going to be about millions of people and harnessing the power of those ideas."[14]

Align People to Strategy and Strategy to People

Top-performing firms understand that it is as hard to find and replace a talented employee as it is to find and replace an important customer. In his best-selling book *Good to Great*, Jim Collins examined 1,435 large firms. Of these, he found that eleven had obtained and sustained "greatness" and that all of these concentrated on "getting the right people on the bus in the right seats and only then deciding where to drive it."[15]

Organizational structure defines how companies divide basic tasks (e.g. finance, marketing, operations), and working relationships between people and activities.

Based on his experience at General Electric, Larry Bossidy came to believe that people are the most important part of the business model. As he said, "after all, it's the people in the organization who make judgments about how the markets are changing, create strategies based on those judgments, and translate the strategies into operational realities."[16] A critical part of the people management process is holding people accountable for results, and if they are nonperformers, the leader must be able to move poorly performing people out of the organization. When Bossidy became CEO of Honeywell, he spent 30 to 40 percent of his time during the first two years and 20 percent thereafter dealing with people issues: identifying, developing, and evaluating human resources.

Functional structures divide work into specialized units (marketing, finance, operations, etc.).

Align Structure to Strategy

Structure defines how companies divide basic tasks, how far authority is delegated, and the working relationships between people and activities in the organization. *Organizational structure* has two purposes. First, it identifies what people do, dividing tasks across units in order to accomplish strategy; second, it identifies how people coordinate activities—how they work together to achieve the organization's goals.

Divisional structures divide work based on products or markets.

There are many different combinations, but three basic types of formal structure are the most common: *functional, divisional*, and *matrix structures*.

Matrix structures are hybrids in which both functional and divisional orientations govern the work that people do.

In order to decide which of these is appropriate for a given strategy, senior executives need to determine the relative importance of technology and efficiency in comparison to speed and responsiveness to change. Functional forms tend to be more efficient and helpful in developing technical expertise, while divisional units are more responsive to change in external markets. Strategy in many firms demands a combination of speedy responsiveness, high levels of creativity and innovation, and the development of new technologies—all with tight controls on cost and productivity. In these cases, the matrix form, which overlays product-market focus onto functional units, seems to work best.

In addition to combining organizational forms, many companies have sought to curb organizational formalities by purging unnecessary bureaucracy. They are flattening hierarchies, which includes not only eliminating layers of management, but also pruning rules, procedures, and other formalities. To execute strategy, leaders are trying to make structures and processes as simple to navigate as possible for employees, customers, and suppliers. Often this decreases response times, increases levels of innovation, and reduces layers of management. In the Harvard study referred to earlier,[17] researchers found that it did not seem to matter which structure the highest-performing firms used (functional, divisional, or matrix). What did matter was whether they simplified the structure in terms of layers of management and work processes.

Nucor Steel provides a short example. With only four management layers (supervisor, department head, plant manager, and CEO), Nucor has pushed substantial decision-making authority down to line employees working in teams. In addition, it has eliminated most of the bureaucracy. Managers spend very little time supervising employees. Instead, when asked, managers provide coaching and assistance. It is assumed that employees will be able to work together to solve their own problems. As a result, decision making is faster, and employee-driven solutions are usually more innovative.

Besides the three classical forms of organization structure (functional, divisional, and matrix), two new forms have emerged in the last decade: network and boundaryless organizations. Though we discussed these developments in Chapter 7, it is worth remembering them as increasingly popular structural choices.

Network organizations operate with a central core group composed of a relatively small staff of full-time employees. This slim organization creates a system of relationships with outside contractors and suppliers. The firm maintains control of key strategic activities but outsources all other functions. Organizations adopting this form have realized that although it might be more convenient to have personnel employed full-time, it is more cost effective to keep them outside the organization, hiring them part-time, or using them as independent contractors only when needed.[18] Perhaps even more important than lower costs, network organizations have more flexibility in responding to change.

There are some downsides. When management converts employees to contractors they lose the advantages that come from more direct control. Apple Computer recently decided to make the customer service function part of U.S. operations rather than relying on a contractor in India to answer customer calls, for example. The reason? Loss of control over quality simply was not worth the cost savings offered by outsource services in other countries.

Network organizations operate with a small central group that is responsible for key strategic activities and outsource all others.

Nike is an example of an organization that has more aggressively pursued a networked strategy. The company maintains control over activities it defines as critical to its competitive advantage, such as shoe design and marketing. All other activities are outsourced, including manufacturing, accounts receivable, and even the sales force.

Network organizations like Nike have two important advantages:

1. They operate with fewer full-time employees and less complex internal systems. This reduces overhead and increases efficiency to maintain cost competitiveness. The firm can then find the "best-in-class" partners for outsourced activities.

2. Because they are focused only on those activities that create the most value for customers, networked firms can respond more quickly than larger, more complex organizations when conditions change.

These choices are not just firm-level choices, they are structural forms that influence whole industries. In fact, they dominate entire clusters of organizations. Activities in Silicon Valley provide a perfect example.

The Diffusion of Silicon Valley

Silicon Valley has developed a new, alternative model of how technology businesses can organize internally and collaborate with supplier and competitive firms. Rather than becoming vertically integrated, they outsource many functions, relying on a network or cluster of firms located nearby.

These networks include venture capitalists, bankers, and regional institutions such as libraries, universities, local government, business associations, and competitive firms. The geographic proximity of many network members provides regular, sustained social interaction, encouraging an exchange of information, new ideas, and collective learning. The result is that there are few boundaries between technology firms, venture capitalists, local government officials, the university research community, and the banking community. People move freely between organizations, exchanging ideas and shifting places of employment.

In Silicon Valley a regional culture has emerged, one in which shared understandings and practices exist. This not only serves to unify the community; it also encourages members to collectively learn and take risks. The management practices that have become part of this culture include open-mindedness, creativity, meritocracy, high tolerance for failure, collaboration, risk taking, enthusiasm for change, and a love for the product.

Governments around the world have been trying to foster the development of these networks in their country or region. In the United

States, four examples are Silicon Desert (Utah and Arizona), Silicon Alley (New York), Silicon Hills (Austin), and Silicon Forest (Oregon and Washington). Models in other countries include Egypt's Smart Village, Hong Kong's Cyberport, Malaysia's Multimedia Super Corridor, the United Kingdom's Cambridge Cluster ("Silicon Fen"), and high-tech clusters in India's Bangalore and Hyderabad.[19]

In addition to some loss of control, a network strategy means limited ability to coordinate activities within the value chain. If one part of a network fails to deliver, the core organization may not be in a position to do much about it. If the needed activity were part of a traditional, hierarchical organization, on the other hand, management would have more ability to command performance.

An even more important disadvantage of a network strategy is that one or more members of the network may become a competitor. For example, in the 1990s, Schwinn bicycles outsourced its production to Giant Manufacturing of Taiwan and the China Bicycle Company. Unfortunately, Schwinn failed to protect its technology or invest in the improvement of its core competencies. Both Giant Manufacturing and China Bicycle entered the world bicycle market selling products based on Schwinn's technology. Schwinn lost market share and later filed for bankruptcy. Today, Giant and China Bicycle dominate the bicycle industry.

Structure is a strategic issue because it affects process. Although hierarchical differences and dividing lines between the units of an organization may seem necessary to alignment and control, these boundaries often get in the way of change. Thus, to create an organization that is both aligned to strategy and responsive to change, managers may need to examine organizational boundaries, in some cases making them more permeable and in other cases eliminating them. Use Worksheet 10.1 to explore how a network structure can enhance firm performance.

It is interesting to think about organizations as a set of boundaries that divide people vertically (the hierarchy), horizontally (functional and divisional units), geographically, and externally (separations between the organization and its customers and suppliers). By carefully assessing such boundaries in light of the organization's strategy, managers are likely to make better choices about organizational structure. Some are choosing to create a *boundaryless organization*. Tactics for reducing boundaries include rotation assignments that provide employees with multiple connections outside of their normal work group, broad distribution of information, and de-emphasis of managerial and supervisory authority.

The Chrysler division that developed the Neon was based on the idea of a boundaryless structure. The head of small-car engineering for Chrysler, Robert Marcell, supervised a core group of 150 colleagues.

Worksheet 10.1: Network Organization Structure—A Tool for Assessing Enhancement through Networks

. . . .

Boundaryless organizations can easily move information and people throughout their system.

These employees were engineers, marketing and production employees, and union production workers. The core team brought together an additional 600 engineers from 289 suppliers to design and deliver the Neon. They developed the prototype in only forty-one months, from project approval to the first day of production, as opposed to the eighty-four months (seven years) that once characterized bringing a new model to market. Concurrent engineering required personnel from external suppliers and different internal Chrysler departments to work together to solve problems in order to eliminate delays and disagreements.[20]

HOW IS STRATEGIC PLANNING CHANGING?

Strategic planning is the process by which most organizations try to align vision, culture, people and structure with strategy. As depicted in Figure 10.1, the planning process typically is organized around an annual cycle whereby managers reflect on their vision, analyze the business and corporate environment, formulate alternatives, select strategies, and then develop action plans to implement them.

Figure 10.1 — Typical Flow Diagram of the Strategic Planning Process

Involvement describes the extent of participation in the strategic planning process across multiple levels in an organization.

Although the range and amount of *involvement* varies, this kind of strategic planning often engages a very large number of managers and executives. Those at the top of the organization take responsibility for developing key premises and targets, while the formulation and selection of strategies is negotiated in dialogue with middle managers. Lower-level managers get involved in helping to develop budgets and operational plans. These specifics are then subjected to further negotiation and approval by top managers. Ideally, this approach to planning helps ensure that strategic decisions satisfy both the criteria articulated by top management and the need for feasibility as seen from middle and lower levels of management.

Over time, however the linear and hierarchical process just described has become more interactive and involving. Figure 10.2 reflects the top-down, bottom-up planning process at Allianz, a financial services firm based in Germany. This process represents a change in both the formality and timing of planning, and the way in which resources are allocated.

Figure 10.2 — The Annual Planning Cycle at Allianz
Source: Allianz company documents.

Formality and Timing of Strategic Planning

Although the *formality* of a planning process varies considerably from company to company, companies are increasingly adopting a less formal approach. The reason is that too much adherence to a formal process undermines flexibility by fixing operational plans and resources. A process like that outlined in Figure 10.1 can award resources (for example) according to an analysis conducted ten or eleven months earlier. If things change in the interim, such plans and budgets may no longer be desirable or feasible.

In light of this, many organizations have not only reduced the degree of formality in the planning process but shortened the time over which planning is conducted. In a study of large oil companies (which have traditionally been big proponents of formal planning), Robert Grant found that many companies had replaced formal tools and techniques with more free-flowing discussion in planning sessions. Doing so, he observed, encouraged dialogue about strategy that was more in keeping

Formality
describes the extent of regulation in the strategic planning process.

with current events and facilitated a kind of "planned emergence" in strategic planning.[21]

In addition to less formality, a recent article by Michael Mankins and Richard Steele shows how companies such as Boeing Commercial Airplanes and Microsoft have abandoned the calendar in relationship to strategic planning and adopted a continuous approach.[22] Seeking a similar outcome, units within IBM have adopted a planning cycle wherein information input, decision making, and action taking occur continuously throughout the year. Figure 10.3 depicts the process at IBM.

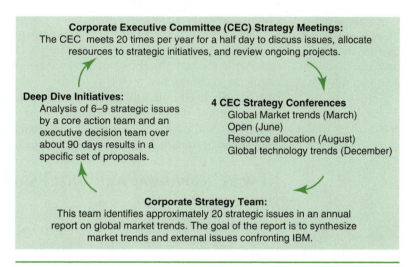

Corporate Executive Committee (CEC) Strategy Meetings:
The CEC meets 20 times per year for a half day to discuss issues, allocate resources to strategic initiatives, and review ongoing projects.

Deep Dive Initiatives:
Analysis of 6–9 strategic issues by a core action team and an executive decision team over about 90 days results in a specific set of proposals.

4 CEC Strategy Conferences
Global Market trends (March)
Open (June)
Resource allocation (August)
Global technology trends (December)

Corporate Strategy Team:
This team identifies approximately 20 strategic issues in an annual report on global market trends. The goal of the report is to synthesize market trends and external issues confronting IBM.

Figure 10.3 — Continuous planning at IBM
Source: McKinsey & Co.

Planning and the Resource Allocation Process

Notice the emphasis on resource allocation at the top of IBM's continuous planning process. Resource allocation is a critical part of all strategic planning processes. In more traditional planning processes, resources are allocated through operating and capital budgets. Essentially, these decisions are made toward the end of the planning cycle and launch a series of initiatives called *induced initiatives* geared to achieve the targets developed in the strategic plan. In a more continuous planning process, however, resources are allocated and re-allocated throughout the year depending on management's current assessment of the viability and desirability of an initiative given current circumstances. In IBM's planning model (see Figure 10.3), for example, the corporate executive council meets twenty times per year to review progress and allocate resources across the organization's portfolio of initiatives.

Not all initiatives are induced as a part of strategic planning. Many of the ideas that spark initiatives develop as the result of operating-level

> **Induced initiatives** are carried out within the official resource allocation process.

employees experimenting with new ways of doing things. A salesperson, for example, may recognize an opportunity to explore a new market, and may bring this idea to the sales manager and ask for a small amount of resources to pursue it. Then, if the initial approach seems successful, the sales manager may decide to pursue official endorsement for the initiative, and in the process, seek additional resources. Initiatives that start in this way—that spring from the bottom up—are called autonomous initiatives. *Autonomous initiatives* are important because they tap into the creativity of employees and help move the organization outside its "comfort zone," thereby learning competences beyond those anticipated in the formal plan and expanding the organization's strategic flexibility. That's called "bootlegging" in many companies, and it can be sanctioned. For example, BMW encourages people to try things out without necessarily asking for permission. That paid off when a small group of engineers made the first prototype for the 3 Series station wagon with parts cannibalized from other cars. Most decision makers thought that kind of vehicle did not fit the company image of high-performance, sporty cars and planned accordingly (by doing nothing). Today the vehicle has an important place in the company lineup.

> **Autonomous initiatives** emerge as the result of experimentation outside the official resource allocation process.

How Is Individual and Unit Performance Improved?

> **Control systems** measure the extent that actions and decisions in the organization are consistent with management intent.

Control systems gauge the extent to which the actions and decisions taken within the organization are consistent with management intent. In this sense, control systems are like the speedometer in an automobile. They tell the driver whether the vehicle is performing as expected. Control systems serve two key purposes in organizations. First, they measure performance and compare it with expectations, thereby allowing firms to determine whether resources are being used efficiently and in ways that contribute to the implementation of strategy.

Second, control systems give executives the information needed to determine whether current strategies are still appropriate. Thus, if a measure falls below expectations, it means one of two things: either sufficient action is not being taken to implement a strategy (e.g., the wrong structure has been put in place) or the strategy itself is not appropriate given conditions in the environment (e.g., customers are not buying the product in expected volumes). In either case, such feedback is invaluable in helping managers take corrective action, either by reformulating strategy or by working harder to seek alignment to an existing strategy.

Financial Control Systems

Most organizations use financial measures as a key part of their control system. Indicators such as sales revenues, expense ratios, and profits provide one way to examine the extent to which an organization is on its intended course. One limitation of financial measures, however, is that they are lagging indicators—that is, they focus on assessing the results of past action. Thus, whatever caused profit to decline has already happened by the time a strategist examines the financial statement, and valuable time for corrective action has been lost.

A second limitation is that financial measures tend to concentrate managers' attention on short-term results, such as quarterly profit. Although short-term results are important, strategies often take time to have an effect on financial indicators. As part of an innovation strategy, for example, the bottom-line results of investments in research and development may take several years to materialize. Thus, too much emphasis on financial performance may cause managers to take action that improves short-term results but damages the organization's ability to achieve its strategy. As another example, executives may reduce spending on discretionary items such as employee training to achieve short-term financial targets, even if the strategy calls for significant investments in new knowledge and skills.

The Balanced Scorecard

In the early 1990s, two Harvard Business School professors, Robert Kaplan and David Norton, argued that as a result of an overreliance on financial controls systems, some 90 percent of U.S. firms were unable to execute their strategies.[23] Their prescription for change starts with a firm's strategy and vision, and on this basis develops a list of key performance indicators in four categories: financial, customer, internal business processes, and learning and growth. [24]

The *balanced scorecard* provides an opportunity to move beyond the use of financial measures as a basis for strategic control. The idea, summarized in Figure 10.4, is simple: Use the four parts of the balanced scorecard to translate the organization's vision and strategy into quantifiable objectives and measures.

The process shown in Figure 10.4 involves the development of four sets of measures in a way that makes them consistent with one another and with vision and strategy:

The **balanced scorecard** is a management tool that enables organizations to clarify vision and strategy and translate them into action.

- *Financial* measures summarize whether the firm's strategy and its execution are contributing to creating shareholder value. The financial component includes measures of efficiency, such as how much activity is obtained for every dollar of cost.
- The *customer* category includes measures such as customer satisfaction, customer retention, and new customer acquisition. This category should also include measures of the value the firm is delivering to the customer, such as the perceived quality of the product, customer service, and innovativeness.
- The *internal business processes* category evaluates the processes that the firm uses to deliver its product or service to its customers.

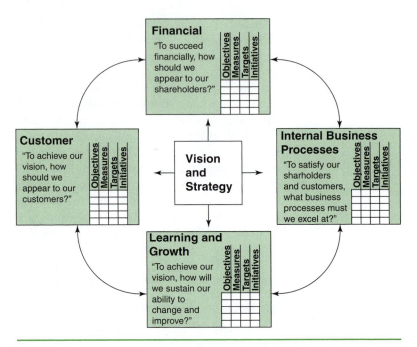

Figure 10.4 — Key Components of the Balanced Scorecard

New product development is an example of an internal process that is often closely related to strategy. Developing measures for such processes includes examining the firm's value chain and setting objectives for continuous improvement.

• The final category, *learning and growth*, sets objectives and measures for how the firm is building its knowledge base. This component asks: Is the firm developing its people, systems, and organizational procedures so that it will have the strategic flexibility necessary to compete in the future?

Now used by many organizations, the balanced scorecard provides information for the organization's executives to monitor and adjust the execution process. Many examples are available on the Web. An example of the strategic outcomes connected to a balanced scorecard review by Oak Knoll Academy is provided in Figure 10.5.

The balanced scorecard has several advantages. First and perhaps most important, it helps focus attention on the key strategic issues that will determine the firm's future success. The balanced scorecard reminds all organization members about the big picture and encourages people to focus on strategic issues. Otherwise, people tend to get lost in day-to-day detail and lose sight of what the organization is trying to accomplish over the long term.

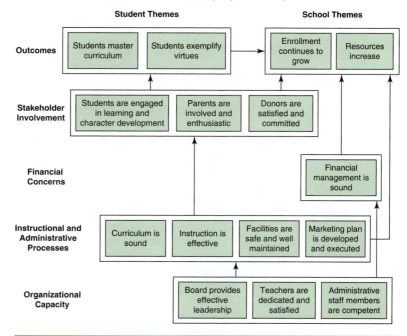

Figure 10.5 — Oak Knoll Academy Strategy

Source: http://www.balancedscorecard.org/Portals/o/PDF/Oak_Knoll_Academy_ Map.pdf, accessed January 12, 2008.

Second, as the name suggests, the approach is balanced. Executives measure how their business units create value for current and future customers while enhancing their internal capabilities. This avoids the trap of putting an exclusive emphasis on financial measures.

Third, this control framework promotes strategic learning and growth. It reminds members of the organization that in a dynamic environment they must continually invest in its people and core competencies in order to create or maintain a competitive advantage.

Worksheet 10.2 provides an opportunity to relate these ideas to a specific organization that interests you.

Worksheet 10.2: Balanced Scorecard—A Tool for Assessing Key Strategic Issues

Linking Data, Decision Making, and Performance

Strategic control is a difficult but critical task in the execution process. Today, organizations are increasingly decentralized, and lower-level managers and employees are taking on more responsibility. To maintain a control and a consistent strategy in this context, people need to understand and become committed to goals and strategies. A good example of combining decentralization with strategic control is provided by the New York City Police Department.

Performance Management in the New York Police Department

In 1994, William Bratton became the new commissioner of the New York Police Department (NYPD). He found an organization in which powerful vested interests prevented any significant change. The staff was demotivated. Police officers felt that their superiors valued loyalty and reducing overtime more than anything else. Staying out of trouble seemed more important than reducing crime. The only data that was collected to measure performance was the amount of effort (in person-hours) each unit expended in fighting crimes and a statistic on the number of crimes committed across various categories.

One of Bratton's most important steps in turning around the NYPD was to implement a new performance management system called Compustat. This database tracked weekly crime and arrest activity and measured associated enforcement activities at the precinct, borough, and city levels. With the system in place, Bratton delegated substantial decision-making authority to precinct commanders, each of whom managed 200–400 officers. The data helped precinct commanders deploy their officers in high-crime areas more effectively.

To motivate precinct commanders, Bratton instituted semiweekly strategy review meetings. The meetings took place in a large auditorium and attendance was mandatory—even for top brass. At each meeting, a selected precinct commander was put in front of the room, and a panel of senior staff questioned him or her about the precinct's performance. Commanders were asked to explain patterns of crime in their precinct and how they were deploying their resources in response. These strategy review meetings allowed Bratton and his staff to monitor how well commanders were motivating and managing their people and how they were meeting the strategic objectives of the police department. The meetings helped develop a performance culture, in which precinct commanders were being held accountable for results. And, because all of the precinct commanders were in attendance, they learned which practices were working and which were not.

The results were spectacular. In less than two years, from 1994 to 1996, and without an increase in budget, felony crime fell 39 percent, murders fell 50 percent, and thefts dropped 35 percent; Gallup polls conducted at the time reported an increase in public confidence in the police from 37 percent to 70 percent.[25]

Clearly much more could be said about the connection between data and performance. The trick, however, is not to let the data and the system impede the recognition of environmental change and new opportunities. It has long been observed that people respond to the way they are assessed. Given human and structural limitations, strategists often hope they can gain benefits from observing what they can measure.

But sometimes an overemphasis on measurement reinforces behavior that does not fit strategy. The title of a classic article by Steven Kerr is instructive: ". . . the folly of rewarding A, while hoping for B."[26]

The article was recently reprinted, along with the results of a poll of members of the Executive Advisory Panel for the *Academy of Management Executive.* Ninety percent of the respondents said that Kerr's folly is prevalent in corporate America today, and more than half concluded that the folly is widespread in their own companies. Some of the examples given by these respondents are shown in Table 10.1.

TABLE 10.1 THE FOLLY OF REWARDS BASED ON QUANTITATIVE MEASURES

We Hope For . . .	But We Reward . . .
Teamwork and collaboration	The best team members
Innovative thinking and risk taking	Proven methods and not making mistakes
Development of people skills	Technical achievements and accomplishments
Employee involvement and empowerment	Tight control over operations and resources
High achievement	Another year's effort

The editors also asked about the obstacles to addressing this mismatch and summarized the results in terms of three general themes:

1. The inability to break out of the old ways of thinking about reward and recognition practices. In particular, there appears to be a need for the definition of new goals and target behaviors, including non-quantifiable behavior . . . which is system focused rather than job or functionally dependent. Among the deterrents to change are the entitlement mentality of workers and the reluctance of management to commit to revamping or revitalizing performance management processes and systems.
2. Lack of a holistic or overall system view of performance factors and results. To a great extent, this is still caused by organizational structures that promote optimization of subunit results at the expense of the total organization.
3. Continuing focus on short-term results by management and shareholders."[27]

The editors felt strongly about these results, as indicated by their final statement: "To say that Kerr's folly is alive and well is an understatement. Hopefully, some future managers will hear this wake up call. Just in case they're not listening, we'll say it again: IT'S THE REWARD SYSTEM, STUPID!"

CONCLUSIONS FOR THE STRATEGIST

Executing strategy is not simply about aligning organizational structure to strategic intent. Alignment is important, but the key message in this chapter is that a changing environment demands flexible organizations that can respond to events that are not anticipated in the formal strategic plan. Such organizations are likely to be populated by people who share an understanding and commitment to their organization's vision and strategy. When people understand and believe in what their organization is trying to do, they are much more likely to work toward strategic objectives, even when no one is telling them exactly what to do.

Key Concepts

Strategic flexibility, the ability to respond to unanticipated situations in ways that are compatible with the organization's strategic vision, has become imperative for most organizations. It is the primary reason why strategists now talk about execution rather than strategy implementation. **Strategy execution** is an interactive process of putting structures and routines into place that help an organization refine strategic direction. **Strategy implementation** refers to a more linear process of first formulating strategy, and then translating it into action.

Execution requires aligning the organization's culture, people, and structure to strategic intent, but doing so in a way that encourages responsiveness to change. Developing a shared strategic vision and a high-performance culture serve this purpose by developing people's understanding of strategy and holding them accountable for creating it. Cultures are likely to be diluted by the wrong mix of people, however, so "getting the right people on the bus in the right seats" has become a top priority. Although **organizational structures** are aimed at creating focus, most large firms have moved away from the three traditional types of formal structures; **functional, divisional,** and **matrix structures.** Instead they are relying on simplified structures that possess fewer layers of management and work processes, such as **network** and **boundaryless organizations** to facilitate greater flexibility.

Strategic planning is the mechanism used by organizations to align culture, people, and structure to strategy and to generate change. The **formality** of the planning process varies considerably. The more formal planning process creates a high degree of involvement in developing strategy, and this helps both to deepen understanding of the strategy in the organization and to commit people to its execution. Some firms follow a less formal approach but have adopted continuous strategic planning as a way to increase flexibility in the face of change. This approach is focused on defining, launching and evaluating **strategic initiatives.** There are two different kinds of initiatives, **induced** and or **autonomous,** which combined can create promising new strategic directions, or **strategic options.**

Control systems are based on defining and measuring key performance indicators to gauge the success of strategy execution. In addition to financial controls, many large firms have adopted the **balanced scorecard** or similar approaches as means to broaden the scope of controls and to prevent overemphasis on short-term performance.

Questions for Further Reflection

1. Choose a product or service that you care about. Identify several major players in this field and find statements about their strategies and mission. Can you as a consumer see differences in the way they execute their strategies? If you were a consultant to the firm you care most about, how would you advise them to improve their performance?

2. Imagine that you are Michael Dell at the beginning of 2008. How would you evaluate changes made in the last year? What more needs to be done?

3. Think of a product you like, but think could be better, and assume you are in charge of executing improvements. What types of people would you like to work around you? How will you develop a high-performance culture? What types of rewards would you want for yourself and the people who work with you if your efforts prove successful?

WORKSHEET 10.1
Network Organization Structure—A Tool for Assessing Enhancement through Networks

Think of a firm that you would like to work for. How could the firm be enhanced by a network organization structure?

Step 1: What are some of the key components and systems of the organization? Put your answers in column 1.

Step 2: How could a network organization enhance these? Write your ideas in column 2.

Network Organization Structure Worksheet 10.1	Strategy Summary:
Key Components and Systems	**How Could a Network Organization Enhance These?**

WORKSHEET 10.2
Balanced Scorecard—A Tool for Assessing Key Strategic Issues

How could a firm you know be enhanced by the use of a balanced scorecard?

Step 1: Choose a firm you are familiar with, would like to start, or would like to work for. Identify four key components and systems of the organization in column 1.

Step 2: What are the key objectives of each of these components or systems? Fill in column 2.

Step 3: How could each of these components or systems be measured? Fill in column 3.

Step 4: What targets might be put into place to meet these components or systems? Fill in column 4.

Balanced Scorecard Worksheet 10.2	Organization:
Analyst(s):	Strategy Summary:

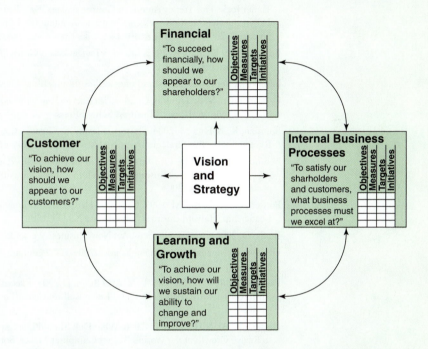

Key Components	Key Objectives	Measurements	Targets

NOTES

[1] Kaplan, R., & Norton, D. 2001. *The Strategy-Focused Organization*. Boston: Harvard Business School Press.

[2] Quoted material can be found at http://www.traderjoes.com/contact_us.html, accessed March 21, 2008. Other information is from Lewis, L. 2005. Fostering a Loyal Workforce at Trader Joe's. *Workforce Management Online* (June). http://www.workforce.com/section/06/feature/24/06/51/, accessed January 9, 2008; Armstrong, L. 2004. Trader Joe's: The Trendy American Cousin. *Business Week* (European edition, April 26). http://www.businessweek.com/magazine/content/04_17/b3880016.htm, accessed January 9, 2008; http://en.wikipedia.org/wiki/Trader_Joe's, accessed January 9, 2008.

[3] Bossidy, L., & Charan, R. 2002. *Execution: The Discipline of Getting Things Done*. New York: Crown Business.

[4] http://www.honeywell.com/sites/honeywell/ourhistory.htm, accessed March 21, 2008.

[5] Govindarajan, V. & Trimble, C. 2005. *Ten Rules for Strategic Innovation: From Ideas to Execution*. Boston: Harvard Business School Press.

[6] Shimizu, K., & Hitt, M. 2004. Strategic Flexibility: Organizational Preparedness to Reverse Ineffective Strategic Decisions. *Academy of Management Executive* (18) 4: 44–59.

[7] Beinhocker, E. D. 2006. Creating Strategy in an Unknowable Universe. *Working Knowledge*. (June 19). Harvard Business School. http://hbswk.hbs.edu/archive/5387.html, accessed March 21, 2008.

[8] Bartlett, C., & Wozny, M. 1999. GE's Two-Decade Transformation: Jack Welch's Leadership. Harvard Business School Case No. 399150.

[9] Brady, D. 2004. Change Happens: Act Now. Business Week Online (October 18).

[10] http://www.chinadaily.com.cn/english/doc/2004-12/09/content_398733.htm, accessed March 21, 2008.

[11] Dell, M., Rollins, K., Stewart, T. A., & O'Brien, L. 2005. Execution without Excuses: An Interview with Michael Dell and Kevin Rollins. *Harvard Business Review* (March–April): 1–9.

[12] Hesseldahl, A., & Holahan, C. 2006. What Dell Should Do: Experts Weigh In on Ways to Revive Growth at the World's Biggest Computer Maker. Some Ideas: Rethink Retail and Bring Back Mike. Business Week Online (July 21).

[13] Hesseldahl & Holahan, What Dell Should Do.

[14] Jarvis, J. 2007. Dell Learns to Listen. *Business Week* (October 17). http://www.businessweek.com/bwdaily/dnflash/content/oct2007/db20071017_277576.htm?chan=top1news_top+news+index_top+story, accessed January 12, 2008.

[15] Collins, J. 2001. *Good to Great*. New York: HarperBusiness.

[16] Bossidy & Charan, *Execution: The Discipline of Getting Things Done*, p. 141.

[17] Nohria, N., Joyce, W., & Roberson, B. 2003. What Really Works. *Harvard Business Review* (July–August): 1–13.

[18] Handy, C. 1989. *The Age of Unreason*. Boston: Harvard Business School Press.

[19] Saxenian, A. 1994. *Regional Advantage: Culture and Competition in Silicon Valley and Route* 128. Boston: Harvard University Press.

[20] A compendium of resources describing the Neon can be found at http://www.allpar.com/neon/design.html, accessed January 12, 2008.

[21] Grant, R. M. 2003. Strategic Planning in a Turbulent Environment: Evidence from the Oil and Gas Majors. *Strategic Management Journal* (June): 491–518.

[22] Mankins, M. C., & Steele, R. 2006. Stop Making Plans, Start Making Decisions. *Harvard Business Review* (January): 76–84.

[23]Kaplan, R., & Norton, D. 1996. *The Balanced Scorecard.* Boston: Harvard Business School Press. We are not experts in this aspect of strategic management, but were interested to read the account of developing the balanced scorecard in the 1980s at http://www.schneiderman.com/Concepts/The_First_Balanced_Scorecard/BSC_INTRO_AND_CONTENTS.htm, accessed January 12, 2008.

[24]Kaplan, R., & Norton, D. 2001. *The Strategy-Focused Organization.* Boston: Harvard Business School Press.

[25]Kim, W., & Mauborgne, R. 2003. Turning Point Leadership. *Harvard Business Review* (March–April): 1–11.

[26]Kerr, S. 1995. On the Folly of Rewarding A While Hoping for B. *Academy of Management Executive,* 9 (1). Originally published in 1975. *Academy of Management Journal* (18): 769–783. http://pages.stern.nyu.edu/~wstarbuc/mob/kerrab.html, accessed March 21, 2008.

[27]Kerr, On the Folly of Rewarding A.

11

Managing Knowledge

➔ ➔ ➔

Perhaps you have wondered after completing a task with limited or no success why you did not make better use of your previous experience or the insights available from more experienced actors. Organizational strategists share that frustration far too often, which is why we devote this chapter to an explicit consideration of knowledge management.

It is particularly important for strategists to think about knowledge management because we are becoming a "knowledge society." This label indicates both more intense use of information and the growing importance of knowledge-based (rather than physical) assets. Today, knowledge-intensive industries represent 70 to 80 percent of developed countries' GDP and 50 percent of developing countries' GDP.[1] And at an individual level, knowledge from formal education is associated with increasing income: a recent study by the U.S. Census Bureau showed that people with a bachelor's degree earn over $25,000 a year more than people with a high school diploma, and the gap has been increasing over time.[2]

Clearly, knowledge is a strategic issue. As a result of significant technological and procedural changes, almost all organizations are using knowledge management to run their operations more efficiently and effectively. In fact, many organizations are coming to view knowledge as their most valuable and important strategic asset. Strategists therefore must spend more of their time ensuring that their organization is properly developing and utilizing these resources.

. . . .

In support of that effort this chapter suggests answers to the following questions:

Why is knowledge an increasingly important source of sustainable advantage?

What are the characteristics of knowledge needed by companies?
> Private versus public knowledge
> Explicit versus tacit knowledge

How do strategists manage and use knowledge?
> Knowledge creation
> Knowledge storage
> Knowledge transfer
> Knowledge use

How do organizational systems affect knowledge management?
> Corporate culture and values
> Incentive systems
> Organizational structure
> Recruitment

What are the most important external sources of knowledge?
Benchmarking
Contingent employees
Strategic alliances
Distributed expertise

Microsoft and Google, two companies with vast knowledge assets, are an appropriate first example.

THE VALUE OF MICROSOFT AND GOOGLE

The importance of knowledge is reflected in the current market value of firms. A firm's total financial worth is the present value of the cash flows that will be generated over time. At the end of the twentieth century, Ford Motor Company, Mitsubishi, and General Motors had combined sales exceeding $500 billion and market value and assets exceeding $635 billion. Compare this to Microsoft, which had sales of only $12 billion and assets of $14 billion, but a market value of $375 billion.

A Microsoft investor is not buying traditional assets; for every dollar of market value investors get less than 4 cents of assets. In comparison, a dollar of market value buys $1.27 in assets in Ford, Mitsubishi, and General Motors. The major difference between these firms is the value of Microsoft's *intellectual capital*. Microsoft's basic patents are clearly an important part of the picture. In addition, the firm's value stems from brand name and goodwill. Microsoft valued its brand name alone at just over $65 billion, second only to the Coca-Cola brand, valued at $70 billion.[3] This and other intangible assets enable Microsoft to continually create leading-edge products.

Google is another company that relies primarily on brand and intellectual capital. After Google went public in 2005, it had a market value of $80 billion on sales of $3.2 billion.[4] The spread continued to increase as Google bought fifteen small companies for $130 million in the next year. When Google bought YouTube, the primary site for sharing videos, it incorporated a company often compared to Napster— the file-sharing company we described at the beginning of Chapter 1. Many shared videos are homemade, but commercial music videos and movie clips are also attractive. Chad Hurley and Steve Chen, YouTube founders, appeared to have learned a valuable lesson from history when they announced they had made agreements with Universal Music Group, CBS, Sony BMG, and Warner. Microsoft and other companies were considering buying YouTube, but in the end Google won with a $1.76 billion offer.[5]

Google's stock price was well over $700 in November 2007, though it sank with others over the next months. Still, the company was number 241 in the Fortune 500 for the year (up from 353 in 2006). Not bad for the intellectual capital collected by two 28-year-old entrepreneurs over twenty months.

Intellectual capital is knowledge that can be stored for later use.

Microsoft, Google, and YouTube are three visible examples of companies that spend a good deal of time managing *knowledge*. Law firms and consulting firms are often cited as well, but personal trainers, financial advisors, adventure travel firms, and many other businesses also rely very little on tangible assets they own. In fact, we believe that virtually all companies are becoming more knowledge intensive, as described in greater detail in this chapter.

> **Knowledge** is information that can be connected to intention.

WHY IS KNOWLEDGE AN INCREASINGLY IMPORTANT SOURCE OF SUSTAINABLE ADVANTAGE?

Professor James Quinn from the Tuck School of Business claims that information has become the source of 75 percent of the value added in manufacturing firms.[6] Nucor revolutionized the production of sheet steel, for example, on the basis of superior knowledge assets. Traditionally, steel companies used three to four hours of labor to produce a ton of steel. That doesn't seem like much, but Nucor cut labor input down to forty-five minutes for each ton of steel by using more computers in its production process. Similar examples from industry after industry have led many people to claim that the global economy is becoming a knowledge-based economy.

Today many firms spend more on computers and telecommunications equipment than on other more traditional capital assets—engines, turbines, machinery, materials handling equipment, and equipment for mining, construction, and agriculture. The result is an incredible increase in the speed, processing, and availability of information for the average firm. But do not think that the computer alone is the source of advantage. IBM, the company known for manufacturing computer hardware, now generates more revenues from selling knowledge in the form of computer services than from selling computers.

As we have said in previous chapters, creating advantage from any asset takes continuing strategic attention. The benefits of actively managing knowledge can be found throughout the value chain. As one example, many firms invest in information technology to cut inventory costs. Wal-Mart has spent more than $1 billion on information technology; as a result, it continues to lead the industry in maintaining very low administrative overhead costs while selling more merchandise per square foot than its rivals. Over fifteen years, GE's lighting division similarly used information technology to reduce its inventories and move to a just-in-time system, eliminating twenty-four of its thirty-four U.S. warehouses. The division also replaced twenty-five customer service centers with one high-tech center.

In Chapter 5 we discussed Michael Porter's industrial economics view of the firm and his argument that most of a firm's profitability depends on the industry in which it competes. The power of rivals, suppliers, buyers, substitutes, potential entrants, and complements determines how much of a product's or service's value will be captured by the providing firm and how much will be usurped by these other participants in the market.

As firms learned over time to benefit from these observations, it became increasingly clear that the unique characteristics of particular firms within an industry could make a significant difference in terms of profit performance. This has led strategists to focus on the internal side of the equation—the firm's resources and capabilities.

Remember that the resource-based approach suggests that firms should position themselves strategically based on their unique and valuable resources and capabilities rather than the products and services derived from those capabilities. Knowledge is seen as a competitive advantage for firms if it takes on this character. Critically, many observers are arguing that knowledge is the most likely resource to be unique and therefore the most likely to create sustained advantage.[7]

Knowledge is the result of a learning process. One conception is shown in Figure 11.1.[8] Because experience on the job is inevitable and individuals who do their jobs well are able to observe, reflect on, and improve their performance, strategists can count on the first two steps of learning occurring in their organization. However, they cannot assume that steps 3 and 4 will take place.

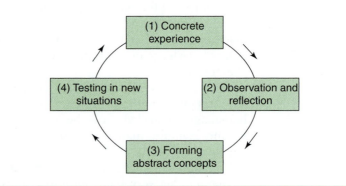

Figure 11.1 — Kolb's Model of Experiential Learning

Knowledge management focuses on connecting all four parts of the learning process, which are required to pass the benefits from one individual's learning to others. When this is accomplished, the value of individual and collective learning increases with use—as opposed to the value of most assets, whose value diminishes with use. In fact, knowledge has been said to appreciate at every stage in the value chain.[9] Firms need to find ways to leverage such resources and capabilities across many markets and products. Products and markets will likely come and go, but resources and capabilities are considered more enduring. Competitive advantage based on resources and capabilities therefore is potentially more sustainable than competitive advantage based solely on product and market positioning.

Many researchers in the field of strategic management who focus on resource theory believe that the focus on knowledge evolved naturally. The tragic loss of lives in World War II prompted economists to consider the role of education and training and the development of human capital theory. Before World War II, most economists were concerned with the economic returns generated by physical capital such as property, plant, and equipment. The benefits of education and training were ascribed to politics and morals, rather than economic returns. Well-educated individuals were thought to make more rational choices and to be better citizens than those with less schooling. Although the role of education in leading to well-paid jobs was acknowledged, few scholars linked education and economic impact. *Human capital theory* considers how knowledge is developed and used at the individual level.

In the 1990s, resource theorists developed the language we have been using in this book, including a focus on core competence.[10] These concepts evolved into a focus on knowledge management.[11] As outsourcing, alliances, and other trends make many companies in developed countries less capital intensive, the focus on knowledge is becoming increasingly important.

In a static or slow-changing environment, Porter's 1980s recommendations (outlined in Chapter 5) for developing a sustainable competitive advantage by developing and defending profitable positions in attractive industries might remain viable. But as we said in Chapter 6, most firms around the world face industries characterized by more dynamism, in which there are frequent and rapid changes in technology, customer preferences, and competitive responses. In these industries, firms establish a competitive advantage that hopefully can be sustained over time by continually creating temporary advantages. In this chapter we explore how firms in knowledge industries try to learn quickly and apply their unique knowledge to build new resource configurations that create market changes and to adapt to the changes made by others.

Knowledge is the only asset that can help a firm adapt to radical change as markets shift, uncertainty dominates, and technologies proliferate. The firms that succeed in these difficult, sometimes hypercompetitive environments are able to create and disseminate new knowledge

Human capital theory examines the role of the individual's competence, focusing on how an individual's knowledge enhances cognitive abilities and can result in more effective activities.

quickly and embody knowledge in their products and services. Radical change regularly renders products obsolete, necessitating that firms reshape or abandon their products or services. Knowledge-based systems and processes have the greatest promise for long-term growth because they facilitate these needed transformations.

However, firms have, to a large extent, been unable to establish successful approaches to knowledge management. During 2003, for example, U.S. firms spent $4.5 billion on software and other information technologies to enable information sharing.[12] Yet a Harris poll of 536 professional, managerial, and technical knowledge workers from companies with 1,000 employees or more reported the following percentages of employees who agreed with five telling statements:

- Some people in the company can help me do my job better—67 percent
- I do not know how to find these colleagues—39 percent
- Work is often duplicated because people are unaware of each other's work—60 percent
- Opportunities to innovate are missed because the right people do not work together—54 percent
- Wrong decisions are regularly made because employee knowledge isn't effectively tapped—51 percent.

That's a very depressing set of statistics. We hope you will do a better job as a strategist.

WHAT ARE THE CHARACTERISTICS OF KNOWLEDGE NEEDED BY COMPANIES?

Data
is the raw input to knowledge, including, facts, words, and numbers.

Information
is data connected with a context that enables insight, analysis, and conversation.

In simple terms, knowing how to use information is what makes knowledge a resource. As an example, a sales director may have sales statistics, but that data becomes information only when it is put into the context of past sales, competitor sales, and so on. Knowledge is created when the strategist uses this information to do things such as decide on tactics for the coming year or prepare training support materials. In other words, knowledge (as defined earlier) uses information to support direction or intent. *Data* (e.g., facts, numbers, or even guesses) are in the background and rarely valuable in and of themselves. *Information* requires a context that enables insight, analysis, and conversation. Knowledge is built on both data and information, as can be seen in the hierarchy presented in Figure 11.2.

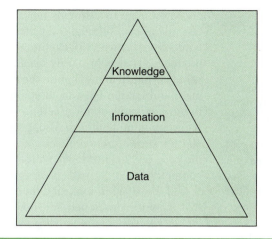

Figure 11.2 — Hierarchy of Knowledge, Information, and Data

Figure 11.2 implies that strategists must manage data and information in order to reliably draw conclusions about strategic direction. They should make sure that statistics (*data*) are collected about sales, for example, and that salespeople and other experienced observers put that data into context, thus creating useful information. But only when that information is put to use for current and future company direction does *knowledge* come into play.

As we've already said, knowledge is unlike any other asset. One particularly interesting feature is that most of the cost to develop and distribute knowledge is in the creation process, not in use, while manufacturing and distribution is the primary source of cost in utilizing most other assets. As a result, once knowledge is created, initial development costs can be spread across rising volume, and advantages from its use can endure over time. In fact, knowledge is an asset that can become more valuable as more people use it and add to it. For example, the value of entries in the online encyclopedia Wikipedia increases as users add, refine, and manage content.

Of course, the value of some knowledge can decline as it becomes known to other firms. When trade secrets become known and widely practiced, or when patents expire, initially valuable information becomes available to all and what was once a knowledge advantage becomes standard operating practice in many firms. In consequence, strategists who hope to be successful over a long period of time must continually update their organization's knowledge base. The capability to rapidly and effectively re-create knowledge is the source of competitive advantage.

Knowledge investments require a different sort of protection than tangible assets. Although they create considerable value, it is more difficult to predict who will capture the lion's share of the value knowledge produces. That is primarily because most knowledge is embedded in people's minds, and so cannot be owned and controlled in the way that plant and equipment can. It is difficult for people to articulate everything they know about a certain process, so it is difficult to pass that information on to others. Also, people are not always willing to divulge all they know. And people come and go from firms, now more than in the past, taking knowledge with them and sometimes transferring it to competitors.

All these factors make it difficult to determine who owns knowledge that is jointly developed and how to trade or sell knowledge. For example, *intellectual property rights* are hard to retain when a knowledge artifact such as a report or a software program can be copied readily without detection. Because knowledge assets are a tricky business, there are few tested models to help managers understand how to use and capture their value, but theorists have argued that valuable knowledge tends to be private and tacit.

Private versus Public Knowledge

The distinction between *public knowledge* and *private knowledge* is important, because only private knowledge can be a source of competitive advantage. Private knowledge includes such items as a firm's unique routines, processes, documentation, and trade secrets.

Public knowledge includes industry and occupational *best practices*. Total quality management (TQM), just-in-time (JIT) inventory management, and lean manufacturing techniques are examples of proven ideas that are now available to all firms, even though at one point many of these practices were private knowledge. The application of public knowledge pertaining to best practices is necessary for survival in a highly competitive marketplace. However, strategists cannot expect to benefit without significant adaptation to their own circumstances, which is why the term *promising practices* is sometimes used instead. The idea is that it is worthwhile to study the various ways that benefits are achieved.

Widely available knowledge is not a source of competitive advantage unless the company figures out a different way to use that knowledge or applies it more faithfully than competitors. On the other hand, failure to apply public knowledge can be a source of competitive *disadvantage*. For example, the Japanese developed just-in-time inventory practices, which gradually became well documented in publicly available articles and books. Firms that do not use these practices today cannot beat rivals who do use these approaches and are likely to go out of business.

Intellectual property rights are knowledge resources that can be legally protected and thus potentially used for competitive advantage.

Public knowledge is openly available and not the unique property of any one firm.

Private knowledge can be protected from others, and includes a firm's unique routines, processes, documentation, and trade secrets.

Best practices are methodologies or techniques that have, through research and experience, been proven to lead to desired results.

Promising practices is an alternative label for proven practices that emphasizes the importance of adaptation to local circumstances.

Explicit versus Tacit Knowledge

Explicit knowledge is based on objective information and observable skills that can be easily taught or written down.

Another way to define knowledge is by categorizing it as either explicit or tacit.[13] *Explicit knowledge* consists of knowledge and skills that can easily be taught or written down. It is "capable of being clearly stated."[14] Collective explicit knowledge resides in standard operating procedures, documentation, information systems, rules, blueprints, and computer code—all of which means that its transfer does not depend on specific individuals. Large multinational firms can have hundreds of thousands or even millions of documents worldwide that contain explicit knowledge, readily available through intranets. Though we discussed this idea in Chapter 7, it is worth repeating when emphasizing knowledge as a key resource.

Tacit knowledge is developed through experience and depends on an individual or group's insight and intuition. It is more difficult to transfer to others and often requires interactive experience.

Tacit knowledge is knowledge learned through experience and includes an individual's insight and intuition. It is very difficult to describe tacit knowledge to another individual, let alone to record it formally. In the words of Michael Polanyi, "We can know more than we can tell."[15] Tacit knowledge is found within organizational routines and developed from experience. This tacit knowledge can be held by individuals or held collectively through shared experiences and interpretations of events.

Though more difficult to strategically manage, tacit knowledge can be the most valuable knowledge to a company because it can create sustainable competitive advantages. Unlike other resources, no other firm can easily purchase and employ tacit knowledge. Normally, as we described in Chapter 2, many firms engage in activities that are similar to those of their competitors, but as they learn from their own experience they are building their own tacit knowledge. But it takes valuable time to share tacit knowledge through interactions.

Social capital theory is concerned with an individual's position in a social network of relationships and the resources embedded in, available through, or derived from these networks.

While human capital theory is mostly concerned with an individual's set of knowledge and skills, *social capital theory* is concerned with an individual's position in a social network of relationships.[16] Social capital theory emerged from the need to account for the role of social processes that were not addressed in early economic theory, including the accumulation of shared knowledge. A basic principle of social capital is that individuals interact when their social networks are characterized by trust, reciprocity, and cooperation.

Social capital theory incorporates a group and an individual perspective and covers prescribed (based on formally specified relationships) as well as emergent (informal) relationships. The group perspective dwells on "(1) how certain groups develop and (2) how such a collective asset enhances group members' life changes."[17] In contrast, the individual perspective is concerned with how "individuals access and use resources embedded in social networks to gain returns in instrumental actions (e.g. financing, better jobs) or to preserve gains in expressive actions."[18]

Because individuals and not the organization possess information, a critical element of developing sustained competitive advantage is first to foster sharing specialized and tacit knowledge among individuals, and then to promote the application of this knowledge to the development of new products and services. These are the topics we address next.

How Do Strategists Manage and Use Knowledge?

Taking the new learning of employees and making it available to others in the organization is the central activity of the knowledge-creating company. It requires finding methods to combine traditional resources and capabilities in new and unique ways. An organization's ability to acquire, integrate, share, and apply knowledge becomes the most important strategic resource for creating a sustainable competitive advantage. Organizations need to develop a formal *knowledge management* process by identifying what information a company has and developing approaches to make useful information available to organization members. Accenture is a good example of profiting from good knowledge management.

Knowledge management is an organization's ability to acquire, integrate, share, and apply knowledge resources for sustainable advantage.

Accenture Profits from Well-Managed Knowledge

Accenture is a knowledge company that focuses on global management consulting, technology services, and outsourcing to help improve client companies' performance. Over the past fifteen years, Accenture has built elaborate knowledge management capabilities, beginning with a rather rudimentary office file system in the early 1980s. The consultants grew frustrated with "checking out" paper knowledge files from office repositories, and the system became unmanageable. Furthermore, employee turnover tended to be high, and Accenture did not want all of its knowledge walking out the door.

In 1991, Accenture's partners established a "Horizon 2000" task force and crafted a knowledge management strategy. An electronic database, the Knowledge Exchange (KX), was created, and consultants were encouraged to contribute client information, company methodologies and tools, and examples of project deliverables. The database also included industry best practices, external information, discussion forums, company-wide policies, and "Yellow Pages" of employee skills and knowledge. Knowledge management caught on, and at one point the firm had as many as 16,000 databases.

In parallel, the firm created "Centers of Excellence" (CoE), groups of people geographically or virtually positioned who gather and distribute leading information in a given discipline and are assigned other knowledge roles. Two hundred "Knowledge Managers" work across industries, competencies, and geographic locales, tasked with knowledge creation, database management, and content management. "Knowledge Integrators" develop deep expertise in a given field and help determine and synthesize the most valuable knowledge. They also conduct secondary research and provide help desk support and external content acquisition and management services. Knowledge management employees also began to "clean the KX"—eliminating data that did not offer value and highlighting "best practice" knowledge.

Accenture has continued to be innovative with its knowledge management practices. The firm created an Internet-based internal company-wide portal, available via a secure Internet connection, in 2001. Employees have instant access to an ever-growing selection of databases, some of which are available via PDAs and mobile sources.[19]

The Accenture case illustrates the importance of processes in knowledge management. There are four essential knowledge processes, as shown in Figure 11.3. First, knowledge must be created. Second, useful information must be captured and stored. That might mean creating a database of information about best practices or getting an employee who has specialized knowledge to articulate to others what he or she knows. Third, the organization must establish processes for transferring this learning or information among employees throughout the organization. The information has no value unless it can be accessed by other organization members when they need it. Finally, management must develop formal procedures and processes to ensure that the firm is using this knowledge in areas critical to sustaining the company's competitive advantages in the future.

Figure 11.3 — Knowledge Management: Processes and Components

Knowledge Creation

Based on their research that examined the knowledge management practices of very successful Japanese global corporations, Ikujiro Nonaka and Hirotaka Takeuchi[20] proposed a model of knowledge creation, which we will describe and then illustrate in Figure 11.4. Nonaka and Takeuchi began with the idea that the organization cannot create knowledge without individuals. The organization provides the structure and support for individuals to create knowledge. Then the process of capturing that knowledge and making it available to others is the central activity of knowledge management.

Nonaka and Takeuchi contend that human knowledge is created through a social process among individuals, during which tacit and explicit knowledge interact. From this assumption they developed a four-category typology of knowledge creation: socialization (tacit knowledge to tacit knowledge), externalization (tacit knowledge to explicit knowledge), combination (explicit knowledge to explicit knowledge), and internalization (explicit knowledge to tacit knowledge).

Socialization describes the experience-sharing process of conveying tacit knowledge from one person to another, whereby a more experienced individual communicates mental models, technical skills, and other tacit knowledge. This occurs not through dialogue, but through observation, imitation, and practice. In some cases, however, new knowledge can result when an individual obtains information from another person, and this triggers an entirely new idea. An example is what happens between the new-product development team of a firm and its customers. After the product is introduced to the market, based on customer behaviors, the product development team can learn and make additional improvements to the new product based on observing its use. As firms interact more with their customers, a socialization process is occurring.

Externalization is defined as the process of translating tacit knowledge that some individuals possess into knowledge that can be readily understood by others; that is, explicit knowledge. Because tacit knowledge, informal "know-how," is hard to define, this process requires that the firm attempt to conceptualize employee subjective insights and images. The firm needs to test that knowledge and then put it in a form that can be transferred to other individuals throughout the organization. It is usually a group process in which people reflect on their experiences. Business process modeling is one way in which tacit knowledge is made more explicit;[21] story-telling in organizations can also be seen as a way in which organization members pass on less formal understanding.

Combination refers to the process of transferring explicit knowledge to explicit knowledge, usually into a new whole. Existing explicit knowledge is often recataloged and expanded into new explicit knowledge—for example, when a comptroller puts together information from across

Socialization occurs as employees share tacit knowledge.

Externalization occurs as employees translate tacit knowledge into more explicit knowledge that can be more readily shared.

Combination occurs as explicit knowledge is integrated and recombined.

a corporation and creates a financial report. However, this financial re-port may not really extend the organization's knowledge base. Individu-als share knowledge through documents, meetings, telephone conversa-tions, and computer networks. A second example is a formal education program that combines and integrates knowledge, such as a master of business administration (MBA).

Internalization describes the process of taking explicit knowledge and translating it into tacit knowledge, which can make it easier for individu-als to act upon. Internalization can be understood as a "trial by error" or "learning by doing" approach. For example, when explicit knowledge is shared, employees internalize the information, extending their own knowledge and, in many cases, reframing their own tacit knowledge. An example is when a firm documents all customer complaints and service questions and makes those available to the new-product development department.

Internalization occurs as individuals augment explicit knowledge with their own tacit knowledge gained from experience.

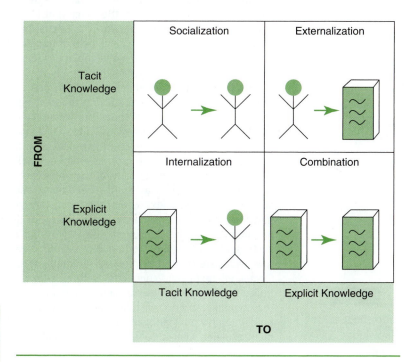

Figure 11.4 — Nonaka and Takeuchi's Knowledge Creation Model

Spirals of knowledge occur when socialization, externalization, combination, and internalization become an ongoing interactive process of learning.

As he worked with the ideas in this figure, Nonaka found that many successful global Japanese firms had been able to develop an ongo-ing interaction of the four forms of learning, which created a *spiral of knowledge*.[22] He defines the spiral as using all four different types of knowledge to create activities that are simultaneously occurring and interacting with each other. As each spiral occurs, the employees gain even greater insights and higher levels of understanding. For example, employees may gain new tacit knowledge in one process and apply it to other processes throughout the corporation, and in so doing they discover new insights that allow them to improve the original process. Brooks Sports provides a good example.

Brooks Sports: Creating New Knowledge In-House

Running shoe and apparel manufacturer Brooks Sports recently in-sourced its research and development, creating a giant biomechanics lab for shoes in its Seattle headquarters. A team of five designers and engineers use more than forty machines to develop, test, and refine running shoe prototypes. In the past, Brooks designers would formulate an idea for a shoe in the Seattle office and then send it to Asia to be manufactured as a prototype. Now the Seattle-based Brooks team uses an in-house, rapid prototype machine that transforms a two-dimensional drawing into a three-dimensional object made out of resin material. This technology enables the team to see how the pieces of the shoe fit together and make further refinements in order to create biomechanically superior shoes for runners with different needs. As well as undergoing external testing, the shoes are wear-tested internally by Brooks employees, often on local trails during their lunch hours, and feedback is shared immediately. The team can also wear-test the latest apparel designs. The new in-house process enables Brooks to save a lot of development time and better control the process.

All 140 employees at Brooks headquarters, as well as customers and other visitors, regularly tour the laboratory to witness firsthand the new innovations. The company also reports that the in-house laboratory has helped educate Brooks employees in other divisions, such as the customer relations and international development departments, about how shoes are created, reinforcing commitment to the brand and the informal, energetic, and connected culture. Brooks fosters an "open door" policy in which employees are encouraged to talk to other members of the company about their roles, including CEO Jim Weber. The firm also holds monthly all-headquarters meetings during which a specific department explains what it does and how this links to firm strategy.[23]

Worksheet 11.1:
Knowledge Creation Process—A Tool for Understanding how Firm Employees Can Create Knowledge

Worksheet 11.1 provides a set of questions for analyzing how a specific firm might create knowledge.

Knowledge Storage

Storing knowledge is a critical second step in the ongoing knowledge management process. Organizations that create or acquire knowledge also have the capacity to forget or misplace these valuable insights.[24] *Organizational memory*, a firm's collective knowledge from past experiences, can influence an organization's present actions and activities.[25] Organizational memory can take various forms: written documentation, structured electronic databases, documented firm processes, and tacit knowledge. ShareNet, an extensive project of Siemens Information and Communication Networks group, is one example of the many formal systems that organizations have used to try to collect experience from one part of an organization and make it available to other organizational members.

> **Organizational memory** is the collective knowledge available from a variety of explicit and tacit knowledge resources.

Memory is important as unanticipated events require new actions. We are all aware of the waste that occurs by "reinventing the wheel." Memory may not supply the exact solution to a new problem, but it facilitates "absorptive capacity," the firm's ability to evaluate, assimilate, and apply new externally gathered information that is dependent on prior related information.[26] As discussed in Chapter 2, individuals and their respective organizations are more capable of storing new knowledge if they have sufficient prior knowledge to evaluate and apply potentially useful information in a given domain.

There are two primary strategies for storing knowledge: *codification* and *personalization*. The codification strategy is computer-centric; firm knowledge is stored in electronic databases. Large organizations such as Siemens generally take this approach and consulting firms such as McKinsey and Bain seem to have been the most active developers. A personalization strategy is people-focused; knowledge is shared through personal contacts. Consulting firms typically establish strong networks of individuals within and outside the firm. Consultants in one part of the world can ask questions concerning client problems, and consultants who have insights on how they might approach the client issues respond. The firm assesses the quality of the knowledge sharing of its consultants, and this is incorporated into the consultants' annual performance review.

> **Codified knowledge** is that which is put into systematic form.

> **Personalized** knowledge shared among individuals is often more compelling, and more likely to be used, than codified knowledge.

Electronic databases store three general classifications of information: external knowledge (e.g., Gartner Group reports), formal internal knowledge (e.g., client deliverables, best-practice methodology), and informal internal knowledge (e.g., discussion databases, expert databases). Effective IT tools and powerful user-friendly search engines are increasing the capacity of organizations to store knowledge. In addition to technology, effective storage relies on the availability of time, money, and staff resources.

Knowledge Transfer

The third phase of knowledge management concerns the firm's ability to retrieve and distribute this knowledge. Transfer conduits can be informal or formal, personal or impersonal. Informal methods (e.g., water cooler conversations) promote socialization, but are not effective for firmwide transfer. Formal transfer (e.g., group training sessions) guarantee widespread transfer but may inhibit creativity. Personal channels (e.g., apprenticeships, shadowing) enable sharing of context-specific knowledge. Impersonal means (e.g., electronic knowledge databases) are effective for explicit, easily transferable knowledge. Explicit knowledge embedded in technology is easier to transfer than knowledge that is not coded technically.[27]

Professors Sumantra Ghoshal and Lynda Gratton at London Business School described the importance of *signature processes* for creating strategic advantage.[28] Their case studies of successful organizations indicate that best practices are recognized and widely used in competitive organizations. Those that do especially well, however, develop practices that are unique to their organization's values and history. One of the organizations they studied is British Petroleum (BP).

Signature processes are unique value-creating practices that resonate with the leaders' values and the unique history of the organization.

Advantage from Peer Assist at British Petroleum

John Browne joined British Petroleum (BP) as a "university apprentice" in 1966 and was named CEO in 1995. His extensive experience in BP convinced Browne that people learn more from their peers than they do from their bosses. As CEO he built on this conviction to help his organization take advantage of a series of acquisitions in the 1990s.

The peer assist program is a particularly important part of a process that BP calls "learning by doing," or gathering knowledge before beginning a project or work engagement. At BP, a peer assist is organized by a team of people on the project, requesting a meeting or workshop with individuals from other teams who can provide knowledge and insights. A facilitator guides the meeting, sets the ground rules, and assists the knowledge-sharing process. In the next stage of the meeting, the assisting team discusses the problem and possible surprises and may wish to contact others or request additional information. The new project team may opt to leave the room at this stage. The visiting team analyzes the situation, reflects on the discussion, and presents feedback. Together the project and visiting peer assist team members agree on actions. The length of the peer assist varies from a half day to two days long. The peer assist program involves explicit procedures for sharing knowledge across divisions, but is also supported by strong BP cultural expectations of support.[29]

Peer assist is a response to the key challenge of knowledge management. Encouraging people to reveal tacit knowledge they may have acquired through painful learning experiences is difficult. Often people want to hold on to knowledge because they feel it will secure their jobs. To share knowledge is not a natural thing for most people to do. Often the only way to encourage exchange throughout the organization is to create opportunities for interpersonal interaction and social relationships. Otherwise, important new information and learning taking place on the job is not reliably passed on to others and incorporated into the firm's decisions and practices.

Organizations develop these interactions through internal and external approaches. Internally, many organizations are experimenting with new organizational cultures, structures, and reward systems to enhance these interactions and to encourage creating and sharing tacit knowledge across the organization. To build their intellectual capital, those organizations are utilizing the "social capital" that develops from people interacting repeatedly over time. Firms need to set up internal procedures to capture learning experiences (e.g., knowledge gained from executing a project, or solutions to problems reported by customers). Externally, firms are engaging in an increase in relational networks that cross organizational boundaries. These activities include alliances, outsourcing, and the use of external consultants, as discussed in the last section of this chapter.

Transfer is critical but can prove costly in terms of wasted employee time and mistaken interpretations. Inaccurate message translation can result from cognitive, social, and structural obstacles. Individuals require time to access electronic databases or colleagues within the firm. Often, as articulated by the late Carnegie Mellon professor Herbert Simon, a winner of the Nobel Prize in economics, there is "a wealth of information and a poverty of attention."[30] Individuals must choose among dozens, hundreds, or even thousands of potential resources whose value is yet unknown.

Knowledge Use

Knowledge acquisition is not adequate in and of itself. Employees must be able to apply what they know—thus, the importance of the fourth and final process, knowledge use. There are two general knowledge management approaches: technological and organizational.

Technological Components of Knowledge Use Knowledge management is made possible by information systems of related components acting together to accumulate, process, store, retrieve, and deliver information in order to facilitate planning, control, coordination, analysis, and decision making. Knowledge management–oriented technology options include groupware, integrated e-mail, discussion groups or newsgroups, videoconferences, electronic databases, intranets, and extranets. Equipped with the necessary analysis, graphics, document management, and communications tools, these systems provide easy access to external and internal databases. Good systems should support large numbers, data manipulations, and high-speed access through a user-friendly interface.

Effective and implementable knowledge management technical solutions are comparatively easy to evaluate and purchase, and they provide multiple benefits to the firm. Technology-based communication may also increase knowledge creation quality by providing virtual spaces in which to express and share ideas. Information systems encourage teamwork and increase individual-to-individual contact in the form of e-mail, discussion databases, and voice messaging.

These technical systems can also be problematic. Effective information systems may not be built because of an unclear understanding of how IT can improve managers' and professionals' tasks.[31] Furthermore, some knowledge is not easily captured or codified or may become outdated if it is documented in an organization's knowledge system. These systems also may be difficult to understand, and users may choose not to contribute.

Companies tend to initiate a knowledge management strategy with technology implementation first and later focus on the necessary people-oriented elements.[32] This may be because technological solutions are easier to apply than human-resource-intensive implementations.[33] Good knowledge management information technology systems must be paired with organizational elements to create a solid, well-rounded program.

Organizational Components of Knowledge Use Organizational (nontechnical) infrastructure is the "glue" that holds organizations together; it includes organizational culture, incentive systems, compatible organizational design, and individual competencies. These behaviors, roles, norms, and internal rules are embedded in knowledge management processes.

Many organizations are trying to become learning organizations. These firms are experimenting with new organizational cultures, structures, and reward systems to enhance these interactions and to encourage the creation and sharing of tacit knowledge across the organization.

In *Learning in Action*, Harvard Business School professor David Garvin defines a *learning organization* as a firm that is "skilled at creating, acquiring, interpreting, transferring, and retaining knowledge, and at purposefully modifying its behavior to reflect new knowledge and insights."[34] In *The Fifth Discipline*, MIT's Peter Senge describes learning organizations as places "where people continually expand their capacity to create the results they truly desire, where new and expansive patterns of thinking are nurtured, where collective aspiration is set free, and where people are continually learning how to learn together."[35]

Learning organization is an organization that is able to create, acquire, interpret, transfer, and retain knowledge to purposefully improve the value they create.

From these definitions, it is clear that generation of new ideas within the organization is essential if learning is to take place. This learning must be shared throughout the organization so that the way work is done is changed. If it does not result in change, then the learning has only created the potential for improvement.

An interesting point about organization learning is that most of it is done as people are actually doing their jobs, not in training sessions. People learn most effectively by doing, not by sitting in a classroom. Therefore, learning may not always be intentional. It often happens as an accident or from a failure, insights, intuition, and hunches.

How Do Organizational Systems Affect Knowledge Management?

Although this entire chapter focuses on the strategic management of knowledge, it is important to emphasize several explicit tools that help bring together the information described so far.

Corporate Culture and Values

An important management tool for establishing a supportive learning environment is developing a corporate culture capable of promoting innovation, risk taking, and collaboration. Perhaps most important, the culture must encourage individuals to share their knowledge and learning throughout the organization.

This starts by permitting discussion of half-baked embryonic possibilities. Companies need to develop and experiment with new ideas that can possibly create new products or services that perhaps current customers have not yet even thought that they need. This requires an open, supportive climate in which expressing differing opinions and points of view is encouraged. All employees need to get involved in product development and offer important feedback, regardless of their positions. Customers, suppliers, and venture partners are important sources of ideas for innovation.

Minnesota-based manufacturer 3M long has been known for its corporate culture that supports entrepreneurship and new ideas. 3M requires all new employees to attend a training session on risk taking. Executives set goals as to how much of 3M's annual revenue must be generated from new products. Employees know that if they want to be promoted, they must participate in developing and bringing to market a new product idea. The company designates funds and time for all employees to spend developing new ideas of their own choosing. National Semiconductor is another company that institutionalizes innovation. National Semiconductor emphasizes diversity in ideas and skills, makes innovation its top corporate priority, openly tolerates risks and celebrates failure as a learning opportunity, stimulates new ideas and avoids ridicule or fault finding, and promotes an innovation process that is clear, well funded, and supported at all levels of the corporation.[36]

Failure is one likely outcome of risk taking and experimentation with new ideas, and thus tolerating failure is important to learning. There is a wonderful story involving Thomas Watson, Sr., the founder of IBM. One day he called into his office a young manager who had lost $10 million in a risky venture. The young man was totally intimidated and said to Watson when he entered his office, "I guess you want my resignation." Watson reportedly said, "You cannot be serious. We just spent ten million dollars educating you!"[37]

An effective culture that transmits knowledge about success and failure must be embedded in the entire organization—from executive management to workers on the front line. Management needs to engage in social activities such as mentoring and training programs. In addition to goal status review, project debriefings can be used to emphasize the importance of lessons learned and acknowledge key contributors. Individuals should recognize the multiple roles in the transfer process and the possibility for mutual benefit. For example, if a manager contacts another manager to gain insights on a particular client solution (knowledge buyer), he or she may also be in a position to share key lessons learned (knowledge seller) or direct the individual to another source (knowledge broker).

Finally, a firm should provide employees with time to create, share, learn, and utilize knowledge. A firm that espouses the importance of knowledge management must support this strategy with policies that enable individuals to spend time specifically on knowledge-sharing tasks. Firms could set aside "learning time" through internal billing-charge numbers for training or dedicated periods during meetings.

Incentive Systems

A firm's capacity for knowledge sharing depends critically on incentive systems.[38] Incentives can be tangible or intangible, intrinsic or extrinsic. Intrinsic rewards are internally focused and based on personal motivations such as a desire to help others or to build self-esteem. These rewards include informed personal satisfaction from serving as a subject-matter expert and being assigned more challenging tasks.

Extrinsic rewards are externally focused and visible to others. These rewards include financial incentives and public recognition. Academics and practitioners caution against the predisposition to throw money or gifts at a knowledge-sharing problem. Long-term knowledge management success hinges on intrinsic "feel-good" returns, not a one-time-only free pen, mousepad, or T-shirt.

Organizational Structure

To be successful, companies must use structures that allow for quick response times to customer needs and changes in market conditions: shorter time to market, higher levels of creativity and innovation, mechanisms for ongoing learning, and the quick adoption of new technologies.

Organizational structures that facilitate these practices involve less bureaucracy, which means faster decision making with fewer levels of approval, higher levels of employee empowerment that delegate decision making to those closest to the customer, and open communication in all directions, including outside the company, to provide employees with the information they need to make decisions. These organization structures result in higher levels of innovation and create a need for fewer managers. Increased levels of learning and technology adoption also occur in shorter time spans under these flatter organizational structures.

Organizations that encourage learning and innovation have two important characteristics: an increasing reliance on networks of personal relationships and the use of smaller operating units. Increasingly, organizations rely on a relatively small staff of full-time employees, maintaining control of all key strategic activities but outsourcing all nonessential functions. Decisions are placed in the hands of the managers who are the most familiar with the details of the business, which enhances access to the needed knowledge and increases flexibility.

The major challenge with this structure is providing sufficient coordination to make these structures successful. Executives need to encourage the different units to share information and knowledge and to cooperate extensively. If there is no cooperation, the firm may lose opportunities to generate and utilize knowledge with tremendous value elsewhere within the organization.

Several solutions help meet these goals. One is developing new positions within the organizations responsible for coordination. Another is empowering and rewarding employees at all levels to search for new ideas, from constant improvements to dramatic breakthroughs. Previously this had been under the purview of product developers only. In addition, these innovative activities will take place outside the research and development department. Different sites will take on the responsibility for developing new knowledge and innovations, which have the potential to be useful throughout the corporation.

Quite a few corporations have created a chief information officer (CIO) position that reports to the firm's chief executive officer (CEO). Global energy giant Chevron, with annual revenues exceeding $30 billion and operations in more than 100 countries, created a position called *process master*. This position oversees the different processes used in its six refineries. Process masters take innovations developed in one refinery and work with managers at other refineries to adapt and implement them.

Recruitment

Companies today must become adept identifiers of talent. Knowledge workers need to have the technical skills to understand how to apply new technologies within the business context. But even more important for a learning organization is employees' ability to be self-learners and their willingness to share that knowledge and work in teams. Given the need for autonomy in learning and decision making, knowledge workers must be comfortable with working in ill-defined and ambiguous situations. Recruiters, therefore, seek employees with a track record of acting entrepreneurially and handling a high degree of responsibility and authority.

Apart from knowledge and skills, employees must demonstrate enthusiasm. Valuable skills are valuable to a company only if the prospective candidate has the drive and ambition necessary to perpetually learn new skills. Southwest Airlines is an example of a firm that focuses explicitly on individual enthusiasm as part of its hiring process.

Worksheet 11.2 provides a tool to help identify structure, staffing, culture, and compensation to encourage these behaviors.

Worksheet 11.2:
Knowledge
Management
Culture—A Tool
for Encouraging
Behavior

WHAT ARE THE MOST IMPORTANT EXTERNAL SOURCES OF KNOWLEDGE?

The resource-based and recent knowledge-based views of the firm have emphasized the importance of paying attention to internal activities and resources. Knowledge management has an equally important external face: acting as the connection between the firm and its stakeholders, especially customers. It is also the distinguishing factor among competitors in a knowledge economy.

Firms use three major approaches to gather information and knowledge from their external environment. The first is having organization members gather information from external contacts, through such approaches as benchmarking, trade shows, and conferences. The second approach uses contingent employees (independent contractors) as a flexible resource. Third, firms can develop cooperative arrangements with other organizations, such as research consortiums and joint ventures (strategic alliances) and through acquisitions or mergers, which also tend to have a strong knowledge component.

Benchmarking
is used by
organizations to
compare their
activities and
outcomes with
the activities
and outcomes of
successful firms.

Benchmarking

Benchmarking focuses on collecting data and other intelligence that permits comparisons with other firms within or outside an industry to identify how well one's firm is performing its basic functions or activities. Activities can include examining materials handling and purchasing and creating new product-development processes. The objective of benchmarking is to identify best (or promising) practices and to take actions that improve the firm's competitive position.

Ideally, observation of others helps turn often tacit knowledge into something more explicit. Xerox provides an early example of strategic benchmarking use. The company found that several Japanese competitors were selling copiers in the United States for less than Xerox's manufacturing cost. A team of engineers went to Japan to work with the company's joint venture partner Fuji Xerox to benchmark Japanese production processes. Xerox learned that its production costs were excessive compared to those of its Japanese competitors, and something about alternative procedures. The result was a corporate-wide benchmarking program with the objective of establishing Xerox as a world-class manufacturer.

General Electric also has an ongoing benchmarking program. The firm regularly sends GE engineers to Japan to learn new techniques and bring these ideas home to GE. More than 80 percent of all Fortune 500 firms have implemented benchmarking programs.

Contingent Employees

As we noted in Chapter 8, contingent employees are independent contractors who are brought into the firm as consultants or on-call workers to accomplish specific tasks. Some companies contract with firms to handle something an internal unit previously would have, such as information technology or customer service.

According to the *Christian Science Monitor*, 90 percent of all U.S. firms use contingent employees and 43 percent of these firms use contingent workers in key professional and technical departments.[39] Contingent workers can cut the firm's operating costs by reducing benefit costs, recruitment costs, employee turnover, and paid-yet-underutilized hours. If these workers do not deliver, there are no firing costs or lost training time. In addition, such workers can bring to the firm important knowledge from outside quickly and cheaply, whether it be specific technical knowledge or perhaps knowledge of industry best practices. This is a quick way for the firm to gain needed important technical expertise without a long, expensive development period. Most contract employees have worked with many other firms and have developed knowledge of many firms' practices.

There are two key disadvantages of using contingent workers, however. First, these workers may learn about your firm and transfer important competitive knowledge from your firm to your competitors. Secondly, the firm may not have the processes in place to capture the knowledge and learning that the contingent workers have to offer, so once their job is finished, continuity is lost. Despite the downsides, evidence suggests that in the face of technological change, firms benefit from hiring contract employees. Firms can gain this knowledge more quickly by hiring contract employees rather than trying to develop this information internally. In addition, by hiring these contract employees, firms can immediately sever their relationship with this type of employee if the employee does not have the necessary information or training. Hiring permanent employees would entail a more time-consuming process.

Strategic Alliances

We have discussed the role of alliances in several previous chapters. Strategic alliances can increase a firm's knowledge base more quickly and cheaply than outsourcing. They include research consortiums, joint ventures, long-term supplier relationships, and licensing arrangements. These cooperative arrangements allow firms to extend their spheres of influence beyond the assets they own and to leverage the assets of others to create greater value while minimizing their own capital outlays. For example, in recent years, American and Japanese firms established joint ventures with Chinese firms to help them understand how to deal with Chinese government regulations, set up local production operations, and learn how to adapt their products to various Chinese tastes.

A group of potential competitors sometimes combine resources and knowledge to develop and transfer technology across organizational boundaries through joint R&D partnerships. An example involves U.S. semiconductor manufacturers that collaborate on research and development in response to significant Japanese competition. Unfortunately for U.S. firms, the Japanese and Europeans have been more successful using these collaborations than their American counterparts.

The most important problem when obtaining information from external sources is the transfer process. Identifying important knowledge and transferring it from the outside environment does not take place automatically. A firm must develop mechanisms to bring appropriate knowledge inside, transmit this knowledge within the firm, and incorporate new knowledge into existing stocks of knowledge. These mechanisms include boundary-spanning positions, a formal strategy for acquiring knowledge, and rewards for employees who successfully attain and share information.

If experience shows that it is difficult to transfer information within one organization, imagine how difficult it is to transfer information *across* organizations. Each organization has its own objectives, culture, and processes. Executives may not even know exactly what knowledge they should be capturing because it is difficult to clearly identify strategic information among large amounts of available information. Making the task even more difficult, the desired knowledge is usually highly tacit, deeply embedded in individuals' experiences and organizational context.

Clearly strategic alliances can have some disadvantages. It is particularly important that firms participating in alliances consider their partners' strategic intent in cooperating on the venture. Of course, these intentions are likely to evolve. Alliances require careful monitoring and planning. A partner can become knowledgeable about a production process or industry and decide to terminate its cooperative agreement and enter the market on its own.

Alliances Aren't Always Fun and Games

In 2000, the agreement between Amazon and Toys "R" Us seemed an ideal partnership. Both companies had been losing money in an area in which the other had considerable knowledge. Amazon had stocked too many of the wrong toys for Christmas 1999 and written off $40 million in losses. Toys "R" Us had been fined by the U.S. Federal Trade Commission for failing to deliver merchandise as promised during the 1999 holiday season. Its website, toysrus.com, was still hard to use after two years of development and had not generated expected sales.[40]

The ten-year agreement involved an icon for Toys "R" Us on the Amazon site. That cost the company an initial investment of $200 million, an annual payment of $50 million per year, and a payment per unit sold and a percentage of the overall price. Toys "R" Us had responsibility for choosing products, buying, and maintaining inventory. Amazon managed the site, took orders, and handled distribution, shipping, and returns.[41]

Observers at the time saw the deal as a forerunner of new relationships between brick-and-mortar companies and e-retailers, especially Amazon. CEO Jeff Bezos said, "While [Amazon] aspires to have the merchandising skills of Toys 'R' Us, it would be foolish to believe that we have them today."[42] John Eyler, CEO of Toys "R" Us, claimed, "What this does is allow us to offer better service, better fulfillment and [reach] profitability sooner."[43]

Within four years, however, the courts were involved. Amazon initiated a lawsuit to end the partnership, indicating that Toys "R" Us had not kept 90 percent of the products listed on Amazon's website in stock at all times, and that it had reduced the number of products that sold for under $5, which accounted for a significant portion of Amazon's toy sales.[44] Two years later, after an acrimonious exchange, Toys "R" Us won its bid to end the partnership. It argued that its toys were not prominent enough on Amazon's site and that other alliances, including agreements with Target,[45] had undercut the exclusivity of the original agreement. Perhaps most important, Amazon was launching a new service for outsiders to establish their own websites on Amazon. Although described as a boon to small entrepreneurs, Toys "R" Us saw the new website as a back door for long-time rival Wal-Mart.

As soon as Toys "R" Us won its suit, it relaunched toysrus.com with the help of new partners. Amazon immediately appealed but had to lower expected earnings, given lost revenue. Interestingly, this turn of events, which might be seen as mixed for both principals, was clearly positive for the toy market as a whole. The fact that Toys "R" Us and Amazon were quickly adding products to their websites was welcome news to toymakers who had faced declining sales for several seasons. Even better, the toy wars quickly spread to other retailers with an online presence, including eBay, Wal-Mart, and Target.[46] Their results adds to the evidence of an increasingly complicated picture for retail sales.

Distributed Expertise

Not all of the smart people work for one company. First expressed by Bill Joy when he was vice president of research and development at Sun Microsystems, this idea has important consequences, outlined by Henry Chesborough and David Teece:

> Because an outside developer of workstation software can obtain great-er rewards by selling software to Sun customers than by developing the same software as a Sun employee, he or she will move faster, work harder, and take more risks. Using high-powered, market-based incentives such as stock options and attractive bonuses, a virtual company can quickly access the technical resources it needs, if those resources are available. In situations where technology is changing rapidly, large companies that attempt to do everything inside will flounder when competing against small companies with highly trained and motivated employees.[47]

We've already described the idea of open innovation in earlier chapters, which is the process Chesborough and Teece are moving toward in this description. InnoCentive goes beyond the virtual company they praise to take advantage of smart people working in many different settings around the world.

InnoCentive

Distributed computing allows individuals to contribute idle CPU resources to collaborative projects, enabling cost-efficient access to massive processing power without fixed infrastructure investments. Similarly, InnoCentive provides a way to search for solutions to technological problems among existing resources outside the conventional internal research and development structures of a firm.

InnoCentive posts its clients' (called "seekers") problems on its website, without any hint of the seeker company's identity, together with a financial reward for the best solution delivered within a given timeframe. Seeker companies are mostly large R&D operations at companies such as Procter & Gamble, Dow, Eli Lilly, and BASF. They use InnoCentive when they are looking for brand-new approaches and new ideas, especially when they are stumped in a particular research area.

InnoCentive provides access to a global network of more than 100,000 scientists who offer solutions in the hope of winning the offered reward. The company facilitates problem formulation and posting, solution screening, confidentiality, intellectual property agreements, and award payments. Using this approach, seeker companies get access to the specialized talents of tens of thousands of scientists without adding to their fixed costs.

Recent research by Karim Lakhani for his dissertation at MIT shows that the InnoCentive model is not just different, but also highly efficient. He studied 166 problems that had been posted on InnoCentive by large corporations from the chemical and pharmaceutical industry. The corporations previously had spent six months to two years trying to solve the problems internally without success. Offering on average $30,000 for a successful problem solution, these firms posted their problems on InnoCentive. In general, solutions had to be submitted within six months of the initial posting.

Of the 166 problems Lakhani studied, 49 (29.5 percent) were solved by the InnoCentive community. This is an impressive percentage, given that individual solvers were competing with organized corporate research labs. But even more impressive is Lakhani's finding that on average a winning solver spent just seventy-four hours to solve the problem—compared to six to twenty-four unsuccessful months by the big corporations. The reason for this almost unbelievable result is rather simple: winning solvers already knew the solution. InnoCentive helps seekers by leveraging preexisting knowledge distributed in its broad community of scientists. In 72.5 percent of all cases, the winner just reused an existing solution from a previous task he or she had solved in a different context. In most cases, the solution was outside the seeker's field of expertise, which means that the seekers would have been very unlikely to find the solutions on their own.[48]

CONCLUSIONS FOR THE STRATEGIST

Whatever the source of data, information, and knowledge, organizational learning is critical to any firm's ability to survive in the current dynamic environment characterized by increasing competitiveness and the rapid development and diffusion of new technology. Perhaps knowledge is the one sure source of lasting competitive advantage. Jack Callahan, recently retired CEO of the Allstate Business Insurance

Group, has stated: "You will only win in the 21st century by building knowledge, growing knowledge workers, and putting knowledge workers at the center of organization."

Successful companies empower people to innovate. They leverage relationships across boundaries and throughout the extended enterprise. They connect their people and partners globally, using networks to tap learning opportunities from suppliers, customers, and alliances to create value for end users. This requires new skills, new behaviors, and new roles to support communication and forge the human connections that lie behind effective knowledge creation. An important part of the learning organization is sharing knowledge.

Learning cannot happen by itself. Organizations need to incorporate knowledge creation objectives into the strategic planning process. The organization must identify the most important challenges and greatest opportunities in its competitive environment. The second step is to translate that into what we need to learn in order to meet these challenges and exploit the opportunities, skills, and knowledge the firm already possesses or can develop. Thirdly, the firm needs to develop a plan for acquiring the necessary abilities to pursue knowledge through multiple approaches, rather than just education and training programs.

Key Concepts

Intellectual capital is knowledge that can be stored for later use. **Knowledge** is information with direction or intent. Unlike traditional firm assets such as equipment, knowledge assets appreciate with use as employees add to and adapt the firm's knowledge base. **Data** is the raw input into knowledge bases, including facts, words, and numbers. **Information** is data in context that enables insight, analysis, and conversation. **Intellectual property rights** are knowledge resources that can be legally protected, and thus used for competitive advantage. **Best practices** are methodologies or techniques that have, through research and experience, been proven to lead to desired results. **Promising practices** is an alternative label for proven practices that emphasizes the importance of adaptation to local circumstances.

People who think about knowledge as the source of advantage distinguish **private knowledge,** which includes a firm's unique routines, processes, documentation, or trade secrets that can be used to create competitive advantage, from **public knowledge** that is in the public domain and is not the unique property of any one firm. As first discussed in Chapter 2, it is unlikely that **explicit knowledge,** which includes knowledge and skills that easily can be taught or written down, will be used to create advantage, even if it is private. **Tacit knowledge,** which is learned through experience and created with an individual's or group's insight and intuition, is much more likely to be a source of advantage.

At the individual level, **human capital theory** examines the role of the individual's competence, focusing on how an individual's knowledge enhances cognitive abilities and can result in more effective activities. **Social capital theory** is concerned with an individual's position in a social network of relationships and the resources embedded in, available through, or derived from these networks.

Organizations use **knowledge management** to acquire, integrate, share, and apply knowledge resources. The knowledge acquisition process involves the following:

- **Socialization** as employees share tacit knowledge
- **Externalization** as employees translate tacit knowledge into more explicit knowledge that can be more readily shared
- **Combination** as explicit knowledge is integrated and recombined
- **Internalization** as individuals augment explicit knowledge with their own tacit knowledge gained from experience

Ideally all four processes create a **spiral of knowledge,** or ongoing organizational learning.

To be useful, past experience must be available in **organizational memory,** which is the collective knowledge available from various explicit and tacit knowledge resources. Storage of past experience is often done by **codification** into systematic form. Although this makes explicit computerized knowledge bases possible, **personalized** knowledge shared among individuals is often more compelling, and more likely to be used, than codified knowledge.

Transfer of knowledge among individuals is a key aspect of knowledge management. However, recent research points to the utility of **signature processes** that uniquely create value from practices that resonate with leaders' values and the unique history of an organization. The key step, however, is ongoing knowledge use, supported by both technological and organizational tools.

Strategic knowledge management is required to create a **learning organization**—one that can create, acquire, interpret, transfer, and retain knowledge to purposefully modify its activity. Strategists depend on several levers to create this ideal situation, including corporate culture and values, incentive systems, organizational structure, and recruitment. They also look externally, **benchmarking** their activities and outcomes against the activities and outcomes of successful firms. Independent contractors can also be used as an external source of knowledge, as can alliances with other organizations, and networks of relevant experts.

Questions for Further Reflection

1. Go to the Web and find a company that interests you.

    a. Describe the role of knowledge in the firm. Does the company have specific knowledge roles or processes?

    b. How would you suggest that a firm try to measure the value of knowledge?

    c. How would you benchmark this firm against other firms? What resources and tools would you use?

2. Think of a company or organization you have worked for full time, part time, or as a volunteer. Did you create new knowledge in your role? How? Were systems in place to capture your learning and pass it on to others? What would you do if you were charged with improving knowledge management in this firm?

3. Imagine that you are a project manager bringing a new member to your team in an organization you have worked for or would like to work for. How would you share tacit and explicit knowledge with the new team member?

WORKSHEET 11.1

Knowledge Creation Process—A Tool for Understanding How Firm Employees Can Create Knowledge

Consider how firm employees can create knowledge.

Step 1: Identify a knowledge-based company you might like to work for and list the types of knowledge that make this company successful in column 1.

Step 2: Brainstorm possible ways that firm employees, at any level, might contribute to each knowledge area through socialization processes and fill out column 2.

Step 3: Could knowledge also be created through externalization? Think of how an employee might externalize his or her knowledge. Complete column 3 with these ideas.

Step 4: Might new knowledge be created through combination? Fill in column 4 with your ideas.

Step 5: Is there also a role for internalization of knowledge in the firm? Think of how an employee might internalize his or her knowledge. Complete column 5 with these ideas.

Knowledge Creation Process Worksheet 11.1	Organization:
Analyst(s):	Summary:

Knowledge	Socialization	Externalization	Combination	Internalization

WORKSHEET 11.2
Knowledge Management Culture—A Tool for Encouraging Behavior

Identify structure, staffing, culture, and compensation to encourage learning behaviors.

Step 1: Identify a company you have worked for or might like to work for. Identify specific examples of knowledge required for this company to succeed in column 1.

Step 2: Indicate the way structure facilitates current knowledge management in the top half of the boxes in column 2, and then brainstorm possible ways that the firm could encourage and manage knowledge through structural changes.

Step 3: Summarize how staffing and other HR practices currently facilitate knowledge management in the top half of the boxes in column 3. Then consider how knowledge management could be enhanced by staffing.

Step 4: Fill in column 4 in the same way with your ideas about knowledge culture.

Step 5: Then consider the current role of compensation in knowledge management (if any) and decide whether you would suggest changes in this area in column 5.

Knowledge Management Culture Worksheet 11.2	**Organization:**
Analyst(s):	**Summary:**

Knowledge	Structure	Staffing	Culture	Compensation
	Current _____ Recommended	Current _____ Recommended	Current _____ Recommended	Current _____ Recommended
	Current _____ Recommended	Current _____ Recommended	Current _____ Recommended	Current _____ Recommended
	Current _____ Recommended	Current _____ Recommended	Current _____ Recommended	Current _____ Recommended
	Current _____ Recommended	Current _____ Recommended	Current _____ Recommended	Current _____ Recommended
	Current _____ Recommended	Current _____ Recommended	Current _____ Recommended	Current _____ Recommended
	Current _____ Recommended	Current _____ Recommended	Current _____ Recommended	Current _____ Recommended

	Current	Current	Current	Current
	Recommended	Recommended	Recommended	Recommended
	Current	Current	Current	Current
	Recommended	Recommended	Recommended	Recommended

NOTES

[1] World Trade Organization, http://www.wto.org, accessed March 21, 2008.

[2] http://www.census.gov/Press-Release/www/releases/archives/facts_for_features_special_editions/010218.html.

[3] The Interbrand study is cited at http://news.bbc.co.uk/1/hi/world/americas/839439.stm, accessed March 21, 2008. Interbrand bases its calculations on the future value of the brand.

[4] $80bn Google Takes Top Media Spot. 2005. BBC News (June 8). http://news.bbc.co.uk/2/hi/business/4072772.stm, accessed March 21, 2008.

[5] Associated Press. YouWin: YouTube Founders, Investors Got More Than One Billion in Google Stock. http:www.foxnews.com/story/0,2933,250889,00.html, accessed March 11, 2008.

[6] Quinn, J. B. 1992. *Intelligent Enterprise*. New York: Free Press.

[7] Chesbrough, H. W., & Teece, D. J. 1996. When Is Virtual Virtuous? Organizing for Innovation. *Harvard Business Review* 3: 65–73.

[8] Kolb, D. A. (1983). *Experiential Learning: Experience as the Source of Learning and Development*. Upper Saddle River, NJ: FT Press. David Kolb is a professor at Case Western University who has spent many years developing his theory of experiential learning and learning styles. There are many discussions and resources available on the Web. See, for example, http://www.businessballs.com/kolblearningstyles.htm and http://www.haygroup.com/tl/Questionnaires_Workbooks/Kolb_Learning_Style_Inventory.aspx, accessed January 12, 2008.

[9] Stabell, C. B., & Fjeldstad, Ø. 1998. Value Configuring for Competitive Advantages: On Chains, Shops and Networks. *Strategic Management Journal* 19: 413–437.

[10] Hamel, G., & Prahalad, C. K. 1996. *Competing for the Future*. Boston: Harvard Business School Press.

[11] See Kogut, B., & Zander, U. 1992. Knowledge of the Firm, Combinative Capabilities and the Replication of Technology. *Organization Science* 3: 387–399; Grant, R. 1996. Toward a Knowledge-Based Theory of the Firm. *Strategic Management Journal* (Winter Special Issue): 109–122.

[12] Gilmour, D. 2003. How to Fix Knowledge Management. *Harvard Business Review* (October): 1–4.

[13] Polanyi, M. 1966. *The Tacit Dimension*. New York: Doubleday.

[14] Polanyi, *The Tacit Dimension*, p. 22.

[15] Polanyi, *The Tacit Dimension*, p. 4.

[16]Nahapiet, J., & Ghoshal, S. 1998. Social Capital, Intellectual Capital and the Organizational Advantage. *Academy of Management Review* 23(2): 242–266.

[17]Lin, N. 2001. *Social Capital: A Theory of Social Structure and Action.* New York: Cambridge University Press.

[18]Lin, *Social Capital.*

[19]Terjesen, S. 2003. Knowledge Management at Accenture. In P. Gooderham & O. Nordhaug (eds.), *International Organizations.* London: Blackwell.

[20]Nonaka, I., & Takeuchi, H. 1995. *The Knowledge-Creating Company: How Japanese Companies Create the Dynamics of Innovation.* New York: Oxford University Press.

[21]For one description of business process modeling as a way of externalizing knowledge, see Kalpič, B., & Bernus, P. 2006. Business Process Modeling through the Knowledge Management Perspective. *Journal of Knowledge Management* 10(3): 40–56. Available at http://www.emeraldinsight.com/Insight/ViewContentServlet?Filename= Published/EmeraldFullTextArticle/Articles/2300100303.html, accessed January 10, 2008.

[22]Nonaka, I. 1991. The Knowledge-Creating Company. *Harvard Business Review* (November–December): 1–9.

[23]Personal conversation with Dan Rickfelder, Brooks employee.

[24]Darr, L., Argote, S., & Epple, D. 1995. The Acquisition, Transfer, and Depreciation of Knowledge in Service Organizations: Productivity in Franchises. *Management Science* 41: 1750–1762.

[25]Stein, E., & Zwass, V. 1995. Actualizing Organizational Memory with Information Systems. *Information Systems Research* 6(2): 185–217.

[26]Cohen, W. M., & Levinthal, D. A. 1990. Absorptive Capacity: A New Perspective on Learning and Innovation. *Administrative Science Quarterly* 3: 128–152.

[27]Zander, U., & Kogut, B. 1995. Knowledge and the Speed of Transfer and Imitation of Organizational Capabilities: An Empirical Test. *Organizational Science* 6: 76–92.

[28]Ghoshal, S., & Gratton, L. 2005. Beyond Best Practice. *Sloan Management Review* (Spring): 49–57.

[29]Ghoshal & Gratton, Beyond Best Practice.

[30]Simon, H. 1997. Designing Organizations for an Information-Rich World. In D. M. Lamberton (ed.), *The Economics of Communication and Information.* Cheltenham, England: Eigar, p. 40.

[31]Sheng, O. R. L., Motiwalla, L. F., & Nunamaker, J. F. 1989/1990. A Framework to Support Managerial Activities Using Office Information Systems. *Journal of Management Information Systems* 6(3): 45–63.

[32]Ruggles, R. 1998. The State of the Notion: Knowledge Management in Practice. *California Management Review* 40: 80–89.

[33]Rogers, E. M. 1983. *The Diffusion of Innovations.* New York: Free Press.

[34]Garvin, D. 2000. *Learning in Action.* Boston: Harvard Business School Press.

[35]Senge, P. 1990. *The Fifth Discipline.* New York: Doubleday, p. 1.

[36]Marquardt, M. 1996. *Building the Learning Organization.* New York: McGraw-Hill.

[37]Bennis, W., & Nanus, B. 1985. *Leaders.* New York: Harper & Row, p. 76.

[38]Lord, M., & Ranft, A. 1998. Transfer and Sharing of Local Knowledge within the Firm and Entry into New International Markets. *Academy of Management Best Papers Proceedings* 58: H1–H7.

[39]Coolidge, S. D. 1996. Temping Is Now a Career—with an Upside for Workers. *Christian Science Monitor* (October 7).

[40]Sandoval, G. 2000. Is Toys "R" Us Heading for E-Commerce Sidelines? CNet News.com (August 18): http://news.com.com/Is+Toys+R+Us+headed+for+e-commerce+sidelines/2100-1017_3-244654.html, accessed March 21, 2008.

[41]Ouchi, M. S. 2006. Toy story winds up leaving Amazon grim. *Seattle Times* (March, 3). http://seattletimes.nwsource.com/html/businesstechnology/2002840626_amazon03. html, accessed March 21, 2008.

[42]Helft, M. 2000. Amazon.com: Toy Story 2—Company Business and Marketing. *Industry Standard* (August 21). http://www.findarticles.com/p/articles/mi_m0HWW/is_32_3/ ai_66672328/pg_, accessed March 21, 2008.

[43]Helft, Amazon.com—Toy Story 2.

[44]Hines, M. 2004. Amazon Says "Game's Over" to Toysrus.com. Online Giant Asks Court to OK Divorce from Toy Seller—and to Award $750 Million in Damages. CNet News.com (June 28). http://news.com.com/Amazon+says+games+over+to+ Toysrus.com/2100-1038_3-5250411.html, accessed March 21, 2008.

[45]Target Corporation. 2006. *Target Corporation and Amazon Enterprise Solutions Extend E-Commerce Agreement to 2010.* http://news.target.com/phoenix. zhtml?c=196187&p=irol-newsArticle&ID=883195&highlight=amazon, accessed March 29, 2008.

[46]D'Innocenzio, A. 2006. Once Partners, Amazon.com and Toysrus.com Become Rivals. *USA Today* (October 5). http://www.usatoday.com/tech/news/2006-10-05-amazon-toysrus_x.htm?POE=TECISVA, accessed March 21, 2008.

[47]Chesborough, H., & Teece, D. 1996. When Is Virtual Virtuous? Organizing for Innovation. *Harvard Business Review* (January–February): 65–73. See excerpt at http://harvardbusinessonline.hbsp.harvard.edu/hbsp/hbr/articles/article. jsp?articleID=R0208J&ml_action=get-article&print=true, accessed January 12, 2008.

[48]Case written by Frank Piller (2008). In Anne Huff (ed.), *Leading Open Innovation.* Munich, Germany: Peter-Pribilla-Foundation. Available at http://www.lulu.com.

12 Providing Leadership

As a reader of this book, you are likely to have leadership skills that help you identify a positive course of action and persuade others to follow your lead. Or perhaps you have the managerial ability to add detail to and execute an idea that others have more loosely identified. We conclude this book by giving more attention to both critical roles, but emphasize the importance of leadership because (as you know from reading previous chapters) we believe your personal contributions to the organization you join are important and we want you to pay attention to what leaders around you are trying to accomplish.

We believe the ability to find and develop leadership talent at multiple levels is important in both new and existing organizations. More than ever before, leaders are needed to coordinate responses to situations that those at the top cannot fully anticipate. It is the responsibility of today's leaders, especially those in positions of authority, to make sure that this depth of talent is in place.

• •

In this chapter, we focus on answers to the following questions to support this important strategic activity:

What are contemporary definitions of leadership?
Discovering mutual meaning that can support change when necessary
The responsibility of a top management team and other leaders

What are the most important activities of strategic leaders?
Articulate and execute a vision
Establish a supportive culture
Invest in human capital

How are high-performance organizations created and maintained?
Communicate high expectations
Support leaders throughout the organization
Establish leadership systems

Muhammad Yunus exhibits many of the leadership capabilities that we will discuss in this chapter. He established an incredibly successful organization based on an idea that almost everyone around him thought was impossible and expanded it into a worldwide association over the next thirty years. The details can be found on the website of the Grameen Bank.

• •

LOANING MONEY TO THOSE WITHOUT CREDIT: AN IMPORTANT CONTRIBUTION TO WORLD PEACE

In 1974, Muhammad Yunus, a Bangladeshi economist from Chittagong University, led his students on a field trip to a poor village. They interviewed a woman who made bamboo stools, and learned that she had to borrow the equivalent of 15 [pence] to buy raw bamboo for each stool made. After repaying the middleman, sometimes at rates as high as 10 percent a week, she was left with a penny profit margin. Had she been able to borrow at more advantageous rates, she would have been able to amass an economic cushion and raise herself above subsistence level. Realizing that there must be something terribly wrong with the economics he was teaching, Yunus took matters into his own hands and from his own pocket lent the equivalent of £17 to forty-two basket weavers. He found that it was possible with this tiny amount not only to help them survive, but also to create the spark of personal initiative and enterprise necessary to pull themselves out of poverty.[1]

From this first experience, Yunus gradually developed the idea of the Grameen Bank, which makes small loans to individuals who are clustered in groups of five prospective borrowers. Initially only two of the five receive a loan. The branch manager observes the group for a month to see if the members are conforming to the rules of the bank. Only if the first two borrowers begin to repay the principal plus interest over a period of six weeks do the other members of the group become eligible themselves for a loan. As a result there is substantial group pressure to repay the loans. The Grameen Bank believes that the collective responsibility of the group serves as the collateral on the loan.

Loans are small, but sufficient to finance projects such as rice husking, machine repairing, purchase of rickshaws, buying of milk cows, and making cloth and pottery. As of 2007, the Grameen Bank had 7 million borrowers, with 2,381 branches in more than 75,000 villages. Ninety-seven percent of the borrowers are women. Yunus found that they had the highest rate of repayment and were most likely to use their profit to help their families. The Grameen Bank has a monthly average loan disbursement of $58.9 million with a repayment rate of 98 percent. The Grameen Bank Replication Program (GBRP) facilitates 138 microcredit programs in thirty-seven countries, and many other organizations have adopted the idea of making small loans at reasonable rates to the poor as a means of economic development.

The significance of Muhammad Yunus's effort was recognized by the 2006 Nobel Peace Prize. The announcement indicated that

> Muhammad Yunus has shown himself to be a leader who has managed to translate visions into practical action for the benefit of millions of people. . . . Loans to poor people without any financial security had appeared to be an impossible idea. From modest beginnings three decades ago, Yunus . . . developed micro-credit into an ever more important instrument in the struggle against poverty. Grameen Bank has been a source of ideas and models for the many institutions in the field of micro-credit that have sprung up

around the world. . . . [They have] proved to be an important liberating force in societies where women in particular have to struggle against repressive social and economic conditions. . . . Yunus's long-term vision is to eliminate poverty in the world. That vision cannot be realized by means of micro-credit alone. But Muhammad Yunus and Grameen Bank have shown that, in the continuing efforts to achieve it, micro-credit must play a major part.[2]

The combination of a compelling idea and the capacity to develop and replicate it makes this a good example of leadership for all kinds of organizations—including profit-making firms.

WHAT ARE CONTEMPORARY DEFINITIONS OF LEADERSHIP?

Muhammad Yunus's achievements depend on attention to detail. For example, the philosophy of the Grameen Bank is articulated in sixteen decisions that are pictorially presented so they can be understood by those who do not read. Attention is spent on the family and community impacts of microcredit as well as banking basics of repayment.[3] His leadership, in short, cannot be totally separated from tasks that fall into the categories of management and supervision.

All three of these roles have similarities in that they involve working with people to obtain information about an organization's goals. However, leadership usually involves seeking and implementing adaptive change, whereas management and supervision are focused on providing stability and consistency.

However, *leaders* raise questions about what should be done and why and then try to answer them. They influence others and create visions for change.[4] *Managers* turn these ideas into practice, assigning individuals to tasks and helping them understand what should be done and how. It is almost inevitable that problems will arise in day-to-day operations, which are typically addressed by people with *supervisory* responsibilities.[5] Table 12.1 identifies how these roles differ across several important dimensions.

Leaders are responsible for setting direction and aligning and motivating people to obtain organizational goals.

Managers are responsible for staffing and task definition, directing, and controlling.

Supervisors have responsibility for solving immediate task-related problems.

TABLE 12.1 IMPORTANT DIFFERENCES BETWEEN SUPERVISORS, MANAGERS, AND LEADERS

	Supervisor	Manager	Leader
Focus	Problem solving	Doing things right	Doing the right things
Time Perspective	Immediate	Medium-term	Long-term
Analysis	Gaps between desires and outcomes	Who? How?	What? Why?

But what is "direction setting"? During the last twenty years there has been a significant change in ideas about leadership, most important a move away from defining leadership in terms of "command and control." Although this approach, rooted in the requirements of warfare, is occasionally effective, we agree with Wilfred Drath that the primary challenge for practice (and leadership research) now lies to the right in Table 12.2.

TABLE 12.2 EVOLVING MODELS OF LEADERSHIP

	Ancient	Traditional	Modern	Future
Idea of Leadership	Domination	Influence	Common goals	Reciprocal relations
Action of Leadership	Commanding followers	Motivating followers	Creating inner commitment	Mutual meaning making
Focus of Leadership Development	Power of the leader	Interpersonal skills of the leader	Self-knowledge of the leader	Interactions of the group

Source: W. H. Drath, Approaching the Future of Leadership Development. In C. D. McCauley, R. S. Moxley, & E. Van Velsor (eds.), *The Center for Creative Leadership: Handbook of Leadership Development* (San Francisco: Jossey-Bass, 1998), pp. 403–432.

Discovering Mutual Meaning That Can Support Change When Necessary

More specifically, we believe that contemporary leadership is more likely to focus on change. In many organizations, *strategic leaders* need to consider the need for increased flexibility and innovation. They have to discover a point of view that will help themselves and others know when and how to change organizational direction. To do so, leaders often need to create a new organization mindset, one that exploits opportunities and threats that emerge as a result of constant technological and competitive change.[6] This has led to the development of the concept of strategic leadership—that is, leadership focused on positioning the organization in its environment.[7]

> **Strategic leaders anticipate the future, maintain organizational flexibility, and most important, manage through others to reach organizational goals.**

Activities often associated with strategic leadership include creating and communicating a vision of the future; making strategic decisions; developing key competencies and capabilities; developing organizational structures, processes, and controls; selecting and developing the next generation of leaders; sustaining an effective organizational culture; and infusing ethical value systems into an organization's culture. In addition, as discussed in Chapter 9, strategic leaders must manage the organizations external stakeholders, such as representatives of financial institutions, government agencies, customer interest groups, and labor, to ensure that the organization can obtain the resources and legitimacy it needs to continue to survive and succeed.

The Responsibility of a Top Management Team and Other Leaders

Top management teams are small groups with responsibility for key strategic decisions in an organization.

Strategic leadership is embodied in individuals, and we often refer to individual leaders such as Muhammad Yunus. Although it is critical to understand these pivotal individuals, it is often more appropriate to consider strategic leadership as the responsibility of a *top management team*.[8] Strategies can emerge from any level of an organization, but top managers are in a unique position to have the most impact on the organization's overall strategy.

It is impossible for a CEO, or even a top management team, to review all information that is pertinent to a strategic decision. To develop a strategy, top-level managers must understand where the firm, technology, and industry are headed and anticipate the likely actions of competitors and consumers. They are flooded with information—but much of it has questionable reliability. They often feel they have little time to choose a course of action. How can leaders find patterns in the midst of a changing global environment, articulate strategies and action plans, communicate them clearly throughout the organization, experiment, and learn—all quickly enough? It makes sense to draw on others within the organization.

Not only do leaders increasingly need other members of the organization to identify critical information, they also need to recognize them as partners participating in "real time" and continuous strategy formulation and implementation processes.[9] This requires that the top management team delegate more responsibility and empower employees throughout the organization. Control by supervisors and managers becomes less critical as individuals are given the ability to respond to changing competitive conditions quickly as long as they are moving in the general direction defined by organizational strategy.

Shared leadership requires that organization members understand and share a commitment to the organization's goals. The successful strategic leader is the person who inspires and obtains this commitment to transform the organization. The major focus of strategic leaders is increasingly on developing the organization's vision and culture and increasing organization members' skills and abilities. Strategic vision and organization culture set a framework, or decision context, within which organization members make daily tactical decisions that are consistent with chosen strategic directions.[10]

WHAT ARE THE MOST IMPORTANT ACTIVITIES OF STRATEGIC LEADERS?

Leadership is one of many human activities that are easier to describe than define. Therefore the following examples provide some useful detail for understanding the critical skill we hope you are working to develop.

The Best and Worst Leaders

At the end of every year, the *Business Week* staff chooses the top leaders of the year.[11] These are people who build their firms by treating employees well, change corporate cultures, and/or develop and execute successful new strategic plans. At the beginning of 2008, *Business Week* chose Hewlett-Packard's CEO, Mike Hurd, who led HP to an earnings increase of 17 percent as a result of internal housekeeping and improving external connections with both consumers and corporations. The company is praised for "decommoditization"—adding features and improving the look of key products.

In 2006 *Business Week* chose Jim McNerney, who took over a troubled Boeing Corporation after two top executives left the firm as a result of allegations that Boeing was involved in questionable practices dealing with the Pentagon. McNerney quickly implemented a new management culture that focused on ethical practices for the defense division, which resulted in Boeing being able to obtain major new Pentagon contracts. In the commercial division he supported the development of the carbon fiber 787 Dreamliner, which is extremely fuel efficient. Due out in mid-2008, the 787 was unveiled in mid-2007, with more than 500 orders in hand.

In contrast, one of the bad managers picked by *Business Week* is Ray Gilmartin, the former CEO of Merck, the pharmaceuticals firm, who appears to have made a bad situation catastrophic. Merck's best-selling painkiller, Vioxx, had been generating $2.5 billion in annual sales, although there was preliminary evidence that the drug might be raising the risk of heart attacks and strokes. Despite this information, Gilmartin and his executive team argued that the drug was safe and continued to aggressively promote its sale. In September 2004, a study was released that confirmed Vioxx was dangerous, and the drug was taken off the market. Merck's legal liability was initially estimated to be as high as $38 billion.[12] The company, still struggling to regain public confidence, offered to pay $4.85 billion to end thousands of state and federal lawsuits over the painkiller. If accepted, it would be one of the largest drug settlements ever.[13]

This kind of assessment is always risky, and even a few months can provide evidence that might lead to different judgments. But clearly leaders are judged by what they try to do and how they do it. We suggest that leaders who are successful focus on three critical leadership activities: articulating vision, establishing a supportive culture, and investing in human capital.

Articulate and Execute a Vision

Howard Gardner, a nationally known psychologist, has studied how leaders successfully change people's minds—which is what leadership is all about. He concluded that successful leaders must be able to envision an altered state of affairs and then create a convincing narrative that is presented to the people that they hope to change.[14] As briefly mentioned in Chapter 1, *strategic vision* of an altered future can be the glue that holds an organization together. The vision should describe what members of the organization are trying to do and provide an overview of how they are going about it. To the extent that employees share this vision, it provides a general framework that guides decision making. It also gives the organization a yardstick against which they can measure their present performance.

James Collins and Jerry Porras say that vision has two primary components: core ideology and envisioned future.[15] *Core ideology* defines the enduring character of the organization—it defines who the organization is and what it stands for. The core ideology transcends purely economic goals; it establishes broader, more meaningful goals. An example is Akio Morita's statement of Sony's core ideology:

> Sony is a pioneer and never intends to follow others. Through progress, Sony wants to serve the whole world. It shall always be a seeker of the unknown. . . . Sony has a principle of respecting and encouraging one's ability . . . and always tries to bring out the best in a person. This is the vital force of Sony.[16]

Collins and Porras suggest that ideology can be further divided into two parts, which are core values and purpose. *Core values* are guiding principles that the firm will live by. For example, David Packard of Hewlett-Packard shaped the "HP Way"—a set of clearly defined values for organization members that included a deep respect for the individual and a dedication to creating products and services that are affordable, high-quality, and reliable. Core values for participants in Grameen Bank programs include a commitment to improving family housing, diet, and health.

Purpose identifies the organization's fundamental reason for existing. Contrary to recent business school teaching, "maximizing shareholder wealth" was not often a driving force for the firms Collins and Porras studied. Leaders of the outstanding firms they studied articulated a broader, more meaningful purpose, which excited and motivated organization members. Hewlett-Packard is again a good example: its purpose is to make technical contributions for the advancement and welfare of humanity. General Electric's purpose is to improve the quality of life through technology and innovation. These are the kinds of values and purposes that leaders develop to guide and inspire organization members for decades.

Vivid examples help organization members envision the future. Collins's website (http://www.jimcollins.com/lab/buildingVision/p2.html#) uses a statement by Henry Ford as an example:

Strategic vision defines a desirable future concept of what your organization wants to become.

Core ideology defines what the organization is—what its purpose is and what it stands for.

Core values more specifically define principles that guide behavior.

Purpose or the reason a firm exists, must excite and motivate most stakeholders.

> I will build a motor car for the great multitude. . . . It will be so low in price that no man making a good salary will be unable to own one—and enjoy with his family the blessing of hours of pleasure in God's great open spaces. . . . When I'm through everybody will be able to afford one, and everyone will have one. The horse will have disappeared from our highways; the automobile will be taken for granted. . . . [and we will] give a large number of men employment at good wages.

We thought of this statement just before going to press when Ratan Tata, a modern-day Henry Ford from India, announced that his company was ready to produce "the world's cheapest auto," the Tata, for a base price of 100,000 rupees (a little more than $2,000). The announcement was a major move toward making Ford's vision a worldwide reality.[17]

Not all leaders are like Henry Ford, Akio Morita, Ratan Tata, or Muhammad Yunus—willing to spend decades to develop detailed procedures to accomplish their goals. Some leaders seem to think that their primary responsibility is to articulate a vision of the future. In fact, they have to work hard to have their ideas accepted by organization members and made the basis of their activities. Because close supervision over time is impossible for most tasks, employees have to voluntarily follow the vision that leaders articulate. This can be difficult, and asking for support of organizational members often makes those in authority feel vulnerable. However, they need employee commitment and cooperation if the organization is going to be successful.

In his book *The Fifth Discipline: The Learning Organization*, Peter Senge identifies shared vision as one of the most powerful forces in society. He notes that people have a desire to be connected to an important undertaking that is larger than themselves. A critical part of being a strategic leader is communicating the firm's strategic vision to all the firm's stakeholders in a way that makes this connection. Jack Welch provides a compelling description of what is required: "Good leaders create a vision, articulate the vision, passionately own the vision, and relentlessly drive it to completion."[18]

The task is complicated because different stakeholders want different things from the organization. Even people in the same stakeholder group have varied needs and desires. Successful leaders must be attuned to these differences. Table 12.3 provides one particularly influential summary of diverse desires of employees, articulated by MIT professor Ed Schein as "career anchors."[19]

**Worksheet 12.1
Motivation
Alternatives—A
Tool for Strategic
Leaders**
. . . .

We encourage you to consider the implications of these alternatives by going through Worksheet 12.1. It asks you to consider how you are most likely to be motivated as an employee. It will be easiest for you to lead people who are like you, because their needs are similar to your own. The more difficult task, and the one many otherwise impressive leaders are not good at, is leading people who are very different from themselves. It may be easiest to grasp these differences if you think in terms of leading a particular organization with a well-articulated purpose.

TABLE 12.3 SCHEIN'S EIGHT CAREER ANCHORS

Career Anchor	Components
1. Technical/functional competence	Desire to excel (money and promotions do not matter as much as opportunity to improve)
2. General managerial competence	Opposite of anchor 1; desire to learn many functions, synthesize information from many sources, supervise increasingly large number of people
3. Autonomy/independence	Operate according to own rules and procedures Desire freedom more than prestige
4. Security/stability	Value a predictable environment Identify strongly with the organization, at any level
5. Entrepreneurial creativity	Obsessed with need to create, otherwise easily bored
6. Sense of service	Money is not the primary issue; a specific cause is
7. Pure challenge	Seek ever tougher challenges
8. Lifestyle	Work gives freedom to pursue private concerns

Source: E. H. Schein, *Organizational Culture and Leadership* (San Francisco: Jossey-Bass, 2004).

Establish a Supportive Culture

The odds of achieving a challenging vision are significantly increased by a supportive *organizational culture*. As more "rational approaches" to strategy implementation have failed, many corporate executives have spent an increasing amount of time on the development of an effective corporate culture.

Culture is sometimes described as "the way we do things around here." It is a social control system in which shared expectations influence the decisions and behaviors of organization members. An effective corporate culture can hold people together and give them a sense of belonging and purpose. It can establish the consistency that is required to ensure effective implementation of strategy throughout the organization. Culture provides an invisible framework that guides the actions of managers and employees, helping them understand what is expected of them. Newcomers learn about these expectations and ways of doing things primarily from observing what happens around them.

It is impossible for management to observe precisely what individuals or organizational units do or know what individuals have in mind

Organizational culture is an organization's internal work climate, created by shared assumptions, core values, beliefs, norms, and practices of its employees.

when they take an important action or make an important decision. Their assumptions, values, and beliefs will drive their behavior when they are not directly supervised, influenced by the norms and customs they observe around them. In other words, if strategists want employees to behave in a way that is best for the firm, they cannot simply tell people what to do and check to see if they do it. They must try to influence culture.

Research has shown that firms with common values operating in global markets outperform firms with more diverse values.[20] Think about the organization that can draw together expectations and norms around fast response to customers, for example. This is the kind of social norm that is especially important in global corporations, where corporate culture provides an invisible bond to hold together diverse subsidiaries in different countries.

However, culture is a double-edged sword, because it can also inhibit the ability of the firm to be strategically flexible when the environment changes. Changing a corporation's culture to support changing strategy is a time-consuming and difficult task, but it can become a competitive advantage in itself. Lou Gerstner found this out when he became CEO of IBM in 1993 and tried to change well-established company strategy.

Culture Defines the Game

When Lou Gerstner took over IBM, its market share had fallen so low that analysts called for the company to be split up before it went bankrupt. Employees felt entitled to lifetime employment and a complete package of benefits, regardless of their individual performance. They tended to believe that customer needs had already been identified—all they had to do was develop a computer system and ship it. The general definition of customer service was to service those IBM machines on the customer's premises. Employees were not focused on trying to understand customers' changing needs or develop new solutions to fit new needs. Gerstner noted later that "at IBM culture isn't one aspect of the game—it is the game."[21] Because the company seemed unable to create products and services that were valued by customers, Gerstner started by talking to customers and ended up making a very dramatic change at IBM. Customers said they wanted service on the variety of machines they bought. To everyone's surprise, Gerstner helped IBM reinvent itself to respond to that need.[22] The strategy involved providing "complete solutions." An example that shows how far it departed from internal development is the company's support for Linux; IBM invested billions of dollars in services and software based on Linux through the IBM Linux Technology Center.[23]

By 2002, when Gerstner retired, company revenues came more from consulting than from hardware sales. His successor, Sam Palmisano, is listening to employees as carefully as Gerstner listened to customers. According to a recent entry in Wikipedia, the year after Gerstner retired "IBM embarked on an ambitious project to rewrite company values. Using its Jam technology, the company hosted Intranet-based online discussions on key business issues with 50,000 employees over 3 days."

Jam technology uses sophisticated text analysis software (eClassifier) to identify online comments for common theme. As a result of the 2003 Jam, the company values were updated to reflect three . . . views: 'Dedication to every client's success,' 'Innovation that matters—for our company and for the world,' 'Trust and personal responsibility in all relationships.'[24]

A post-Jam Ratings event in 2004, was convened to allow IBMers to develop ideas that supported these corporate values.[25] In 2006, Palmisano launched another jam, called InnovationJam. Its most innovative aspect was that members of IBM employees' families, together with employees from IBM's customers—i.e., most of the world's largest corporations—could join in and discuss future products.[26]

The Jam technology is now becoming a service in itself. The company supported Habitat Jam, "an unprecedented global dialogue that took place on the Internet in December 2005. Sponsored by the Government of Canada in partnership with UN-HABITAT and IBM, the goal of Habitat JAM was to engage, empower and stimulate tens of thousands of global citizens, rich and poor alike, with the ultimate goal of turning ideas into actions. In just over 72 hours, the participants produced over 4,000 pages of dialogue and generated hundreds of actionable ideas on critical issues related to urban sustainability, including ideas for empowering women and the youth and suggestions for the opening of 'technology hubs' to give the urban poor access to meeting space, and the Internet."[27] More recently, IBM announced a Jam to support suppliers of the automotive industry.[28]

Several leadership tasks are involved in creating results like these:

- Leaders (at multiple levels of action) must articulate simple and clear values. It is important that everyone be able to understand these values. Leaders often rely on stories and symbols to convey meanings. McDonald's, for example, uses QSCV to summarize its key values. The acronym stands for *quality* in all ingredients, the fastest possible *service*, highest standards of *cleanliness*, and good *value* for the price. It is expected that these four ideas will influence the practices of every McDonald's restaurant regardless of where it is located in the world.
- Strategic leaders must sincerely believe and continuously practice the values they define. They must lead by example. Employees (and other stakeholders) will quickly observe whether executives are sincere about corporate values or whether

those values are just words. Anyone who has spent some time in different organizations knows how difficult this is. Senior managers often contradict what they say by their actions. It soon becomes clear to the firm's employees that the unspoken values driving behaviors around them are ideas like "follow orders," "do not take risks," and "please the boss." However, in some firms, executives live the values they espouse. For example, Nucor Steel pursues a low-cost provider strategy. Its executives have eliminated perks. They have conservative expense accounts and spartan offices. They do not tolerate waste and constantly scrutinize cost budgets.

- Values and culture must remain consistent and stable over a long period of time. This is not a short-term exercise; it takes time for the culture to become accepted and shared. Perhaps the saddest aspect of organizational life today is "banner fatigue." So many leaders have come and gone, each with a different strategy and a different way of trying to support it, that the next effort has little chance for success. Instead, employees wait out what they see as the latest enthusiasm. Their experience tells them that this effort will not last long.

Invest in Human Capital

Larry Bossidy was a successful CEO who turned around the troubled AlliedSignal and then merged it with Honeywell. During his tenure he increased shareholder return nine times. He identified his key to success as spending 30 to 40 percent of his time recruiting and hiring great leaders during his first two years.[29]

Human capital is the set of skills and abilities found in an organization's employees.

We have already observed that strategists are paying increasing attention to building the firm's *human capital*. Effective strategic leaders maximize employees' skills rather than minimize employee costs. This means that top managers must be sure that managers recruit and select quality employees and invest in training and development to continuously build these assets.

Jim Collins and Jerry Porras reported in *Good to Great* that when they began work, they thought that "great" firms would be those that chose a new vision and strategy and then obtained the commitment of the organization's employees. Instead they found that great firms started by getting great people—"they got the right people on the bus (and the wrong people off the bus) and then they figured out how to drive it."[30]

Southwest Airlines is a great example of a firm that has successfully outmaneuvered competitors such as United Airlines and Delta. Did it do so by clever strategic maneuvers or advanced use of technology? There were some clever uses of new technology, but the key to Southwest's success is typically seen as the capacity to leverage its people.

Southwest Airlines

Southwest Airlines started as a small regional airline in 1971, with three aircraft serving three Texas cities. Today Southwest operates more than 400 aircraft flying to sixty-three cities. In an industry characterized by billions of dollars in losses after the September 11, 2001, terrorist attacks, Southwest continued to report profit.[31]

As noted in previous chapters, Southwest has always pursued a low-cost, low-fare, frequent-flight business strategy. Typical flights are about eighty minutes long and land in underutilized airports located close to major metropolitan areas. As a no-frills carrier, Southwest Airlines does not provide assigned seats or meals.

The mission of Southwest Airlines is articulated in this short statement:

> . . . Southwest Airlines is [dedicated] to the highest quality of Customer Service delivered with a sense of warmth, friendliness, individual pride, and Company Spirit.
>
> To Our Employees: We are committed to provide our Employees a stable work environment with equal opportunity for learning and personal growth. Creativity and innovation are encouraged for improving the effectiveness of Southwest Airlines. Above all, employees will be provided the same concern, respect, and caring attitude within the organization that they are expected to share externally with every Southwest Customer.[32] LUV is our stock exchange symbol, selected to represent our home at Dallas Love Field, as well as the theme of our Employee and Customer relationships.[33]

These basic ideas have been transformed into a corporate culture that creates a competitive advantage other carriers have been unable to imitate: a remarkably productive workforce. Southwest staffs each gate with one attendant and a ground crew of six. Other competitors have three attendants and ground crews of twelve for similar aircraft. Southwest personnel routinely turn around aircraft in fifteen minutes, from the time of the plane's landing to its takeoff. During this short period they change flight crews, unload, and reload about 135 passengers and their baggage, transfer hundreds of pounds of mail, and refuel the plane. Compare these figures to your last experience on another carrier and you will have tangible proof of what the company routinely achieves.

There are many stories concerning how Southwest employees have assisted passengers. An example that we particularly like concerns a passenger who arrived at the airport to go on vacation with his dog. He was told he could not take his dog with him. But rather than have the customer cancel his trip, the gate agent offered to take care of his dog for two weeks so he could enjoy his holiday.

How did Herb Kelleher, until recently CEO of Southwest Airlines, support this achievement? One thing he did was take one day per week to be visible. He served drinks and snacks and told jokes to passengers who were flying Southwest. He exemplified the friendly and fun service that he wanted all Southwest employees to provide.

How Are High-Performance Organizations Created and Maintained?

Some organization observers believe that leadership is not important. They argue that the internal and external environment in which the organization operates largely determines its results. The firm is subject to government, consumer, and competitive actions that it does not control. These observers typically believe that the leader's possible actions and decisions are constrained by existing personnel, political coalitions, and culture.

We have already established that we take the opposite view: leadership is even more important in the new competitive landscape than it was in less interactive environments. Leaders must establish strategic coherence in the organization so that employees' actions and decisions are consistent with the organization's direction. Simultaneously, leaders must ensure that the organization is developing or maintaining its ability to be strategically flexible so that it can respond to changes in technology and competitive interactions.

> **High-performing organizations** do a better job of reliably creating valued outputs than peer organizations.

Nowhere is the role of leadership clearer than in *high-performing organizations*. Herb Kelleher is certainly one example. So is Jack Welch at General Electric, Richard Branson at Virgin, and John Chambers at Cisco Systems. These executives have all consistently focused their time and energy on the people in their organizations. They have been able to establish shared strategic visions and have empowered and energized their respective workforces to achieve consistently better than "normal economic" profits. The key tasks are to communicate high expectations, promote leadership throughout the organization, and establish leadership systems.

Communicate High Expectations

Creating a high-performance organization begins with setting high expectations. Trying to understand what will motivate those around you is only part of the leadership task. What you *do* in interaction is also critical. One critical aspect of behavior is the evidence it provides of your attitude about those around you. The implications of expectation were vividly illustrated by Harvard professor Robert Rosenthal, who told students in his psychology class that he had developed "superintelligent" rats and asked for help testing them. The group with "maze-bright" rats found that their rats improved daily—running faster and more accurately. The second group, who were assigned "dull rats," found that they did not perform well. In fact their rats refused to run the maze used to test their abilities 29 percent of time, while smart rats only refused 11 percent of the time.

But all rats were normal rats, assigned to the students at random! It became obvious in variations of this experiment that students unknowingly communicated their expectations to the rats they tested, leading to differential performance. The research showed that students with "superintelligent" rats liked their rats better. They found them more pleasant to work with, were more relaxed around them, treated them more gently, and were more enthusiastic about the experiment.[34] This *"Pygmalion effect"* (named after the mythological artist who fell in love with the sculpture he created) has been found in many different situations, including classrooms and organizations.

The Pygmalion effect refers to high performance produced by expectations for high performance.

On the downside, supervisors, managers, and leaders can unconsciously act to lower the performance of those they work with, precisely as the students with rats they thought were "dull" did some time ago in Professor Rosenthal's experiments. Here are some problematic behaviors:

- Seat low-expectation employees in low-prestige offices far from managers and leaders
- Pay less attention to "Lows"
  - Smile less often
  - Maintain less eye contact
  - Give less information
- Call on "Lows" less often to
  - Give their opinion
  - Give presentations
  - Work on special projects
- Give "Lows" less time to perform
- Provide less help to "Lows" in failure situations
- Criticize "Lows" more frequently/praise them less frequently
- Demand less work and effort from "Lows" than "Highs"
- Interrupt "Lows" more frequently than "Highs"
- Provide feedback on job performance to "Lows" that is
  - Less frequent
  - Less accurate
  - Less detailed[35]

Not surprisingly, research also has shown that leaders, managers, and supervisors with high expectations help create the results they hope for. Leaders who want to achieve the most from those they work with use the following approaches:

- *Decentralization and Delegation*: Decentralize control and reduce the number of levels of management; delegate some responsibility and decision making to others.
- *Job Enlargement*: Broaden the scope of an employee's job to add variety and create opportunities to satisfy ego needs.
- *Participation Management*: Consult with employees in the decision-making process to tap their creative capacity and provide them with some control over their work environment.

Effective actions in these areas are likely to inspire followers to be involved in their tasks and focus on group and organizational goals rather than their more selfish concerns. When successful in achieving distinctive results, leaders are sometime called *transformational leaders*. They make managerial decisions that lead those who work for them to generate impressive results.

What makes a spirit of high performance come alive? According to Charles O'Reilly and Jeffrey Pfeffer, it is the reinforcing and consistent set of organization practices—values, staffing, training, information sharing, team-based organization, and reward systems.[36]

> **Transformational leaders** are able to inspire others to work beyond their previous levels of accomplishment.

1. These firms tend to have *horizontal structures* with few boundaries between departments and divisions. The building blocks for getting work done are *self-managed teams.* These firms believe that teams are the most effective way to stimulate creativity and individual energy. In addition, they create a sense of ownership or belonging and accountability.

2. High-performing firms are *customer-focused*. They understand the importance of speed in solving problems to provide a better product or service to their clients. These organizations are therefore constantly looking for ways to break down the barriers between their internal departments, customers, and suppliers so that they can be in closer and more constant contact.

3. As we have already discussed, great firms establish strong vision, values, and culture. They are intensely *people oriented*. They reinforce the value they place on their people in every way conceivable, especially by treating them with respect and dignity. These firms spend considerable resources in developing their employees' skills and knowledge. Managers are held accountable for training and coaching their subordinates.

4. High performance firms *share information* concerning the operations and finances of the firm. The assumption is that if employees are going to contribute to the decision-making process of the firm, they must understand in detail how the firm is doing and what it is trying to do. For example, at Southwest, all employees have access to critical data concerning aircraft

turnaround times, lost baggage, customer complaints, and on-time performance.

5. Strategic management is most important. The different things that leaders do are *aligned*; values, strategies, systems, culture, and core competencies of the firm point in the same direction. The senior management team helps people in the organization understand how what they do makes a difference. These executives do not get lost by focusing on managing the day-to-day business, or conversely by formulating grand strategy. Instead, they set and reinforce the vision, values, and culture of the organization.

Support Leaders throughout the Organization

We believe that a "pipeline" of leadership talent is also critical to high performance. Ram Charan, Jim Noel, and Steve Drotter suggest that "[e]stablishing a leadership pipeline is a key competitive advantage. . . . Companies that can grow their own leadership at all levels and recognize the unique requirements at each level will have a decided edge." Their approach aims for systematic strategic leadership development. It is based on the key idea that what is needed at one level of leadership is not what is needed at other levels, as summarized in Figure 12.1.

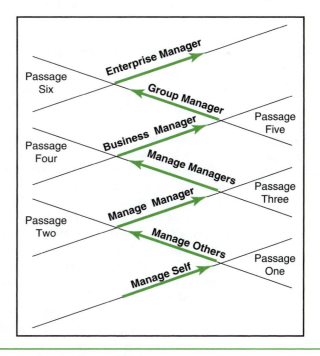

Figure 12.1 — The Leadership Pipeline

Source: R. Charan, S. Drotter, & J. Noel, *The Leadership Pipeline* (San Francisco: Jossey-Bass, 2001), pp. 7, 145.

According to the authors, "each passage requires that people acquire a new way of managing and leading and leave the old ways behind" in the following three areas:

- Skill requirements—the new capabilities required to execute new responsibilities.
- Time applications—new time frames that govern how one works.
- Work values—what people believe is important and so becomes the focus of their effort.

> The challenge for organizations is to make sure that people in leadership positions are assigned to the level appropriate to their skills, time applications, and values. . . . If you keep the metaphor of a pipeline in mind, you can see how things might become clogged at the turns. Imagine a company where more than half the managers at each turn are operating with skills, time applications, and values inappropriate to their level; either they've skipped a level and never learned what they need to know or they're clinging to an old mode of managing that was successful for them in the past.[37]

In Worksheet 12.2, you will assess your own capabilities in these areas.

Worksheet 12.2 Capabilities of Middle Managers—A Tool for Assessing Strategic Leadership

Establish Leadership Systems

The development of leadership talent throughout an organization is not primarily a matter of charisma, but of *leadership systems* that connect and align employee selection, appraisal, reward, and development. Organizations of any size have at least rudimentary systems in place. The question for leaders is how these routines can be strengthened and aligned with strategy.

Corporate leadership systems were the subject of a recent two-year study of thirty-seven large multinationals in Germany, Great Britain, the United States, and the Netherlands. The companies came from a broad range of industries, including automobile (e.g., BMW, DaimlerChrysler), IT, electronics and software (e.g., Cisco Systems, HP, IBM, Philips, SAP), telecommunications services (e.g., BT, Deutsche Telekom), energy (e.g., Chevron Texaco, E.On), risk, insurance and financial services (e.g., Allianz, Deutsche Bank, JP Morgan Chase, Liberty Mutual, Marsh, Munich Re), systems and solutions (e.g., BAE Systems, Siemens), and travel/tourism (e.g., Lufthansa, TUI). The study found that the companies contacted used a broad range of tools and processes to support the management of their leaders. They differed in the extent to which these practices were implemented and integrated, but showed common patterns as of the overall design of the leadership systems in place.

Leadership systems are organizational routines for selection, support, and evaluation of leaders at multiple levels within the organization.

Figure 12.2 shows the generic pattern that can be used to describe the core fields addressed by corporate leadership systems:

- Identify leadership talents and promote them to excellence (selection of leaders and leadership development)
- Support executives in their everyday tasks (leadership as a day-to-day interactive process)
- Evaluate and measure leadership performance (leadership metrics)
- Use the evaluation results more broadly in order to develop leadership as a systemic capacity in the organisation (leadership deployment)

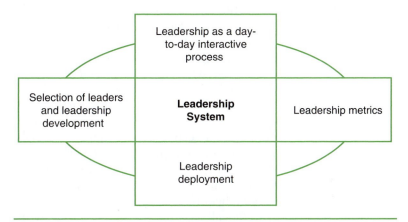

Figure 12.2 — Leadership Systems that Support Performance

Source: A. S. Huff & K. Möslein, An Agenda for Understanding Individual Leadership in Corporate Leadership Systems. In C. Cooper (ed.), *Leadership and Management in the 21st Century* (Oxford, England: Oxford University Press, 2005), pp. 248–270.

CONCLUSIONS FOR THE STRATEGIST

As can be seen by the dramatic increase in CEO salaries, effective leadership is in high demand. However, leadership of any organization—large or small, profit or nonprofit, high-tech or low-tech—is not an easy task. There is no "one size fits all" solution or style that is successful for every person in every situation. Great leaders often have very different styles. The last three successful CEOs of GE have been Reginald Jones, who was known as a statesman; Jack Welch, a dynamic change agent; and Jeff Immelt, a leader who empowers his top management team. That's an interesting example of our primary point: effective leadership styles have to fit a specific context or situation and need to change over time. Warren Bennis, one of the leading scholars on leadership, also suggests that how a person responds to context separates managers versus leaders: "I tend to think of the differences between leaders and managers as those who master the context and those who surrender to it."[38]

Leadership development and training is a growth industry. There is no shortage of books written by scholars and business leaders calling for a new leadership style to be compatible with current organization needs. Writers question whether organizations can be managed with a traditional top-down, command-and-control approach. Today it is generally accepted that leadership is needed at all levels of the organization.[39] As a result, a critical task of leadership is to empower and develop organization members to move beyond their self-interests for the greater good of the group, the organization, or society.[40]

Consistent with that call, dozens of best-selling business books prescribe a transformational (Warren Bennis), authentic (Bill George), or servant leadership style (Richard Greenleaf). Gary Hamel's new book, *The Future of Management*, discusses the importance of creating a community of purpose within the organization. Common purpose gives meaning, motivation, and coherence to organization members' actions and behaviors.[41]

For Bill George, former chairman and CEO of Medtronic, a $12 billion medical equipment manufacturer, leaders must have high integrity, possess a deep sense of purpose, and display the courage to build and change their organization so that it is better able to meet the needs of all of its stakeholders.[42] He also emphasizes that today's employees demand a more personal relationship with their leaders before they will commit themselves to the organization's vision and purpose.

Although these ideas can be appealing, we need to repeat our warning that there is no "silver bullet" solution to identifying leadership styles or behaviors that work in more than one situation. Although we cannot identify an optimal style, we have discussed the tasks strategic leaders need to address in every organization, especially paying attention to strategic vision, corporate culture, and development of human talent.

Key Concepts

Organizations exist to help multiple individuals work together to achieve a desired outcome. This chapter distinguishes three important roles that help that happen. **Supervisors** have responsibility for solving immediate task-related problems. **Managers** are responsible for staffing and task definition. **Leaders** are responsible for positioning the organization in its environment. They do not work alone. The **top management team** is responsible for key strategic decisions.

Today's turbulent environment requires **strategic leaders** whose most important tasks include developing their firm's **strategic vision,** creating a supportive **organizational culture** and building **human capital.** This is a powerful mental image of what the organization can and should be in the future. It defines what the organization is—its **core ideology**—which consists of **core values** or principles that guide behavior and purpose.

The **purpose** of a firm, or its reason to exist, must excite and motivate most stakeholders. But leaders do much more than verbalize a mission statement. They must be aware of the **Pygmalion effect,** which refers to the likelihood that performance outcomes will be influenced by their expectations (positive or negative) and related behaviors. **Transformational leaders** inspire others to work beyond their previous levels of accomplishment. Their tasks include fostering an **organizational culture** of shared assumptions, values, beliefs, norms, and customs that affect employees' activities and decisions. **High-performing organizations** do a better job at creating valued outputs by these and other means than peer organizations. They do this more effectively via **leadership systems** that routinize the selection, support, and evaluation of leaders at multiple levels within the organization.

Questions for Further Reflection

1. Do you think that the characteristics of an ideal leader are changing?

2. Think of a diversified firm operating in several countries (Nestlé, for example). Should it choose different kinds of leaders for different products? For different regions of the world?

WORKSHEET 12.1
Motivation Alternatives—A Tool for Strategic Leaders

Consider how you can be motivated and how you can motivate others.

Step 1: Choose three descriptions of what you want from work from the career anchors listed in column 1.

Step 2: How could a manager motivate you to achieve these three goals? Write your ideas in column 2.

Step 3: Now examine the other five competencies in which you are less interested. How would you motivate employees who are interested in these five competencies? Put your answers in column 3.

ALTERNATIVES:

- Think of an example from a work experience in which a manager motivated you to perform your task. What specific things did he or she do?
- Think of a situation in which you were not motivated to complete a task. If you had to manage yourself in that situation, what would you do?

Motivation Alternatives Worksheet 12.1	Strategy Summary:	
Career Anchors	**How Could a Manager Motivate You to Achieve These Goals?**	**How Would You Motivate Others to Achieve These Goals?**
Technical/functional competence		
General managerial competence		
Autonomy/indepen-dence		
Security/stability		
Entrepreneurial creativity		
Service		
Challenge		
Lifestyle		

Consider the leadership opportunities of a middle manager.

Step 1: Identify a middle manager who is willing to talk about his or her experience. (Or, if you have middle management experience, interview yourself.)

Step 2: In Part 1 of the worksheet, read each of the statements in column 1.

Step 3: Ask your respondent to indicate how frequently he or she has observed each activity in his or her organization. Record the answers in column 2, using 1 = never, 2 = rarely, 3 = occasionally, 4 = regularly, and 5 = frequently.

Step 4: Now ask your respondent how frequently each activity *should* be performed. Record the responses in column 3 using the same scale: 1 = never, 2 = rarely, 3 = occasionally, 4 = regularly, and 5 = frequently.

Step 5: In Part 2, add up the totals for each row. Circle the row with the greatest number of points, the recommended role.

Step 6: Read the description of the recommended role and advice. Discuss how this advice might be put into action and put your answers in column 4.

Capabilities of Middle Managers Worksheet 12.2	**Role:**
Organization:	**Summary:**

Part 1: Assessment of Current and Required Activities in Your Organization.

1 = Never　　2 = Rarely　　3 = Occasionally	4 = Regularly	5 = Frequently
	Currently	**Required**
	In your experience, how frequently have you observed the following activities in your organiza- tion?	In your opinion, how frequently should the follow- ing activities be performed at your organization?
1. Monitor and assess the impact of changes in the organization's external environment.		
2. Implement action plans designed to meet top management objectives.		
3. Integrate information from a variety of sources to communicate its strategic significance.		
4. Evaluate the merits of new initiatives and approaches that allow the firm to do different things.		
5. Evaluate the merits of initiatives and approaches generated in my unit, encouraging some, and discouraging others.		
6. Translate organizational goals into objectives for individuals.		
7. Provide a safe haven for experimental programs.		
8. Assess and communicate the business-level implications of new information to higher-level managers.		
9. Search for new opportunities and bring them to the attention of higher-level managers.		
10. Communicate and sell top management initiatives to subordi- nates.		
11. Define and justify the role of new programs or processes to upper-level managers.		
12. Encourage multidisciplinary problem-solving teams.		
13. Proactively seek information about your business from custom- ers, suppliers, competitors, business publications, and so on.		
14. Monitor and communicate to higher-level managers the activities of competitors, suppliers, and other outside organizations.		
15. Justify to higher-level managers programs that have already been established.		
16. Provide resources and develop objectives/strategies for unofficial projects.		
17. Translate organizational goals into departmental action plans.		
18. Relax regulations and procedures in order to get new projects started.		
19. Propose new programs or projects to higher-level managers.		
20. Monitor activities within your unit to ensure that they support top management objectives.		

Part 2: Determine Appropriate Role and Action Items.

Rows	Total	Role	Advice	Actions You Can Take
4, 9, 11, 15, & 19		Champion strategic alternatives	Persistent and persuasive communication of proposals that either provide the firm with new capabilities or allow the firm to use existing capabilities differently.	
1, 3, 8, 13, & 14		Synthesize information	Derive strategic meaning from operational information and communicate it to top management.	
5, 7, 12, 16, & 18		Facilitate adaptability	Encourage cross-functional problem solving, experimentation, and learning, and create arrangements that increase organizational flexibility.	
2, 6, 10, 17, & 20		Implement deliberate strategy	Align your organization's actions with the firm's strategic intent.	

NOTES

[1] *Banker to the Poor: Autobiography of Prof. Muhammad Yunus, Founder of the Grameen Bank.* http://www.grameen-info.org/book/index.htm, accessed October 19, 2006.

[2] Announcement on the Grameen Bank website, http://www.grameen-info.org/Media/mediadetail6.html, accessed November 3, 2007.

[3] http://www.grameen-info.org/bank/index.html, accessed November 3, 2007.

[4] Kotter, J. P. 1990. *A Force for Change: How Leadership Differs from Management.* New York: Free Press.

[5] In very small organizations, leadership, management, and supervision can be carried out by the same individual, as Muhammad Yunus did before the Grameen Bank was established. But in this chapter we will focus on leadership as a separate and critical aspect of organizing, typified by Yunus's more recent activities.

[6] Ireland, D., & Hitt, M. 1999. Achieving and Maintaining Strategic Competitiveness in the 21st Century: The Role of Strategic Leadership. *Academy of Management Executive* 13(1): 43–57.

[7] Ireland & Hitt, Achieving and Maintaining Strategic Competitiveness.

[8] Finkelstein, S., & Hambrick, D. 1996. *Strategic Leadership: Top Executives and Their Effects on Organizations.* St. Paul, MN: West; Hmieleski, K., & Ensley, M. D. 2007. A Contextual Examination of New Venture Performance: Entrepreneur Leadership Behavior, Top Management Team Heterogeneity and Environmental Dynamism. *Journal of Organizational Behavior* (forthcoming).

[9] Ensley, M. D., Hmieleski, K. M., & Pearce, C. L. 2006. The Importance of Vertical and Shared Leadership within New Venture Top Management Teams: Implications for the Performance of Startups. *Leadership Quarterly* 17(3): 217–231.

[10] Baum, J. R., Locke, E. A., & Kirkpatrick, S. A. 1998. A Longitudinal Study of the Relation of Vision and Vision Communication to Venture Growth in Entrepreneurial Firms. *Journal of Applied Psychology* 83(1): 43–54.

[11]The Best & Worst of 2006. *Business Week* (December 18). http://www.businessweek.com/magazine/content/06_51/b4014001.htm, accessed March 24, 2008.

[12]Merck's Vioxx Liability Could Reach $38 Billion. 2004. *Forbes* (December 3). http://www.forbes.com/markets/bonds/2004/12/03/1203automarketscan13.html, accessed March 24, 2008; Berenson, A. 2006. Merck Suffers a Pair of Setbacks over Vioxx. 2006. *New York Times* (August 8). http://www.nytimes.com/2006/08/18/business/18merck.html?ex=1161489600&en=696c654d8999dec7&ei=5070, accessed March 24, 2008.

[13]Merck to Pay $4.85 Billion over Vioxx Suits: Drug Firm Will Settle Thousands of Claims Drug Fatal, or Injured Users. 2007. MSNBC (November 9). http://www.msnbc.msn.com/id/21701212/, accessed January 29, 2008.

[14]Gardner, H. 2006. *Changing Minds.* Boston: Harvard Business School Press.

[15]Collins, J., & Porras, J. 1994. *Built to Last: Successful Habits of Visionary Companies.* New York: HarperCollins.

[16]Collins & Porras, *Built to Last,* p. 51.

[17]Chang, R. S. 2008. Tata Nano: The World's Cheapest Car. *New York Times* (January 8). http://wheels.blogs.nytimes.com/2008/01/10/tata-nano-the-worlds-cheapest-car/?hp, accessed January 12, 2008.

[18]Bartlett, C., & Wozny, M. 2002. *GE's Two-Decade Transformation: Jack Welch's Leadership.* Boston: Harvard Business School Press.

[19]Schein, E. H. 1990. *Career Anchors: Discovering Your Real Values.* San Diego, CA: Pfeiffer.

[20]O'Reilly, C., & Pfeffer, J. 2000. *Hidden Value: How Great Companies Achieve Extraordinary Results with Ordinary People.* Boston: Harvard Business School Press.

[21]Gerstner, L. 2002. *Who Says Elephants Can't Dance?* New York: HarperCollins, p. 183.

[22]Lundquist, E. 2003. Gerstner's Vision Got IBM on Course. *eWeek* (February). http://www.findarticles.com/p/articles/mi_zdewk/is_200202/ai_ziff22344.

[23]http://en.wikipedia.org/wiki/IBM#history, accessed March 24, 2008.

[24]http://en.wikipedia.org/wiki/IBM#history, accessed March 24, 2008.

[25]Palmisano, S., Hemp, P., & Stewart, T. 2004. Leading Change When Business Is Good: The HBR Interview—Samuel J. Palmisano. *Harvard Business Review* (December 1).

[26]http://en.wikipedia.org/wiki/IBM#History, accessed March 24, 2008.

[27]http://www.ibm.com/news/ca/en/2006/06/2006_06_20.html, accessed March 24, 2008.

[28]http://www.ibm.com/news/be/en/2007/02/27_3.html, accessed January 12, 2008.

[29]Bossidy, L. 2001. The Job No CEO Should Delegate. *Harvard Business Review* (March): 119–121.

[30]Collins, J. 2001. *Good to Great.* New York: HarperCollins, p. 41.

[31]Schlangenstein, M. 2005. Southwest Airlines Profit Jumps: Lower Fuel Costs Let Carrier Nearly Triple Its Bottom Line. *Washington Post* (April 15). http://www.washingtonpost.com/wp-dyn/articles/A55140-2005Apr14.html, accessed March 24, 2008.

[32]http://www.southwest.com/about_swa/mission.html, accessed March 31, 2008.

[33]http://www.southwest.com, accessed November 3, 2007; O'Reilly, & Pfeffer, *Hidden Value.*

[34]http://www.psichi.org/pubs/articles/article_121.asp, accessed March 24, 2008.

[35]http://en.wikipedia.org/wiki/Pygmalion_effect, accessed March 24, 2008.

[36]O'Reilly & Pfeffer, *Hidden Value;* Elenkov, D. S., Judge, W., & Wright, P. 2005. Strategic Leadership and Executive Innovation Influence: An International Multi-Cluster Comparative Study. *Strategic Management Journal* 26(7): 665–682.

[37]Charan, R., Drotter, S., & Noel, J. 2001. *The Leadership Pipeline*. San Francisco: Jossey-Bass, pp. 7, 145.

[38]Bennis, W. 1986. *The Strategies for Taking Charge*. New York: Harper & Row.

[39]Western, S. 2008. *Leadership: A Critical Text*. London: Sage.

[40]Bass, B. 1990. From Transactional to Transformational Leadership: Learning to Share the Vision. *Organizational Dynamics* 18: 19–31.

[41]Hamel, G. 2007. *The Future of Management*. Boston: Harvard Business School Press.

[42]George, B. 2003. *Authentic Leadership*. San Francisco: Jossey-Bass.

13

Personal Strategizing

All of us want to achieve something important—though definitions of success vary significantly. For some, success is defined by salary size and physical goods. For others, recognition or fame lights the fire. Perhaps you want to make a difference in the lives of others because of the work you do. Or your most important desire may be to have time to pursue activities outside work. Most of us want to combine all of these desirable things. Our efforts and their outcomes are shaped by chance. But most successful people also act strategically; they usually have a conscious plan to develop the skills and experience to reach desired goals and take advantage of unexpected opportunities.

We know that our readers are talented, well educated, and ambitious. You have enormous potential to live a happy and productive life. We believe the ideas found in this book are relevant to making the most of the opportunities you encounter and create during your career. In this epilogue we discuss how strategic management can help you become more successful in your job and promote greater harmony between your work and personal life.

However, you are also entering a work culture and economic era with significant challenges. Today's workers bear greater risk in terms of job security, income, health insurance, and retirement than recent generations. As we have discussed throughout the book, the current and future environment has rarely been so uncertain. One consequence of this uncertainty is that employees are more likely to experience career disruptions.

As you probably already know, the emotional and economic links between employees and employers are weakening, and workers are increasingly responsible for managing their own careers. Opportunities for personal development will not be handed to you. The overall direction of your continuing education is your responsibility. You will need to intelligently formulate your career plans and frequently revise them based on new information and emerging opportunities. We hope you can choose employers who facilitate these efforts.

· ·

This epilogue will help you think about answers to the following questions:

What are the trends shaping future work opportunities?
Growth industries
Smaller, more entrepreneurial firms and more entrepreneurial workers
A global labor market

WHAT ARE THE TRENDS SHAPING FUTURE WORK?

Just as strategists in a company need to continually scan their environment, individuals need to continually identify and analyze the implications of major trends in the national and international economy, their firm, and the industry. As the strategist in charge of your own career, you should compare emerging opportunities and threats against your career objectives and the nature of your current job. The objective is to identify additional skills and abilities you need to succeed in the future you want for yourself.

Three trends are especially important to your career planning: differential growth in the economy, increasing entrepreneurship, and globalization of labor markets.

Read

Growth Industries

Economic activity has always changed the fortunes of companies and their employees. As some economic activities grow, others decline and ultimately disappear. For example, typewriters have become obsolete, family farms have largely disappeared, and a host of businesses as diverse as newspapers, recording companies, and travel agencies have been diminished by the Internet. What's next? Few careers are as secure as they once were. If you are an accountant, as just one telling example, you should know that in 2006 nearly 400,000 U.S. tax returns were processed by accountants in India, and by 2011 the estimates for how many tax returns will be processed in India range from 1.6 million to more than 20 million![1]

Although a limited number of opportunities remain in stable or declining industries, on balance the job outlook is not attractive when the revenue stream is shrinking. In declining industries, the law of supply and demand works against you—driving wages down and depressing opportunities for advancement.

It therefore makes sense to seek employment in industries that have future growth potential. Robert Reich, labor secretary during the Clinton administration, identified domains he expected to offer increasing employment opportunities.[2] The logic he uses, based on so-cial and technological trends, is as instructive as the specific industries.

- The first opportunity should be obvious—**health care,** the largest industry in the United States. According to the U.S. Department of Labor, more new jobs—about 19 percent, or 3.6 million—will be created in health care between 2004 and 2014 than in any other industry.[3] That's because millions of aging baby boomers will need more attention. They tend to be demanding, but eager to purchase new products that may help them live longer and improve the way they feel. At the same time, medical science is continuing to develop new products for the population as a whole, and innovations in treatment (from new forms of drug delivery to cosmetic surgery in Dubai) also contribute to overall employment growth. Other opportunities are fueled by a grow-ing crisis in basic health care in poorer countries. In addition to service providers, there is a need for research and delivery pro-grams to address persistent diseases[4]—and of course expansion in each of these areas will require management skills.
- A very different opportunity can be found in the **entertainment** industry. Almost 2 million people are employed in this sector, but 85 percent are in establishments that employ fewer than 20 people.[5] The opportunities for growth come from consum-ers searching for new experiences. They expect greater access to video and audio creations of all kinds, more engaging live theater, and interactive art exhibits and museums, among many other kinds of diversions. The industries seeking to meet these needs are becoming more global as companies bring novel content to current consumers and try to entice new ones.[6]

The growing entertainment content of other products and services is perhaps even more important. Entertainment is an increasing part of a very wide range of activities, including hands-on scientific education and extreme sports. It is hard to know what will be attractive in a few years, given the trendy nature of some forms of entertainment, but it is worth thinking about pleasure-seeking as a continuing driver of consumption.

- **Personal care** is a third growth industry. We live in a world infused with the desire to be attractive and fit. Dietary supple-ments, fashionable sportswear, nutriceuticals, anti-aging creams, and hair replacement/removal are all part of a growing inventory that is blurring the line between beauty and health. Already, botox treatments, laser eye surgery and liposuction are mass marketed. As disposable incomes increase, growth in this sector is expected to accelerate.

- A fourth area of opportunity involves **intellectual stimulation.** In addition to the increasing need for formal education and training of all kinds, lifelong learning is on the rise, and new delivery mechanisms are being developed to meet this need.[7] For example, a U.S. survey found that more than 3.5 million people were taking online courses in 2006.[8] In many ways, ongoing education has become non-negotiable, because technology and the abilities required to understand and utilize it are changing so quickly. Learning also is changing in form. It is often part of work; in fact, companies now spend more on education than institutions of higher learning. Learning is also becoming more interactive, and many new players are entering the market in response to the transformation of traditional learning models.
- The fifth area of growth is driven by the desire for **social contact.** People want to be connected, have friends, feel pampered, and be sexually delighted. Many innovations respond to these desires. The relocation of telecommunication and all forms of media from the household to the individual is both a driver and an important outcome of these developments. Think about how cell phones have increased information exchange and impromptu meetings at work and play.

Similar opportunities for social contact are being created in more traditional industries as well. Pharmaceutical firms now host websites that offer people who have a given aliment the opportunity to learn about their condition and interact with one another. Televised news programs encourage viewers to share their opinions in text messages that are sometimes read on the air. Another response to the need to connect can be seen in the growth of reality TV—audiences not only drive the format of the show but expand the experience by interacting in chatrooms. Traffic reporters and news organizations increasingly rely on reports from private parties; the response is more than altruistic, it is a way of connecting with other drivers. The growing popularity of websites like MySpace not only emphasize the growing importance of this aspect of current culture but point to a growing source of career opportunity.

- A related area of growth is found in Reich's sixth area: products and services that help us obtain **financial security.** As people age they tend to increase their personal wealth and have more money to invest. In addition, as a result of more employees having to fund their own pension and health care needs, more people are investing in the bond and stock markets. Insurance and investment planning are two examples of products and services that respond to this need. This significant driver of globalization makes this area a worldwide opportunity.

Our advice to think about long-term growth when making career plans may seem obvious, but many people do not spend enough time taking a broad and long-range view of their job decisions. Niche opportunities can be found in unexpected places, even in declining industries. For example, even though the recording industry as a whole saw revenues decline by more than 20 percent from 1999 to 2006,[9] for example, workers with the technical and design skills required to help major record companies move to the Internet have enjoyed plenty of opportunity.

Our advice is to lean toward growth industries, but whatever industry you enter, in today's economy jobs cannot be expected to last forever. It therefore makes sense to think about how your skills can be transferred from one job to another. Ask yourself the questions we asked about companies in Chapter 2:

- What resources will I need over my career and how can I collect them?
- Do I have the capabilities needed for the job market I hope to enter?
- Am I fully utilizing them?
- What (if anything) is my competitive advantage?
- How long will it last?

A career-based resource analysis (using the worksheets found in Chapter 2) may be a good way to start thinking about your career.

Smaller, More Entrepreneurial Firms and More Entrepreneurial Workers

Fewer than 1 in 10 Americans are employed by a Fortune 500 firm. Even more interesting, 97.5 percent of all the businesses in the United States employ fewer than twenty employees.[10] This is largely a positive picture; from 1980 to 2005, the U.S. Small Business Administration reported that 65 percent of all new jobs were created by small businesses, while the proportion of job growth from small entrepreneurial firms is even higher in emerging economies.[11] Calculating the benefits of this growth to employees is somewhat controversial because of "churning"—new small businesses open, contract, and close more frequently than larger more established firms. However, no one doubts the importance of small business to the world economy. Small businesses can respond more quickly to market changes than most large firms and consistently account for many innovations.

Smaller firms are not necessarily mom-and-pop corner-store businesses. We've already mentioned that most entertainment firms are small, but did you know that more than 90 percent of all engineering firms employ four people or fewer? As a result of information technology and the Internet, small firms can successfully compete against major international corporations. According to the U.S. Small Business Administration, from 2000 to 2004 the number of small business incorporations grew at five times the rate of population growth.

One of the reasons for this dramatic growth is corporate outsourcing and increasing use of contracted employees. Management thinker Daniel Pink calls these independent workers "free agents." He says:

> They are free from the bonds of a large institution, and agents of their own futures. They are the new archetypes of work in America. Today . . . America's new emblem is the footloose, independent worker—the tech-savvy, self-reliant, path-charting micropreneur.[12]

Entertainment provides an example of an industry once dominated by major studios that controlled technology, talent, and distribution. Today it is increasingly characterized as a dynamic network of small businesses. Talented individuals and small firms come together for a film project. When it is completed they disband. Each small firm (and individual free agent) has hopefully developed new skills and completed a project that will enhance its reputation so it can bid on the next project. In Los Angeles, the center of this industry in the United States, more than 90 percent of roughly 7,000 entertainment firms employ fewer than ten employees.

But increasingly, this industry has no geographic center. Higglytown Heroes, a television cartoon series, provides an interesting example. The producers have recording studios located near artists in New York City and Los Angeles. Design and production are done in San Francisco. The writers for the series network electronically from their homes in Florida, London, New York, Chicago, Los Angeles, and San Francisco. There are eight different animation teams in Bangalore, India, each working with a different writer. Firms in other industries as diverse as construction, consulting, and even manufacturing are developing similar business models.

A Global Labor Market

In a business landscape of increasingly dispersed microenterprises, one of the most important trends is the globalization of labor markets. This means that all of us are in competition with the best and brightest from all over the world. According to Harvard economist Richard Freeman, in 1985 there were 2.5 billion people involved in world trade and commerce. By 2000, as a result of the collapse of communism and increasingly liberal government economic policies in many countries, the number of people involved in the world economy had increased to 6.5 billion people.[13] Perhaps only 10 percent of these have the education and connectivity to collaborate and compete with the American labor force. However, that 10 percent represents 600 million people — four times the workforce of the United States.

Many knowledge jobs that were formerly held by workers in the United States and a few other well-developed countries are now being carried out by bright, affordable, and productive professionals from a much broader set of countries. Analysts at the consulting firm Forrester Research project that by 2015 more than 3.3 million white-collar jobs and more than $136 billion in wages will shift from the United States to low-wage countries such as India, China, and Russia.[14]

The economic logic for this relocation is hard to refute. In 2004, a chip designer in the United States earned $7,000 per month compared to $1,000 in India. Boeing Aircraft completes a large portion of its aerospace engineering work in Russia, where it pays $650 per month for an aerospace engineer versus $6,000 stateside. Accountants in the Philippines are performing audits for Cap Gemini and Ernst & Young at a cost of $300 per month versus $5,000 for an accountant in the United States.[15]

In short, when international firms send jobs overseas, they save up to 75 percent on wages. Even more important, the transfer is often accompanied by increases of up to 100 percent in productivity. An example can be found in customer service call centers. In the United States, this is a low-wage, low-prestige job; in India the same job is well paid and enjoys high prestige.[16] No wonder better-educated and more highly motivated workers in other countries are attractive.[17]

New entrants into the global labor force tend to be very ambitious, excited about the opportunity to earn higher incomes, and thus willing to work long hours to learn new skills. Most are eager to adapt new technology and management approaches to their local situation. The bottom line is that American, Japanese, Western European, and other workers with well-paid jobs cannot expect that they will continue to be employees of choice. In fact, they are already sharing the rewards of a globalizing economy.

We hope readers of this text will pay serious attention to the globalization of the labor market when planning their careers. The past is not a good predictor of the future, and workers in the United States are particularly at risk if they do not respond to changing conditions. Thomas Friedman, a reporter for the *New York Times*, interviewed an international IT system designer who teaches in the United States. He was very concerned about the motivation of American students compared to international workers, indicating that he would consider hiring only two of the many American students he had taught over the years. The rest lacked creativity, problem-solving abilities, and passion for learning when compared to students in other countries.[18]

Friedman also interviewed U.S. consular officials in China. After working for years in China, one official concluded:

Americans are oblivious to the huge changes [that have taken place in the labor market]. . . . Your average kid in the U.S. is growing up in a wealthy country with many opportunities . . . many are the kids of advantaged, educated people . . . [many] have a sense of entitlement. Well, the hard reality for that [average] kid is that fifteen years from now, Wu is going to be his boss and Zhou is going to be the doctor in town. The competition is coming, and many. . . . [American] kids are . . . clueless about the rising forces [involved].[19]

In other words, you will have to work much harder than previous generations, not only on your job, but preparing for that job and maintaining your competitiveness as you carry it out. To understand this new deal it is important that you understand how the workplace has evolved; you might reread Chapter 5's advice on understanding your rivals from an individual point of view.

HOW IS THE EMPLOYMENT RELATIONSHIP CHANGING?

Over the past three decades, employers have developed a new relationship with their employees. This change sometimes gives you greater earning potential, but there is definitely less financial and job security than many employees enjoyed in the past.

The Old Deal: IBM's Lifetime Employment Practices

After World War II, IBM was considered one of the best places to be employed in the United States. The most talented students from the best colleges and universities applied for jobs. The company dominated the world market for mainframe computers and was known for having sophisticated corporate strategic planning. In retrospect it was very easy for IBM to develop strategic plans; technology was developing and markets evolving, but not at today's pace.

IBM invested enormous training dollars in its employees to develop their skills. Training never ended, and the company only promoted candidates from within the company. The possibility of moving up IBM's corporate ladder was a real incentive. As demand for IBM's products and services gradually changed over time, employees in areas of declining demand were moved to other facilities or divisions where demand was growing.

IBM felt that it benefited from these practices because turnover was reduced. Employees were committed to the firm and likely to stay with IBM for their entire work careers. There was very little chance of employees being fired as long as they exhibited a satisfactory performance level.

In return, employees exhibited a strong sense of loyalty and commitment to carrying out firm objectives. They knew that if they worked hard and were loyal, IBM would take care of their careers, families, and retirement.

All of this changed for IBM in the 1980s. By 1985, personal computers began replacing mainframes, which had generated most of IBM's revenues and profits. Initially, IBM redeployed more than 20,000 employees from declining areas into businesses it deemed more stable or growing. Wall Street investors didn't buy that strategy, causing IBM's stock price to dive. The company then offered financial incentives for employees to seek employment elsewhere and initiated its first round of significant firings, weeding out poor performers. Even so, IBM's global position continued to decline, causing IBM to lay off more than 100,000 employees in 1992 and 1993 alone. Lifetime employment had become too expensive.

As we indicated in Chapter 12, Lou Gerstner took over as CEO of IBM in 1993. Wall Street analysts believed that the firm needed to be broken into separate units and sold. Gerstner made the strategic decision to keep the company intact, but he knew that IBM's human resource polices had to be dramatically altered. Gerstner laid off people who did not have the new skills that rapidly changing technology and new markets demanded, and he hired people from outside the organization. The hierarchy was flattened by eliminating half of the managerial workforce. Many support operations were outsourced; for example, all positions below executive secretary were staffed by employment agencies.

Today IBM has a new relationship with its employees. CEO Sam Palmisano stresses personal empowerment whereby employees are responsible for their own careers. IBM provides a framework so that its employees can build the knowledge and experiences necessary to make them employable, either at IBM or, if necessary, at other employers.[20]

Many companies have been making the same kind of decisions that IBM did, and we described the pressures of past financial commitments to employees as one cause of the breakup of DaimlerChrysler in Chapter 8. Another telling example of the consequence of changes in the employment contract is found in the story of New York City taxi drivers. Back in 1980, it was illegal for firms to lease out taxis to individuals. Most taxi firms relied on full-time company employees. Retirement plans and health benefits were common. Within twenty years, however, most drivers were independent operators paying $105 per day to lease a cab. They have the opportunity to earn more than their counterparts from the past if they hustle, but they pay for their own vacations, medical benefits, and retirement. Average take-home pay in 2006 was below the 1980 rate in nominal dollars, despite a fare increase, while drivers on average worked 15 percent more than commissioned drivers in 1980.[21]

In other words, as a free agent you sell your services to whoever you believe may give you the greatest return in terms of wages, learning, and development. However, your income will be much less predictable than the income of educated workers in the past, and in many industries it appears to be going down in terms of buying power.

The New Employment Contract

We are merely saying for one last time that business has entered a new era. The use of benchmarking has forced individual internal operating units to recognize and adapt best practices or their operation will be eliminated and contracted out to any corner of the world where higher skills can be found at a lower cost. Advances in information technology have reduced the costs of monitoring these outsourced operations. As we have already indicated, an increasingly skilled, global workforce is eager for employment.

The impact reaches beyond individuals. Companies that supply other firms with products and services are selling to buyers that regularly scan the environment for a better deal. Many firms learn the hard way that relying on a few customers is risky. Tomorrow their clients are quite likely to shift their business to a different contractor with a lower price point or a more attractive offering. In other words, employment volatility is increasing because employers themselves have less assured work.

The increasing speed of transactions increases this volatility. Firms look beyond their current labor pool for new skills from subcontractors, joint ventures, or independent workers because it takes too long to develop new skills internally. The result in the United States is that more than one-third of the workforce is now "contingent"—a term that includes workers who are temporary, part-time, freelance, or contracted independently.[22] Many contingent workers work out of their homes on a contract, which blurs economic and emotional comparisons with past employment. In 1997, 11.6 million people in the United States worked at home; by 2005 the number had almost doubled—to 21 million.[23]

Compensation and Benefits

An obvious risk of the changing employment picture is steady income. In addition to less job security, today's employees are required to take more risk with regard to compensation, health coverage, and retirement benefits. Not long ago compensation policies were based on job evaluation systems designed to produce internal equity between employees in different jobs and to reward individuals who have greater seniority. Most corporations are no longer concerned about these equity issues. Today, wages tend to be set by prevailing national and international labor markets, not internal pay grades. Employees with unique skills that are currently in demand are paid competitive wages and benefits to keep them from leaving the organization for better offers. When other employees complain that younger people make more money, employers respond that older employees tend to have lower-value skills.

Another change in the landscape is that many firms reward a higher percentage of annual wage increases on the basis of overall company performance. These systems include profit-sharing programs, stock options and commissions. An employee who did an outstanding job may get a substantial bonus, but if the firm does poorly in the next year, regardless of how well that individual performs, he or she can earn less; it's not unheard of for compensation to drop 30 percent from one year to the next because of changes in company profits.

A third important change involves the availability of retirement benefits. In 1980, 83 percent of all employees in the United States had defined benefit programs; they guaranteed that no matter what happened to the firm or the general economy, long-term employees (typically those who had been with the company for twenty-five to thirty years) would receive a predetermined income after retirement for as long as they lived. A common formula ensured that retirees would receive 70 percent of the average of their last three years' wages. Someone who averaged $100,000 would therefore be entitled to receive $70,000 every year until he or she died, often with guaranteed lifetime health benefits.

These defined benefit programs proved very expensive for companies. If the firm's investments in its employee pension fund didn't perform (or the fund was "raided" for other purposes), the employer was responsible for covering guaranteed pension payments. When stock prices declined in recessions, firms found themselves obliged to increase contributions to employee retirement funds while simultaneously suffering a recession-fueled decline in sales and earnings.

By the 1990s, many U.S. firms were shifting this risk to their employees. Currently, most corporate pension funds are called defined contribution (or 401 [k]) programs. This means that what goes into the program is determined, but what comes out in terms of benefits varies depending on investment performance. Employees decide how many pretax dollars they will set aside from their wages. In many cases the employer provides matching contributions, normally 25 to 50 percent of the employee's contribution. For example, employees in many Fortune 500 firms can contribute up to 10 percent of their gross annual income to a 401(k) program, with their firm matching 50 percent of the employee's contribution. If you earned $50,000 in this kind of company, you could save up to $5,000 of your income before taxes. If you did so, your employer would contribute $2,500 and your overall retirement benefit would be 15 percent of your annual gross income.

Employees decide how they want to invest contribution funds among different investment options designated by the plan (usually mutual stock and bond funds). The employer has no further responsibility to the employee. If the value of the employee's stock or bond investments declines, the employee must deal with the consequences.

This has proven devastating for some individuals who retired in the late 1990s and saw their retirement assets decline 40 to 50 percent in value during the 2000–2003 recession. As baby boomers retire in the United States, an increasing portion of the population will be significantly affected by stock market volatility, which amplifies concerns about another recession as we go to press.

One of the greatest benefits of the traditional employment contract is medical coverage. Since 2000, premiums for employer-sponsored family health programs have increased by at least 87 percent in the United States.[24] That is large enough to have a major impact on the price of goods. Going back to the automotive industry, General Motors recently revealed that the cost of employee health care for current and retired employees had reached $1783 per car.[25] Compare this to Toyota, which pays health care costs equivalent to $200 per car.[26]

The rising costs of health care have caused most organizations to force employees to share an increasing portion of the costs of insurance and care, while a number of employers have dropped health benefits for many employees. In 1980, more than 70 percent of workers in the United States received some form of health care benefits from their employers; in 2004, less than 50 percent received these benefits. Even the programs that continue have become substantially less generous, with employees having to pay an increasing share of costs with higher co-payments, deductibles, and monthly premiums.

Our intent in this epilogue is to remind you that strategic planning is relevant to your life and career, but planning for medical care is a particularly difficult task, given the potential size of the costs involved. Supporting health with sensible diet and exercise is obviously strategic, even though it may be difficult to schedule in a busy life. Employment that covers some health care costs and insures against the high cost of "catastrophic" illness or accident is obviously valuable. Those who do not have this support can seek similar programs from other associations (such as professional organizations or AARP) to lower the high cost of medical insurance available to individuals. Savings to cover household expenses when earners cannot work is also desirable, but all too rare. Strategy is about managing risk—this is a major area of risk in the United States and is increasingly being felt in other countries.

WHAT ARE THE MOST IMPORTANT CAREER-PLANNING ACTIVITIES?

Throughout this book we have argued that strategists define their direction by considering what they want their organization to become. It is an ongoing activity symbolized by chapter headings that emphasize *defining* strategy, *seeking* opportunity, *ensuring* execution, and so on. Individuals who take responsibility for their career must similarly continue to develop new skills and ideas for how to use them. If you do not do it, no one else will. In fact, one study showed that 94 percent of employees already see themselves as being responsible for their employability.[27]

Because you can expect to change jobs and employers many times during your lifetime, you must act strategically to make this sequence of changes into a coherent career. A vision of what you want to become is the place to start.

Defining and Updating Your Career Strategy

The ideal career vision is based on what you are passionate about and what you would be proud to accomplish. Vision is the basis of an intended strategy that can guide your day-to-day decision making. As described in Chapter 1, it can help you decide what to do and why, when and where to act, and who might receive the results of this activity. But, as we also discuss in Chapter 1, you should also anticipate that important aspects of your career will emerge from learning and unanticipated conditions that develop along the way. As with business strategy, it is important to be flexible and take advantage of opportunities as they arise. Factor into your plan the reality that you are likely to face setbacks. Understand that market forces may call for a change in your personal goals and even your vision.

Changing conditions will be easier to deal with if you regularly (but not obsessively) scan the environment. We think it makes sense to keep track of day-to-day business news from trusted sources, augmented by more specific information about your industry and company. Professor Peter Drucker, perhaps the most famous management scholar of the twentieth century, wrote, "Success in the knowledge economy comes to those who know themselves—their strengths, their values and how they best perform."[28] Learn to accurately determine how colleagues and superiors perceive you. This reflection is a critical part of your learning and developing process.[29] And don't forget that many of your rivals come from an international labor market. They, too, are anticipating how you will try to compete, and as a result they are adjusting their career strategies.

Your SWOT analysis might start with past successes. Try to identify *why* you were successful. Take a critical look at patterns. What do you truly enjoy doing? Are you a natural coach to others? Do you thrive under the guidance of a mentor? What kinds of issues do you like to resolve: structured or unstructured? Do you like to work independently or with others on teams? Do you tend to become the leader in groups, or are you more naturally a supporter of others? Your strengths are not likely to change dramatically in a short period of time, but in the longer term, you can develop them and deploy them with greater sophistication if you have a plan.[30] At a minimum, you can avoid selecting careers that run counter to your nature.

It's also important to position yourself in the marketplace—to differentiate yourself from your competitors and colleagues. Management author Michael Goldhaber wrote in *Wired* magazine, "If there is nothing very special about your work, no matter how hard you apply yourself you won't get noticed and that increasingly means you won't get paid much either. In times past you could be obscure yet secure—now that's much harder."[31]

Finally, you should develop a habit of reviewing or evaluating your performance. Self-feedback improves learning. You need to examine the effects of your decisions and actions. Peter Drucker believed that he became successful as a management consultant because of his personal feedback technique. When he made a key decision or took an important action, he recorded it along with his outcome expectations. Six to twelve months later, he examined what actually occurred compared to his expectations.[32] You might try the same technique for self-evaluation and augment it with honest performance reviews from your peers and superiors.

Maximizing Career Options

We have been describing the process of recognizing and developing resources in the light of a specific career plan. As a strategist, you also have to think about the activities that will implement or execute that plan.

Marketing   Once you have developed your strategy, you need to learn how to market yourself. In the past, a good reputation was often evident to the relatively stable set of co-workers and supervisors who surrounded an employee. In a more dynamic, competitive, and fickle environment, the people around you constantly change. As a result, you need to make sure that a changing set of co-workers and bosses see and recognize your performance and talents.

Management consultant Tom Peters suggested in his seminal article "The Brand Called You" that we need to think of ourselves as our own brand—just like Coca-Cola or Nike. The current popularity of this idea can be seen by the many books recently published with titles such as *Me, Inc; You, Inc.; Brand You; Be Your Own Brand;* and *Become the CEO of You, Inc.* Seth Godin, a best-selling author and entrepreneur, believes that you must take control of your brand: "Many of us are taught to do our best and then let the world decide how to judge us. I think it is better to do your best and decide how you want to be judged. And act that way."[33] We think this advice needs to be adopted with a good measure of humility (and some humor), but it points to a necessary strategy.

Martha Stewart is cited as one of the best examples of someone who has created a brand around herself. She literally has incorporated and sold shares in herself. Her brand includes her personality and her homespun but elegant taste. Many politicians, relying on a growing number of political consultants, similarly market themselves on the basis of their personalities, rather than their beliefs or platforms. We suggest that you learn from those whose accomplishments you genuinely admire.

Personal marketing has an impact on job selection. Your goal should be to learn—which means that your job's contribution to your résumé is at least as important as salary. More specifically, good strategists will negotiate with a potential employer more about the nature of the job experience than about the salary they will be making.

We have mentioned the trend toward graduates taking jobs with small, entrepreneurial start-up firms. These strategists often pass up higher-paid jobs for the possibility of future high compensation when or if their employer becomes successful. They believe there is less downside to taking such a risk early in their careers, and they approach such opportunities as accelerated learning. An alternative strategy that also can be recommended is to work for a larger firm that is already doing well in an industry that attracts you. The idea behind this choice is that it is easier to learn from success than from failure, and an established company has a higher probability of teaching you about successful practice. Indeed, many entrepreneurs start by "learning on someone else's payroll."

Once on the job, career management really begins. Two key activities are continued professional development and intentional networking. It is easy to say that you should always be observing and learning on the job; however, relatively few workers proactively select projects that will develop new skills and have high visibility. Our advice is that you build a portfolio of skills and experiences on your résumé that demonstrates different talents. Use the diversity of jobs that you've had to emphasize your overall skill set and your adaptability. Think of the résumé as a marketing tool that expresses your offer to help solve a potential employer's problems.

Teamwork   White-collar work is being fundamentally transformed, and project work is fast becoming the primary vehicle that organizations use to solve complex problems. That means you must become an expert at working in and managing teams. As a strategist, you should carefully consider and evaluate the different projects that are available to you. When you can, choose projects with the potential to create the highest value for your personal career as well as your firm. It is not enough to manage any project that is dumped into your lap; every project offers some possibility to create new value both for the firm and for your career. Become the driver that helps your team look at an assigned project in new ways. Tom Peters provides the following example:

> A team was assigned the task of cleaning up a warehouse. The project leader saw the assignment as a chance to rethink the distribution

system. Her team realized that they needed to take into account both the incoming parts from suppliers and the outgoing parts to customers. The project leader not only cleaned up the site, she made the case for a new distribution system that would feed flawlessly into the reorganized warehouse. The result was a warehouse that stayed clean because of newly designed processes.[34]

Networking   Few successful people achieve significant career goals by themselves. We rely on others to help us to get the jobs we want, accomplish our work, and provide learning opportunities.

The authors of this textbook have taught many students in many different countries. In recent years, working for a consulting firm has often been the top choice of our most ambitious students. These jobs can provide incredible learning experiences in different industries. Working with different clients facilitates building a network of contacts and friends across companies and industries; it provides experience and information that informs subsequent job searches.

Other good students make a more targeted first choice. Their interests and past experience take them into a particular industry or a well-specified profession. This too can be a smart choice. Some first jobs offer far more responsibility and variety than the average consulting job. You may be able to discover more about your current and needed skills and build a network of connections that facilitate future employability in a desirable industry.

No matter what job you choose, you need alliances—just as the companies you work for do. Good alliance partners fit your goals and help you augment your skills. At the same time, you will be chosen as a partner only if you have something to offer.

The first network you need to build is inside the organization that employs you. Your peers and superiors are likely to be your primary contacts. Try to connect with people who have perspectives and experiences that augment your own. It is worthwhile to seek appropriate relationships that will help you be more effective in your job by providing information about strategies that the organization is pursuing and why these strategies are important. But don't forget that accurate foresight is not always possible in a changing world. The most helpful contacts cannot all be identified beforehand.

Your boss is an important part of your network because he or she will almost certainly have a major impact on your next move. Your boss also is a source of developmental opportunities and constructive feedback on how to improve your job performance. But in a network, you have to do more. You need to observe your superiors to better understand how they work and identify how you can help them become more effective.

In addition, you need to build a network of contacts outside the organization for which you work. This can be more difficult and take more time than networking within the organization, but it is no less important. Outside networks are a pipeline to identifying innovative ideas and practices as well as new employment opportunities. Identify ways in which people in your profession meet each other—for example, at trade shows and professional organizations. Think about how you can provide useful information and help to others.

With electronic technology, employers have access to a universe of candidates for any given job. However, no corporate personnel departments can review all available résumés. The result is that more and more organizations rely on the recommendations of trusted friends and associates. The seminal book in seeking jobs and careers which you will find personally satisfying is Richard Nelson Bolles's *What Color is Your Parachute?* Bolles contends that less than 4 percent of all jobs come through the Internet. The two hiring methods that he finds companies use most often are (1) finding someone they know from within the organization, and (2) finding someone who is recommended by another employee within the organization, a friend, or a known colleague.[35] That information alone is a compelling reason to make networking part of your strategic agenda.

Evaluating Employers

Business Week conducted a study in 2007 to identify the fifty best places for new college graduates to go to work.[36] It surveyed career services directors and 44,000 undergraduate students from universities around the country to determine their top employer choices. It then asked each nominated firm to fill out an extensive survey on salaries, benefits, corporate culture, and training programs. The top ten firms are as follows:

1. Deloitte & Touche
2. PricewaterhouseCoopers
3. Ernst & Young
4. IBM
5. Google
6. Microsoft
7. Walt Disney
8. Accenture
9. Lockheed Martin
10. Teach for America

It is interesting that Teach for America was in the top ten; the U.S. State Department was ranked 19 and the CIA was ranked 50. Though not at the very top of the list for many graduates, these and other government and nonprofit organizations do have some advantages over for-profit firms. They offer employees an opportunity to contribute to society in meaningful ways. In addition, they often offer more reasonable hours, and in the case of government employment, higher benefits.

Again our advice is obvious, even though we know from experience that few students are as strategic as they might be at the beginning of their careers. It is worth taking the time to think about how the first companies you work for will affect your career trajectory. Read surveys like the one we have just described, not only for the companies they list, but the questions they ask. Get advice from people who have jobs like the one you hope to have. They are often flattered to be considered experts, and indeed they have expertise that you need. Most especially, do not jump at the first job that becomes available before making a strategic assessment of what it has to offer you. Of course, a good choice depends on what *you* have to offer as well.

WHY BE PURPOSEFUL ABOUT WORK/LIFE BALANCE?

Before ending this book, we want to step back from the nitty-gritty kinds of questions we have just been discussing to think about the broader issues raised by the changing world of work. As just described, we believe most employees will work harder than their counterparts in the past. For most of us, the forty-hour workweek has become extinct. We need to put in more late nights and early mornings to find new ways to cut costs and add value. The standard of performance we met last year may have been difficult, but the next standard is likely to be even more challenging.

This time on the job does not include time spent at home answering cell phones, pagers, and e-mail—the devices that keep many of us connected with clients, customers, and the office 24/7. We previously mentioned that the average American works 350 more hours annually than the average European. But, the average workweek in Europe and the United States is increasing as we work harder to compete with other workers located all around the world.

If you are serious about your career, you are likely to be afraid to cut back the hours you spend on the job. You will want to be part of many networks. You won't want to be invisible at an important meeting, miss learning about a new program, or be late learning about a new market development. However, there is a steep cost to this "always on" mentality, often exacerbated by work shared with international colleagues and relevant events that happen even as we sleep.

A globalizing economy takes more of our time and often pressures us to define success only in working terms. At this early point in your career, you are especially likely to erode relationships with family and friends and not attend to health and wellness, personal fulfillment, financial planning, spiritual development, and service to others. We are all at risk of developing a shortsighted strategy that does not serve our broader, longer-term human needs.

One research study, conducted by Harvard professors Laura Nash and Howard Stevenson, uncovered four components of enduring success:

1. Happiness (feelings of contentment about your life)
2. Achievement
3. Significance (the sense that you have made a positive impact on people you care about)
4. Legacy (a way to establish values or accomplishments that can help others find future success or happiness)[37]

Nash and her colleagues argue that we need to establish a balance among the four factors, although the proportions allotted to each will shift at different stages of life.

Can you truly do this and still be successful at work? Their study found that some high-achieving, successful people accomplished great things for themselves and others by recognizing that they had multiple goals that were critical to their personal definition of success. They were fully committed to every activity they engaged in. They also achieved a sense of renewal by being involved in different activities, while others just felt pressured by the multiple expectations around them.

The approach taken by the most successful employees in Nash and Stevenson's study suggests adopting "multiple strategies"—similar to the kind of planning that some companies carry out when they commit to the triple bottom line, which includes financial performance, environmental impact, and social impact, as mentioned in Chapter 9. As an example of life balance, we can think of one young professional who has achieved early career success but also maintained balance in her life.

The Running Professor

After three years of management consulting work in the United States and Europe, a 25-year-old American woman decided to pursue her MBA. She joined the university's informal running club for Tuesday and Thursday night runs, training for an end-of-school-year relay race against students from a rival MBA program. After the relay, she continued to run on the nearby mountain trails and participated in a few local races. She moved to another country to start a Ph.D. in management and continued to run, where her performances caught the eye of fellow runners and a coach who encouraged her to enter the national championship in the 50-km "ultramarathon." She won that race, and many others—completing more than sixty marathons during the four years of her Ph.D. studies, but also managing to publish several articles and book chapters and her very long thesis!

She described the balance that she manages in this way:

> "I really enjoyed my MBA and Ph.D. studies, but at times it could be stressful, and I needed to get away. I found myself running every day for an hour or so. At the weekend, I wanted to escape the city, but I needed an excuse to get out, so I would find a marathon somewhere and just travel by bus or train and stay in a local hostel or bed and breakfast. I would spend all traveling time focusing on my studies, and then when the race started, I would just concentrate on it. Running enabled me to think through my ideas better, but equally, after reading and writing so much, I felt that I deserved a break, and made the most of it!"

The running professor's times improved so much that she was invited to represent her country in the world championships on several occasions, and she won the bronze medal in September 2006. Five days the United States, she interviewed successfully for a job as an assistant professor in Texas. Almost every day, she wakes up around 5 a.m. to run for a few hours and then cross-trains on a bicycle at the gym, usually reading the latest management research. She showers, eats, and heads into the university to teach her classes. Although she has an athletic shoe contract and gets to travel to as many as ten different countries each year for competitions, the running professor balances her love of sport with her commitments to research, teaching, and service to her university and her students.

We hope that you find a similarly diverse set of activities in your life. Whatever model you use to help establish happiness and success, consider the perspective of Charles Handy, an internationally respected management thinker. He argues that the purpose of a career is the pursuit of meaning, which comes to those who develop a personal sense of direction, continuity (a legacy), and connection to their work.[38] We also recommend that you take the time to read Viktor Frankl's short yet important book, *Man's Search for Meaning*.[39] Frankl was a Jewish psychologist arrested and sent to a concentration camp by the Nazis. The theme of his book is that "man's main concern is not to gain pleasure or to avoid pain but rather to see meaning in his life."[40] If a prisoner of Auschwitz can find meaning after the deaths of close family members and friends, we can certainly do it in the comfort of our abundant lives. We all have the time and resources to determine what is important to us and then consciously plan how to live a deeply satisfying life.

CONCLUSIONS FOR THE STRATEGIST

We began this chapter with concerns generated by the globalizing labor market. We still have them, but there is potentially a happier story to tell, one that could facilitate your search for a meaningful career and work/life balance.

In 1998, McKinsey Corporation released a study called *The War for Talent.*[41] After a year of gathering data from 6,000 managers working in seventy-seven companies, the researchers concluded that talent was the scarce resource most impeding companies. Their informants were searching for more "smart, sophisticated businesspeople who are technologically literate, globally astute, and operationally agile."[42] The idea that captured broad attention was that as the demand for talent increased in a globalizing economy, the supply was going down. The "war" metaphor, it was reported,

> has to do with demographics. In 15 years, there will be 15% fewer Americans in the 35- to 45-year-old range than there are now. At the same time, the U.S. economy is likely to grow at a rate of 3% to 4% per year. So over that period, the demand for bright, talented 35- to 45-year-olds will increase by, say, 25%, and the supply will be going down by 15%. That sets the stage for a talent war.[43]

The dot-com boom reached its midpoint in 1998. Interest in the war for talent subsided as unemployment increased after the bust. But by 2006, the "War for Talent" had assumed a global face. McKinsey looked at talent shortfalls in India and China and provided ideas for developing internal talent markets in companies.[44] *The Economist*'s multiple-article survey on the "Battle for Brainpower" reports:

> Obsession with talent is no longer confined to blue-chip companies such as Goldman Sachs and General Electric. It can be found everywhere in the corporate world, from credit-card companies to hotel chains to the retail trade. Many firms reckon that they have pushed re-engineering and automation as hard as they can. Now they must raise productivity by managing talent better.[45]

That's good news for employees, and demographics will continue to be in your favor. By 2010, it is estimated that two baby boomers will be retiring in the United States for each college student who will be entering the workforce. As college graduates become a more valued asset, they may be able to bargain for what recent surveys indicate they (you?) want most:

- Balance between work lives and personal lives. Many students are concerned about their parents' working seventy-hour weeks.

They want liberal vacations, and they want to make sure they will be able to use them.

- Frequent performance appraisals and a mentor to help them get settled in their new position and provide long-term guidance.
- A chance to work on important projects early in their careers.
- Opportunities for community service. Twenty-seven percent of current undergraduate students listed contributing to society as a top career goal.[46]

That's a good list. We hope you are strategic enough to achieve all that and more. Good luck!

NOTES

[1] http://www.rediff.com/money/2006/nov/24bpo.htm, accessed October 25, 2007.

[2] Reich, R. 2000. *The Future of Success*. New York: Knopf.

[3] http://www.bls.gov/oco/cg/cgs035.htm, accessed October 25, 2007.

[4] Announcement of World Health Day 2006. http://www.who.int/mediacentre/news/releases/2006/pr19/en/index.html, accessed March 24, 2008.

[5] http://www.bls.gov/oco/cg/cgs031.htm, accessed October 25, 2007.

[6] Pine, B., & Gilmore, J. 1999. *The Experience Economy: Work Is Theatre and Every Business Is a Stage*. Boston: Harvard Business School Press.

[7] An interesting overview of the links between technology and education can be found at http://en.wikipedia.org/wiki/Educational_technology.

[8] Allen, E., & Seaman, J. 2007. Online Nation: Five Years of Growth in Online Learning, 2007. Needham, MA: Sloan Consortium. http://www.sloan_c.org/publications/survey/index.asp.

[9] Testimony of Mitch Bainwol, Chairman and CEO, Recording Industry Association of America (RIAA) before U.S. Senate Committee on Appropriations Subcommittee on Commerce, Justice, State, and the Judiciary. April 29, 2004. http://www.riaa.com/news/keystatistics.php?content_selector-consumertrends.

[10] SBA. 2005. *The Small Business Economy: Data for 2005*. Washington, DC: U.S. Government Printing Office.

[11] Reynolds, P., Bygrave, W., & Autio, E. 2004. *Global Entrepreneurship Monitor*. London: London Business School and Babson College.

[12] Pink, D. 2001. *Free Agent Nation*. New York: Warner Books, p. 14.

[13] http://esa.un.org/unpp, accessed November 5, 2007. See this URL for the United Nations online estimator.

[14] Pink, D. 2005. *A Whole New Mind*. New York: Riverhead Books.

[15] Pink, *Whole New Mind*.

[16] Friedman, T. 2005. *The World Is Flat*. New York: Farrar, Straus & Giroux.

[17] Special Report—Outsourcing. 2006. *Business Week* (January 30). http://www.businessweek.com/magazine/content/06_05/b3969401.htm, accessed March 24, 2008.

[18] Friedman, *The World Is Flat*, p. 261.

[19] Friedman, *The World Is Flat*, p. 264.

[20] This section is adapted from Gerstner, L. 2002. *Who Says Elephants Can't Dance?* New York: HarperBusiness. See also *2006 Annual Report*. http://www.ibm.com/investor, accessed March 24, 2008.

[21] Schaller Consulting. March 2006. *The New York City Taxicab Fact Book*, p. 40. http://www.schallerconsult.com/taxi/taxifb.pdf, accessed March 24, 2008.

[22] Cappelli, P. 1999. *The New Deal at Work*. Boston: Harvard Business School Press.

[23] http://www.bls.gov/cps, accessed November 6, 2007.

[24] Kaiser Family Foundation: Employer Health Benefits 2007 Annual Survey. http://www.kff.org/insurance/7672/index.cfm, accessed March 24, 2008.

[25] http://www.medicalnewstoday.com/articles/64104.php, accessed October 25, 2007.

[26] http://money.cnn.com/magazines/fortune/forune achive/2007/04/30/8405437/index.htm, accessed October 25, 2007.

[27] Cappelli, *The New Deal at Work*.

[28] Drucker, P. 1999. *Management Challenges for the 21st Century*. New York: HarperCollins, p. 163.

[29] Bennis, W. 1989. *On Becoming a Leader*. Reading, MA: Addison-Wesley.

[30] Buckingham, M. 2005. *The One Thing You Need to Know*. New York: Free Press.

[31] Peters, T. 1999. *The Brand You 50, or, Fifty Ways to Transform Yourself from an "Employee" into a Brand That Shouts Distinction, Commitment, and Passion!* New York: Knopf, p. 21.

[32] Peter Drucker on Leadership. Forbes (November 19). http://www.forbes.com/management/2004/11/19/cz_rk_1119drucker.html, accessed April 28, 2007.

[33] Brady. D. 2007. Creating Brand You. *Business Week* (August 20): 72–73.

[34] Peters, *The Brand You 50*, p. 41.

[35] Bolles, R. 2007. *What Color Is Your Parachute?* Berkeley, CA: Ten Speed Press.

[36] Gerdes, L. 2007. The Best Places to Launch a Career. *Business Week* (September 24): 49–60.

[37] Nash, L., & Stevenson, H. 2004. Success That Lasts. *Harvard Business Review* (February):30–37.

[38] Handy, C. 1995. *Age of Paradox*. Boston: Harvard Business School Press.

[39] Frankl, V. 1984. *Man's Search for Meaning*. New York: Pocket Books.

[40] Frankl, *Man's Search for Meaning*, p. 136.

[41] Michaels, E., Handfield-Jones, H., & Axelrod, B. 2001. *The War for Talent*. Boston: Harvard Business School Press.

[42] Fishman, C. 1998. The War for Talent. *Fast Company*. (July). http://www.fastcompany.com/magazine/16/mckinsey.html.

[43] Fishman, The War for Talent.

[44] http://www.mckinseyquarterly.com/PDFDownload.aspx?L2=18&L3=31&ar=1765, accessed March 24, 2008.

[45] The Battle for Brainpower. 2006. *The Economist*. (October 5). http://www.economist.com/surveys/displaystory.cfm?story_id=7961894, accessed March 24, 2008.

[46] Gerdes, L. 2006. 50 Best Places to Launch a Career. *Business Week*. (September 18): 64–78.

Index

Bold page numbers indicate locations of defined terms.